THE HISTORY OF
BLACK CATHOLICS
IN THE UNITED STATES

THE HISTORY OF BLACK CATHOLICS IN THE UNITED STATES

CYPRIAN DAVIS, O.S.B.

CROSSROAD • NEW YORK

This printing: 1998

The Crossroad Publishing Company
370 Lexington Avenue, New York, NY 10017

Printed in the United States of America

Library of Congress Cataloging-in-Publication Data

Davis, Cyprian.
   The history of Black Catholics in the United States / Cyprian
Davis.
     p.   cm.
   Includes bibliographical references and index.
   ISBN 0-8245-1010-0; 0-8245-1495-5 (pbk.)
   1. Afro-American Catholics   I. Title
BX1407.N4D38   1990   90-36503
282'.73'08996073—dc20   CIP

To Mary
Virgin and Mother

O Mary, immensity of heaven,
foundation of the earth....
You are greater than the cherubim,
more eminent than the seraphim,
more glorious than the chariots of fire....
Your lap held the glowing coal.
Your knees supported the lion....

Ethiopian liturgy

CONTENTS

PREFACE

Some time around the first quarter of the sixth century in the North African city of Carthage, a wealthy landowner (presumably a member of the Afro-Latin aristocracy, which at that time was Catholic in religion and Roman in culture) had an adolescent slave, a black youth from the interior of Africa. The slaveowner had him enrolled among the catechumens of the city so that he might receive baptism on the night before Easter. The young black man had gone partway through the various stages of the catechumenate when he fell ill. As his illness progressed, he became paralyzed and unable to speak. Nevertheless, he received the waters of baptism on the night before Easter with the other catechumens. Shortly thereafter he died.

Ferrandus, the archdeacon of Carthage, was troubled by the incident because the young African had not been able to respond to the questions preceding the baptism. Did he have the capability of making the intention to receive baptism? How could one presume that he wished to enter the church when he could give no sign? Ferrandus wrote down his questions in a letter to the leading theologian of the North African Catholic church of the time, St. Fulgentius (d. 527), the exiled bishop of Ruspe. Fulgentius answered the letter of Ferrandus from his see city of Ruspe in North Africa, where he had returned to live out his days. It was a time when much of North Africa was gripped by the harsh rule of the Vandals, a Germanic tribe that had conquered North Africa at the time of the death of St. Augustine a hundred years before, in 430.

The lengthy response of Fulgentius to the letter not only set forth a theological principle that we all find useful still today, but he immortalized in the pages of history this nameless black teenager. The letter of Ferrandus and the reply of Fulgentius bore the title throughout the Middle Ages "Concerning the Salvation of an Ethiopian on the Point of Dying." (In the ancient world the word "Ethiopian" designated black skin color and not a nationality.) In his response Fulgentius spoke of the power of baptism and solidarity with the

ix

church. This young boy was rightly judged to have persevered in his desire for baptism. Once having made a right intention, its good purpose lasts — despite illness, loss of consciousness, or distraction of mind.[1]

We do not know the name of this black teenager who was initiated into the Christian Mysteries one Easter in the city of Carthage in the early sixth century. Although we do not know his name, this book is about him. Like so many blacks who appear in the early Christian sources, sometimes named and more often nameless, this young man of Carthage is a fleeting presence in a theological treatise, an anonymous person with a racial qualification, a passing reference in an ancient text — all reminding us that in the rich background of church history, there are images that we have chosen not to see, figures that have been allowed to blur, characters passing through center stage for a brief moment with no supporting cast. Still, they have been there, and the church has been marked with their blackness. Yet, too often the presence of black Catholics through the centuries has been a muted one, a silent witness, an unspoken testimony. It is the historian's task to make the past speak, to highlight what has been hidden, and to retrieve a mislaid memory.

The history of the black Catholic community in the United States has never really been told. In the first part of this century, the learned Josephite John T. Gillard published two books on black Catholics in the United States: *The Catholic Church and the American Negro*, and *Colored Catholics in the United States*.[2] Gillard deserves credit for his pioneering effort to treat black Catholics as a community with a history within the American Catholic church. While giving much information that was valuable for the time, he presented his own views with vigor and assurance. Today these views are no longer fully tenable. Moreover, few historians would feel it necessary to defend the church in its relationship to the black community in such an apologetic way as Gillard did.

Historical studies have appeared dealing with specific elements in the history of black Catholics, such as Albert Foley's biographical sketches of black priests from the mid-nineteenth century to the mid-twentieth as well as his life of James Augustine Healy, the first black bishop.[3] More recently there has appeared the excellent study by Marilyn Nickels on Thomas Wyatt Turner, the great black Catholic lay leader of the first half of this century.[4] Finally, we have the study on blacks and the Roman Catholic priesthood that Stephen Ochs presents in his book *Desegregating the Altar: The Josephites and the Struggle for Black Priests, 1871–1960*. As a result, less space has been given in this work to the growth of a black clergy around the turn of the twentieth century.

We have lacked a historical overview of the black Catholic community in this country. In 1974 Maria Caravaglios published *The American Catholic Church and the Negro Problem in the XVIII–XIX Centuries.*[5] Despite many factual errors and methodological deficiencies, it was a serious attempt to provide such an overview. Caravaglios treated the problem, however, not the people. She gave an account of the institution and the object of that institution's attention.

Although the Catholic church is an institution, it is also a community of people with a shared faith and a shared tradition, making their pilgrim's progress through space and time. The people who are the subject of this history were quite conscious of their position within this great community; not only were they conscious of it, they shared a pride in it. The Catholic church was theirs, and they saw themselves as an integral part of that church. For this reason many details regarding the missionary activity of white priests, sisters, and male religious have not been recorded in detail. This is a story yet to be told. The focus in this book is narrower and more direct, concentrating on the story of black American Catholics in the historical context of Roman Catholicism in the United States.

Ideally, the history of the black Catholic community should be the synthesis of carefully researched histories carried out on the local level. To a large extent this research is still lacking. The present history, therefore, is an attempt to give the larger framework within which future historical research can develop. For a people whose past has been systematically ignored, it is important to start at the beginning and reveal its existence. We must have some idea of how blacks got here and what they found. Hence, the story of the black Catholic community in the United States begins with the story of the Catholic church in Africa. The community itself began with the first baptized black, and it continued with faith and hope and not a little love as the image of God revealed in black.

ACKNOWLEDGEMENTS

The research for this book has been made possible through a generous grant by Lilly Endowment, Inc., and through the continued interest of its program director in religion, Jacqui Burton. Acknowledgement with appreciation is made of the confidence shown me by Professors C. Eric Lincoln of Duke University, Lawrence Mamiya of Vassar College, and Doris Sanders of Jackson State College in Mississippi. A special debt of gratitude is owed to the Most Reverend Moses Anderson, auxiliary bishop of Detroit, and Professor Albert Raboteau of Princeton University for their recommendation and assistance.

Both encouragement and assistance were given me by the administration and faculty of the St. Meinrad School of Theology. Again a special thanks is due to the former president-rector, the Most Reverend Daniel Buechlein, O.S.B., now bishop of Memphis who arranged a study leave, and to the Very Reverend Eugene Hensell, O.S.B., the present president-rector, who read the manuscript chapter by chapter and urged me in season and out to complete the task. Thanks are also due to Dexter Brewer, former student and now priest of the diocese of Nashville, who gave indispensable aid as research assistant; and to Victoria Woody, who graciously typed the manuscript. In so many intangible ways the monks of St. Meinrad Archabbey, my colleagues on the faculty, and the students of St. Meinrad Seminary provided the incentive for this work by their continued interest. I am especially grateful to my superior, the Right Reverend Timothy Sweeney, O.S.B., the archabbot of St. Meinrad, whose sympathy and understanding from the beginning made the research and the writing of this book possible.

Research for this book took me to archives and libraries in Rome and throughout the United States. Interest and even enthusiasm for the subject on the part of so many made the research exciting and rewarding. No one who ventures into the field of black Catholic history can ignore the resources of the Josephite Archives in Baltimore or dispense with the assistance of the archivist, Father Peter Hogan, S.S.J.

The resources of these archives and the wise counsel of Father Hogan, who patiently read the manuscript, were made available from the beginning. Research into the history of black Catholics in this country took me to Rome, to the Vatican Archives and the Congregation for the Evangelization of Peoples Archives. A special word of thanks is due to the personnel and staff of both archives. Special mention must be made of Monsignor Charles Burns, who patiently explained the research potential of the Vatican Archives, and Signor De Dominicis, who opened up a vast field of black Catholic sources. Without this help, the research for this book would have been incomplete.

My thanks go to the Sulpician archivist, Father John Bowen, S.S., and to Christopher Kauffman at the Sulpician Archives in Baltimore for invaluable assistance and encouragement; to Sister Catherine Markey, M.H.S., Diocese of Little Rock Archives, who first alerted me to the documentation available that opened the way to this present work; to the Most Reverend Oscar Lipscomb of Mobile, archbishop and historian who gave me both hospitality and access to the Archdiocese of Mobile Archives, and to Mrs. Rehm and Mrs. Zieman, archivist and assistant archivist respectively; to Father Philip Gagan of the Diocese of St. Augustine Archives; to Sister Charlene Walsh, R.S.M., who made available her documentation on Mother Mathilda Beasley and most especially to Sister Felicitas Powers, R.S.M., who was of invaluable assistance both in the Archdiocese of Baltimore Archives and the Diocese of Savannah Archives; to his Eminence, Cardinal O'Connor of New York, who granted me access to the Archdiocese of New York Archives, and the archivist, Sister Marguerita Smith, O.P., to Sister Wilhelmina Lancaster, O.S.P., and Sister Mary Alice Chineworth, O.S.P., archivists at the motherhouse of the Oblate Sisters of Providence in Baltimore; to Sister Margaret O'Rourke, S.B.S., archivist of the Sisters of the Blessed Sacrament at Bensalem, Pennsylvania, and Sister Georgiana Rockwell of the same community with her rich knowledge of the history of the Blessed Sacrament Sisters.

My thanks also to Sister Boniface Adams, S.S.F., the archivist of the Holy Family sisters in New Orleans; to Charles Keyes of the Knights and Ladies of Peter Claver, who granted me access to the organization's archives in New Orleans; to Monsignor Earl Woods and Charles Nolan of the Archdiocese of New Orleans Archives, to Father Edward McSweeney, of the Diocese of Pittsburgh Archives, and Father Henry Koren, C.S.Sp., of the Spiritan Archives, Pittsburgh; to Brother Philip Hurley, O.S.B., of the St. Vincent Archabbey Archives; Father Paul Nelligan, S.J., of the Holy Cross College Archives;

and Sister Maureen Thornton, R.S.M., of the Diocese of Portland Archives; John Treanor and Timothy Slavin of the Archdiocese of Chicago Archives; Sister Connie Supan, I.H.M., and Sister Celeste Rabaut, I.H.M., archivist, who allowed me access to the Sister Servants of the Immaculate Heart of Mary Archives in Monroe, Michigan; Father William Faherty, S.J., of the Jesuit Archives of St. Louis and Ivan James of the same city; Joseph Casino of the Archdiocese of Philadelphia Archives and Historical Collections; to the archivists at Marquette University, the University of Notre Dame, the Beinecke Library at Yale, the staff at the Schomburg Center for Research on Black Culture and the Manuscript and Rare Book Division of the New York Public Library. I owe particular thanks to Margaretha Childs at the South Carolina Historical Society in Charleston for the enormous help over the years and to Monsignor Richard Madden, priest of the diocese of Charleston, who was so generous with his time and information. Many thanks again to H. Warren Willis, archivist for the National Conference of Catholic Bishops, who gave kind assistance for research on Thomas Wyatt Turner.

Various persons granted me personal interviews or access to their own papers and research. I especially want to thank Ellen Tarry, Roy Foster, Frederick Foster, Roberta Rudd Lawson, the sisters at the motherhouse of the Franciscan Handmaids of Mary in New York City, Father Robert Emmett Curran, S.J., of Georgetown University, Father Robert Carbonneau, C.P., Jane Landers, Sister Alberta Hubner, O.P., Stephen Ochs, Marilyn Nickels, Brother Thomas Spalding, C.F.X., Sister Mary Anthony Scally, R.S.M., Sister M. Roland Legarde, S.B.S., and Edward Purnell.

Moreover, I cannot omit mentioning those who aided me with their observations and suggestions, especially the Most Reverend James Lyke, O.F.M., apostolic administrator of Atlanta; and Sister Jamie Phelps, O.P., of the Catholic Theological Union; and my editor at Crossroad, Justus George Lawler. Their support was invaluable.

Last, I wish to acknowledge the help given by my students in black Catholic history at St. Meinrad Seminary and at the Black Catholic Studies Institute at Xavier University in New Orleans and to the many African American Catholics who helped me clarify my thoughts and conclusions through the many lectures and discussions on black Catholic history in which I was involved. So many made me welcome and granted me hospitality. Let them know that whatever merit can be found herein is a tribute to their generosity and magnanimity.

RELIGIOUS ORDERS AND CONGREGATIONS

C.M.	Congregation of the Mission. Vincentians.
C.SS.R.	Congregation of the Most Holy Redeemer. Redemptorists.
I.H.M.	Sisters, Servants of the Immaculate Heart of Mary.
M.H.M.	Mill Hill Missionaries.
O.D.C.	Order of Discalced Carmelites. Carmelites.
O.F.M.	Order of Friars Minor. Franciscans.
O.F.M. Cap.	Order of Friars Minor Capuchins. Capuchins.
O.P.	Order of Preachers. Dominicans.
O.S.B.	Order of St. Benedict. Benedictines.
S.A.M.	Society of African Missions. (Today the initials are S.M.A.)
S.M.	Society of Mary. Marists.
S.P.M.	Society of the Fathers of Mercy.
S.S.J.	St. Joseph's Society of the Sacred Heart. Josephites.
S.V.D.	Society of the Divine Word.

Chapter 1

AFRICAN ROOTS

All black history begins in Africa. In one way or another, Africa became part of the self-understanding of American blacks throughout the nineteenth century. The black Catholic community in America was no exception. It sought its roots in the religious experience of Africa and its self-definition in the African saints of the early church.[1] American blacks, both Protestant and Catholic, found their roots in the black Africans who appeared in the pages of the Scriptures, both in the Old Testament and the New, and most particularly in the many references to Ethiopia in the Psalms and the Prophets.

Origen, the great Alexandrian church father of the third century, paved the way with his famous commentary on verse 5 of chapter 1 in the Song of Songs ("I am very dark, but comely, O daughters of Jerusalem"). For Origen the bride in the Song of Songs was the church. Famous for his spiritual interpretation of Scripture, Origen believed (as most did in his day) that the great love poem of the Old Testament was a composition by King Solomon, in which was set forth the love songs between Solomon and the queen of Sheba. Origen followed the traditional belief of the time in seeing the queen of Sheba as an Ethiopian queen, a beautiful woman with black skin. The Septuagint version of the Scriptures in fact uses the wording: "I am black and beautiful." Commenting on this verse, Origen wrote in his commentary on the Song of Songs:

> Let us look at the passage which we quoted...about the queen of Sheba, who also was an Ethiopian; and concerning whom the Lord bears witness in the Gospels that in the day of judgement she shall come together with the men of this faithless generation, and shall condemn them....

1

This queen came, then, and, in fulfilment of her type, the
Church comes also from the Gentiles to hear the wisdom of
the true Solomon, and of the true Peace-Lover, Our Lord Jesus
Christ.[2]

Solomon is a type of Christ, and just as the queen of Sheba came
to Solomon to consult him because he was wise, so the church comes
to Christ who is Wisdom himself. As a result, since the queen of
Sheba is black, so must the church be black and beautiful. Her very
blackness is the symbol of her universality; all nations are present in
her. "She came to Jerusalem, then, to the Vision of Peace, with a single
following and in great array; for she came not with a single nation, as
did the Synagogue before her that had the Hebrews only, but with the
races of the whole world, offering moreover worthy gifts to Christ."[3]
Origen looks to the Old Testament for examples of blackness that
foreshadow the mystery of the church. For him, there are two: the
wife of Moses and Ebed-Melech, the Kushite who saved the life of
Jeremiah when the latter had been abandoned in an empty cistern.[4]

I

In the Old Testament, the land of Kush usually meant Nubia, the land
south of Egypt from the first cataract of the Nile to the point south
of the sixth cataract, now the modern city of Khartoum, where the
Blue and White Nile come together as one river flowing northward.
In other words, it is the northern part of the country now known
as the Sudan. The black-skinned people of Nubia were the earliest
beneficiaries of Egyptian civilization. They in turn were the corridor
between Egypt and the interior of Africa, a corridor that brought the
civilization of Egypt to sub-Saharan Africa and the riches of Africa
to Egypt.

The Nubians, on the other hand, were not only a colony of Egypt
that received from it its culture but a people who took that culture
and made it an integral part of their own. Nubia was a black African
nation with its own pharaohs. The people built their own pyramids,
constructed their own majestic temples with their own style of architecture, developed their own writing — in fact, founded their own
empire.

By the eighth century before Christ, the former colony of Egypt
became the dominant power. Shortly before the middle of the century,
the Nubian king Kashta assumed power in the region of Upper Egypt.

He died in 750 B.C., having returned to his home in the south. That same year his son Piankhi (or Peye) assumed the title and the trappings of office of the pharaoh of both Upper and Lower Egypt. With Piankhi began the XXVth Dynasty, the reign of the black pharaohs, who would rule Egypt and Nubia together for almost a hundred years.

During this period Nubia and the black pharaohs made their appearance in the Old Testament. Isaiah speaks of the powerful Nubian warriors:

> Ah, land of whirring wings
> which is beyond the rivers of Ethiopia;
> which sends ambassadors by the Nile,
> in vessels of papyrus upon the waters!
> Go, you swift messengers,
> to a nation, tall and smooth,
> to a people feared near and far,
> a nation mighty and conquering,
> whose land the rivers divide. (Isa. 18:1–2)

In chapter 19, Isaiah speaks of Egypt and its eventual defeat by Assyria. This critical juncture in the history of Egypt was described in 2 Kings 19 (repeated in Isa. 37:5–11). The prophet Isaiah promised Hezekiah, the king of Judah, that the Assyrians would abandon the siege of Jerusalem because the king of Assyria had been called to meet an invasion of Egyptian troops under Tirhakah (or Taharqa). This ruler was the next to the last and perhaps the greatest of the black pharaohs; he ruled from 690 to 664 B.C. In 663, under the rule of Tanoutamon, nephew of Tirhakah, the Assyrians invaded Egypt and took over the empire, seizing the city of Thebes, the home of the black pharaohs. With this defeat, the Nubians returned to Nubia and never again held power in Egypt.[5]

It is, however, a Nubian who emerges from the pages of the New Testament as the one person there who was undeniably black. He is often referred to as the "Ethiopian Eunuch," and his story appears in Acts 8:26–40. This text is significant, since it places this individual of non-Jewish origin as a proselyte, or believer in the Jewish religion, in the chapter before the conversion of the apostle Paul and two chapters before the Roman centurion Cornelius, who is converted by the apostle Peter.

The text in Acts describes a very wealthy and powerful man who was definitely black, yet it never gives us his name. We know that he was wealthy because he journeyed in a chariot, not on foot like

Philip the Deacon, who baptized him. We also know that he was wealthy because he was a royal treasurer in a country that clearly from the text is not Ethiopia but Nubia. "Ethiopian," as pointed out, is the generic name in Greek for a black African. In fact, the text indicates that this man is from Nubia inasmuch as he is described as the treasurer of the "kandake," a title used in Nubia at the time to refer to the queen mother or perhaps a queen reigning in her own right. At any rate, it seems that in Nubia at this time the mother of the sovereign wielded much influence.[6] Another sign of this man's wealth is his possession of a personal scroll of the prophet Isaiah, which he read in the Greek Septuagint version. Like most people of ancient times, he was reading aloud, so that Philip was able to hear him and use the text that was cited as the beginning of his catechesis.[7]

This unnamed African is the first black to enter the Christian faith. It was more than five hundred years, however, before Nubia itself accepted Christianity. When the Christian faith arrived, it came already divided.

II

Justinian, the Byzantine emperor who ruled the Roman Empire from Constantinople between 527 and 565, sent missionaries to Nubia in the middle of the sixth century; his wife, the beautiful and resourceful Theodora, also sent missionaries. Theodora supported the cause of the Monophysites — those holding the doctrine that Christ's human nature had been swallowed up by his divine nature, making him not human and divine but only divine. The Council of Chalcedon in 451, however, had solemnly declared that Christ had two natures, human and divine. The church of Alexandria in Egypt and other large groups of Christians, for reasons partly doctrinal and partly political and social, rejected Chalcedon's definition and became known as Monophysites, from the two Greek words meaning "one nature." Apparently, the first missionaries to arrive in Nubia were Monophysite priests sent by the authority of Theodora. Justinian, on the other hand, supported the teaching of Chalcedon, the official teaching of the Catholic church. His missionaries finally reached Nubia about 570.

By the sixth century the original kingdom of Nubia had broken up into three kingdoms: Nobatia in the north, Makouria in the center, and Alwa in the south. Details regarding the movement and extension of conversion are not known, but by the final quarter of the sixth century, Nubia had become Christian. Apparently both the northern and southern kingdoms were Monophysite, and the middle kingdom of Makouria was Chalcedonian (or, as the supporters of Chalcedon would be known in Egypt, Melkite). By the next century the kingdoms of Nobatia and Makouria were united under one king, and the church was Monophysite, although there are indications of a Melkite episcopal see that lasted for some time.[8]

Much of our knowledge about Christian Nubia has only recently been acquired. Unlike Egypt, which was excavated and studied in the course of the nineteenth century, most of the Nubian treasures and ruins remained covered over by sand until the middle of this century. Only in the last half century and especially in the last twenty years (stimulated in particular by the construction of the Aswan Dam, which meant the submergence of many of the temples and churches) has the serious study of Christian Nubia been made. Hence, only in the last several decades has it become clear that in a black African nation in large measure cut off from the rest of the Christian world, an ancient people built their churches with murals depicting the Virgin and the saints (usually with white skins) and their kings, queens, bishops, and nobles (with dark skins), clad in rich vestments and royal insignia in the stylized and hieratic Byzantine manner.

The Nubians left their leather manuscripts and documents, both liturgical and legal, written in several forms of Nubian script, some of which still remain undeciphered. The Byzantine influence was unmistakable in this country in the heart of Africa. Not only did the art bear the mark of Constantinople, but the Byzantine titles of the imperial government were reduplicated in the royal administration of Nubia. For instance, the royal governor of the area known as Nobatia was called an *eparch*; at the court there existed an official called the *domestikos*, and another was the *protodomestikos*. Evidence suggests that the upper classes of Nubia used the Greek language as well as the Coptic of Egypt and their own Nubian tongue. Very likely the church also used Greek, at least in certain periods. It is unclear how long the Nubian church remained under the jurisdiction of Constantinople. Certainly, it was under the influence and probably the jurisdiction of Alexandria in Egypt by the eighth century. In 641 the Arab conquest of Egypt was complete, and the church of Alexandria was under the control of the Islamic governor of Egypt. Nubia as a Christian kingdom was in many respects an independent entity cut off from the great Christian centers.

Yet this Christian nation survived with its liturgy, which may very well have long been the liturgy of Constantinople rather than that of the Copts of Alexandria; with its monasteries, some of which were very large and extensive; with its cathedrals (at one point, it seems Nubia had thirteen episcopal sees);[9] and with its military forces and fortifications, which stood as a barrier against Islam.[10] A great deal remains to be discovered about this unique African church. There are still sites to be excavated and many manuscripts to be deciphered and studied. One thing is certain, however; recent evidence makes it clear that the Nubian church remained as an outpost of Christianity much later into the Middle Ages than was hitherto believed.

In 1964 a corpse was discovered in the rubble of a crypt at the church at Q'asr Ibrim (or Kasr Ibrim), a fortified city in the northern part of Nubia. The body had seemingly been buried in haste. Attached to the thighs of the skeleton were two scrolls, one written in the Coptic dialect of the delta region of Egypt and the other in Arabic. They were ordination documents attached to the dead body of a bishop attesting to his episcopal ordination; they gave his name — Timotheos — and his see, the joint episcopal sees of Faras and Ibrim (originally two separate sees). The documents also attested that the ordination took place in the presence of other Nubian bishops in the city of Fustat (now called Old Cairo) by the patriarch of Alexandria, Gabriel IV, whose episcopacy lasted from 1372 to 1380.[11]

The remains of Timotheos, bishop of Faras and Ibrim, are a mute testimony to the survival of a Christian church almost to the end of the Middle Ages, a church that existed on the frontiers of Christianity for almost eight hundred years. It is the testimony of an African Christianity and an African Christian culture that is, despite its Monophysite orientation, part of the Catholic tradition in the same way that all of Eastern Christianity is. We do not know exactly when Christianity died out completely. There were rumors of Christian villages surviving in remote areas as late as the middle of the eighteenth century.[12] What we do know is that the story of one of the world's oldest civilizations is also one of the forgotten dramas of church history.

III

Yet Nubia was not the most ancient Christian community in black Africa. Ethiopia was converted to Christianity some two centuries before the kingdoms of Nubia. A mountainous kingdom in the horn of Africa, across the Red Sea from the more ancient kingdoms of southern Arabia, this earlier civilization was apparently established by Semites from the south of Arabia.[13] A great civilization of indigenous black peoples came into existence in the first century A.D. The major sources for our knowledge of this civilization are the massive archaeological remains at the site of what was the royal capital, Axum. Here a centralized monarchy evolved, and here the language of the people, Ge'ez, received an alphabet and a written form. Ethiopia had a written language with its own alphabet from the second century A.D., having used the South Arabian script in the previous period. By this time also the mountain kingdom had emerged as a commercial center, trading with countries from the Mediterranean to the Indian Ocean, as well as with the interior of Africa. Merchants and travelers from all parts of the civilized world came to Adulis, the harbor, and Axum, the capital.[14]

The Ethiopian kings located at Axum gradually extended their dominion over parts of Nubia, northern Ethiopia (Eritrea), and parts of southern Arabia. By the fourth century, the king of Axum had the title "king of kings," for he had become the overlord of other kings in the area. In the first part of the fourth century, the king of kings was Ezana, an excellent and powerful military leader.

Ethiopia became a Christian country in the first part of the fourth century through the activity of Frumentius and Edesius, two Syrians who had been slaves at the royal court of Axum during the reign of Ezana's father, whose name it seems was Ella Amida. At his death the queen became regent during the minority of Ezana. It seems very likely that the influence of both Frumentius and Edesius led to the conversion of Ezana and the royal court. Ezana freed them both at his accession, and they were able to return to Syria. Frumentius, who is honored as a saint in both the Catholic and Ethiopian churches, visited St. Athanasius, the patriarch of Alexandria, on his way to Syria in order to apprise the patriarch of the growth of Christianity in Ethiopia, especially at the royal court. He requested Athanasius to ordain a bishop and send him to Ethiopia. Athanasius made Frumentius a bishop and sent him back. Thus he is rightly considered the founder of the church in Ethiopia. Inscriptions on the monuments of Axum and elsewhere in the country as well as the symbols on the coins of the time (Ethiopia was one of the first black nations to have its own coinage) indicate the conversion of Ezana to Christianity. It is not at all clear how rapidly Christianity spread in the countryside among the ordinary people. It is certain, however, that by the last quarter of the fourth century, Ethiopian pilgrims were a frequent sight in Jerusalem. Their presence is attested in documents of the period.[15]

By the end of the fifth century, Christianity became firmly established in the country, and by the middle of the sixth century, Ethiopia was a powerful nation whose rulers were militant protectors of Christianity in the neighboring areas, including southern Arabia and Nubia. In the first part of the sixth century, the Ethiopian king, Caleb or Elesbaan, led an expedition into southern Arabia to punish those responsible for the massacre of Christians at Najran in 523.[16]

Ethiopia became a Christian nation with its own tradition and culture. By the fifth century it had its own liturgy, derived from the Coptic liturgy of Alexandria. This liturgy had its own unique characteristics in terms of liturgical texts, sacred rites like the dance, music (including the use of the drum that was unique to Ethiopia), and artwork and architecture, like the famous churches hewn out of the living rock at Lalibela. Ethiopia has made its own unique contribution to the Christian heritage with its own translation of the Scriptures, its own version of several patristic texts, and its own rich tradition of monasticism and asceticism. Monasteries began to be established as early as the fifth century, and monks continued to play an important role in the spiritual life of the people throughout Ethiopian history. Liturgically and canonically, Ethiopia was part of the patriarchate of Alexandria. Down to the middle of the present century, the head of the Ethiopian church, the *abuna*, or the metropolitan ordained by the patriarch of Alexandria, was always an Egyptian. This practice ceased finally in 1951, when an Ethiopian was chosen.

Theologically also, Ethiopia (like Nubia) followed the Egyptian church in rejecting the position of Rome and Constantinople in the Council of Chalcedon in 451. As a result, the Ethiopians to this day are Monophysites, except for the several thousand members of the Eastern Rite Ethiopian Church, which is joined with Rome.[17] Politically, however, from the fourth to the seventh century, Ethiopia was a partner with the Byzantine Empire in the Red Sea area. At the same time, Greek influence was very strong, and that language was spoken at the court and by the upper classes. With the rise of Islam and its spread into Africa in the seventh century, links with the Byzantine Empire and the Mediterranean world were almost completely broken.

In the history of the church, Ethiopia occupies a special place. Here we have an African church that has its roots in the early church. Before the church was established in Ireland or Anglo-Saxon England or in any country of northern Europe, a Catholic church linked to St. Athanasius blossomed in an African culture. Despite any doctrinal differences that arose later, the Ethiopian church is a reminder that Africa forms part of the rich heritage of Catholicism.

IV

Africa is the home of monasticism, and an extraordinary black saint was one of its leaders during the first century of the Christian monastic experience in the Egyptian desert. His name is St. Moses the Black. Much of the historical information regarding him comes from a source rich in legendary material woven around a core of historical fact, *The Lausiac History of Palladius.*[18]

In the Egyptian desert just south of the delta region, men and women began living the monastic life singly or in twos or threes as hermits in small dwellings far enough apart for solitude but nevertheless located around a central oratory or church. These colonies of hermits had already begun to develop by the middle of the fourth century when St. Athanasius wrote his life of St. Anthony of Egypt, usually considered the founder of Christian monasticism. The hermits were not the only dwellers in the Egyptian desert. During this period of history many citizens from the municipalities who could no longer support the heavy taxation found their way to the desert. Finally, outlaws and bandits also sought refuge in the desert wilderness. One of these outlaws was a strong, athletic black man who had been a slave; he was difficult in character — perhaps even a murderer — and was too much for his owner to control. His name (or the name he took later) was Moses. Moses went to the desert and became the leader of a band of outlaws. Under circumstances that are not known, he was converted and became a monk. Eventually, he was ordained a priest. This was a singular honor, for at that time monks were not normally ordained.[19]

St. Moses the Black became the spiritual leader of a group of hermits in the desert of Scete, about a hundred miles south of Alexandria. It was there that he and his monks were martyred around the year 410. We have about forty sayings, or *apophthegmata* of the Abba Moses. The title "abba" (from the Aramaic word for "father") was given to monks who were spiritual teachers.[20] The sayings attributed to St. Moses the Black would be sufficient to place him among the spiritual teachers of early monasticism; however, present-day scholarship also attributes to him the first two chapters in the collection known as the *Conferences*, by Cassian,[21] which deal with the ends and purposes of the monastic life.

The monastic writings of the early monks in the period between the fourth and seventh centuries have had a great influence on the spirituality of the church. Both in the East and in the West, these writings laid the foundation of future ascetic and mystical writings. It

is important to note the role of an early black monk in this movement.
Just as we know from the sources that in the Egyptian desert of the
fourth and fifth centuries there were many men and women from all
parts of the Christian world seeking a life of prayer in the eremitical
way of life, so the presence of Moses the Black is a good indication
that more than likely there were other black Africans in the desert
whose names have not been recorded.[22]

In the south of Egypt, the cenobitic (or community) form of
monastic life was established by St. Pachomius. These were large
villages of monks and separate monastic villages for women. This
Pachomian form of monasticism, as well as the traditions of the
eremitical form, found a home in Ethiopia. More than likely both
Ethiopians and Nubians were found in the Pachomian monasteries
of Upper Egypt.

V

The history of blacks in the early church is clearly documented in
Ethiopia and in Nubia, and in the identity of an individual such
as the Abba Moses. The picture of black Africans in North Africa
and in Egypt is less clear and more uncertain. The population of
Egypt was African; the racial characteristics of the indigenous peoples
of Egypt have been the subject of much discussion. Certainly, the
black African element became more pronounced as one advanced into
Upper Egypt. In the period of early Christianity, the delta region and
particularly Alexandria were Greek-speaking centers with a highly
cosmopolitan population, among whom were many black Africans
from Nubia and present-day Ethiopia and other areas of sub-Saharan
Africa. Many of them were slaves and descendants of slaves, soldiers
and their descendants among the troops from the South who had
fought for centuries on behalf of the Egyptian pharaohs and later
Egyptian rulers, as well as ambassadors and legates, freedmen, and
their families. As a result, it is the consensus of historians that Egypt
has for centuries been a region of mixed peoples both racially and
culturally.[23]

On the other hand, it is not easy to draw hard and fast conclusions regarding the racial characteristics of historical personages, to
say with certainty who was actually black or who was of racially mixed
ancestry, or who was of non-Egyptian origin. The Abba Moses was certainly a black African, for the texts describing him make more than
a passing reference to his complexion. There is no way, however, to

determine whether St. Cyril of Alexandria (ca. 375–444), father of
the church, bishop and theologian, was black or even dark-skinned.
The same uncertainty exists regarding Origen (d. ca. 250). Still, they
were Africans. Perhaps what is important to remember is that no
matter how much Hellenistic Egypt may have looked outward to the
Mediterranean world, it remained an African country with an African
past. Neither the Egyptian church nor the leaders of that church were
European in thought and culture; they were Egyptian — that is to
say, African.

The same problem regarding the black presence in the early church
is encountered in North Africa. While evidence of skeletal remains
may show that the earliest inhabitants of North Africa were Negroid in physical characteristics and that the subsequent invasions of
tribal peoples from the eastern part of Africa were dark-skinned,[24] the
Berber population made up of Mauretanians, Numidians, and other
tribal groups that never fully submitted to Roman authority was not
necessarily considered black by ancient authors, though intermarriage
with the population south of the Sahara had taken place for centuries.
North Africa was a crossroads of ethnic groupings, cultures, civilizations, and religions. Carthage, the great maritime city-state of North
Africa, was founded by the Phoenicians in what is now Tunisia in
814 B.C. It was finally destroyed by Roman armies in 146 B.C., to be
rebuilt as a Roman city by Augustus in 29 B.C. The presence of black
Africans in Carthage is well attested by documents. These black Africans were not only slaves, but many were part of the military force
of Carthage. Black troops accompanied Hannibal in his European
campaigns against Rome in the third century B.C.

The victory of Rome over Carthage made Rome an African power.
North Africa became Roman Africa. The territory was eventually divided into such Roman provinces as Proconsular Africa, Mauretania,
Numidia, and Cyrenaica. These divisions and names underwent modifications later. It is in this North African area, especially the region of
the restored city of Carthage in Proconsular Africa and Numidia, that
a church was established, Latin in language and Roman in culture.
The landed aristocracy was basically Roman, made up of families
from Italy that had established themselves in the "colonies." There
were also the descendants of the Roman soldiers who had been given
lands in Roman Africa. The urban population was mainly composed
of descendants of the Roman or Italian population or Romanized
Berbers who had established themselves in cities like Carthage. The
rural population was essentially of Berber stock.

Individual North African Christians like Tertullian and St. Cyprian left a lasting mark on the development of Christianity. Tertullian (ca. 160–ca. 220) was the son of a Roman soldier; Cyprian (d. 258) was a convert from the aristocratic society of Carthage. Both spoke Latin and culturally were Romans. It is not likely that they were black. Two of the greatest martyrs of the early church were two North African women, Perpetua and Felicitas, courageous women whose martyrdom account, written perhaps originally in Latin but translated into Greek, occupies an important place in early Christian literature. St. Perpetua was a member of the Carthaginian upper class, and St. Felicitas was a slave, probably in the same household.[25] The martyrdom took place about 203.[26] There is nothing to indicate the racial characteristics of the two saints. It is very unlikely that a wealthy family of Carthaginian landholders were black Africans, but it is quite possible that a slave girl in the household was. In any case, there is no evidence for saying one way or another with certitude. And yet this is in a city where blacks had become famous, as for example the great athletic hero Olympius, who fought animals with his bare hands in the arena and was immortalized in Latin poetry by Luxorius.[27]

For many, St. Augustine and his mother, St. Monica, are two examples of black Africa's contribution to history and world civilization. Certainly, Augustine can be ranked as one of the most brilliant theologians and ecclesiastics of all times. For African American Catholics in the nineteenth century, there was a singular pride in being able to point to Augustine as one of their own. But was he in fact black?

Augustine was born in 354 in a small provincial town some two hundred miles southwest of Carthage. It was named Thagaste and is now located in Algeria. He was a townsman but not rich. His father had the Roman name Patricius and was perhaps of Roman extraction. He was a man of very modest means. Augustine's native tongue was Latin. He did not know any other language well. Augustine's mother had a Berber name and perhaps was of Berber stock. Physically, he probably resembled the typical Algerian of today. He was not a European, despite his long sojourn in Italy.[28]

Augustine wrote about black Africans in a commentary on Psalm 73 (Psalm 74), using the words of the old Latin translation: "You have broken the head of the dragon. You have given it as food to the Ethiopian peoples."[29]

What is this? How do I understand the Ethiopian peoples? In what way, unless through them, all the nations? And well it is through the blacks; for the Ethiopians are black. They who have been black are called to faith; they precisely, as it is written: For you were at one time darkness but are now light in the Lord (Eph. 5:8). They are especially called black, but they shall not remain black; for from them is the church made, to whom it is said: Who is this who ascends all lightsome (Song of Songs 8:5)? What is made of the color black except that which is said: I am black and beautiful (Song of Songs 1:4)? And how have they received this dragon as food? I think they have received Christ as food.[30]

For Augustine, the Ethiopians — those who are black Africans — are the sign of the church, and in particular, of its universality.

VI

Three popes of the early church are said to have been Africans: St. Victor I (reigned ca. 186–ca. 197), St. Miltiades (311–14), and St. Gelasius I (492–96). Victor I was pope during the quarrel between those in Asia Minor who celebrated Easter on the day of the first full moon of the vernal equinox, which could be any day of the week, and those in the rest of the church, who celebrated Easter on the first Sunday after the first full moon of the vernal equinox. By this time Sunday was the weekly commemoration of the Resurrection, the day of rest. Victor tried desperately to make the churches of Asia Minor conform to the general usage, which in time did prevail.[31]

Pope Miltiades is especially important because he was pope at the time of the Peace of Constantine in 313. Although not baptized until much later, Constantine's conversion had begun, and with it, the long process whereby the Catholic church would become the only recognized religion of the Roman Empire. Miltiades was also the first pope who had to deal with the schism caused by the Donatists in North Africa, a split in the North African church that would last for several centuries.[32]

Gelasius I was probably the most significant of the three in that his strong declaration to the Byzantine emperor Anastasius I spelled out the right of the Roman pontiff to exercise jurisdiction in all parts of the church. He also vindicated the papal right to be judged by no one, including the emperor. In a sense he laid the foundations for the primacy of the see of Rome. Pope Gelasius I also played a role in the elaboration of the Roman liturgy during a period of increased splendor in the liturgical ceremonies. While they are not known in detail, the reforms that Gelasius introduced, one of the oldest collections of prayers and texts for the Mass, bears his name.[33]

The *Liber Pontificalis* gives the birthplace of these three popes as Africa. This work is a collection of biographical notices of all the Roman pontiffs beginning with St. Peter. These notices are extremely short for the early popes, but for those of the early Middle Ages the notices become longer and more detailed. For each of the three pontiffs in question, the *Liber Pontificalis* uses the formula *natione Afer*, "in nation an African." As we have seen, the designation "African" did not necessarily mean a black African. In a document of the late Roman Empire, the term "African" would mean most likely an inhabitant of Proconsular Africa, the province around Carthage. It is not out of the question that a black man from this area could have been pope, and yet it does not seem likely. At any rate, the text itself does not say so.

Some historians raise a question regarding the credence one should place in the description given regarding Africa in the *Liber Pontificalis*. The fact is that this source cannot be trusted completely for its historical accuracy. Abbé Duchesne, who produced a critical edition, came to the conclusion that the first section was composed in the second quarter of the sixth century. He based this conclusion on the internal evidence in the text. It is only about thirty years after the pontificate of Pope Gelasius I (d. 496) that the biographical notices seem to become contemporaneous with the writer of the *Liber*. As a result, much of the information found in the earlier notices must be treated with caution.[34]

It is not beyond the realm of possibility that a black man of African origin would be a leader in the church in Rome.[35] The historical research of Frank Snowden, Jr., *Blacks in Antiquity: Ethiopians in the Greco-Roman Experience*, proves through his detailed and careful examination of different artworks depicting the human figure through the Hellenistic period that men and women with obvious Negroid features and skin coloration were to be found in almost every large city of the Roman Empire from Gaul to Asia Minor from the sixth century B.C. to the third century A.D. In the city of Rome blacks were found as actors, entertainers, public and household slaves, gladiators, soldiers, charioteers, religious attendants for the cult of Isis, and even as emissaries of foreign governments.

In a famous passage in his *Life of Constantine*, Eusebius of Caesarea described the court of Constantine the Great in Constantinople.

Ambassadors were continually arriving from all nations, bringing for his acceptance their most precious gifts.... I myself have sometimes stood near the entrance of the imperial palace, and observed... barbarians in attendance, differing... in costume and decorations... some of a red complexion, others white as snow, others again of an intermediate colour. [There]... might be seen specimens of the Blemmyan tribes,[36] of the Indians, and the Ethiopians, "that widely divided race, remotest of mankind"... some offering crowns of gold, others diadems set with precious stones.... Some appeared with horses, others with shields and long spears, with arrows and bows,... offering... services and alliance for the emperor's acceptance... He also honoured the noblest among them with Roman offices of dignity; so that many... preferred to continue... among us, and felt no desire to revisit their native land.[37]

Constantine died in 337. Some thirty-five years later, about 372, St. Zeno died, bishop in the city of Verona. For some unknown reason, he had left his home in Africa and found his way to a remote north Italian town where the populace elected him bishop and where he left the memory of a holy shepherd and preacher — the latter is evident from the small number of his homilies that have survived. Zeno is considered the patron of Verona. By his own account, he was from Africa. Was he black? We have no firm evidence, but there may be a tradition regarding his dark complexion.[38]

About a century before the death of St. Zeno, a group of Roman soldiers were put to death in the mountains of present-day Switzerland. These soldiers, according to the account written some 150 years after the event, formed the Theban Legion, and their leader was a soldier named Maurice. These soldiers had accepted death at the hands of other soldiers rather than deny their Christian faith. Their martyrdom took place in a narrow valley in the canton of Valais in what is now the French-speaking area of Switzerland. By the fourth century the tomb of these martyrs had become a great shrine and center of pilgrimage. It became the site of a monastery that has survived to this day as one of the oldest in the Christian world. In medieval art St. Maurice and his soldiers were often depicted as black men. (The name "Maurice" is from the same root as the English word "moor," meaning "dark.") Several Roman legions were named Theban, one of which was composed of soldiers from the interior of Egypt. Coupled with the fact that the presence of black soldiers in the Roman armies is well attested, it is logical to assume that many of the soldiers were dark-skinned Egyptians or Nubians and that a man with a name meaning "dark" was dark in complexion. On the façade of the thirteenth-century Gothic cathedral of Magdeburg in northern Germany, there is a stone statue of a knight in chain mail. The knight, a black man who is one of the patron saints of soldiers, is St. Maurice.[39] The black presence in the early church in North Africa and Europe may be a shadowy one, its extent may be measured more by legend than by verifiable data, but the reality of this presence is undeniable, even when only symbolized by Melchior (or Balthasar), the exotic black king usually pictured among the Magi at the Christ Child's crib.[40]

VII

The church reappeared in Africa at the very beginning of modern times. This was the result of Portuguese activity at the end of the fifteenth century, in what is now the country of Angola, at the mouth of the Congo River. Portugal, the first of the maritime powers that opened up the great age of exploration in modern times, had allied itself with one Afonso, the eldest son of Nzinga a Nkouwou, king of the Congo. Afonso, known as Afonso the Good, had wholeheartedly accepted the Catholic faith, and in a war with rival claimants to the throne, his forces won with Portuguese help. He ruled as the king of the Congo from 1506 to 1543.

Afonso's rule was marked by two concerns. The first was to convert his people to Catholicism and to profit from the technological knowledge of the Europeans. The second was to control the rapacious appetite of the Portuguese for riches and especially for slaves. The tragedy of Afonso, a man of extraordinary ability and wisdom, was his failure to accomplish either of these goals. The scope of the tragedy is laid bare in letters between him and the kings of Portugal, Manuel I (1495–1521) and João III (1521–57). The royal correspondence is preserved in the Archives of Simancas in Portugal. Afonso had Congolese scribes who wrote the letters in Portuguese. These letters and the copies of the letters from the Portuguese kings have been edited and translated into French.[41]

Afonso was sincere in his zeal for religion. A Portuguese missionary described him as follows in a letter to King Manuel I in 1516: "It seems to me that his Christianity is not that of a man but of an angel whom the Lord would have sent to convert this kingdom. I can in fact testify to your Highness that he teaches us and that he knows better than we do the prophets, the Gospel..., all the lives of the saints, and everything that relates to our Holy Mother the church."[42] He goes on to point out that Afonso would preach to the people after Mass was over. He was also determined to stamp out the practice of the traditional religions, and he burned the images.

In one very bitter letter Afonso expressed his disappointment regarding some of the Portuguese clergy who had been sent to evangelize the people. The king had sent a group of canons regular from Lisbon, known familiarly as the Fathers of St. Elias. After their arrival in the kingdom of Afonso, they ceased to live the common life, began to live in concubinage with the women of the country, and started to traffic in slaves.[43] Afonso had requested the services of stone masons from Portugal. No sooner had they arrived than they demanded slaves, money, and wine; they ultimately accomplished little of the work the king desired. The same held true for the shoemaker to whom the king had given leather to make shoes; there was much waste and poor workmanship.[44]

In the end, slavery meant the undoing of all that Afonso had tried to accomplish. It must be admitted that Afonso had agreed from the beginning to supply slaves as part of the regular trade agreement. Slavery was found in practically all of the African civilizations. The African form of slavery resulted primarily from being captured in war or being punished for crimes.[45] It might be said on Afonso's behalf that he probably did not know that slavery in Portugal meant something other than the kind of slavery found in Africa. The king soon found out that the appetite for slaves was insatiable. He found out also that nothing would stop the Portuguese from expanding the slave trade, even if it meant seizing Afonso's own people, and even members of his family. In fact, the king of Portugal made clear to him that slavery, like a narcotic, sucked every party into its corruption. In a letter written sometime in 1529, João III wrote Afonso, noting that in his last letter Afonso wished to stop the sale of slaves, as it was "depopulating your country." The Portuguese king pointed out that there was an endless supply of slaves outside of the Congo as well as of slaves captured in war; thus Afonso would not need to worry about his own subjects being sold as slaves. He also made it clear that if the slave traffic were to be stopped, commerce with Portugal would be reduced to only one ship per year and suggested that this arrangement would procure little honor and wealth for the African king.[46]

The one hope for Afonso was the establishment of the Catholic church in his kingdom as an institution independent of the Portuguese crown. He wanted his own bishop for a diocese within the Congo. He wanted his own communication with the pope without depending upon the generosity of the Portuguese. He had sent his eldest son, Henrique, to Portugal to study for the priesthood along with other noble Congolese children who were to receive an education and bring Western culture back to the Congo. Henrique was ordained a priest sometime before 1518. In that year Pope Leo X gave him permission to be consecrated a bishop, despite his young age. The prince was about twenty-three years old. It seems that he actually was made a bishop in 1521. Leo X made him a titular bishop to act as the auxiliary of the bishop of Funchal in the Madeira Islands.[47] Henrique resided in the Congo, and he died in 1531.[48] With him died the hope of a Congolese church with direct access to Rome, and likewise the hope of an indigenous clergy. Thus, at the very time when the Catholic church was losing northern Europe to the Protestant reform, an African king had wished to win his people to that same church. It was the curse of the slave trade that drove many of Afonso's subjects against the church after his death in 1543.[49]

VIII

The slave trade, of course, was not new to the European continent. It had existed since Roman times. It continued, to a lesser degree, along with serfdom through the Middle Ages. A large proportion of the traffic involved men and women of the Slavic nations in the East, hence the derivation of the word "slave" from "Slav" in all of the major European languages.[50] Nonetheless, it is the opinion of Charles Verlinden, the historian who has written the most on medieval slavery, that black Africans were imported as slaves into southern Portugal and Spain during the Moslem period — that is, before the twelfth century.[51] By the fourteenth century there is more extensive documentation regarding the sale and possession of blacks from Africa. Most were imported from North Africa and were part of the spoils of the intermittent warfare that Christian Spain carried on with the Moslem peoples both within the Iberian Peninsula itself and in what is now Morocco.[52]

In time a substantial part of the population, both slave and free, was African or of African extraction. Obviously they were Catholics and are part of that long history of the black presence in the Catholic church. In Barcelona and in Valencia in the fifteenth century, there existed a confraternity or *cofradía* of blacks, both male and female, freed persons and slaves. A confraternity in the medieval church was a union of laypersons organized for mutual support, mutual security and protection, professional aid, and religious fervour.[53] This increase of African slavery, specifically of black Africans, at the end of the Middle Ages was evident in other Mediterranean countries. From his own research, Verlinden has pointed out the increase in black slaves working as laborers in the agricultural economy of Sicily. He estimated that in the first part of the fifteenth century, two-thirds of the male slaves in Sicily were black.[54]

It was from this milieu of agricultural slaves that one of the most famous black saints arose. The man now known as St. Benedict the Moor was born near Messina in Sicily in 1526; he died in the city of Palermo in 1589. His lifetime spanned the Reformation and the first activities of the Counter-Reformation. It also spanned the opening of the New World to exploration and exploitation. Benedict's parents, Diana and Cristoforo Manassari, were both slaves; as a youth, Benedict was a shepherd and was remarked for his piety. Freed by his slaveowner, Benedict joined a group of hermits who followed the Rule of St. Francis, though they were not members of the Franciscan Order. The superior was a certain Jerome Lanza, whom Benedict succeeded as superior.

Such hermits were in many ways fringe groups, often enough representative of more radical attitudes among the people in the face of established practice and faith. Pope Pius IV (reigned 1559–65), the pope who convened the third period of the Council of Trent and who presided over its completion, charged the hermits to join one of the branches of the Franciscan Order. St. Benedict the Moor entered the reformed branch, which was known as the Order of Friars Minor, or the Observant branch, commonly known today as the Brown Franciscans. Benedict was never ordained a priest. Nevertheless, he served a term as superior of his community and then novice master and also as cook. He became renowned as a counselor and adviser to many of the laity and the clergy; at one point, he advised the viceroy of Sicily. At the time of his death in 1589, his reputation for holiness was well established. Even before his eventual canonization, he was chosen as the patron of Palermo. Popular devotion to him was widespread not only in Italy but also in Spain and in the New World, where he became the patron of the black population, most of whom were slaves. Benedict was canonized in 1807 by Pope Pius VII, not only because of his sanctity, but also because his canonization was a statement regarding the evils of the slave trade. His feast day was established on April 4, the date of his death.[55]

St. Benedict the Moor is a witness not only to the fact that in the Catholic church a black slave could be raised to the altars as a saint, even a very popular saint, but also to the widespread presence of a black Catholic population in southern Europe at the beginning of the modern period. It is also paradoxical that at the time when black Africans were increasingly being enslaved not only in Europe but especially in the newly discovered territories in the Americas, a black African and former slave was venerated for his holiness and revered for his sanctity even before his canonization in the very countries engaged in the slave trade.

Slavery was very much an accepted institution in the world of the sixteenth and seventeenth centuries. It was accepted as an institution by the church leaders of the time, despite the efforts of popes to regulate trafficking in slaves and of Catholic theologians to determine the legitimate basis for the enslavement of certain peoples.[56] Very likely the institution would have petered out in Europe had not the discovery of a vast new world in the Western Hemisphere created a demand for cheap and abundant labor.

Roman law, and the jurisprudence resulting from it, governed the institution of slavery in such Catholic nations as Spain, Portugal, and France. Even when these nations introduced special legislation regarding the institution of slavery, Roman law tradition still served as its basis. The legislation of the church had insisted upon the obligation of slaveholders to baptize their slaves and to ensure their right to religious practice, including marriage and family life. Roman law tradition also listed the legitimate reasons or titles by which certain categories of persons could be enslaved, such as prisoners of war, those guilty of criminal acts, and the condition of birth. As is often the case, however, there was often a vast discrepancy between the theory and the practice. The fact that one individual had ownership of the person and the labor of another provided the framework for inevitable acts of oppression and brutality.[57]

IX

In the Western Hemisphere, however, there was another factor: to exploit the mineral riches and to work the vast plantations required cheap and abundant labor. Slavery was the answer. At first, the native population was enslaved by both the Spaniards and the Portuguese in what is now Latin America. Both the physical labor and the psychological constraints of bondage led to the death of much of the

Indian population. On the other hand, black Africans provided an inexhaustible supply of laborers for work in the mines and in the fields. African slaves arrived in the New World with the Spanish conquerors. These slaves were already part of the population in Spain. By 1510 slaves were being imported from the African mainland. Early on, however, Spanish theologians, basing themselves on Roman law teaching, questioned the legitimacy of enslaving the Indians. What crimes had they committed? What was the justification for waging war against them? On the other hand, the Africans south of the Sahara were considered as being Moslems — erroneously in fact, since at that time little Moslem influence was found in the general population outside of North Africa. In the Middle Ages, Christians were considered to have a legitimate right to enslave the Moslems of North Africa who waged war on them. Moslems made Christians slaves, and Christians in turn enslaved their Moslem prisoners.

It is in this context that the remarkable figure of Bartolomé de Las Casas must be seen. De Las Casas was born in 1474 in Seville to a family that had been associated with the second voyage of Columbus to America in 1493. In 1502 he himself migrated to the island of Hispaniola, now comprising Haiti and the Dominican Republic. At the time he was already a cleric, and on his ordination to the priesthood in 1512, he would be the first priest to be ordained in the New World. As a landowner, he was the owner of Indian slaves. Shortly after his ordination he underwent a conversion experience and became convinced that he had no legitimate title to own slaves. He came to the decision that the enslavement of the Indians was immoral. He also saw the enslavement of the Indians as slowly destroying them as a people. De Las Casas was a man of tireless energy and unflagging determination. He traveled back and forth between Spain and the Spanish colonies to plead before the Council of the Indies on behalf of the Indians. In the end he entered the Dominican Order because the Dominican friars were outspoken in their criticism of the exploitation of the Indians. He began writing his famous treatise on the history of the Indies, in which he documented the brutality and injustices inflicted on them by the Spaniards. In 1537 Pope Paul III issued the bull *Sublimis Deus*, which detailed the rights of the Indians and the injustice of their enslavement. Yet, in many respects the papal bull remained a dead letter.

In 1544 De Las Casas was named bishop of Chiapas, in what is now southern Mexico. As bishop he issued instructions to the priests who heard the confessions of slaveholders. Those who owned slaves could not receive absolution for their sins until they promised to grant them freedom and — perhaps this was the greatest threat — made restitution to slaves from whom the slaveholders had unjustly profited. At Easter 1545, rioting ensued as many of the Spaniards found themselves without absolution and consequently unable to fulfill their Easter duty. De Las Casas, facing violent opposition from both his clergy and his people, had to return to Spain, and in 1547 he resigned his see.

Bartolomé de Las Casas played an important role in the history of black Catholics in the New World because of an opinion that he expressed on two separate occasions concerning the enslavement of Africans. In writing his *History of the Indies*, de Las Casas wrote that he regretted the opinion that he had given when still a young priest. In 1516 he had urged the Crown to grant a licence to the Spanish colonists to import Africans into the colonies to replace the Indians who were being destroyed by the harshness of slavery. De Las Casas wrote later that he was unaware that the African slaves were as unjustly treated as the Indians.[58]

There is little to prevent us from believing de Las Casas in this regard. He had a single-minded devotion to the Indians; he was willing to go to any lengths to protect them. At the same time, he was under the impression that the enslavement of prisoners of war, when the war was a just war, was justified. In the sixteenth century a Spaniard would have believed that a war with the Moslems was always justified. Black Africans were seen as inhabitants of Moslem territory. Hence, they could be enslaved like the North African Moslems. The tragedy of Afonso reminds us of the catastrophic results of such a belief. It was typical of de Las Casas, however, to acknowledge his failing and to regret it publicly. In any case, de Las Casas himself was not responsible for the importation of black slaves into the New World. In fact, licences for the introduction of black slaves there had been given as early as 1511.[59]

It is perhaps more important to remember de Las Casas for his conviction regarding what is today called human rights. On his return to Spain in 1547, de Las Casas took part in a famous disputation held at Valladolid in 1550–51 before Emperor Charles V. His opponent was the famous priest and humanist Juan Ginés de Sepúlveda. The question was whether the warfare against the Indians by the Spaniards was a just war. The contention of Sepúlveda was that the war was just, since the end was the conversion of the Indians. This position was supported by the teaching of Aristotle that some men and women are naturally born slaves. They must be ruled by force. The argument of de Las Casas was that Aristotle was wrong. For him all people are one. In the argumentation he used and in the lines of reasoning set forth, one can say that in a real sense de Las Casas helped lay the foundation of modern conceptions of racial justice.[60]

Over 1.5 million blacks were imported into Latin America during the period between 1595 and 1773.[61] By and large, these slaves had some connection with the Catholic church. Both for the Spaniards and the Portuguese, the law demanded that all slaves be baptized and opportunities for religious worship be granted. For the Portuguese this baptism was to take place at the port of embarkation.[62] The Spaniards often baptized the slaves at the port of entry.

The story of black Catholicism in the Western Hemisphere would not be complete without mentioning St. Peter Claver, a Jesuit priest, born about 1580 in Verdù, in the Catalan-speaking section of northeast Spain. Peter Claver came to the Spanish colony of New Granada in South America (today the country of Colombia), where he was ordained a priest in 1616, and where in the port city of Cartagena he began his life's work of ministry to the slaves as they arrived from Africa. The slaves were systematically baptized upon disembarkation. Many were suffering both psychologically and physically. The terrible middle passage, the Atlantic voyage of the slave ship, often resulted in the loss to disease of a large portion of both the human cargo and the crew. For over thirty years under the most harrowing of circumstances, Peter Claver ministered to the spiritual and bodily needs of the slaves, not only the newcomers, but those who lay ill, the prisoners, those condemned to death, the lepers, and the abandoned. He learned at least one African language, and for the others he used the services of interpreters. He made an effort to teach using illustrations and sketches and sought to do more than just baptize or give a few simple instructions. Following the lead of the great Jesuit defender of the blacks Alonso de Sandoval, Peter Claver also sought to improve the physical conditions of the African slaves. He died on September 8, 1654. Pope Leo XIII canonized him in 1888 and made him the patron of missions to blacks. His life was lived in accord with the motto he inscribed at the time of his solemn profession: "Peter Claver, ever the slave of the Ethiopians!"[63]

A recent history of black slavery in Peru describes the social and religious conditions of these transported Africans.

Concerned men like Sandoval have left us a grim picture of conditions under slavery. By his account, the typical African, whether agricultural laborer or household servant, toiled from dawn to dusk, went about almost naked unless he worked on

Sunday and feast days to obtain money for clothing, was miserably fed, received no medical attention, and was harshly, even sadistically, punished for the most frivolous reasons. Sandoval quotes (and supports) the observation of an acquaintance that the Christians punished their slaves more in a week than the Moors did in a year.[64]

Alonso Sandoval (1576–1652), a Jesuit, was a colleague of St. Peter Claver who spoke out forcefully against the conditions of black slaves in the Spanish colonies. Sandoval was among the Jesuits who ministered to the slaves and also wrote a treatise excoriating the treatment they received at the hands of the slaveholders.[65]

One of the means used to evangelize the blacks, both slave and free, in the Spanish and the Portuguese colonies was the *cofradía*. These confraternities were brotherhoods of lay men and women bound together by some common tie who had a chapel where Mass was offered for deceased members, where the feast of the patron saint was annually celebrated, and where the funerals of members were carried out. These confraternities were numerous in the Latin countries of medieval Europe and were transplanted to Latin America. Members of the confraternities assured the funeral rites and the annual suffrages or prayers and Masses for the deceased members and engaged in other charitable works. Many of them were powerful and wealthy.[66]

A recent study has given some idea of the confraternities for blacks in the city of Bahia in colonial Brazil.

Many coloured brotherhoods were established in Bahia in the seventeenth and eighteenth centuries — there were some five for mulattos and six for Negroes dedicated to the Virgin Mary alone — and testified to the social consolidation achieved by the coloured populace. In some cases the brotherhood was founded with the object of freeing its members from bondage: once free, a member contributed to the liberation of his brothers. The majority had wider terms of reference to protect the interests of their members during life and to give them a decent burial at death. The most powerful colored brotherhood of Bahia was that of Our Lady of the Rosary, the only brotherhood to hold annual elections of a king and queen.[67]

We also have a description of the confraternities of blacks and mulattoes in the city of Lima. The oldest confraternity for blacks was founded in the 1540s and was named in honor of the Most Holy Sacrament. By 1619 there were some fifteen in the city, some exclusively for either blacks or mulattoes respectively; others for both blacks and mulattoes together. Many provided religious instruction for their members every Sunday. They engaged in charitable activities such as feeding the poor in hospitals and prisons. They held processions and celebrated the feast of Corpus Christi with public dancing and processions. Once each year or sometimes more often they met for confession and communion. Most were under the protection of a religious order. The richest and most splendid in terms of ceremonies was the *cofradía* of Nuestra Señora de los Reyes (Our Lady of the Kings), under the protection of the Franciscans.[68] How many blacks, either slave or free, were actually members of a confraternity in the various Latin American cities must still be determined. Bowser is of the opinion that only a minority of the blacks actually belonged to a confraternity.[69]

The black confraternities are an aspect of black Catholicism that needs further study. Questions still need to be asked about the Afro-Latin spirituality that was expressed in the life of the confraternities. Further study of the religious ceremonies and devotions peculiar to each *cofradía* needs to be made. Finally, the impact of these organizations specifically for blacks and mulattoes on Latin American Catholicism needs to be measured.

X

Certainly the impact of one Afro-Latin on Catholicism in our day can be measured. St. Martin de Porres, born in Lima in 1579, where he died in 1639, was the illegitimate son of a Spanish nobleman, Juan de Porres, and a freed black woman originally from Panama, Anna Vásquez. Anna Vásquez had likewise given birth to a daughter of Juan de Porres, a younger sister to Martin. At first, Juan de Porres gave no recognition to his son. Finally, he took both children to Ecuador and saw to their instruction. Juan de Porres eventually was named governor of Panama. The young boy, Martin, was returned to Lima, where he was allowed to apprentice himself as a barber-surgeon.

In the meantime, Martin was also attracted to the religious life. He sought to enter the Dominican friary of Our Lady of the Rosary. As a young adolescent Martin was received into the Dominican Order as a *donatus*, that is, in the status of nonfree servant. Juan de Porres was utterly opposed to this status for his son. Martin nonetheless remained. In 1603 Martin made vows as a Dominican lay brother. It seems that this profession was highly unusual because by this time the Council of the Indies had decreed more than once that no African, Indian, mestizo, or mulatto could be ordained a priest or professed as a religious in the Spanish colonies. Ostensibly it was to maintain respect for the religious and priestly office and to maintain doctrinal purity. In the end it was a form of racism that eventually crippled the South American church. Although there were at times priests of mixed blood, they would remain few.[70] It is quite possible that the influence and the dignity of Juan de Porres combined with the evident holiness and charity of the young Martin persuaded the Dominican community to accept him as a lay brother and admit him to solemn profession.

Whatever the circumstances that permitted him to become a Dominican lay brother, Martin soon became a one-man charity agency in the city of Lima. As infirmarian, barber-surgeon, and pharmacist, this dark-skinned friar in his black and white habit stalked the streets of a cruel and indifferent city to bring healing and compassion to the Indian outcast, the abandoned slave, the forgotten child. He inspired others in works of charity such as in the erection of the first foundling hospital in the New World. He was responsible for the disbursement of enormous sums of money. During the day St. Martin de Porres was a man of action; in the night he was a man of prayer, a mystic. For more than forty years he literally lived out his calling as the "Father of the Poor."[71]

Preparations for his eventual canonization took place some twenty years after his death. With the process began the stories and anecdotes that often, perhaps at times too often, centered on the miraculous and the marvelous. In actual fact, despite the almost instant and widespread veneration for Martin as a saint, he was not declared a blessed until 1837 by Pope Gregory XVI, who two years later would condemn the slave trade and by inference slavery itself. Only in 1962 did Pope John XXIII canonize Martin de Porres, during a period that saw the rise of the civil rights movement in the United States and the movement for independence from colonial domination in Africa.

Obviously Martin de Porres, like every saint, was an individual molded by his own age and culture. He was, in fact, fashioned by the historical matrix of the sixteenth and seventeenth centuries. Like every saint also, he has become a symbol, a model for all to relate to, each in his or her way. Martin de Porres was a man of African ancestry, son of an aristocratic father, educated as a Spaniard, yet never escaping the stigma of dark-colored skin and slavery. No matter what may have been his father's influence, he made his choices with independence and determination. No matter what may have been the external expressions of humility and self-effacement, nonthreatening virtues in a black saint fulsomely recorded by his biographers, the persistence and strength of character required for such an arduous ministry as he exercised revealed a Martin both mature and heroic, not a boy but a man, not a tentative novice but a powerhouse of ministry, who by the grandeur of his holy life became the embodiment of a people and the revelation of another side to the Catholic church in New Spain. In him, Africa's roots bore fruit in holiness. Through him, Africa's sons and daughters made the Catholic church their own. It is this church, both African and Spanish, that later was to lay the foundation of the black Catholic community in what is now the United States.

Chapter 2

CATHOLIC SETTLERS
AND CATHOLIC SLAVES:
A CHURCH IN CHAINS

In 1536 four men arrived in Mexican territory after a harrowing trek through lands that are now Florida, Texas, and Arkansas. They were all Spaniards — three were white, and the fourth was black. Their odyssey is one of the epics of early American history. The account is entitled "The Relation that Alvar Nuñez Cabeza de Vaca gave of what befell the armament in the Indies whither Pánfilo de Narváez went for Governor from the year 1527 to the year 1537 when with three comrades he returned and came to Seville."[1] At the end of his narrative Cabeza de Vaca, who had been the second-in-command of Narváez's ill-fated expedition, gave the names of his fellow survivors. The name of the black man was Esteban, often called Estevanico (Spanish variants of the name Stephen), a Spanish-speaking slave, described by Cabeza de Vaca as an Arabian black, native of Azamor in Morocco.

Esteban was a resourceful, intrepid explorer who survived shipwreck, disease, captivity, and physical hardship as much by his wits as by his personal courage. Unlike his fellow survivors, he was a slave. For us, he is a reminder that the first black man to traverse what is now the territory of the United States was Spanish-speaking and a Catholic. With his three companions, he is at the beginning of the story of Catholicism in the United States.

Quite often it is stated that Esteban was a Moslem, since Cabeza de Vaca indicated that he was born in Morocco.[2] It is not likely that a Moslem would have borne the Christian name of Stephen. It is even

28

more unlikely that the Spaniards would have employed a Moslem in an expedition that had evangelization of the Indians as one of its goals. Although we know little about the early history of Esteban, we can assume that as a black slave — there were blacks in North Africa, and he is consistently described as a black man — he was baptized when brought to Spain and was a Catholic when made part of the expedition.

I

In 1539 the viceroy of New Spain, Don Antonio de Mendoza, sent a Franciscan friar, Fray Marcos de Niza, northward into the present-day southwestern part of the United States to report on certain fabled cities of gold. Fray Marcos was also to investigate the possibilities of missionary activity. Mendoza chose Esteban to go as guide and scout for the friar because during previous journeys in that area he had acquired much wilderness experience. It seems that the Indians trusted the Spanish African. Fray Marcos de Niza set out with Indians and Esteban.[3] The latter was to push on ahead of Fray Marcos, who was making slower progress. As Esteban proceeded to reconnoiter the land, it was agreed that he would signal to the Franciscan the importance of the places visited by the large or small dimensions of the crosses he sent back. When Esteban arrived at the first of the famous seven cities, Cibola, he did not receive a favorable reception, as had been the case heretofore. In fact, he was imprisoned for a night and then put to death by the Zuni Indians. The Indians who accompanied him were not killed, and they returned and reported the event to Fray Marcos. They explained that the Zuni Indians did not believe that Esteban was the messenger of white men. Because of their suspicion, they killed him.

In the following year, the expedition of Francisco Vázquez de Coronado set out to retrace the footsteps of Esteban and Fray Marcos. The author of the narrative recounting this journey, a soldier on the expedition, Pedro de Castañeda,[4] reported the death of Esteban, claiming that he demanded women and turquoises at every stop he made. Still, he reported that the Indians got along with him because they had known him previously. Castañeda reports the death of Esteban as a result of the Zuni Indians' mistrusting his account of who he was and why he had come.[5] Spanish-speaking blacks were also present in the expedition of Coronado in 1540. They are described only briefly, however, in Castañeda's account.[6] The presence of blacks, Spanish-speaking and Catholic, is rarely noted, which is perhaps one of the most glaring omissions in the story of Catholicism in the United States. Their presence was not peripheral but essential. Theirs was a supporting role without which the drama would have been incomplete.

A Spanish colony was established by 1565 in what is now northern Florida through the efforts of Pedro Menéndez de Avilés. St. Augustine was the center of this colony on the northeast coast. Today St. Augustine is the oldest non-Indian town in the continental United States, and its church, the oldest parish. From the beginning Florida was primarily a military outpost to protect Spanish holdings in the New World from the threatening presence of the English and the French to the north and west.[7] As military post and Spanish settlement, St. Augustine is the oldest home for African Americans in the United States. Blacks, both as slaves and free persons, were part of the population in the city and of a settlement to the north of St. Augustine.[8]

As the English settlements in the Carolinas and Georgia provided a base for English and Indian raids on the Florida colony, especially after 1700, the Spanish authorities invited the slaves in those territories to escape their slaveholders and find refuge in Florida, where they would receive their freedom — provided they converted to the Roman Catholic faith. From the end of the seventeenth century to 1763, these escaped slaves found a home in a free black settlement, known in Spanish as a *palenque*, just to the north and east of the town of St. Augustine and its fort, the Castillo de San Marcos.

Recent excavations have thrown new light on the daily life of what can now be considered as the oldest black town in the United States. It is significant for us to remember that it was a black Catholic township. Even before its establishment in 1738, a significant number of escaped slaves had arrived from the English settlements. The name given to the settlement was Gracia Real de Santa Teresa de Mose. In 1740 General Oglethorpe, the English governor of Georgia, led a military attack on the Florida colony. Oglethorpe's men took Fort Mose, and the women and children found refuge in the Castillo de San Marcos. The blacks formed part of the fighting force that defended St. Augustine and eventually drove the British away from Fort Mose and the Florida coast.[9]

In both the eighteenth and nineteenth centuries, the population of St. Augustine included not only slaves and free blacks but also a garrison of black soldiers from Cuba. These soldiers were mulattoes and were often designated in the sacramental books by the Spanish word *morenos*. The parochial registers for the two-hundred-year period 1565–1763 are still extant. These are the oldest ecclesiastical documents for the United States. Blacks are mentioned in all of them.

In 1763 Spain signed the Treaty of Paris, which brought an end to the Seven Years' War and ceded the colony of Florida to the British, while winning back the port of Havana in Cuba, which the British had seized. All Spaniards, black as well as white, mestizo as well as mulatto, slave as well as free, civilians as well as soldiers, moved from Florida to Cuba. From 1763 to 1784 Great Britain controlled Florida, and Catholicism practically disappeared.[10]

The second Spanish period began in 1784 and lasted some thirty-five years until 1821, when Florida became part of the territory of the United States. Again it is clear that the return of Spaniards meant blacks as well as whites not only in St. Augustine but also in Pensacola, which by that time was a small frontier town in West Florida with one parish. In 1791 Pensacola included 114 black Catholics and almost 300 white Catholics.[11] Thanks to the parish registers that were segregated by race in St. Augustine, as elsewhere in the South, historians possess a picture of the black Catholic population of St. Augustine at the end of the eighteenth century and the first half of the nineteenth century. The early records were kept in Spanish. We meet again black slaves who had left the Carolinas, slaves and free persons with Spanish names and recognizable families, soldiers from Cuba, many of whom married or met death and were buried in this Spanish colony. (See table 1.)

The number of baptisms indicates at least that there were a substantial number of blacks, both slave and free, who were Catholics. In the first decade after the reestablishment of Spanish rule, there were almost 400 baptisms, and this number was doubled in the second decade. It seems that this can be attributed to the activity of Bishop Cyril de Barcelona, the auxiliary bishop of Havana, who conducted a visitation of Florida in 1788. During the visitation, the bishop insisted upon the duty of slaveholders to baptize their slaves. There were approximately 650 slaves in St. Augustine at this time.[12]

In the following decade and a half the number of baptisms almost doubled. This would seem to indicate that the black Catholic community in St. Augustine and possibly also in Pensacola was substantial. This community, of course, was both slave and free. Further examination of the baptismal registers is needed to tally the number of baptisms for free blacks in proportion to the number of slaves. Unfortunately, we do not have accurate statistics of the overall black population in this period. We also lack any precise information regarding the number of blacks who received communion or made their

Table 1

St. Augustine Church Records of Blacks

CATEGORY	DATES	NUMBER OF ENTRIES
Baptisms I	1784–1793	389 baptisms
Baptisms II	1793–1807	818 baptisms
Baptisms III	1807–1848	394 baptisms[a]
Baptisms IV	1848–1885	175 pages[b]
Marriages	1784–1882	88 pages[c]
Burials	1785–1821	224 burials

Source: Spanish Colonial Parochial Registers of St. Augustine, Diocese of St. Augustine Archives, Jacksonville, Florida.

[a] Two pages of baptisms are missing.

[b] Each page lists approximately two baptisms.

[c] Each page lists one or two marriages.

Easter duty. It would be valuable to compare the frequentation of the sacraments by blacks in relation to the reception of the sacraments by the rest of the population. For the time being, such data are not available.

The number of marriages recorded of blacks is much lower than the number of baptisms. The approximate number of marriages was between one and two hundred, which indicates that some of the black population did have their marriages recognized by the church. This number was certainly higher in Florida than in the general population of slaves in the United States at the same period. This would indicate that the church did not neglect the black population and that the black population was more than merely Catholic in name. The marriage register also indicates that a good proportion of this black Catholic population was mulatto soldiers from Cuba. This population of soldiers is made all the more evident by an examination of the burial register. The number of those who were buried from the church is approximately the same as the number of those married in the church. This balance confirms the fact that the black Catholic population of this Spanish colony was not inactive in terms of religious practice.

What is the general conclusion that can be drawn from a look at the sacramental books of black Catholics? We see a church in the

Spanish colony of Florida with a mixture of black and white, slave and free. It is clear from the number of baptisms that after Florida became a territory of the United States, the number of active black Catholics over a thirty-year period was less than half of what it was before.

If St. Augustine was an outpost of Spain with a large black Catholic presence, Los Angeles was an outpost of New Spain built on a black and Indian presence. In 1775 Don Felipe de Neve became the governor of Alta California, the present-day state of California. Although long neglected by the Spanish crown, it became apparent by the end of the eighteenth century that Spaniards would need to settle the area to prevent the infiltration and ultimate takeover by other foreign settlers. For this reason Governor de Neve wished to establish an agricultural *pueblo*, or village, that would be independent of the Franciscan missions established by the friars for the conversion of the Native Americans in the territory. In 1781 some eleven families were recruited mainly from the villages of Sonora and Sinaloa in what is now northern Mexico. The majority of these civilian recruits were of mixed ancestry, either mestizos or people of Indian and Spanish ancestry and mulattoes, or Indians and Africans.[13] Moreover, as in Florida, many of the Spanish soldiers sent to California for the protection of the missions and the pueblos were mulattoes.[14]

In September 1781 the eleven families of settlers arrived with their military escorts at their new home on the banks of the Porciuncula River not far from the Mission San Gabriel.[15] The census taken in November 1781 gives the names of the original settlers, known as *Los Pobladores*. The Spanish recorders were punctilious in giving the specific terms designating the exact racial mixture of each individual. Only two of the original settlers were white. (See table 2.)

Thus was founded, about two centuries ago, the town of Nuestra Señora de Los Angeles. The eleven founding families were all Catholics; over half of the adults were black, two were Spanish, and the rest were Indians. The story of Los Angeles is that of many of the cities of California.[16] In time the African element would evolve into mestizos and Indians, but the fact remains that Spanish California would be in large measure Afro-Hispanic in its racial heritage, Hispanic in its culture, and Catholic in its faith.

Table 2
The Original Settlers of Los Angeles

FAMILY MEMBERS	AGE	RACIAL CHARACTERISTICS
1. Josef de Lara	50	Spaniard
Maria Antonia Campos	23	India Sabina[a]
3 children		
2. Josef Antonio Navarro	42	mestizo
Maria Rufina Dorotea	47	mulatto
3 children		
3. Basillio Rosas	67	Indian
Maria Manuela Calixtra	43	mulatto
6 children		
4. Antonio Mesa	38	Negro
Ana Gertrudis López	27	mulatto
2 children		
5. Antonio Villavicencio	30	Spaniard
Maria de los Santos Seferina	26	Indian
1 child		
6. Josef Vanegas	28	Indian
Maria Maxima Aguilar	20	Indian
1 child		
7. Alejandro Rosas	19	Indian
Juana Rodriguez	20	Coyote Indian (mestizo and Indian)
8. Pablo Rodriguez	25	Indian
Maria Rosalia Noriega	26	Indian
1 child		
9. Manuel Camero	30	mulatto
Maria Tomasa	24	mulatto
10. Luis Quintero	55	Negro
Maria Petra Rubio	40	mulatto
5 children		
11. José Moreno	22	mulatto
Maria Guadalupe Gertrudis	19	[no indication]
— Antonio Miranda Rodriguez[b]	50	Chino (Indian and *saltatrás*[c])
[daughter] Juana Maria	11	

Source: David J. Weber, ed. *Foreigners in Their Native Land: Historical Roots of the Mexican Americans*, 6th ed. (Albuquerque: University of New Mexico Press, 1981), 34–35.

[a] Seemingly a reference to dark brown skin color.

[b] Antonio Rodriguez and his daughter never actually settled in Los Angeles. See Harry Kelsey, "A New Look at the Founding of Old Los Angeles," *California Historical Quarterly* 15 (1976): 331.

[c] A *saltatrás* was a Negroid child of white parents.

II

In the spring of 1785, John Carroll, superior of the priests working in the missions of Maryland, nearly all of them, like himself, former members of the suppressed Society of Jesus,[17] wrote to Leonardo Cardinal Antonelli, prefect of the Congregation of the Propaganda.[18] The year before, Carroll had been made prefect apostolic, and in this letter he described the situation of the Catholics in the newly established United States. "The Catholic population in Maryland is about 15,800. Of this number nine thousand are adult freemen, that is above twelve years of age; about three thousand are children, and the same number are slaves of all ages, come from Africa, who are called 'Negroes' because of their color. In Pennsylvania there are at least seven thousand but very few Africans."

A little later in discussing the moral tone of the Catholic population, he added, "There is a lack of care in educating the children in religion, especially the African slaves." Moreover, in speaking of pastoral concerns regarding requirements for marriage, Carroll requested certain extraordinary faculties enabling him to dispense couples seeking marriage from certain marriage impediments: "My colaborers most earnestly wish that dispensation could be granted here for the first degree of affinity resulting from illicit sexual intercourse. This impediment often obtains among the Africans, especially before marriage is entered into; and it is discovered by the priest accidentally only after the lapse of an extended period of time and many years of co-habitation."[19]

In this first letter as ecclesiastical superior for the newly formed United States, Carroll laid open for the Roman Curia the composition of the American church. The African slaves were one of the main components of the nascent church. Twenty out of every one hundred Catholics in Maryland (the only state where Catholics were more numerous) were black. The peculiar conditions of American slavery made this Catholic population a particular concern for Carroll. Neither the conditions nor the concerns would change for Carroll and his successors in the episcopate until slavery disappeared from the United States over seventy-five years later. American slavery existed in the United States in one of its most brutal modern forms and marked the American Catholic church in a way that no other American institution would do.[20]

Maryland itself, where Cecil Calvert, the second Lord Baltimore, founded a proprietary colony in March 1634, was exceptional in that freedom of religion for all Christians was permitted, and the public practice of Catholicism was taken for granted. By the first quarter of the eighteenth century, slaves began to be imported into the colony at a very rapid rate. By the middle of the century the state had become an agricultural center based on a slave economy.[21] Catholic families like the Carrolls were slaveholders, and religious corporations like the former Jesuits owned slaves to work their estates.

They had received some twelve thousand acres in land grants from Cecil Calvert in 1636; they had estates in four counties in the southern part of Maryland and also two in the peninsula known as the eastern shore. The estates brought them revenue, which was used to further their pastoral and mission activity. The labor on the estates was supplied in the beginning by indentured servants, men and women who came to America mainly from England and Ireland and who worked for nothing except their board and keep to pay back those who had sponsored their voyage. It was a form of limited slavery. By the end of the seventeenth century, the Jesuits had introduced on their lands African slaves, which meant that the Jesuits would now learn firsthand the disadvantages and moral ambiguities that affected every slaveholder attempting to align conscience with slavery.

As a financial enterprise, slavery could hinder as well as help. If care for the slaves entailed a greater charge than the profit received from the land, they became a burden. If there were a large number of children and elderly who were not yet or no longer productive, then the profits from the estate were seriously diminished. It cost money to have and maintain slaves. The more practical among the Jesuits wished to rid themselves of the slaves. In his moving account of Jesuit slaveholding in Maryland, Emmett Curran, S.J., describes the struggle that took place within the Jesuit community in Maryland over the question of its ownership of slaves.[22]

By 1819 the Maryland Jesuits were in serious financial trouble. From 1773, when the Society of Jesus was suppressed by Pope Clement XIV, to 1814, when the society was reestablished by Pope Pius VII, the Jesuits existed in legal form as the Corporation of the Roman Catholic Clergyman. Later when the society was restored, the corporation as a legal body continued to be composed of the American Jesuits who had survived as secular priests during the time of the suppression. They were Americans, distrustful of their European confreres, many of whom had been aristocrats who survived as Jesuits in Russia under the protection of Catherine the Great. The sentiment of many in the Jesuit community in the first period of the nineteenth century was for emancipating the slaves. They did not do so because of litigation with the archdiocese of Baltimore over who had the right to the property owned and operated by the original society of clergymen of Maryland.[23] As a result, the Jesuits continued as slaveholders. Many of the older Jesuit priests, especially the Europeans, saw the slaves as a responsibility; but by 1830 the question shifted, as many of the young American Jesuits demanded that the Jesuits get out of the agricultural enterprise, sell the slaves, and devote themselves to education. The older Jesuits considered the elderly and infirm as a liability that conscience demanded should be borne by the society. They saw all the slaves as a trust, for whose salvation they would have to answer. No financial considerations should override this concern.

In the end, however, they did. In 1833 William McSherry became the first provincial of the newly founded Maryland province of Jesuits. In 1835 the sale of some slaves took place. In 1836 the general of the Jesuits, John Roothaan, approved the sale of slaves, provided the practice of the Catholic faith by the slaves was assured and that families were not separated.[24] In 1837 Thomas Mulledy became provincial, and the sale of all the slaves on the various estates began. Altogether 272 slaves from the Jesuit estates in southern Maryland were sold to purchasers in Louisiana. They were not necessarily sold to Catholic slaveowners, and in the end families were separated. While many Catholics would have argued that slavery could be justified under certain conditions, all theologians would have insisted that the salvation of souls was still to be of paramount concern to the slaveholder. Separation of families and subjection to non-Catholic slaveholders spelled the end of Catholic practice by Catholic slaves. That the Jesuits should have carried out such a transaction became a scandal to the Catholics in southern Maryland and was roundly denounced by Samuel Eccleston, the archbishop of Baltimore.[25] In the end the provincial, Thomas Mulledy, was forced to go to Rome, where the general received his resignation. For a time under disgrace, Mulledy returned to the States three years later to active service in the province.[26]

At the time when the slaves were being rounded up for sale, some of the Jesuits aided them in escaping the agents. In this way perhaps a dozen or so avoided the trip south. The tragic story of the Jesuit slaves presents to us not only the harshness of slavery as it really existed but also the moral quicksand of expediency and inhumanity that sooner or later trapped everyone who participated in the ownership and buying and selling of human beings.

The Maryland Jesuits were not the only religious slaveholders. The Vincentians in Missouri were major slaveholders in Perry County, south of St. Louis, where they first settled in 1818. Here the Vincentians under Joseph Rosati, the future bishop of St. Louis, began St. Mary's Seminary, which became an important center for the training of priests all over the Midwest. In an illuminating study on the slaves owned by the Vincentians in Missouri, Father Stafford Poole, C.M., and Father Douglas Slawson, C.M., point out that the Vincentians became slaveholders because they needed domestic help when they opened the seminary. It was Louis William DuBourg, the first bishop of New Orleans, who supplied the Vincentians with their first slaves.[27] In 1820, at the time DuBourg left St. Louis to establish his see at New Orleans, he left some slaves both at his property in St. Louis and in Perry County. In both instances he donated these slaves to the Vincentians.[28]

Already in 1819 there were women who worked in the seminary kitchen. The Vincentian superior, Felix DeAndreis, justified the ownership of slaves because there were no lay brothers to perform the manual labor and because other seminaries, such as those run by the Sulpicians, had female slaves for the domestic work.[29] By 1827, when there were more lay brothers, the latter refused to do certain tasks because such was "slave work."[30] By 1830 the Vincentians had the largest number of slaves among the slaveholders in the area.[31] According to the census records for 1830, cited by Poole and Slawson, the seminary possessed twenty-seven slaves — fourteen men and thirteen women. Seven of these were actually rented from neighboring slaveholders.[32] A few years later the Vincentians acquired more slaves in order to reunite some families.[33] The Vincentians had the policy of selling, hiring, and lending their slaves among their various houses and parishes, not only in Missouri but also in Louisiana, where they also owned many slaves. Beginning in 1840, the Vincentians followed a policy of divesting themselves of their slaves through sale to the Catholic slaveowners in the neighborhood. They continued, however, to hire the slaves of others. Nonetheless, it seems that the Vincentians in Missouri owned some slaves until the beginning of the Civil War.[34]

Other religious orders of men possessed slaves. The Sulpicians had slaves in their seminaries in Baltimore and Bardstown, Kentucky. The Capuchins in Louisiana owned slaves as well. Further research on the slaveholding practices of the various religious orders in keeping with the scholarship of historians like Curran, Poole, and Slawson is needed for a more complete picture of the black Catholic community prior to the Civil War, a community that was itself an image of the church — the Catholic church in chains.

Women religious also figured in American church history as slaveowners. The Ursuline nuns who came to New Orleans in 1727 owned slaves from the beginning. Many young girls who entered the community brought slaves with them as a portion of their dowry. This was a practice carried out elsewhere as well.[35] The Carmelite nuns at Port Tobacco in Maryland formed the first contemplative community in the United States in 1791. They too owned slaves, also part of the dowry of incoming novices. Such religious groups as the Daughters of the Cross in Louisiana, the Religious of the Sacred Heart both in Louisiana and Missouri,[36] the Visitation nuns in Washington, D.C., and the Dominican Sisters in Kentucky were all slaveholders, and inevitably they shared the sentiments of the slaveholding class.[37]

Kentucky was the home of two American foundations of sisters that embodied the frontier American spirit. The Sisters of Charity at Nazareth, Kentucky, founded by Bishop Jean-Baptiste David in 1812, had slaves at Nazareth itself and in their various foundations.[38] In the same year and in the same locality, the Belgian priest Charles Nerinckx founded the Sisters of Loretto, who also owned slaves. In the beginning of the convent at Loretto, the sale of her personal slave to Father Nerinckx by Mother Ann Rhodes, the first superior, enabled the sisters to purchase land for the convent.[39]

III

In 1839 Pope Gregory XVI condemned the slave trade in the apostolic letter *In Supremo Apostolatus Fastigio*. He did so, as he explained, in virtue of his position as chief pastor and because it was part of his pastoral concern to turn people away from "the inhuman traffic in Negroes."[40] After reviewing previous statements of Roman pontiffs regarding slavery, which condemned the unjust enslavement of various peoples, Gregory XVI proceeded to condemn the slave trade as it existed then.

> [We] do...admonish and adjure in the Lord all believers in Christ, of whatsoever condition, that no one hereafter may dare unjustly to molest Indians, Negroes, or other men of this sort; or to spoil them of their goods; or to reduce them to slavery; or to extend help or favour to others who perpetrate such things against them; or to exercise that inhuman trade by which Negroes, as if they were not men, but mere animals, howsoever reduced into slavery, are, without any distinction, contrary to

the laws of justice and humanity, bought, sold, and doomed sometimes to the most severe and exhausting labours.[41]

Finally, he forbade any ecclesiastic or layperson to defend or teach anything that supported the slave trade.

Pope Gregory XVI was seemingly an unlikely person to issue such a condemnation of the slave trade and, by inference, of slavery itself. Born in 1765, he had become a Camaldolese monk, an order of monks who followed the Rule of St. Benedict and lived as hermits in monastic villages. He was by all accounts a most austere and rigid man. Elected pope in 1831, he reigned for fifteen years, during a period in world history marked by revolution and crisis. Politically reactionary, Gregory XVI believed strongly in the principles of legitimate authority. No matter what the justification, revolt against legitimate authority, particularly royal authority, was never justified. Moreover, Gregory was conservative in theological matters. His pontificate was marked by intransigence in thought and government. Yet it was this pope who went further than any other in opposition to slavery.

The reason for Gregory's attitude, however, is not difficult to find. Despite his lack of experience with the wider world of political and social change in his youth, he had, when elevated to the rank of cardinal, served in the Roman Curia as prefect of the Congregation of the Propagation of the Faith. Both as cardinal and later as pope, he had a keen interest in missions and in the problems facing missionaries. This experience gave him firsthand knowledge of the depredations of the slave trade. Faced with what he considered an evil, he was intransigent in condemning it.[42]

The attitude of Catholics in the United States was somewhat different. Many bishops were slaveowners. Inevitably some of them did engage in the buying and selling of slaves, just as many priests and religious did. The attitude toward slavery, however, was not uniform. John Carroll, the first American bishop, was a slaveowner. He claimed that he had no slaves of his own, but he did have in his service a slave lent by his sister and a servant to whom he gave a salary.[43] On the other hand, in his will he gave his slave, Charles, to a certain Daniel Brent, with the understanding that Charles was to be manumitted "within twelve months after my decease, unless I should do so previously." Charles was to live in or near Washington and "make a prudent use of his emancipation" and receive fifty dollars.[44] Moreover, Carroll seemed to have disposed of the slaves on the estate owned by the Jesuits at Bohemia Manor according to the "Bohemia Plantation Record, 1790–1815." In this record he estimated the value of one Fanny and her family, which included seven children as well as the infant of Fanny's seventeen-year-old daughter, Polly, all of whom were to be sold and then manumitted after a certain number of years. The list contains the names of other slaves also, many of whom were children. The list concluded with two adult males who were to be manumitted after six years, provided they served faithfully "the reverend gentlemen" at Bohemia Manor.[45]

Despite his involvement in slavery and the traffic in slaves, Carroll took the pastoral care of the slaves very seriously. He expressed the desire that permission might be granted for the United States to have the liturgy of the church in English, as "the poor people, and the Negroes generally, not being able to read, have no technical help to confine their attention."[46] He was concerned about the quality of the spiritual care given to slaves on the estates belonging to the Jesuits.[47] At the same time he could raise money by the "sale of a few necessary Negroes, three or four," from the estate at St. Inigo's belonging to the Corporation of Reverend Gentlemen.[48] Although he claimed not to have any slaves, he was able to rid himself of a problem slave who was an alcoholic, through sale.[49]

Archbishop Carroll once acknowledged frankly his uneasiness over the question of slavery. In a letter to one of his priests who criticized the institution of slavery in the United States, he wrote, "I am as far as you from being easy in my mind at many things I see, and know, relating to the treatment and manners of the Negroes. I do the best I can to correct the evils I see; and then recur to those principles, which, I suppose, influenced the many eminent and holy missioners in S. America and Asia, where slavery equally exists."[50] Carroll no doubt was unaware of the writings of de Las Casas or Sandoval. As the first bishop of the American church, Carroll was faced with the American problem of slavery and racism. In the end, he tried to meet the demands of his conscience, the pastoral needs of all of his people, and the standards of American public opinion. His dilemma and his failure became the dilemma and failure of the American church.

IV

Slavery, even for those who accepted the institution as a necessary evil, raised other moral and canonical problems for the pastor of souls. Louis William DuBourg, S.S., bishop of the Louisiana Territory, broached some of these canonical issues in a series of questions addressed to the Congregation of the Propaganda. The document, which is unsigned and undated, is handwritten in Latin and contains four *dubia*, or problems, offered by Bishop DuBourg. The first query is whether the missionary should "disturb the consciences" of slave-holders "regarding the possession of their slaves" and whether these can "purchase and possess slaves for their service according to the norms of civil law, since it is impossible to find others, except slaves," for domestic work. Furthermore, he asked whether it was permitted to slaves to engage in manual labor on Sundays and feast days — first, because this was the only time they could work for themselves for clothing and food and even gain money and, second, because it preserved public order, as it would be dangerous for so many of "the lowest class of men" to have so much leisure.[51]

Unfortunately, there is no indication as to how the problems were answered. They do make clear the pastoral ramifications of the slavery question. A few years later another set of *dubia* was presented to the Congregation of the Propagation of the Faith. This document, which is also unsigned and undated, is entitled in Italian "Decisions requested by the Bishop of Upper Louisiana from the Congregation of the Propaganda Fide."[52] It is a request from DuBourg, who became bishop of Louisiana in 1815 and served until he resigned in 1826, concerning canonical difficulties regarding marriage and the burial of Freemasons. The questions regarding marriage concern among other things the validity of the marriage of slaves. The problem, according to DuBourg, is that civil laws forbid the marriage of slaves without the prior consent of the owners. The slaveholders will not give their consent because the marriages would not be in their own interest. Slaves, therefore, find it morally impossible to contract a valid marriage. If one is bound to observe the Council of Trent, the slaves are either obliged to celibacy or constrained to concubinage, having absolutely no means of being married validly in the church. The question then is how must one act in this regard, as it is not known whether the decrees of the Council of Trent have been promulgated in the area.

The canonical problem was that the Council of Trent had decreed that Catholic marriages were not valid unless the vows were exchanged before a priest and two witnesses. Clandestine or secret marriages were no longer valid. At the end of the eighteenth century, not all Catholic countries had officially accepted the marriage decree *Tametsi* of the Council of Trent, which had been passed in the twenty-fourth session in 1563. DuBourg was asking, it would seem, whether slaves could have clandestine marriages or whether a priest could consider any slave marriages as canonically valid, inasmuch as the permanent basis for a marriage was lacking because of the arbitrary power of slaveholders.[53] Here again the response to this second set of *dubia* is not known. The questions themselves highlight the consequences of the slave system for the slave, for the slaveholder, and for the spiritual leader who was responsible for the salvation of both. If marriage is a sacred institution to which all have a right, how can one participate in a system that abridges that right to a major portion of society? How can the ministry of the church give its blessing to a sacramental act in which the participants are not free? The further question might have been, How could one defend such a system or refrain from condemning it?[54]

Louis William DuBourg as a bishop in the Louisiana Territory had no problems, it would seem, in profiting from the slavery system. Born into an aristocratic family in Santo Domingo in 1766, DuBourg grew up in France, was ordained a priest in 1790, and emigrated to the United States as a result of the French Revolution, where he became a Sulpician. DuBourg was made bishop of Louisiana in 1815, with both St. Louis and New Orleans in his pastoral care. As a slaveowner, he provided the Vincentians in Missouri with their first slaves and helped them acquire others.[55] He was willing to use his slaves as collateral to borrow money and as investments for other financial ventures.[56]

From the viewpoint of evangelization, slavery was a hindrance to the preaching of the gospel. From the viewpoint of the apostolate, Catholic slaves often were deterred from the practice of their religion by the ill will of the slaveowners. Some three years before the outbreak of the Civil War, William Henry Elder (1819–1904), the future archbishop of Cincinnati, who would give much support to black Catholics at a later date, was the bishop of Natchez in Mississippi. As was often the case for American bishops in the nineteenth century, he received subsidies from the Society for the Propagation of the Faith, located in Lyons, France. Writing in the society's newsletter, Bishop Elder described his Southern diocese, which included the whole state with a Catholic population purported to have been about 10,000. Elder thought this number too small, out of a general population of 606,526. "More than half our population consists of negro slaves, who number 309,878; besides free negroes to the number of 930. These poor negroes form in some respects my chief anxiety. I believe they are generally well cared for, so far as health and the necessaries of life are concerned. But for learning and practising religion, they have at present very little opportunity indeed."[57]

Elder went on to explain that slaveowners did not like the slaves of one plantation mingling with the slaves of another: "If the servants have free intercourse together, they are apt to make each other jealous and dissatisfied." He went on to express his chagrin at not having enough priests to visit the plantations.

> Catholic masters of course are taught that it is their duty to furnish their slaves with opportunities for being well instructed, and for practising their religion. And here is my anxiety, that I cannot enable those masters to do their duty because there are not Priests enough. The negroes must be attended in a great measure on the plantation... because in our case there are so few churches; and even where there is a church, the negroes of four or five plantations would fill it up, and leave no room for the white, nor for the other negroes of the neighborhood.

Elder wrote that he needed a band of "travelling missionaries"; the few priests that he had, needed to remain in their parishes.

Although Elder's report was written with a view to obtaining from the readers increased donations, especially from the Catholic populace in Europe, his concern for the plight of the slaves is from all indications genuine. One might wonder, however, at the rather optimistic view that the slaves "are generally well cared for, so far as health and the necessaries of life are concerned." He indicated that the slaveowners did not trust their slaves to mingle with slaves of other plantations. Slavery meant constraint; constraint meant domination. Without it, slavery could not continue. Constraint meant force, and force meant violence. The slave society was of necessity a violent society. A current of violence underlay all Southern life. Elder certainly knew this, but an article in a newsletter that sought donations from the Catholic faithful abroad would not have been the place for such a discussion.

The article, however, reveals much about the mentality of an antebellum Catholic bishop who was genuinely concerned about the slaves who were a major portion of the local population. For Elder, the African American slave was part child, part animal, part saint.

> The poor negroes very often have at first a fear of a Catholic Priest, or imagine they can never understand him; but they are not ill disposed towards religion. Indeed they often have a craving for its ministrations. Having few comforts and no expectations in this world, their thoughts and desires are the more easily drawn to the good things of the world to come. I say often because often again they are so entirely animal in their inclina-

tions, so engrossed with the senses, that they have no regard for any thing above the gratifications of the body.

Elder saw blacks as "naturally inclined to be dependent on others," which meant that they were open to the ministrations of the priest. "When he resists the teachings of religion, it is not so much from stubbornness as from weakness of mind and will." Elder found them "fickle," unable "to resist temptation," "very much creatures of feeling." Nevertheless, the missionary who is persistent in his ministry to them "may have the unspeakable consolation of finding among them vocations to a high degree of sanctity." Elder attributes this possibility to the fact that God gives his grace to the humble and the lowly. "I have known a case of a servant girl's being really revered as a saint by the family in which she had been reared, and where she was working with all simplicity and fidelity in the lowest offices." Elder concludes by writing, "Oh! what a harvest of souls among these 310,000 negroes; every one of them immortal, made to the image and likeness of God, redeemed by the Precious Blood of the Son of God! Oh! what a frightful havoc Satan is making among them!" He asks for more priestly vocations from Europe who would come to America and do what St. Peter Claver did in ministering to the slaves.

For a truly pastoral bishop like Elder, the needs of the slaves were evident. Still, even he saw them as basically inferior to whites in regard to character and intellect, although, as he clearly pointed out, grace could make up for these deficiencies and make them saints. Elder's pastoral concern for blacks can be seen from extracts in his diary.[58]

August 16th, Sunday [1863]. After dinner I sent Revd. Fr. Finucane [a priest] to the Negro camp or corral as it is called, to see what was to be done for the souls of the poor people especially the dying, infants and others. He baptized he said some thirty infants...[59]

August 17. Went down with Fr. Finucane to the Negro camp on the Old Cotton Press grounds, back to the hills [in the vicinity of Natchez]. Met three or four gangs of Negro men marching under white officers — probably going to work. Negro sentinels at the gate. There seem to be some thousands... Most of the men are gone out to drill or to work. Only the sick and feeble left — but crowds of women and children. Great numbers of the children sick, and they say of those that sicken seriously — very few get well. They seem to have enough of meat and flour furnished

by the Fed. army but no vegetables nor fruit. Diarrhea and
Dysentery prevailing. Some say they saw a Doctor this morning — I suspect it was Fr. Finucane — for we separated to do
more work. No medicine. I baptized twenty-four infants. Found
two or three Catholics; Celestine Craig from Point Coupeé [*sic*]
and her mother, both baptized — but they never went to confession. And Frank Evans who lived at Calvary, Kentucky till
he was 22 years old, and went to the Sacraments frequently.
Since he came South, he was not permitted to go. He promised
to come to the house for confession... Baptized 23 infants in
danger of death.[60]

For the next year Elder detailed the pastoral activity of a Southern
bishop in a state occupied by Union troops. His sympathies lay with
the Southern cause; his concerns went to all. He was always concerned
with the human element and with the human tragedy, much of which
lay with the former slaves who were refugees in a land that had been
a prison more than a home.

                                    V

For some of the Southern bishops, however, slavery was not simply an
evil condition that had to be endured; they considered themselves as
apologists for slavery, obligated to defend it on the basis of Catholic
tradition and Scripture. This was the case for John England, one of
the most brilliant and innovative bishops of the pre–Civil War period.
England was born in 1786 in Ireland, where he was ordained a priest
in 1808. He was a parish priest in the diocese of Cork when he was
chosen to become the first bishop of Charleston in South Carolina
in 1820.

There he introduced such innovations as a written constitution for
his diocese, annual conventions of people and clergy, and a diocesan
newspaper, the *United States Catholic Miscellany*, the first Catholic
periodical in the United States.[61] In 1835 England opened a school to
teach the boys and girls of free black families. The school raised such
opposition from the white people of South Carolina that there was a
riot, forcing England to close down the school.[62] A further attempt
was never made.

Four years later Pope Gregory XVI wrote his above-mentioned
apostolic letter against the slave trade. The following year, an influential Southern political leader, John Forsyth, secretary of state in the

administration of Andrew Jackson,[63] publicly criticized Pope Gregory XVI's letter condemning the slave trade. In the *United States Catholic Miscellany*, Bishop England published a series of eighteen public letters to John Forsyth, in which he attempted to prove to the secretary of state that Gregory XVI meant to condemn the slave trade as practiced by the Spanish and the Portuguese and "not that sale and purchase which must frequently occur in domestic slavery,"[64] referring to the slavery found in the American South. The publication began with letter 1 on September 29, 1840, and ended with the letter of April 23, 1841.

England sought to show with arguments from history, Scripture, the canons of church councils and local synods, and finally canon law and Roman law that slavery has always existed and been accepted as legitimate under specific titles or circumstances. One has to admire the great erudition of the bishop of Charleston as he quotes from diverse historical documents and cites examples from a vast knowledge of late Roman and medieval history to support his contention that slavery was permitted, since it was regulated. As a result, he concluded, it is impossible to believe that the Scriptures or the church would have treated slavery without condemning it, if it was fundamentally wrong.

His very arguments, however, betrayed him. The legislation in the Old Testament, the canons of the church councils, the jurisprudence of Roman law, and the teaching of the popes all sought to ameliorate the condition of the slaves and to recognize the existence of certain rights that accrued to the person of the slave, especially regarding marriage, family life, freedom from sexual exploitation, and even certain property rights. The slavery system in the Southern states recognized no such rights inherent in the slave as a person, no freedom regarding marriage, no freedom regarding religious practice, and turned a blind eye to arbitrary penalties and sanctions by slaveholders, who were in no way bound to respect the personality and humanity of the slave. None of this practice was consonant with Catholic doctrine, but this was the situation of slaves in South Carolina. If Bishop England did not know this, he was remiss; if he knew it, it was certainly reprehensible to neutralize the words of the Roman pontiff so as not to disturb the prejudices of slaveholders.

England never completed his exposition on slavery. In February 1842,[65] he explained in a letter to the newspaper:

My more pressing duties will not permit me…to continue the letters on the compatibility of domestic slavery with practical religion. I have been asked by many, a question which I may as well answer at once, viz.: Whether I am friendly to the existence or continuation of slavery? I am not — but I also see the impossibility of now abolishing it here. When it can and ought to be abolished, is a question for the legislature and not for me.[66]

He could oppose it, yet defend it and have no feeling of responsibility regarding its existence. England died less than two months later.

Peter Clarke, in his excellent study of England's position in the history of American Catholic thought, wrote:

John England's vision of the American church failed to sufficiently appreciate two portions of the American church and their possibilities. These portions were the Indians and the Negroes of the United States. He brought the church's mission among both the Indians and the Negroes to the attention of Propaganda. He also saw to it that these apostolates were discussed by the American hierarchy. This is all to his credit. It would seem, however, that he was uncritical of the transfer of the Indians to western reservations...

The Indians may have been few in the Diocese of Charleston but black people comprised approximately one-half of a population of two-million persons. There does not seem to be any record of England speaking out in favor of emancipation or against the increased restrictions that were placed on black people and on slaves during the time he was Bishop of Charleston... England's strong statements about his disgust for the institution of slavery and the immorality of slavery were made in Europe...

England, it would seem, accepted the structure of the society that he found in the South. In this policy of acceptance, he allowed the church and himself not to be considered as opponents of slavery.[67]

Francis Patrick Kenrick (1796–1863), the archbishop of Baltimore, composed a manual of moral theology for the students for the priesthood in American seminaries (published in Philadelphia in three volumes, beginning in 1840), in which, among other things, he treated the moral aspects of slavery.[68] Kenrick's approach to the questions of morality and particularly the question of slavery was quite different than what would be the methodology today. Kenrick based his moral theology on law. Extremely legalistic, he founded his approach to slavery on the principles of Roman law. At the same time, he in no way took a position that called into question the prevailing system of slavery. He wrote in the section "On Slavery:"

> What must one think about that domestic slavery which flourishes in most of our southern states, the descendants of those abducted from Africa and still subject to the yoke [of servitude]? Indeed in this fulness of freedom, in which we all take pride, it must be regretted that there are so many slave laws which have been passed which forbid the teaching of reading and which impede greatly the exercise of religion at any place so that one must take care from any undertakings [contrary to the laws]. Since, for the rest, such is the state of affairs, nothing against the law must be attempted, neither anything by which the slaves might be set free, nor must anything be done or said that would make them bear the yoke with difficulty. But the prudence and the charity of the sacred ministers must be shown in this, so that the slaves, informed by Christian morals, might show service to their masters, venerating always God, the supreme Master of us all; so that in turn the masters might show themselves gentle and even-handed and might lighten the condition of their slaves with humanity and with zeal for their salvation.[69]

The same tone is maintained throughout by the author in this work. Whatever may have been the reason — perhaps because it was written for the seminarian or future pastor of souls — the author's point of view is extremely cautious in dealing with the slavery issue and in acquiescing in the prevailing conditions, despite the immoral climate of the American situation. Kenrick avoids the slightest hint that might trouble the consciences of those who were slaveowners. He argues that even though the original seizure of the slaves in Africa might be unjust, "the invalidity of the original title [to the possession of slaves] through the lapse of a long period of time must be considered to have been validated"; "they indeed sin who take others by force; but their descendants are not seen to be held unjustly in servitude."[70]

Kenrick's priorities were the tranquillity of civil society first, then the good of the slaveholders who were Catholics, and finally the well-being of the slaves. Hence, he agreed that one could not force the escaped slave to return to the slaveholder.[71] There is little that was original or challenging in Kenrick's work. The Catholic church in nineteenth-century America made no startling new approaches to moral theology. Slavery was the issue that dominated the national scene because it permeated all other questions. Unlike Protestant authors, who were violently divided over the question, the American Catholics, thanks to a theological approach like that of Kenrick, were shielded from the agony and the anguish of the American moral dilemma. As one author wrote regarding Kenrick's opinion on slavery:

> [Kenrick] placed no limits of time on the toleration of slavery... He was content to allow slavery to become a permanent condition...
>   ... Kenrick seemed to have been satisfied to let conditions remain in statu quo... It would seem that a progressive theologian should have thought of social improvement and should have given his pastoral advice accordingly. But a man is influenced greatly by the conditions of the time in which he lives.[72]

Two American bishops, however, did not simply retain a low profile regarding the slavery issue. They did not simply seek to allay the consciences of the slaveholders within their flock or show solidarity with the Southern cause. Rather, they openly embraced the institution of slavery and sought to show how it could be a force for good. Their zeal for the slavery cause was not unnoticed in Rome and did not escape Rome's disapproval. Unfortunately for later history, in this case the condemnation of Rome did not come fast enough. The two bishops were Auguste Marie Martin and Augustin Verot, both born in France and both bishops of dioceses in the Confederate States.

Martin was born in St-Malo in the region of Brittany in France in 1803. He was ordained in 1828 and came to the diocese of Vincennes in Indiana in 1839, where the bishop, Céléstin de la Hailandière, was a fellow countryman and friend. Later Martin joined the archdiocese of New Orleans, where Anthony Blanc was archbishop. In 1853 a new diocese was created in northern Louisiana at Natchitoches, and Auguste Martin became the first bishop. He would remain in this diocese until his death in 1875.[73] Later the see would be changed to Alexandria. Natchitoches was a very old settlement of French Catholics, dating back to the beginning of the French colony in 1714, when a trading post was erected that later became the Fort of St-Jean Baptiste de Natchitoches. At the time of the Civil War, there were seventeen secular priests and thirty thousand Catholics, many of whom were slaves.[74]

In August 1861, four months after the beginning of the Civil War,

Bishop Martin wrote a pastoral letter in French to his people, entitled "A Pastoral Letter of the Bishop of Natchitoches on the Occasion of the War of the South for Its Independence."[75] The bishop began by stating that the war "imposed on all classes of citizens duties that our conscience as a bishop forces us to recall to the Faithful." These duties "arose from the justice...of our cause." The bishop declared that "every man capable of bearing arms and free to dispose of himself must be a soldier." The purpose of the war "that the party brought to power in Washington has declared on us is enslavement and extermination." He went on to ask, "On whom will weigh the responsibility of this fratricidal war?" He suggested that "we will have every right to have it weigh on the shame of those thousands of preachers who from their pestilential pulpits have breathed on the people a spirit of hatred and discord." He was referring here to the abolitionists in the North, many of whom were clergymen. The bishop, however, went on to point out that they themselves had to share some of the blame. At this point he approached the question of slavery.

In the admirable dispositions of His Providence, God, the Father of us all, who loves the souls for whom He has given His only begotten and well-beloved Son, and who uses even purely human motives for the profit of eternal interests, for centuries God snatches from the barbarism of savage morals some thousands of the children of the race of Canaan on whom there continues to weigh nearly everywhere the curse of an outraged father.[76]

For Bishop Martin, slavery is really a disguised blessing for the Africans, "children of the race of Canaan," for through slavery they have received the faith and other advantages.

The manifest will of God is that in exchange for a freedom of which they were incapable and for a labor of the whole life, we should give to these unfortunate ones, not only the bread and the clothing necessary for material life, but also and especially their legitimate portion of the truth and the goods of grace, which consoles them in their present miseries through the hope of rest in the bosom of the Father, to Whom they are called under the same title as us.[77]

Considered from this point of view, according to the bishop, slavery was really not an evil but "a betterment both material and moral for a degraded class." It was "an eminently Christian work, the redemption of millions of human beings, passing from the night of the intellect of the blackest type to the sweet and life-giving brightness of Gospel light."

At this point, Martin rather delicately pointed out that in this matter the slaveowners have failed. "Ah, how noble and beautiful was the mission which our Father had given us," because as slaveowners they were supposed to be "ministers of His goodness, and instruments of His mercy!" Unfortunately, they have understood neither "the divine plan nor the nobility of our mission." Despite the great caution that he took so as not to give the impression that he was using the arguments of the abolitionists against them, Martin admitted that the noble results of slavery had not been achieved. "Let us say that, blinded by materialistic teachings, and without any respect for God, in the image of whom their immortal souls as well as ours have been created; in those very persons that we should have, in regenerating them, raised them up from their original degradation, most of us saw only the means for our own profit and exploitation, too often making them the docile instruments of brutal passions."[78]

He admitted that among the Catholics there were some "consoling exceptions." "But, great God! how they are rare!" And even then the results of faith seemed to Bishop Martin very meager in the diocese. It seems that the Catholics of Natchitoches were not very generous, and Martin pointed out that orphanages, homes for the poor, churches, and schools were lacking. There were no vocations to the priesthood. He ended by exhorting his flock to humble themselves before God and recognize their faults, remembering always that God is merciful. He then closed making certain pastoral provisions for the liturgical prayers for peace.

The extraordinary aspect of this pastoral letter is that the bishop was attempting to introduce a theological justification for slavery — it was something noble because it was God's plan for the conversion of the black race, who were in dependence upon the white race. This was the "white man's burden" with a vengeance, and it would get him into trouble with the Roman Curia. He also was attempting to give a theological rationale for fighting the war, while at the same time admitting that the materialistic preoccupations of the Southern people rendered the cause for fighting less than noble.

With a language that was more eloquent and a reasoning that was less ambiguous, Augustin Verot, another Franco-American bishop, addressed his faithful from St. Augustine Church in St. Augustine, Florida. The occasion for Verot's sermon was the proclamation by

President James Buchanan of Friday, January 4, 1861, as a day of prayer and fasting for the whole nation. The observance took place amid the increasing tension between the Southern states and the Northern states. The question of slavery had now effectively divided the nation. The states in the South were preparing for secession from the Union.

Augustin Verot was fifty-five years old when he preached on the issue of slavery in 1861. He had been made a bishop and appointed vicar apostolic in Florida three years before. He was a blunt, outspoken man, pastoral in outlook, concerned but undiplomatic.[79] Augustin Verot published his sermon in the form of a booklet under the title *A Tract for the Times: Slavery and Abolitionism, being the Substance of a Sermon, Preached in the church of St. Augustine, Florida, on the 4th day of January, 1861. Day of Public Humiliation, Fasting and Prayer, by the Right Rev. A. Verot, D.D., Vicar Apostolic of Florida.*[80] Verot took Proverbs 14:34 as his text: "Justice exalteth a nation, but sin maketh nations miserable." The country was "now undoubtedly under the operation of that stern and inflexible rule of justice...any government that rests upon injustice, must necessarily crumble." Verot continued, "Slavery is the origin of the present disturbances...Injustice has then been committed on this point." Verot charged the abolitionists with causing the present strife by their charges that slavery was evil. He then proceeded to show that slavery has "received the sanction of God, of the church, and of Society at all times, and in all governments."

Verot passed in review all of the titles or legitimate reasons found in jurisprudence to justify the existence of slaves. In this defense he followed the legalistic approach of both England and Kenrick as shown above. These arguments were taken from Roman law. Scripture was used to show that the prophets, apostles, and even the Lord himself spoke of slaves and about slaves and slavery, and in fact ameliorated the condition of slavery but significantly never condemned its existence, although the opportunity was there to do so. The same argument was used from church history. The church called for regulation and never enjoined condemnation, which would have been done were slavery inherently evil.

Verot attacked the abolitionists as the source of the unrest. "There has been, in the northern part of the country, an actual conspiracy against justice and truth...This conspiracy is headed by fanatical preachers...who desecrate and pollute the Divine word." Verot explained why many Catholics were so passionately opposed to the abolitionists: they were considered as anti-Catholics, part of the anti-Catholic movement known as Know-Nothingism. "Now, beloved brethren, they are the same who heretofore assailed, calumniated, vilified our church, and have resorted to the vilest and most iniquitous devices... to destroy our holy religion... It is to their nefarious machinations that we are to ascribe the burning of the Charleston Convent."[81]

In the second part of his sermon, Verot set forth in rather blunt language the circumstances in which slavery could not be considered lawful — namely, where the legitimate rights of the slaves were ignored. Making reference to Gregory XVI's condemnation of the slave trade, which, following England's judgment, did not refer to the buying and selling of slaves within the confines of the United States, Verot did decry any effort on the part of the slave-holding states to legalize the slave trade. "It must be a subject of regret... for the true friends of the Southern cause... that some people have expressed, or hinted, a desire, that the trade should be revived."[82] He concluded that if this trade was reintroduced, it would mean the downfall of the Southern Confederacy. This, of course, was naive thinking on his part, since the clandestine trade had continued and since the agrarian economy of the South was based on slavery in such a way that it needed an ever-increasing labor supply.

Verot called for respect of the rights of free blacks. It was a fact that in many Southern states free blacks were forced out of the state, or their activities were severely restricted. Free blacks were always liable to seizure and kidnapping as escaped slaves because of the presumption that all blacks were slaves. Verot also called for an end to the sexual exploitation of slave women. "I must mention in the name of morality... that the whites do not take advantage of the weakness, ignorance, dependence, and lowly position of colored females, whether slaves or not — availing themselves of the impunity which, hitherto, laws in the South have extended to this sort of iniquity." He leveled a solemn warning to his hearers.

> I am a sincere and devoted friend of the South, to which Divine Providence has sent me, and I am ready to undergo any hardship — to make any sacrifice — for the true welfare of the people among whom I live; still I must say it for conscience sake — who knows whether the Almighty does not design to use the present disturbances for the destruction of frequent occasions of immorality, which the subservient and degraded position of the slave offers to the lewd.[83]

Verot also demanded that the matrimonial rights of slaves be recognized. "All know that there have been, and there are frightful abuses." Slaveowners, he insisted, have only the right to the "obedience, respect, and service" of their slaves; they are not the masters of their slaves' rights regarding marriage. "Slavery, to become a permanent institution of the South, must be made to conform to the laws of God; a Southern Confederacy will never thrive, unless it rests upon morality and order."[84] He insisted that slave families not be broken apart. The sale of spouses to different owners and of children away from their parents should not be allowed. He wrote, "A master ought not to be allowed to do this merely for the sake of greater profit." He said that the husband and wife separated from each other will not live in continency. And he added, expressing the racist convictions of many in that time, "It would be requiring a miracle of fortitude and virtue, which cannot be expected from the generality of men, much less from a race more inclined to pleasures than any other. Indeed, the strength and violence of animal propensities is in the inverse ratio of intellectual and moral faculties, which are decidedly weaker in the African race, as all persons of experience will testify."[85]

Finally, he specified that slaveowners must provide adequate food, shelter, and clothing. And they must be given the "means of knowing and practising religion." He concludes by calling for the establishment of a "servile code" once the Confederacy will have been established. And he adds,

> It is undoubtedly true that the law of God does not reprove Slavery; it is undoubtedly true that now the sudden and abrupt manumission of slaves would be a misfortune of appalling magnitude; more so yet for the slave than for the master. Let then the wise and the virtuous unite and combine their prudence, their patriotism, their humanity, and their religious integrity to divest Slavery of the features which would make it odious to God and man.[86]

Michael Gannon points out in his life of Verot that there was a movement on the part of Southern ecclesiastics to try to humanize the slavery condition through legislation.[87] Such a notion was almost ludicrous, and Verot's considerations were tragically deceiving. The economic conditions that favored slavery and made it profitable demanded a relationship of subordination and domination. It demanded psychological control and psychological submission. It demanded that someone be broken and stay broken. Religious autonomy, a sense of self-esteem, and an independent spirit certainly existed among the slaves; but the institution itself could not champion these values because to do so would be destroying itself.

By the same token, the effort made by both Verot and Auguste Martin to create a kind of theological rationale for "a kind and good slavery" led to a contradiction in terms. Their writings came to the notice of the Roman Curia, and judgment was made upon their orthodoxy. If the Civil War had continued or the Southern cause triumphed, the considerations might have been made public. This did not happen, and it is unfortunate that the Roman authority did not have a chance to articulate its unequivocal position on slavery. It would have provided Catholics with a clear, unambiguous framework for the racial questions that so troubled many Catholics in the mid-twentieth century.

Three years after Bishop Martin published his pastoral letter on slavery, the recommendation was made in Rome that the letter was worthy of condemnation. Perhaps someone in the diocese sent a copy of the pastoral letter to Rome. Some were apparently critical of Martin's pastoral activity. In 1858 Father A. Cauvin, stationed at the cathedral with the bishop, wrote to Propaganda denouncing Martin's neglect of the poor and particularly the blacks.[88]

Vincenzo Gatti, O.P., was delegated by the Congregation of the Index to examine the doctrinal content of Martin's pastoral letter.[89] He made his report to the Sacred Congregation of the Index in 1864.[90] Gatti found most of the bishop's conclusions regarding slavery to be objectionable. The bishop was wrong in stating that blacks were descended from Canaan and therefore were accursed. If such a curse existed, it would not be valid after the redemption of Christ. In saying that Divine Providence has snatched from barbarism the "race of Canaan," Martin seems to make God the author of the slave trade and thereby the bishop seems to approve what Gregory XVI had condemned. He assumes that blacks are incapable of freedom and that it is God's will that they be deprived of it. When the bishop speaks of the "original degradation" of blacks, he seems to make a distinction between blacks and whites, "as if the latter did not have original sin and the former did" or that the blacks with education could not become equal to the whites.

> Experience shows that Negroes, placed among Catholics and educated like them, can become learned and virtuous people, fit for moral dignity and freedom. From this treatment we can easily infer that the Bishop favours the enemies of the Catholic

church who accuse her of approving slavery, which is the origin of the vile trade and of the brutal treatment of the Negroes from Africa. It makes the church unjustly odious; it promotes the mistake of those who believe that the slave trade of the Negroes is lawful and who try to elude the condemnation of the Sovereign Pontiffs with every kind of cavil.[91]

Gatti recommended that the pastoral letter should be placed on the Index of Forbidden Books; before doing so, however, the bishop should be allowed to correct it. Gatti's recommendation was approved by the Congregation of the Index, and it was so recommended to Pope Pius IX in an audience held on December 17, 1864. The pope concurred, and the prefect of the Congregation of the Propaganda was instructed to inform Bishop Martin of the decision. He was asked "to correct the errors and inaccuracies...at the earliest possible time, lest...further and harsher measures be taken by the Holy See."[92]

As Maria Caravaglios observes in her article "A Roman Critique of the Pro-Slavery Views of Bishop Martin of Natchitoches, Louisiana," the apostolic letter of Pope Gregory XVI was interpreted as a condemnation of slavery as well as the slave trade.

In this rather devious, obscure way a small revolution was effected in the Curia's thinking on the subject of human rights. Obviously, then, the liberal spirit still breathed in the Vatican — and this in the very year of *Quanta Cura* and the *Syllabus of Errors.*
...Rome's new stance completely undercut the proslavery arguments of Bishops England, Verot, Elder, and indeed of the whole hierarchy in the southern states...When [Martin's] theories were condemned, so were theirs. In effect, Rome said that they had all been wrong for half a century![93]

It is not known what reply Martin made to the Congregation. By April 1865 the Civil War was ended, and by the end of the year the Thirteenth Amendment to the Constitution had abolished slavery.

There is no evidence, on the other hand, that Bishop Verot was ever censured for his sermon of January 1861. In the Propaganda archives a note was added to the Italian résumé of the sermon: "Not everything it seems can be accepted that is affirmed in this argument."[94] Was this judgment communicated to Verot?

VI

By and large, the Catholic laity who were white accepted the condition of slavery. During the Civil War white Catholics fought on both sides. Yet even in the North the sentiment of the Catholic laity, most of whom were recent immigrants, was decidedly antiblack. This was especially so in regard to Irish immigrants. As many American church historians have pointed out, this antiblack sentiment on the part of the Irish in the period prior to the Civil War was the result of resentment over "the competition of the Negro worker in the labor market."[95] Both the Irish and the free black population in the North were on the bottom rung of the social and the economic ladders. In New York City these conditions resulted in the draft riots in the summer of 1863. The first bill of military conscription in the United States was signed into law in the spring of 1863. Men between the ages of twenty and forty-five were eligible for service unless a draftee paid three hundred dollars or could pay for a substitute. The draft law was thus biased in favor of those with wealth. The Irish were among the poor, and blacks who wished to enlist as soldiers in the Civil War were initially not accepted. The Irish staged a series of riots in the city of New York between July 13 and 16. They brutalized the black community, lynching, burning, killing men, women, and children. Archbishop Hughes of New York was challenged to control the rioters. He addressed them publicly, calling for peace. This was one of his last acts, for he died in 1864.[96]

Madeleine Hooke Rice, in *American Catholic Opinion in the Slavery Controversy*, a book that still remains the only study in the area, details the attitudes of Catholics in both the North and the South. She points out how the antagonism of Catholics toward blacks was the result of their feelings toward the abolitionists. Many of the latter — for example, Lyman Beecher,[97] the president of Lane Seminary in Cincinnati and the father of Harriett Beecher Stowe, the author of *Uncle Tom's Cabin* — were anti-Catholic in thought and word. Many Catholics saw the abolitionists simply as fanatics.

However, there was no uniform type of abolitionism. The abolitionists often had deep religious convictions but were not all attached to recognized Protestant denominations.[98] Nor, indeed, were all of the abolitionists without racial prejudice. There was a decided difference between abolitionists in England and in the United States. Those in England were in some instances opposed to the Catholic Irish and their search for freedom. This also aroused the antipathy of American Catholics.[99]

It would not be an exaggeration to say that the attitude of many Catholics to blacks was as much a result of racism as it was a distaste for abolitionism. In the nineteenth century there were few white Americans who really believed that blacks were equal to whites.[100] The assumption of black inferiority was an accepted part of the social and cultural landscape, a conclusion not to be questioned. On this point the majority of Catholics differed little from their contemporaries, whether in the South or in the North.

A good example of this mind-set is a man who played an important role in nineteenth-century American Catholic thought, Orestes Brownson (1803–76). Brownson had been first a Presbyterian minister and then a Universalist minister. He converted to Catholicism in 1844 when he was forty-one years old. He was perhaps the best example of an authentic intellectual and an original thinker that the American Catholic church possessed in the mid-nineteenth century. More than anyone else he embodied the idea that "American thought" (meaning the intellectual ideas of New England) and Catholicism could be welded together. At the same time, Brownson was opinionated, bigoted, and intolerant. In the pages of his periodical, *Brownson's Quarterly Review,* and in other publications, he treated many issues current in his day from the perspective of his newfound faith. In so doing, he did not always succeed in respecting the beliefs and logic of others.[101] Brownson, for instance, sincerely held that women were inferior to men. He was adamantly opposed to giving women the right to vote. According to Brownson, no one had a natural right to vote. According to his own logic, blacks also, he said, do not necessarily have the right to vote.[102]

As for the Irish, Brownson took a condescending attitude to them as well. For him, Americans of English descent were the original Americans. As he said, "Individuals of other races have done their duty and deserved well of the country, but only by assimilating themselves to the Anglo-Americans and becoming animated by their spirit."[103] After praising the Irish Catholics as "quiet, modest, peaceful, and loyal citizens," he added, "It cannot be denied that hanging loosely on to their skirts is a miserable rabble, unlike any thing which the country has ever known of native growth — a noisy, drinking, and brawling rabble, who have, after all, a great deal of influence with their countrymen, who are usually taken to represent the whole Irish Catholic body."[104]

Brownson was opposed to slavery. He considered it "a great moral, social and political wrong... whatever be the complexion of the slave."[105] He credited the Catholic church with always being opposed to slavery, saying that although the church may tolerate it for a while, "she sets her face against it." Later in the same article he points out that the great evil of slavery was the spiritual and intellectual degradation necessary for slaveholders "to keep their slaves in subjection." He adds, "They must stifle in them the man, and prevent the development in them of that 'image and likeness' of God after which they were created."

Brownson's opposition to slavery was highlighted by his controversy with the colorful and outspoken archbishop of New York, John Hughes (1797–1864).[106] Hughes made no secret of his feelings about slavery. He felt that the lot of slaves in the South was not half as miserable as that of the exploited Irish workers in the North. In an unsigned article in a Catholic newspaper, the *Metropolitan Record*, he spoke about what he considered to be the wretched condition of black prisoners in Africa and affirmed that their condition of being sold as slaves was much better than the alternative, the "butcheries prepared for them in their native land." It was much more humane, he averred, to purchase them "at a sum which prospectively might cover the annual or semi-annual wages given to laborers in other parts of the world."[107] Hughes had criticized an article of Brownson's entitled "Slavery and the War," in which Brownson called for the emancipation of the slaves. He pointed out publicly that since Pope Gregory XVI had condemned the slave trade, it was forbidden for any Catholic, ecclesiastic or lay, to write anything supporting or approving the slave trade. Hughes had more or less implied that there was nothing wrong with this trade.[108] After citing the offending passage, Brownson wrote:

> This, at first sight, looks very much like an apology for the slave-trade, for the writer not only says that he cannot discover the crime in the slaver, or that there would be any moral transgression of the law of God in the act, but even explains away the terrific part of the question that 'not only the individuals brought to the American continent or islands are themselves to be slaves, but their posterity, in like manner, for all time come.' "[109]

Brownson, on the other hand, insisted that slaves were private property. One could not divest someone of his or her property without recompense. It is for this reason that he both opposed the abolitionists and defended the Fugitive Slave Act of 1850. "If the master has a title to the bodily services of his slave which is good in morals, as he certainly may have, he has the right in justice to recover his slave, the same as he would have in the case of any other species of property."[110]

Brownson's feelings and assumptions regarding blacks affected his judgment regarding the significance of black people and their future existence. In an article entitled "Abolition and Negro Equality," written on the eve of the victory of the North in the Civil War,[111] he stated, "We may talk as we will, spin any fine theories we like, praise the negro as we please, and sneer at the boasting Caucasian to our heart's content, but we cannot alter the fact of negro inferiority, or make it not a fact that the negro is the most degenerate branch of our race."[112] As he said, this inferiority is no reason to enslave blacks, but one must insist upon total segregation because one must never permit intermarriage. "Between blacks and whites marriage is anomalous... Both races suffer by it, because the distance between them is too great to be leaped by a single bound." The mulatto, according to Brownson, was "intellectually inferior to the white man, and as an animal, inferior to the black man." He used the barnyard animals as a proof: "Mixed breeds even in animals, without frequent new crossings, soon run out."

Because blacks are inferior both intellectually and physically, Brownson did not believe that they could long survive in the country. He did not believe in deportation, but he believed they would naturally die out. "Hemmed in or crowded out by an ever advancing tide of white population, more vigorous, more energetic, and more enterprising, their numbers will diminish day by day, and gradually the great mass of them will have disappeared."[113]

He proceeded to spell out what he meant by racial inferiority.

The inferior races, the yellow, the red, or the black, nearly all savage, barbarous, or semi-barbarous, are not... types of the primitive man, or so many stages in man's progressive march from the tadpole, chimpanzee, or gorilla up to Bacon, Newton, Napoleon Bonaparte, George B. McClellan... They mark rather so many stages or degrees in human degeneracy. The African negro is not the primitive man, the man not yet developed, the incipient Caucasian, but the degenerate man, who, through causes which neither you nor I can explain, has fallen below the normal human type... He has ceased to be progressive, and when a race has ceased to be progressive, nothing remains for it but to die.[114]

Brownson evidently had no knowledge of black Catholics, black saints, or black religious or priests.

> Why is it that you can rarely get a negro to embrace any thing of Christianity but its animality, ... or its exterior forms, and that after generations of Christian worship and instruction, he falls back to the worship of Obi? Why is it that you can scarcely get a single Christian thought into the negro's head, and that with him religion is almost sure to lapse into a grovelling superstition? Why, because he is a degenerate man, and superstition is degenerate religion, and the religion of the degenerate.[115]

Brownson's racist attitudes must be placed within the context of his own time. His feelings regarding questions of racial equality or the lack of it reflected pretty much the general sentiments of nineteenth-century America. Although in some respects Brownson was not the typical Roman Catholic, nevertheless, his views regarding race were most certainly shared by the majority of Catholics both North and South. It must not be forgotten that this racist ideology was the justification for slavery and, after its demise, for the passage of laws that severely curtailed the opportunities of nineteenth-century American blacks to take advantage of their newly acquired freedom. Ultimately this attitude led to the terrible lynchings and random violence used to intimidate the black population in the second half of the nineteenth century and the first half of the next.

VII

Not all Catholics, however, shared the prevailing American attitude toward slavery and racial equality. Both within the United States and abroad were found vocal opponents of slavery and racism among members of the clergy and the laity.

One man more than others dominated the political arena of England and Ireland in the first part of the nineteenth century. By the middle of the century, that same man became one of the best-known Catholic laymen in Europe. Daniel O'Connell (1775–1847) was a member of an Irish Catholic gentry family that had retained some wealth and influence despite the penal laws. He was born in County Kerry and was educated on the Continent. He led the fight for Catholic emancipation, for the repeal of many of the disabilities from the penal laws that prevented Catholics from participating in public life.

As the first Irish Catholic in the British Parliament since the Reformation and as a master of political organization, by 1828 he became the recognized leader of Catholic Ireland.

Although a pragmatist in terms of political strategy, O'Connell had a deep sense of justice that went far beyond merely political considerations. As a result, he was passionately opposed to slavery, and he joined the antislavery forces in England to abolish slavery in the English colonies. Many Irish Americans and Americans who were not Irish joined with O'Connell in his agitation for a repeal of the political union between Ireland and England. Money flowed in from the United States, but O'Connell made it clear that he as the leader of Irish nationalism would not cease in his outspoken condemnation of slavery in the United States. Many Irish Americans, including O'Connell's friend Bishop John England, criticized O'Connell for his stand against slavery and for what they considered his interference in American affairs. This opposition never deterred O'Connell, and he delivered a strongly worded plea for an end to slavery in his *Address to the Cincinnati Irish Repeal Association*. O'Connell was especially distressed by the antiblack sentiment of his fellow Irishmen. "We conjure you, Irishmen and descendants of Irishmen, to abandon forever all defence of the more hideous negro-slavery system. Let it no more be said that your feelings are made so obtuse by the air of America, that you cannot feel, as Catholics and Christians ought to feel, this truth — this plain truth — that one man can not have any property in another man."[116] O'Connell based his opposition to slavery on his convictions as a Catholic.[117]

Just as O'Connell, the layman, had political influence in all of Catholic Europe by the middle of the nineteenth century, so Félix-Antoine-Philibert Dupanloup (1802–78), bishop of Orléans, was one of the most influential ecclesiastics. By the middle of the century, Dupanloup, who became the first bishop to be received into the Académie Française since the Revolution and in addition served as a deputy in the National Assembly, was also the leader of the liberal Catholic movement in France. Although conservative in some areas of political life, Dupanloup was the voice that championed liberal causes and the herald who sought to make the church more alert to the demands of modern society.[118]

Dupanloup had no hesitation in condemning slavery in the United States. In the middle of Lent 1862, Dupanloup wrote a pastoral letter to the priests of his diocese asking them to pray for those in slavery. Commenting on the Civil War in the United States, he referred to the relative merits of both sides and added, "What I do know is that there are still four millions of slaves in the United States, two millions in the rest of America, together six millions of slaves in Christian countries eighteen hundred years after the Crucifixion."[119]

Commenting on the preliminary moves in preparation for the Emancipation Proclamation by President Lincoln, Dupanloup gave his enthusiastic support, called for compensation to be given to former slaveholders, and refused to deal with theories supporting slavery, except to reject them in the name of the redemption of Christ and the mystery of the unity of the human family in God.

> There are, then, on the same earth with myself children of God and children of men like myself, saved by the same blood that I am, destined to the same Heaven that I am, five or six millions of my fellow-beings, in the United States, in Brazil, in Cuba, in Surinam, who are slaves; aged people, vigorous men, women, young girls, children. Just Heaven! Is it not yet time, after eighteen centuries of Christianity, for us all to begin to practice the ever enduring law, "Do not to another that which you would not he should do to you."[120]

Dupanloup approached the question of slavery not only from the viewpoint of the humanity of those enslaved but also from the Catholic teaching that all are transformed by the redemption of Christ. He insisted that the Catholic church was opposed to slavery and that those who stated otherwise attacked and calumniated the church.

Among the Catholic authorities to whom he referred in his pastoral letter as writing against slavery, Dupanloup mentioned the name of Augustin Cochin (1823–72). Cochin was a layman from an old Paris family of the haute bourgeoisie. Sincerely Catholic, Cochin belonged to the liberal circle of French Catholics that published the newspaper *Le Correspondant*. This circle included such persons as the Count Charles de Montalembert, Albert de Broglie, and Henri Lacordaire, O.P. Cochin was very active in the antislave societies of nineteenth-century France, and in 1861 he published a book against slavery entitled *L'abolition de l'esclavage*. For this work, Pope Pius IX decorated him with a papal medal.[121]

In the United States too, a few Catholics opposed slavery publicly. Such was William Gaston (1778–1844), born in New Bern, North Carolina. He was sent to study at Georgetown College in the District of Columbia when he was fourteen years old. His name is first on the student rolls of the college. He did not complete his college years at Georgetown and ultimately graduated from Princeton. Gaston's public life was as a member of Congress and finally as a justice on the supreme court of North Carolina. He spoke out publicly against slavery. In a commencement address delivered in 1832 at the University of North Carolina, he challenged the students in calling for "the ultimate extirpation of the worst evil that affects the Southern part of our Confederacy."[122] As member of the constitutional convention of 1835 for North Carolina, Gaston led the unsuccessful fight to give free blacks the vote. As justice on the supreme court, he defended on more than one occasion the rights of blacks, both slave and free.[123] It seems fair to assert that Gaston's position on slavery was in part the result of his Catholic beliefs.

Although many Catholic priests were also slaveowners and many priests were committed to the Southern cause in the Civil War, other priests were opposed to slavery. One of the most bizarre incidents concerning an antislavery priest occurred in New Orleans during the war. Claude Pascal Maistre was born in the region of Champagne in France. He became a priest of the diocese of Troyes and after five years of service came to the United States, going first to the diocese of Chicago. By 1856 he was in the archdiocese of New Orleans and later became the pastor of St. Rose of Lima Church in New Orleans. Maistre already had the reputation of being an abolitionist.[124] Father Maistre began preaching against slavery in 1862, and complaints were made to the archbishop, Jean-Marie Odin. He refused to desist when asked, and the archbishop suspended him in 1863. Father Maistre ignored the suspension, and the archbishop placed the church under interdict. Later that year Father Maistre built another church in New Orleans, Holy Name of Jesus, which was considered to be schismatic. Here in keeping with his convictions, Father Maistre noted that in the parish registers there would no longer be a separation between the entries of whites and blacks. Father Maistre was reconciled to the church in 1866, through the intervention of Cardinal Barnabò, prefect of the Congregation of the Propaganda.[125]

The most prominent American bishop to come out publicly for the emancipation of the slaves was John Baptist Purcell (1800–1883), archbishop of Cincinnati. He took a public stand on the issue, however, only in the summer of 1862.[126] His brother, Father Edward Purcell, the editor of the archdiocesan newspaper the *Catholic Telegraph*, used its editorial columns to criticize slavery.[127]

Slavery has cast a long shadow over the history of the United States. It has led to civil strife, racial violence, and ethnic resentments that still fester. American Catholic history is covered by that same shadow. Whether in Spanish, French, or English Catholic areas, slavery was part of the religious scene. Not only laypersons but religious and priests availed themselves of slave labor. Catholics outside of the United States, beginning with the papacy and including both clerics and lay, had developed a moral consciousness that by the middle of the nineteenth century could no longer tolerate slavery. But the Catholic church in the United States found itself incapable of taking any decisive action or of enunciating clearly thought-out principles regarding slavery. This factor unfortunately prevented the American church from playing any serious role until the middle of the twentieth century in the most tragic debate that this nation had to face.

Serious research is still necessary regarding the Catholic reaction to slavery. A more thorough study of the documents of those religious congregations and secular priests who owned slaves may reveal insights into the question of racial feelings and sentiments that lay at the heart of proslavery or antislavery mentality. Did Protestants have a keener sense of social justice than Catholics in the United States? A closer look at the background and teachings of the abolitionists in contrast to the background and theological positions of American priests may reveal more about why American Catholics opposed the abolition movement. Was there a causal link between abolitionism and anti-Catholic prejudice? A more detailed look at abolitionists in this country, white and black, may reveal more about the manipulation of Catholic opinion than the anti-Catholicism of abolitionists. Finally, one may wonder why in the United States there was so little social consciousness among Catholics. Catholic social teaching was in its infancy in mid-nineteenth-century Europe. In the United States it was practically unknown. It is almost half a century since Madeleine Hooke Rice made her study of Catholic sentiment on the slavery controversy. The sources are now more abundant, the questions more relevant, and the interest in mentality and popular thought more important for historical understanding today.

Chapter 3

CHRIST'S IMAGE IN BLACK: THE BLACK CATHOLIC COMMUNITY BEFORE THE CIVIL WAR

Who were the members of the black Catholic community at the end of the eighteenth century and in the period before the Civil War? Can we identify individuals, and do we have names? Do we have some notion of their faith and their position within the Catholic community? Can we identify the various locations of communities that were African American in race and culture and Catholic in religion? Can we get some idea of the origin of the members and of communication between the individual communities of the larger black Catholic community? In many areas, especially in the South, people can be identified because there was a fairly rigid rule about maintaining distinct and separate sacramental books. A careful examination of the registers for black Catholics can often reveal names, family relationships, age, and origin. It can also reveal the extent and frequency of religious practice. In fact, such records represent a historical source that has yet to be exploited to its fullest extent.

I

St. Augustine in Florida was the first Catholic parish in what is now the United States. As noted, it is also the site of the oldest black Catholic community. In 1784, when the Florida Territory had been restored to Spanish rule, many of the British emigrated and more Americans arrived. Some came with their slaves; others who were

67

slaves fled to the Spanish colony from the United States to find freedom. All who were not Catholic were expected in time to convert to
Catholicism. The black population was large in proportion to the total
population; it was Spanish in language, diverse in origin, and Catholic in religion. Those who were slaves numbered about five hundred.[1]
The number of free blacks is not given. The relation of the blacks
to the white population was, it seems, complex and multifaceted.[2]
The white population numbered about nine hundred persons of diverse nationalities, not counting the Spanish soldiers and officials.
Some examples of this complexity will help put flesh and blood on
this outline.

On February 14, 1788, two free blacks named Right, (perhaps
originally spelled Wright), John and Milly, had their week-old son
baptized. He was given the name Robert Joseph Right and baptized
by Michael O'Reilly, a Spanish-speaking Irish priest who had studied in Salamanca at the Irish College of Nobles and who came to
Florida under service to the Spanish crown in 1778.[3] Robert Joseph's
godparents were an Italian man, Roque Leonardii, and a woman,
Agatha Poll, members of the Minorcan colony that had arrived in
Florida in 1768.[4] Thirty-two years later, Francisco José, a native of
the province of Florida and a brother of Robert Joseph Right, married María Petrona Herrera. Both Francisco and María Herrera are
listed as free blacks. According to the records, his parents now have
Spanish names, Juan and Emelia, instead of "John and Milly." His
parents are described as "natives of South Carolina in the United
States of America." María's parents are listed as Thomas, a native
of Guinea (in Africa), and María de los Dolores, a native of Boston
in the United States. They were married on Monday, June 26, 1820,
in the presence of Don Miguel Crosby, the banns of marriage having
been proclaimed on three successive Sundays at the principal Mass. It
is interesting to note that the Right family was now Spanish-speaking
and that the father of the bride was African born, yet free, and the
mother, a free black from Boston, and that both parents' names were
Spanish.[5]

Another example of these complicated interrelations is the Husten family. Prince and Judith are described as "fugitives from South
Carolina." They had a son and a daughter both baptized on the same
day, August 16, 1788. The boy was nine years old and his name had
been Bob, but he was given the Spanish names Francisco Domingo
Mariano Husten; his godparents, both white, were Dominic Marti-
noli and Mariana Cavedo, husband and wife, from the parish.[6] The
daughter was eight and received the name María, the godfather being

Pedro Cotsifakis, a Greek in the Minorcan colony who by this time had managed to become a well-to-do merchant and slaveowner.[7] It is not stated whether the Hustens were slaves.

Manuel de Barcelona, however, was a slave, described as a Bozal (that is, one born in Africa), eleven years old, the slave of Don Cirilo de Barcelona, O.F.M. Cap., auxiliary bishop of Havana, who as vicar was episcopal visitator of the Floridas and Louisiana. In July 1788 Bishop de Barcelona came to St. Augustine for an episcopal visitation. He concluded the visitation in October and prepared to go to New Orleans. He did not leave, however, until the following year.[8] The baptismal register placed the baptism of Manuel on Sunday, November 16, by Don Miguel O'Reilly. Presumably, the bishop acquired Manuel sometime during his stay in St. Augustine.[9]

The census list given to Bishop de Barcelona for his visitation indicates that in 1788 there were a total of 1,078 white persons in the East Florida colony. In addition, there were 284 slaves in St. Augustine and 367 outside of the city. It is not stated how many free blacks there were. It is significant that there were 651 slaves in the colony, or over half as many blacks as whites.[10]

Bishop de Barcelona made several reforms regarding the slaves. The slaveowners were reminded that they had to see to the baptism of their slaves after due preparation. They incurred excommunication if they failed to baptize their slaves within six months of acquiring them. This failure also made them subject to a fine by the secular authorities. Finally, the slaves were to receive religious instruction every Sunday.[11] The baptismal registers indicate that often the slaves were brought in groups to be baptized. Very often the sponsors at baptism were black, slave or free. Josefa Fernández, the slave of Don Pedro Camps, the pastor of the Minorcans, was often a sponsor, as in the baptism on June 24, 1788, of a sixteen-year-old youth from Guinea, Juan José Sánchez, the slave of Juan Sánchez. Josepha Fernández was godmother, and Luís de Almanza, slave of Don Manuel de Almanza, was godfather.[12]

One of the most interesting persons to appear in the sacramental books is María Beatrice Stone. A lengthy baptismal entry is devoted to her under the date February 16, 1788.[13] Don Miguel O'Reilly described Stone as a free mulatto woman, thirty-nine years old, originally from South Carolina, the daughter of John Stone and Regina Stone, the slave of John. She had been a Lutheran, though the term "Lutheran" may have been a general name for Protestant in this Spanish-speaking world. "Embracing piously and devotedly all those things which the Holy Roman Catholic and Apostolic church teaches must be believed and taught and having been found well instructed as a catechumen in the Catechism," she abjured her heresy and was baptized according to the "order and rite in the baptism of adults."[14] Her sponsor was Lawrence Capo, a Minorcan, who served as sponsor for many blacks at that time.

Beatrice Stone was evidently the daughter of the slaveowner John Stone. She was a woman of age and substance when she came to St. Augustine. Perhaps she had been for some time in St. Augustine and acquired some wealth before becoming a Catholic. Her name appeared often in the baptismal book. On July 12 in the preceding year, Don Thomas Hassett, the pastor of the parish of St. Augustine (like O'Reilly, a former student of the Irish College of Nobles in Salamanca serving at the behest of the Spanish crown),[15] baptized a free mulatto infant boy, the "natural" son of Francisco Sánchez and María Beatrice, "free mulatto woman from North America." The infant was given the name Francisco Mattaeo Sánchez. It does not seem that María Beatrice was married to Francisco Sánchez.[16] Francisco Sánchez apparently had many slaves. On that same day a three-year-old boy, the son of Edenborough and Filis, slaves of Francisco, was baptized, and three days later so was a twelve-year-old girl, María del Rosario, the daughter of two slaves of Francisco.

On January 13, 1788, Don Miguel O'Reilly baptized three children — two girls, one seven and the other ten, and one month-old baby boy — all described as slaves of María Beatrice Stone. Their parents were slaves of Francisco Sánchez.[17]

Several years later there is a mention of Catalina Sánchez, the quadroon *(quarterona)* "natural" daughter of Francisco Sánchez and Beatris Piedra, free mulatto woman *(parda libra)*.[18] Piedra is the Spanish word for "stone," and one may speculate that Beatrice Stone had assumed the Spanish form of her name. Her daughter has become almost white. Another daughter, Beatriz Sánchez, is mentioned in the baptismal notice of Esteban José Fernando Pérez, grandson of Beatrice de Piedra, in January 1798.[19] He is referred to as a quadroon. And in 1808 with the birth of María de la Consepción [*sic*] Dolores Sánchez, the mother, Catalina Sánchez, is referred to as "*quarterona*...the natural daughter of Francisco Sánchez and Beatris Piedra, *parda libra*."[20] In 1805 her son José Sánchez married Lucia Iznardy [*sic*]. José is described as a free mulatto, the natural son of Don Francisco Xavier Sánchez, native of St. Augustine, and of Beatris Piedra, free mulatto woman, native of Charleston in the United States of America. The bride, Lucia Isnardy, is identified as a free mulatto from the parish, the illegitimate daughter of Don Miguel Isnardy, deceased, and Isabel Jenkins, free mulatto from South Carolina.[21]

The sacramental books of St. Augustine reveal a complex black Catholic society where there were both slaves and free and various shades of color. There was upward mobility of a sort; there was a mixture of races, recognized if not approved. We know little about individual histories; yet we do know that a woman like María Beatrice Stone, who became María Beatris Piedra, originally from Charleston, South Carolina, thirty-nine at her baptism and fifty-six at the marriage of her son, was the consort of a well-to-do Spaniard and mother of his children. Perhaps she was not legally married; but to all intents and purposes within the limits of the law, she was most likely a woman of means and dignity.

The death registers round out the picture of this black Catholic community. Among the soldiers garrisoned at St. Augustine was the First Company of Free Morenos of Havana. Some were mulattoes; others were blacks originally from Africa, like Francisco de Castro, who died at the age of forty-four years, in communion with "our Holy Mother the church ... having received the Holy Sacraments";[22] and José Melgarejos, soldier of the free black battalion from Havana, son of Balthazar and Josefa Oguendo, forty years old, who died in the Royal Hospital, having received extreme unction and the sacrament of penance on November 12, 1817.[23] Many blacks came from afar, such as Benito Peso de Bungo, a native of Maryland and a widower, who died at the age of forty, having received penance, communion, and extreme unction and who is buried in the church cemetery.[24] Others came from the Caribbean, like Agustín Sánchez Moreno, native of New Providence in the Bahamas, slave of Don Juan Sánchez, who died in January 1798 at the age of fourteen, having received the sacraments.[25]

Slavery and racial prejudice existed in East Florida during the Spanish period, as it did after 1821, when the colony became a territory of the United States. Still, unlike the slaves in many parts of the United States, the sacrament of baptism gave them a status and a name — at times sonorous Spanish names with religious significance — as well as a family and spiritual relations, and even a history. The records certainly indicate that the many who were baptized did not all receive the sacrament of marriage in the church or the last rites of the church with burial in the cemetery. Still many among the slaves were married with due solemnity in the church and also received the last rites on their deathbed. Their names rise out of the

stilted, formal phrases of the ecclesiastical language as persons who
were not without dignity and character.

II

Louisiana as a Catholic settlement was not as old as Florida; but
because of the importance of centers such as New Orleans and Mobile,
it would become much larger and more important as a colony that was
first French and later Spanish. For the same reason it would rank first
in importance as a black Catholic community, unique in its history
and unique in its culture.

The area known today as Louisiana, including also southern Mississippi and the Gulf coast east to Mobile, began to be settled by the
French at the end of the seventeenth century. About 1718 the settlement at the mouth of the Mississippi River to be known as New
Orleans was established. By this time African slavery had been introduced into the colony. The *Code Noir*, the laws governing slavery in
the French regions, was drawn up and promulgated in 1724.[26] The
early missionaries in the region, both the Jesuits and the Capuchins,
ministered to the slaves as well as to the white population. These two
religious orders likewise owned slaves and profited from their labor.

The first religious order of women introduced into the colony
was the community of Ursuline nuns who were established in New
Orleans in 1727. The nuns engaged in educating young girls and op-
erating the royal hospital. The nuns not only gave an education to
the young French women in the city, but they also held classes for
black and Indian girls and women.[27] At the same time, as pointed
out in chapter 2, they, like other religious institutions in the colony,
owned slaves.[28]

The small number of French women in the colony at its beginning resulted in concubinage between the male population of soldiers,
settlers, merchants, and adventurers who flocked to the colony and
the women, mainly Native Americans and slaves of African descent.
The interracial character of these alliances, especially with blacks,
resulted in a mixed population of people of color. In general, this
population was free, but it was nonetheless bound by the rules of
racial segregation.

In 1769 the Louisiana colony was ceded to Spain. It would remain
under Spanish control until 1803, when it briefly reverted to France.
Later that same year the United States acquired the territory. By the
end of the eighteenth century the religious situation in Louisiana and

particularly in New Orleans was desperate. There were never suffi-cient clergy in the colony. In the rural areas many of the Catholic settlers grew accustomed to life without the ministrations of a priest. There was constant bickering between the religious orders and also between the ecclesiastical administration and the provincial govern-ment. By the end of the eighteenth century the French population had embraced many of the anticlerical sentiments from the French main-land at the time of the revolution of 1789. As a result the practice of religion had practically ceased in certain quarters.[29]

The legislation of both the French and Spanish governments stip-ulated that religious ministrations were to be given to the slaves. Despite the written ordinances, the Catholic settlers were often ne-glectful. If the slaves were baptized, they were often spiritually ne-glected in the rural areas; and in failing to grant them access to the other sacraments, they could in no way be considered to have had the fullness of Catholic life. Very often they were forced to work on holy days, no opportunity was given for religious instruction, and marriage was openly discouraged.[30] In a letter to the rector of the seminary at Lyons, Jean-Marie Odin, C.M., the future archbishop of New Orleans, wrote that while the American slaveowners permitted their slaves to marry in the church and to practice their religion, "in southern Louisiana most of the French do not want even to hear about having instruction for their slaves, to have them get married; often they do not even permit them to go to church. You can easily imagine what disorders result from all that."[31]

By the beginning of the nineteenth century, the practice of concu-binage between well-to-do men and free women of culture was well established, especially in New Orleans. From this milieu of "genteel immorality" emerged Henriette Delille, the woman who founded the second black religious congregation in the United States. Her story will be told in chapter 4. In spite of this general religious decadence, it was observed at the beginning of the nineteenth century that the churches in New Orleans were frequented "only by women, the offi-cials of the governor's entourage and Negroes."[32]

The "people of color," later often referred to as creoles of color,[33] or *les gens libres de couleur,* began to form a group apart in the harsh, racially conscious society of Louisiana. There were economic and social advantages in maintaining a distinction based on degrees of blackness or brownness in skin complexion. An example of how this differentiation worked on the parish-church level is the quar-rel between the *marguilliers,* or church wardens, and the pastor of St. Martin's Church in St. Martinsville, located in south-central Louisiana, about fifty miles southwest of Baton Rouge. The *marguilliers* in Louisiana were equivalent to the lay trustees that owned many parishes in other parts of the United States. In Louisiana, especially in the cathedral at New Orleans, they took on an adversarial role with the ecclesiastical authorities.

On June 29, 1843, the church wardens passed a series of resolutions informing the pastor and the then bishop, Antoine Blanc,[34] that "the pastor . . . [is] invited to establish the distinction that exists, even in the church, between whites and persons of color, or slaves, when they approach the holy table or for the veneration of the cross." They went on to add that the law "making it a duty for the free people of color, *gens de couleur libres*, not to presume to make themselves equal to whites" prevents them from "making their devotions" until after every white person will have done so. Even for the veneration of the cross, which was part of the liturgy of Good Friday, they could not approach the cross until after the whites. Finally, it was added that "granted that the free people of color have a distinction over the slaves, these latter cannot fulfill any of these ceremonies except after [the people of color], it being understood that the priest admitting a slave to communion must have him present the permission of his master."[35] There is no indication of the resolution of this conflict at St. Martinsville. The demands of the church wardens do indicate that in the period before the Civil War a distinction was encouraged between the free people of color and the slaves. It would be interesting to know how widespread even in Louisiana was the custom that a slave had to present a permission of the slaveowner granting him or her the right to receive communion.

Another example of the tyranny that Louisiana Catholic slaveholders sought to exercise over their slaves is recorded in a letter of the seminary superior, Anthony Andrieu, C.M., to Bishop Blanc, July 31, 1853. Andrieu had announced one Sunday from the pulpit that catechism would be given to the slaves each Sunday after vespers in the church and urged slaveowners to send their slaves. At that point, according to Father Andrieu, the president of the *marguilliers* of the parish stood up and said in a loud voice, "The Administration is opposed." Andrieu asked for instructions from the bishop. It is not recorded what these were.[36]

A fascinating illustration of tangled family roots and complex racial relationships in the history of Louisiana is the story of a unique black Catholic community in the northern part of the state, some sixteen miles south of Natchitoches in an area known as Isle Brevelle on the Cane River. This extraordinary story begins with a slave woman whose French name was Marie-Thérèze but whose African name was Coincoin. Coincoin's father, François, was a slave born in Africa who belonged to the commandant of Fort St-Jean-Baptiste, Louis Juchereau de St-Denis, at the settlement of Natchitoches. Coincoin's mother, Marie Françoise, was a slave in the same household and would have eleven children. Marie-Thérèze Coincoin was the third child and was baptized August 24, 1742, in the parish of St-François in Natchitoches. The three eldest children had received African names as well. Coincoin, which meant "second daughter," was an African name in the Ewe language of Togo on the West African coast.[37]

With the death of St-Denis in 1744, his widow in 1758, and the parents of Marie-Thérèze in the same year, the young girl was inherited by the younger son of the family, Pierre Antoine Juchereau de St-Denis. Between 1759 and 1761, Coincoin, unmarried, became the mother of three children. Sometime after 1761, she became the slave of Marie des Neiges de St-Denis, the youngest sister of Pierre Antoine. Her husband was Antonio Manuel Bermudez de Soto and her brother-in-law, the commandant of the fort, Athanase Fortune Christophe de Mézières. In 1767, when she was twenty-five, Marie-Thérèze Coincoin met a young French merchant and reserve soldier, Claude Thomas Pierre Metoyer, who had been born into a bourgeois family at La Rochelle in 1744 and had emigrated to Louisiana with his brother. Coincoin became the concubine of Pierre Metoyer through a monetary arrangement with Madame de Soto. It was legally impossible for them to be married, but they lived as husband and wife, Coincoin giving birth to one set of twins and eventually five more children.

Concubinage was against the law, and Father Luís de Quintanilla, O.F.M. Cap., the pastor, baptized the illegitimate children of Coincoin with the notation "father unknown," even though all knew who the real father was. Finally in exasperation, the pastor demanded that the commandant de Mézières do something to break up the cohabitation of Coincoin and Metoyer. The commandant did so. The separation, however, did not last; eventually Madame de Soto came to the defence of her slave and Metoyer, upbraiding Father de Quintanilla for interfering in their personal life. Eventually, in 1778, a partial solution was found when Metoyer arranged to purchase Coincoin and their seven children, who had legally belonged to Madame de Soto. Following the purchase, Metoyer emancipated Coincoin and their last son.[38]

For eight more years Coincoin and Metoyer lived together with their children. One last child, a son, was born in 1784. In 1786 the ménage broke up, apparently by mutual agreement. Several years before, Pierre Metoyer had made a will in which he gave about sixty-eight acres of land to Coincoin and their children, whose manumission he reserved to himself in the future. This testament was drawn up in secret, but in it Pierre Metoyer never legally acknowledged his children by Coincoin. In 1786 the land was given to Coincoin along with a very modest annuity. Claude Metoyer then proceeded to marry a white woman, the widow of an old friend, who bore him three children. The donation to Coincoin and his slave children was carefully protected by a legal document so that his wife would have no legal claims to Coincoin's property or to his slave children, whom he intended to set free. By this time Metoyer was a very wealthy man in his forties and was respected in the community. Coincoin was forty-six.[39]

Amazingly Coincoin with her children worked the sixty-eight acres of land with such shrewdness and diligence that by 1793 she had a thriving business of tobacco, indigo, and bear grease. The next year, with the help of Pierre Metoyer, she received a land grant from the Spanish crown, which enabled her to become a fairly well-to-do woman. She saved her money and invested it back into the land; and with the help of Pierre she was finally able in the first part of the nineteenth century to buy the freedom of those children who were not the offspring of Pierre Metoyer. Eventually more land was purchased in the area of the Cane River. By the beginning of the nineteenth century, Coincoin and her children had themselves purchased more than a dozen slaves. This was now the beginning of a small community.

By the time of her death in 1816 or 1817,[40] her son Augustin had become the head of the community of Isle Brevelle. Family members purchased land and slaves, and in time the community included other free people of color who had married into the Metoyer family. Before the Civil War, Augustin had become one of the wealthiest men in the Natchitoches area. He constructed a church in 1829 named in honor of St. Augustine. It was a mission of the parish of St-François in Natchitoches and is one of the oldest black Catholic churches in the country. It was a symbol of the intense Catholic consciousness that characterized this community. Attached to it still is the cemetery. The present parish church is not the original, but the painting of Augustin Metoyer with the church he built in the background, painted by a visiting artist in 1836, still hangs in the church. In the time of Augustin Metoyer "outsiders [i.e. whites] professing our holy, catholic, apostolic, and Roman religion will have the right to assist at the divine office in the said chapel."[41] St. Augustine's Church, though not a canonical parish church until 1856, was the third church for either whites or blacks constructed in that region.[42] Augustin Metoyer died in 1856 and was buried in a large mausoleum in the cemetery behind the church.

The community at Isle Brevelle on the Cane River survived the Civil War, but it lost its prosperity. Always strong in Catholicity and French culture, it would continue to be so through the twentieth century, preserving much of its ethnic flavor in family celebrations, traditional cuisine, and a unique cluster of buildings now classified as a historical landmark. One might wonder at the mention of this community in a history of black Catholics, inasmuch as in the nineteenth century the Metoyer family and the others would have bridled at such a designation. The fact is that the history of black Americans is a many-textured phenomenon, embracing highly diverse social and cultural segments.

There were other communities of free people of color in southern Louisiana. They too were light-skinned, French, Roman Catholic, and often slaveholding. This phenomenon, perhaps with the exception of the owning of slaves, also existed in Alabama, Maryland, and possibly South Carolina; not all were French in these other places, but they were Roman Catholic. What is more fundamental, however, is the reality of racial ambivalence among many different segments of African American society, and the search for either isolation from or total acceptance by the majority population. The acceptance never really came, and the isolation never really lasted; but what did come was a multilayered African American experience that made "blackness" have a slightly different meaning for each respective group.[43]

III

Mobile had been one of the earliest settlements in what was to become the French colony of Louisiana. A parish had been established as early as 1703. The city was a harbor and a small trading center captured by Spain in 1763. In 1790, when Bishop Cirilo de Barcelona made his visitation, the black Catholics of Mobile numbered 419, and the number of white Catholics 165.[44] The present-day archdiocese also possesses its parish registers, which go back to 1781;[45] until the last quarter of the nineteenth century, they were maintained by race. The registers in Spanish are not as florid or detailed as those of St. Augustine, but they do give some notions of family names, conditions, and relationships.

On Sunday, February 23, 1812, Don Vicente Gerien, the pastor of the parish church of Our Lady's Most Pure Conception of Mobile, baptized an adult black man of the Congo, fourteen years old, his own property, to whom he gave the name Fernando. His godfather was Antonio Frovillet, a mulatto, slave of Don Miguel de Eslavo. Thus, Fernando was the fourteen-year-old slave of the parish priest, and his godfather was the slave of a leading citizen of the small settlement that would come under American control that very year. Father Gerien had become pastor under the authority of the king of Spain in 1808 and would remain until 1823.[46]

On Sunday, March 1, 1812, the same Don Vicente Gerien baptized a male child born on February 8, the son of María, a mulatto slave of Doña Isavel (Isabel) Chastang, widow of Don Rafael Idalgo. The boy was given the name Federico, and the sponsors were Don Miguel Yrigoyen and Hipolita Colen, free mulatto woman.[47] The name Chastang is very important in the history of black Catholics in Mobile. At the end of the eighteenth century, three brothers from France named Chastang settled in southern Alabama. Two of the brothers married white women, but a third, Dr. John Chastang, reportedly married a slave. The mulatto descendants of Dr. Chastang formed a tightly knit community of light-skinned blacks, French in language and Catholic in religion. The name of Chastang is to be found frequently in all of the sacramental books of Mobile.[48] In this instance Doña Isabel Chastang was more than likely from the white branch of the Chastang family. Eighteen years later, on July 14, 1830, another Isabel Chastang was married to Joseph Laurent by the first bishop of Mobile, Michael Portier.[49] Although the entry does not state it, it is reasonable to presume that both Isabel Chastang and Joseph Laurent were free blacks, since otherwise in the marriage register the priest who witnessed the marriage would have indicated that they were slaves and that permission had been granted by the master.

The Chastang family gave its name to the locality north of Mobile where Dr. John Chastang settled and raised his family. To the south of Mobile at the entrance to the bay is Mon Luis Island, where at the beginning of the nineteenth century a young mulatto slave, Maximilien Colin, received land from the Baudin family and became the head of a black Catholic family-based community like Isle Brevelle in Louisiana. Unfortunately, the same kind of historical studies have not yet been completed on the Mon Luis settlement.[50] The name Colin and related forms (Colen, Collins, Colins, and so forth) appear in numerous forms in this community.

It seems very likely that the Baudin family was a free mulatto family that owned slaves. There apparently was a marriage between the families on May 14, 1834. On that day, the vicar-general of Mobile, Matthias Loras, future bishop of Dubuque, witnessed the marriage between Celestin Baudin and Louise Colins, "both coloured persons of this place."[51] On the preceding page of the marriage register that recorded the marriage between the Baudin and Colin families is recorded also the marriage of a slave, Mary, "negro woman, slave to the Bishop Portier," to Richard James (Dick), "negro slave to M. Jhro Shelton," on February 13, 1834, before Matthias Loras, the vicar-general.[52] Two years later, on February 16, 1836, two other slaves of Bishop Portier were married before Matthias Loras. "I have joined in the holy banns of matrimony Charles with Lolotte, both slaves of R.d. Bishop of this place. Were witnesses to it R. M. James McGarahan and Francisque Quigley. The permission of the Master had been previously granted."[53]

There is very little indication that great numbers of blacks migrated from outside the settlement of Mobile into the community, but at least some did. On June 30, 1833, Etienne Lalande of Mobile married Maria Walkins of Nashville. The witnesses were Jhon [*sic*] Colins and Lucienne Durette.[54] The Durette family name was a very common name in the area of Mon Luis Island. There is also the announcement of the death of Françoise Provorène, "free black woman, native of the island of St. Domingo [Haiti], aged about 120 years." She died on August 15, 1829.[55] Françoise Provorène may have come to Mobile in the wake of the revolutions on the island of Haiti after 1796.

The people of color in the area of Mon Luis Island also owned slaves, as is indicated in the burial register for André, who was an infant of fifteen months when he died, the natural son of Marie Louise, "black woman, slave of Mr. Faustin, free colored man," May 17, 1835.[56] Faustin's full name was Faustin Colins. On July 18 that same year was buried Mary, nine months old, "the legitimate daughter of M (crossed out) Faustin Colins";[57] and four weeks later, Mathilde Collins, two years old, "legitimate daughter of M. Faustin Collins, a free colored man of Mobile."[58] The next year, September 18, 1836, two-year-old Nanette died, slave of Faustin Collins.[59] A last example is that of Nancy, who died at the age of two on June 15, 1829, "the negro girl slave to Nanette Duret [*sic*] freewoman of color."[60]

The sacramental books for black Catholics in the diocese of Mobile for the period before the Civil War reveal that many of the blacks, both free and slave, were baptized. On the eve of the Civil War in the last decade of Bishop Portier's administration, it is estimated that about a thousand or so blacks were Catholic. In a letter written to the secretary of the Society of the Propagation of the Faith at Lyons in 1860, Père Jourdan, S.J., of Spring Hill College, comments:

> The black population of this vast state merits to be taken into consideration. The vast majority is stationed very far from the cities, on vast farms or plantations where they engage in agricultural labor, especially in the cotton fields. All of these unfortunates in the actual state of things never see a priest and are bowed down in the most abject ignorance of God and their salvation. It is only by means of the presence of Missions organized for the interior of the country that it is possible to come to their aid. They have Sunday to themselves but it would be necessary that the priest go to them or draw them to himself. As a result they must not have to go too far.[61]

Probably the slaves were not as ignorant of God and the need for salvation as Père Jourdan thought. Still, for Catholics access to the sacraments was essential, and this was lacking. As one looks at the sacramental books, it is evident that although many black Catholics were married, certainly only a small proportion had their marriages blessed by the church, and perhaps only a slightly larger proportion received Christian burial from the church. In fact, one has the impression from the burial register that very few received the last rites.[62]

The early history of the black Catholic settlements at Mon Luis Island and Chastang must still be written. Investigation must still be made of their unique cultural and social development in the period prior to the Civil War.

IV

At the end of the eighteenth century in Savannah, there was a small settlement of Catholics with their slaves. The sacramental register of the Church of St. John the Baptist includes records of the baptisms, marriages, and burials of both white and black Catholics from 1796 to 1816. The first entries are in French, and the rest in English. The third entry records the conditional baptism of Edward on November 13, 1796, the legitimate son of Samuel and Monnica, "both negroe slaves belonging to Joseph Thompson, born on the nineteenth of July," 1795; the godfather was Lewis, and his godmother Anne, "both negroe slaves belonging to ignatius semmes." The priest was a Father LeMercier, canon regular of St. Augustine of the French congregation. Also in 1796 was baptized Frederick, the son of Barbara, a slave belonging to Ignatius Semmes. His godfather was Aaron, also a slave of Semmes, and his godmother was Anne O'Brien, who was white.

Between the years 1796 and 1808 there are 107 entries. Forty-two are baptisms of black infants, both slave and free. Two announce the marriage of free blacks, and one that of a slave couple. There are two notices of the deaths of slaves — one a child, the other a slave named Edward, "a negroe slave of joseph thompson deceased on the twenty third of September or thereabouts, of the year one thousand seven hundred and ninety four in the twenty eighth year of his age, by us priest hereafter subscribed..." (signed) Le Mercier, priest.[63] In this dozen years almost half of the sacramental ministry of Père LeMercier was devoted to blacks. There were many free blacks in the Savannah area; many of them had French names and had probably escaped from Haiti. Many whites were of French origin, and the text reveals that they had left Haiti, more than likely with their slaves.

With the French population there appears in this sacramental register something not seen before, namely, the registering of the infant's baptism as the registration of the infant's manumission. In these dozen years there were five manumissions of newborn infants by French slaveholders. An example of this act is the following for Monday, May 21, 1798, in Savannah: "was baptized... peter natural son of Cicé a negroe slave belonging to Mary Destrée widow prevôt, born in September 1797 et [*sic*] to whom the said widow prevôt has by an act here joined given his liberty for Life. his godfather peter Michael joseph mivault his godmother Nichole Laffit a free negroe."[64] On the next page the act was drawn up in French.

> I the undersigned give for the present freedom to the said Pierre, Negro, aged about eight months, the natural son of the said Cicé, my slave, for him to enjoy during his lifetime, in appreciation of the good services of his mother. And I consent that he be baptized as free to the effect of declaring the liberty and that the present act be deposed in the register of baptisms. Done at Savannah this twenty-first day of May, one thousand seven hundred ninety-eight. (signed) Veuve Prévot.[65]

In this same register there is the unusual mention of a black person's acting as godmother to a white infant. Adele, a mulatto girl, acted as sponsor with Edouard Coppée for Edouard, the son of Claudine Gerau, February 10, 1808.[66]

Prior to the Civil War there was not a large Catholic settlement in Savannah and the outlying areas of Georgia. A large proportion of this small Catholic settlement was black, many of whom were free. In a sense it might be said that the Catholic population of the colonial South and the antebellum South, no matter how small the population, was not pure white. From the records it seems clear that Catholicism was more Africanized than many would believe.

This was certainly the case in the early days of St. Louis in the territory that would become Missouri. The first resident priest arrived in the settlement in 1772. The trading post set up under the leadership of Pierre Laclède on the banks of the Mississippi had already been in existence some eight years. From 1772 to 1775 the Spanish pastor, Father Valentine, baptized 24 blacks, 19 Native Americans, and 64 whites. During the thirteen years of the pastorate of Father Bernard de Limpach under the authority of the Spanish crown, 410 whites, 106 blacks, and 92 Native Americans were baptized. It is significant that during that same time, 60 blacks and 44 Native Americans were buried, along with 222 whites. And perhaps it is not surprising that while there were 115 marriages of whites blessed, there were only 4 involving other races: one black, two Native American, and one mixed marriage of Indian and white.[67] In the last quarter of the eighteenth century, the population of St. Louis, mostly Catholic in religion and French in language and culture, was 30 percent black.[68]

In the area on the eastern shore of the Mississippi in Illinois, the French made settlements at the Indian villages of Cahokia and Kaskaskia during the first quarter of the eighteenth century. Ste. Genevieve on the west bank of the Mississippi was founded about the year 1750 by settlers from the French towns in Illinois.[69] Black slaves made their appearance on the upper Mississippi in 1717. Probably they first were imported by the Jesuit missionaries from the territory of southern Louisiana.[70] The slave community at Perryville, Missouri, attached to the Vincentian seminary of St. Mary's, which was treated in chapter 2 above, began a century later. Carl Ekberg, in his study of Ste. Genevieve entitled "Black Slavery French Style," estimated that blacks composed about 30 percent of the population in the colonial period.[71] He suggests that this is the percentage in general for all the French Illinois region.[72] Certainly, there was a substantial black Catholic community in this region of the western frontier. Ekberg's research led him to conclude that although the slaves were regularly baptized, in general they were not married by the church. There is no indication, he observes, of a spiritual ministry to the slaves in this Catholic region.[73]

The Sisters of St. Joseph opened a school for free black girls in 1845 in Carondelet, near St. Louis, but they were soon forced to close it.[74] About a decade later the Sisters of Mercy opened a school for black children.[75] By 1860 St. Louis had a larger proportion of free blacks than slaves. Many of these were Catholic.[76] A look at this St. Louis black community on the eve of the Civil War is given in a very interesting and highly personal way by Cyprian Clamorgan, himself a black Catholic, entitled *The Colored Aristocracy of St. Louis*.[77]

Although he did not live in the black Catholic community on the Mississippi, Jean-Baptiste Pointe du Sable was buried there in 1818. Du Sable is doubly celebrated by black Catholics in the United States: first as a black man who was an authentic coureur de bois, trapper, trader, and trusted friend of the Indians, and then as a Roman Catholic who was the first settler in the place that would become the city of Chicago. His origins are unknown. It is speculation that he arrived in the Illinois country from Canada or from lower Louisiana and, before that, from Haiti. In the last quarter of the eighteenth century, du Sable was a trapper and trader in the central Illinois area around Peoria, where he owned land. The British imprisoned him briefly in 1779 because of their distrust of him and of his influence with the Native Americans.

Jean-Baptiste had a commodious residence in Chicago. He was married to a Potowatomi woman named Catherine and was an official in the tribe. The exact number of his children is not known, but he evidently had several. His marriage was blessed by the parish priest of Cahokia in 1788. His son Jean-Baptiste settled in St. Charles just north of St. Louis. In 1800 du Sable sold his property in Chicago and moved to St. Louis with his son. After the death of his son in 1814, he had to sue for poor relief because his granddaughter did not assist him as she had agreed. Eventually he died in 1818 and lies buried today in the Catholic cemetery at St. Charles.[78]

The military post of Fort Vincennes, now in Indiana on the Wabash River, became one of the easternmost French settlements. It was established around the middle of the eighteenth century. The early sacramental registers recorded the baptisms and marriages of the French inhabitants, many of whom were from Canada. The registers also included Native American inhabitants in the area. Vincennes also had slaves, some of whom were Indians and others were black. The number of the slaves is not known, but it seems safe to say that it was small.

On January 26, 1773, Father Pierre Gibault, a friend of George Rogers Clark, baptized "two adults, negro slaves, that is to say, Fran-

çois about 40 years old, belonging to Sieur Ste-Marie, whose sponsors
were François Barrois and Jeannette Racine de Ste-Marie daughter of
Jean Baptiste Racine de Ste-Marie. Alexis belonging to Nicolas Cardinal, whose sponsors were Jean-Baptiste St-Dizier and Julie Tartre,
who declared they could not sign (signed) P. Gibault, M.P."[79] Pierre
Gibault also owned slaves. On December 29, 1751, there died the
nine-month-old daughter of "Alexandre and Dorothée, negros [sic]."
The next year there died the six-month-old son of the same Alexandre and Dorothée, "negroes belonging to R. P. G. who,... was born
and baptized privately the 17th of the same month at birth." R. P. G.
is certainly Révérend Père Gibault. A decade earlier the same register recalls the baptism of Pierre Joseph on June 27, 1763, the son
of Joseph and Helene slaves (black) of the Jesuit Fathers; signed by
Jules Devernai, Jesuit.[80]

In the first part of the nineteenth century, the mention of blacks
and Indians, either as slaves or free, becomes less frequent. Still in
1823 there is the mention of the baptism on December 31 of Joseph
Poirier, born December 1, the son of Toussaint Poirier and Silvey Mc-
Cake, "both of color."[81] On November 5, 1832, Eleonore Taylor was
baptized at the age of nine years and four months, "a little negress,
daughter of Johnston Taylor and Dredai Hearter."[82] Finally, on December 29, 1837, was baptized Edward Sims, son of William and
Sarah Sims, "Free Negroes."[83]

V

Of all the thirteen original colonies, Maryland was the home of the
largest community of black Catholics in colonial times and during
the antebellum period. As pointed out in chapter 2, John Carroll informed Cardinal Antonelli in 1785 that there were three thousand
Catholics of African origin in the state. Most of these were ministered to by the former Jesuits. Baltimore received what was to be
the nucleus of the black Catholic community in that city with the
arrival of people of color on July 10, 1793. The Annapolis newspaper
announced the event the following day. "Yesterday at three o'clock,
arrived at Fells' Point, six ships (one a Guineaman, with negroes) four
brigs, and four schooners, being part of the fleet which sailed from
Cape François on the 23d ultimo. The passengers and crews amount
to 619 persons."[84] These were refugees, both whites and blacks, from
the revolution then taking place on the island of Santo Domingo,
in what is present-day Haiti. The French-speaking blacks some time

later found a spiritual home in the basement chapel of the Sulpician seminary on Paca Street.

The baptismal registers of St. Peter's Procathedral and of the Cathedral of the Assumption, although not segregated by race, indicated those who were black and those who were slaves. Many of the entries indicated the large presence of French-speaking blacks in the city at the end of the colonial period in Baltimore. On March 24, 1797, the ceremonies of baptism were supplied by Father Beeston, rector of St. Peter's, to an eighteen-year-old "girl of colour," Jeanne Antoinette Sanite, "born in the parish of St. Peter de l' Archagein [?] St. Domingo"; the sponsors (presumably white) were Judocus Schutte and Catherine Mary LeMonnier.[85] The following month on April 2 was baptized John Gabriel, infant of six weeks, the natural son of Marinette, "french negro, slave of Mrs. Asselin Dessables. Sponsors, Ambrose, free negro, and Mary Louise negro slave of Mrs Creuzé," signed by Father Beeston as rector.[86] On August 1, 1802, Peter, the natural son of Nicole Simonet, "free French negro," was baptized, with Joseph LeClerc and Genevieve Ollive as sponsors; and on the same day, John Baptist, natural son of Zerphine, "negro slave of Madame Landais," the sponsors being Domingue and Marie Noel.[87]

At the same time there were other blacks, both slave and free, with English names. The records mention a Betty, described as "negro slave of Rt. Rev. J. Carroll," who acted as a sponsor for a white infant, Sarah Ramsey, on April 4, 1797.[88] In the same year on November 29, Elizabeth, "negro slave of Bishop Carroll," was sponsor for a black infant, Sophia, "natural daughter of Ruth, negro slave of Mr. Keener."[89]

The Butler family was a very important black Catholic family in Maryland. In the year 1797 the family name appeared several times. On April 13 David Butler, a month-old infant son of Nancy Butler, free mulatto, was baptized. The godmother was Priscilla Berry, a slave of James McSherry.[90] In May, Jane, the natural daughter of Clare Butler, free mulatto, was baptized; Henry, a slave of Robert Walsh, and Joanna Butler, a free mulatto, acted as sponsors.[91] On August 15 there was baptized William, lawful son of Henry, a Negro slave of Robert Walsh, and Joanna Butler, free mulatto. Alice Butler was the sponsor. One is left to wonder at the relationship between Robert Walsh and Joanna Butler. The baptismal registers also inform us that the rector of St. Peter's Procathedral, Father Francis Beeston, was a slaveowner. On April 18, 1802, Eliza, a month-old infant, the natural daughter of Deborah, the slave of Captain Ronald Whelan, was baptized by Father Beeston, the sponsors being "William, slave of Francis Beeston, and Milly Smally."[92] The same year Catherine, "slave of Rev. Francis

Beeston," and Ignatius, "slave of Mr Ghequiere," had their daughter Catherine baptized on July 25 by Father Beeston. George and Catherine were the sponsors.[93]

One of the most precious documents for the history of black Catholics in this country is a small notebook, $8'' \times 6\frac{1}{2}''$, found in the Sulpician Archives in Baltimore. There are sixty-seven pages in this handwritten document. The first page begins: "Journal of the Commencement and of the proceedings of the Society of Colored people; with the approbation of the Most Rev. Archp. Samuel [Eccleston] and of the Rector of the Cathedral Revd. H. B. Coskery."[94] This is the oldest extant written document of a black Catholic society in the United States. It is an account of the weekly meeting of some 150 to 200 black Catholics that was held in the basement of Calvert Hall, the parish hall attached to the cathedral, beginning on the first Sunday of Advent, December 3, 1843, and lasting until September 7, 1845. The journal was kept by Father John F. Hickey, assistant at the cathedral and director of the meeting. It appears that he was the writer of the journal.

The meetings usually lasted an hour and a half to two hours. They met on Sunday evenings at 7:00. The members of the society were all black, but we do not know if any were slaves. A list of the members' names is given twice. They numbered about 270 members. The second list is in alphabetical order and seems the more complete.[95] It is important to remember the historical context. This society was a unique opportunity for black Catholics to exercise some decision making and self-government. It is in the light of this reality that we appreciate reading that the members voted on a name for themselves and for officers in the society. At the second meeting the majority of the members chose the name of the Holy Family as its title. The other choice was the St. Benedict's Society, after St. Benedict the Moor, who had been canonized in 1807. At the third meeting the election of officers took place. John Noel, a member of a prominent Haitian family, was elected president, and Miss Mary Holland was elected first counselor. Later Mr. Washington Ford was elected first vice-president, and William London, the second counselor. The meetings consisted of prayer in common, an instruction delivered by Father Hickey, and hymns. The officers formed a council that met separately and decided on policy. Members were admitted upon the vote of members of the council.

Among the activities, singing was very important. Normally the members were to sing four hymns, but at times they prolonged the meeting by singing more. In fact, the hymns were so important that there was a practice session during the week. At a later time they had the service of a violinist who accompanied the hymns. At times there were solo renditions, or a special group sang. Among the prayers said was the recitation of five decades of the rosary. The instruction was often inspirational and at other times doctrinal. One woman, Jane Thomson, opened up her heart in spontaneous prayer. Father Hickey remarked, "Jane Thomson came out with Gospel of St. John by heart." On another occasion, "Jane came out with something about the rock of Peter."[96]

Each member had to pay dues of 6 1/4 cents per month. In addition, money was collected for the cathedral fund. From the dues collected the members agreed to pay rent for the use of the hall, to buy more chairs and benches, to pay for lamps, and to have two Masses said for each member who died. Harriet Queen died in March 1844, and Lucy Butler a little later. Collections were also made for charitable purposes. The members decided on which needy persons to help.

The society decided to have a lending library. Each person could borrow a book for one cent per month and one cent for each week after that. Later the charge was two cents for more expensive books. Such books as catechisms, devotional literature, lives of the saints, and Catholic hymns were in the collection. The members also purchased a bookcase. They hired a German professor, apparently to teach part singing, and at times they had Protestant visitors.

Father Hickey noted for September 7, 1845: "Today there was no meeting of the Holy Family in the basement of Calvert Hall; as the room, in which the meeting was always held, was filled with Wm Galvin's lumber and as the Brothers had taken possession of the Hall. — It appears that the society can no longer occupy the basement of Calvert Hall, as the Brothers of the Christian Doctrine have taken possession of it."[97] The council met with Father Hickey and decided that they "would not ask for or accept of the Cathedral as a place of meeting of the Holy Family." It would appear that the members, understandably, felt some resentment at the way they were treated. At the end of October 1845, it was decided to dissolve the society. The pastor of St. Peter's allowed them to set up their library in the basement of the church "for the use of Coloured people." The monies were to be distributed "for the relief of the poor coloured people... and in particular [those] who were members of the society." At the end of the journal there was a financial account of monies collected and disbursed and the purpose of each expenditure.

Despite the brevity of the society's existence, this document is of capital importance because it is the first glimpse of how black Catholics in the antebellum period organized themselves and of what their piety was like. We have no records of black Catholic parochial life, but in this document we get some notion of black Catholic spirituality in a parish setting. The devotions were traditional, such as the rosary, the offering of Masses for the deceased, and the singing of hymns. In regard to the hymns, more investigation might be made. Some of them may have been of black origin. What is noteworthy is the high value placed on singing. The members enjoyed the singing and sought constantly to improve it. A catalogue of the subjects chosen for instruction might give some insight into the formation given to black Catholics by a priest who was devoted to them. The presence of spontaneous prayer, which may have caused concern to Father Hickey, was a unique characteristic of a black religious meeting. The concern for the poor by people who were not themselves particularly wealthy is also noteworthy. In fact, there is evident a desire for financial independence, for paying their own way. Also noteworthy is the desire for literature; to have a lending library is extraordinary, given the little formal education available to blacks. It is not surprising that they raised money for a black girls' school — probably the school opened by the Oblate Sisters of Providence, who will be treated at length in chapter 4. Finally, this society indicates a level of fervor that existed among some members of the black Catholic community of Baltimore who were willing to deepen their spiritual life. The question remains as to how many other organizations of this type existed among black Catholics.

The value for historians is that this journal gives us names not only of individuals but of families who made up the black Catholic community. These names can provide a basis for future research. (See table 3.)

Another source for names is a copy of the ledger for Easter confessions for the cathedral parish in Baltimore, 1819–21.[98] The names are listed by race. The following names are those of blacks, members of the Society of the Holy Family:

> Edward Queen (1819 Easter confession register, p. 1)
> Rosetta Livers (1819, p. 5)
> Harriet Berry (1819, p. 5)
> Mary Johnson (1819, p. 5)
> Harriet Berry (1821, p. 22)
> Mary Johnson (1821, p. 22)
> Mary Holland (1821, p. 22)
> Rosetta Livers (1821, p. 22).

Table 3
Some Black Catholic Families in Baltimore

NAME	BAPTISMAL REGISTER
Sidney Queen	Sponsor for Mary Ann Brown, June 20, 1822
Fanny Queen	Mother of Mary Magdalene Queen, July 2, 1822
Edward Queen	Edward Thomas, Son of Edward and Sydney, March 18, 1823
Sophia Queen	Nanny, child of Sophia Queen, June 13, 1823
Lucy Butler	Sponsor for William Johnson, February 8, 1824
Mary Berry	Sponsor for George Vaughn, July 8, 1823
Lucy Butler	Sponsor for Louisa Ann Dorsey, April 19, 1824
Fanny Queen	Mother of Sarah Ann Queen, July 24, 1824
Edward Queen	Father of Mary Elizabeth Queen, September 12, 1824

Source: Baptismal registers of St. Peter's Church, Archdiocese of Baltimore.

Except for Sidney Queen, all persons listed were members of the Holy Family society.

In the period before the Civil War, western Kentucky became a center for black Catholics, primarily slaves in the families of Maryland Catholics who migrated to Nelson County and adjacent areas at the end of the eighteenth century. Many of the black Catholic families bear the same names as the original white families from Maryland. The first bishop of Bardstown, Benedict Joseph Flaget (1763–1850), owned slaves, and there were slaves in the seminary of St. Thomas founded by Flaget. The attitude of Flaget was one of kind paternalism toward the slaves in his diocese and in his household. There are indications that he had little faith in the capacity of blacks to profit from being free.[99]

We do not have much information regarding the religious life of black Catholics prior to the Civil War. There is, however, a very interesting portrait of an elderly slave whose piety was long remembered. In his history of Catholicism in Kentucky, Benedict Webb wrote about an "Uncle Harry," the slave of Father Stephen Badin (1768–1853), the pioneer Catholic missionary in Kentucky.[100] It is recorded of Uncle Harry that he spent most of his nights in prayer. "In the church, he always knelt as immovable as a statue, and was often there for hours before the rest of the congregation. His whole life appeared to be one continual prayer; and he died as he had lived, praying."[101]

VI

One of the first places of worship for the use of black Catholics in a northern city was opened in 1844 in Pittsburgh under the care of Father Robert Wilson, a priest of that diocese. It was known as the Chapel of the Nativity. The black population of Pittsburgh was about three thousand at the time, of whom only about twenty were Catholics. Michael O'Connor, the first bishop of Pittsburgh, who later resigned and became a Jesuit, was interested in the evangelization of blacks and encouraged Father Wilson's ministry.[102]

Washington, D.C., was unique as a black population center at the beginning of the nineteenth century, first because of its large black population and then because of its ever-increasing free black population. In 1800, out of a total population of 14,000, there were 4,000 blacks. Of these, some 780 were free and the rest slaves. In 1850 the total population of 51,000 included 10,000 free blacks and some 3,000 slaves.[103]

Washington, D.C., had many black Catholics because of its proximity to the southern Maryland area — St. Mary's, Charles, and Calvert counties — where there had always been a large black Catholic presence. In the District of Columbia, black Catholics appear to have flourished more than in other southern Catholic areas. Thus, they were not segregated in church during the antebellum period. In Georgetown, blacks attended Holy Trinity Church, which was located very close to Georgetown College. During the first part of the nineteenth century, the parish operated a free school for both white and black children from poor families. At other periods black children attended Sunday school, where reading and writing were taught as well as catechism.[104] Black Catholics also freely attended St. Patrick's, St. Matthew's, and St. Aloysius churches, the latter built shortly before the Civil War. Schools were operated for blacks by the last two parishes in the period before the Civil War.[105]

A well-known black Catholic in early nineteenth-century Washington was Maria Becraft (1805–33), whose father had been a slave in the household of Charles Carroll of Carrollton. Maria Becraft was educated as a young girl in Washington at several of the small privately run schools for free blacks that existed in the city at the time. When she was fifteen, she opened a school of her own in Georgetown, and at the age of twenty-two was invited by the pastor of Holy Trinity Church to open a girls' school in the parish, for both boarders and day students. She was aided in her work by the Visitation nuns who operated a school for white girls in

Georgetown. In 1831 Maria Becraft entered the convent of the Oblate Sisters of Providence in Baltimore, where she died shortly thereafter.[106]

On July 2, 1853, a funeral was held in New York City of a black man who even in his lifetime had begun to be talked of as a saint — Pierre Toussaint. The funeral was held in old St. Peter's Church on Barclay Street. The mourners were both black and white, members of the upper class, religious, and poor blacks. Toussaint was born a slave in 1766 at L'Artibonite near the town of St-Marc on the west coast of the French colony of Santo Domingo. Slavery on the island was particularly harsh and oppressive. Large numbers of slaves had fled into the interior and had become Maroons. Pierre Toussaint had been born on the Bérard estate and presumably enjoyed a privileged position in the household, learning how to read and write and growing up in the practice of the Catholic religion. When it became evident that social unrest was spreading throughout the French colony, the owner of the plantation, Jean Bérard, decided to leave temporarily the island and its troubles and to establish residence in New York City. He and his wife arrived in New York in 1787 along with two sisters of Madame Bérard and several slaves, Pierre, his two sisters, and an elderly aunt. At the behest of Jean Bérard, Pierre, then about twenty-one years old, was apprenticed to a hairdresser in the city. This was the age of elaborate hairstyles for aristocratic women, and the wealthy had the hairdresser come to their residences, often on a daily basis. The result was a trade that enabled Pierre to have a steady and a lucrative position in the society of the time. It also provided him with access to the wealthy and the influential.

Jean Bérard returned to Haiti in 1789 to oversee his properties. He was there at the outbreak of revolution in Haiti, which had been sparked by the revolution in France but was fueled by the utterly inhuman exploitation of the slaves on the island. Jean Bérard lost his property during the uprising, contracted pleurisy, and died. Moreover, the investments that were made by Jean Bérard for the future support of his wife were lost through his financial mismanagement and failure. As a result, Pierre, his slave, became the support for Madame Bérard and the other female slaves in her home in New York. As a hairdresser Pierre was assured of a modest and stable income. One has the impression that Madame Bérard suffered from emotional as well as physical disability and that Pierre was concerned that she be provided for and never suffer anxiety from having too detailed a knowledge of her precarious financial position. Just before her death in 1807, Madame Bérard-Nicolas, who had only recently married another French refugee from Haiti, gave Pierre Toussaint his freedom in a legal document drawn up before the French consul.[107] She died soon thereafter.

Pierre Toussaint did not live in poverty. His income was sufficient that he could give away much of his money to charity. He purchased the freedom of his sister Rosalie, who married another Haitian refugee, Jean Noel. He also purchased the freedom of the woman he married, Juliette, a relative of Jean Noel. It is at this time that he began the remarkable charitable activity that would characterize his whole life. Toussaint was generous with his funds as well as with his time and his friendship. Over eleven hundred documents make up his personal papers preserved in the New York Public Library. We also have a biography, *Memoir of Pierre Toussaint, Born a Slave in St. Domingo*, by Hannah Sawyer Lee, who as a member of the Schuyler family of New York knew Toussaint very well.[108] Most of the papers in the manuscript collection are letters to Toussaint, many of them testimonies from people to whom he had shown friendship or given aid. Many of the correspondents were French refugees from Haiti, such as the members of the Bérard family who had found their way to France; others were expatriates in the United States like Gabriel Nicolas, the second husband of Madame Bérard, who had continued to live with Toussaint and his wife for a while, to whom Toussaint had lent money.[109] Other correspondents were blacks, Haitians, or Americans. There are very few letters or writings of Toussaint himself.

Toussaint not only lent money to various people, he contributed out of his own pocket to many causes such as the orphanage of the Sisters of Charity for whites only, contributions to the Catholic school for black children opened at St. Vincent de Paul Church, and contributions to individuals, including penniless priests. He nursed the victims of various epidemics that periodically swept through early New York.

One lady mentions that when the yellow fever prevailed in New York, by degrees Maiden Lane was almost wholly deserted, and almost every house in it closed. One poor woman, prostrated by the terrible disorder, remained there with little or no attendance, till Toussaint day by day came through the lone street, crossed the barricades, entered the deserted house where she lay, and performed the nameless offices of a nurse, fearlessly exposing himself to the contagion.[110]

When he discovered a poor sick priest, ill of "ship fever," or typhus, Toussaint brought him food and resources, moved him to his own home, where he and his wife nursed the priest. In pre–Civil War New York, there were many homeless black youths on the street. Toussaint would bring them to his home, give them lodging, teach them a trade or send them to school, and even teach them the violin — "if they did not derive profit from it, it would at least be an innocent amusement."[111] When his sister died from tuberculosis, he raised her daughter, Euphémie. He hired a French teacher for his niece and later an English teacher. In his papers is a folder containing the weekly letters Euphémie wrote him as exercises in French composition. Euphémie died tragically of tuberculosis at the age of fourteen in 1829.

Toussaint attended Mass every morning at 6:00 at St. Peter's Church. Then he would begin his visits to his clients. People enjoyed talking to him, and he became the confidant of many. He always walked because blacks were not then allowed to ride the horse-drawn buses. Slavery was finally ended in New York State in 1827, twenty years after his own manumission.

In regard to the evident holiness of this man, two rather special characteristics can be pointed out. Toussaint was a very joyful person who liked to mimic others while enjoying their company.

> His heart was not only kind and affectionate, but gay and cheerful; it was filled with trust and confidence, and gave him the happy power of dispelling gloom and anxiety in others.
> ... He was tall and well made, and with the flexibility of limb which belongs to his race. He was truly an African ...
> Toussaint had a quick sense of the ridiculous, and like most of his race, when he was young, was an excellent mimic; as he grew older he relinquished this power ... He played on the violin for small dancing parties at one time.[112]

Toussaint was about twenty-two years older than his wife. He married her when he was thirty-eight, and she was fifteen.[113] He was very much in love, and he demonstrated openly his affection for his wife. When she went to Baltimore to visit her relatives (she was apparently related to Jean Noel, who later was elected president of the Society of the Holy Family), Pierre wrote her a loving letter, assuring her that he loved her for herself alone.[114] In his papers, we find a poem in French written in his own hand, a testimony to the endurance of this love.[115]

Toussaint was friends with George Paddington, a black man from

Dublin, Ireland, who was ordained to the priesthood by Bishop John England in Port-au-Prince, Haiti, on May 21, 1836. At this time England was serving as a representative of the Holy See in Haiti. This ordination may have made John England the first American bishop to ordain a black man.[116] Paddington is an elusive figure in black Catholic history. He is important for the history of the church in Haiti and significant as a black in nineteenth-century Dublin. There are some seven letters from Paddington to Toussaint. Paddington stayed with Pierre and his wife on his first trip to Haiti. He did not like America because it was "a cursed land of slavery."[117] Juliette, Pierre's wife, died in 1851. Pierre himself died two years later on June 30, 1853. In recent years the cause of Toussaint's beatification has been introduced in Rome. If he is ever canonized, he will probably be the first American black saint.

Few would gainsay the genuine holiness of this remarkably magnanimous and charitable man. Few would deny the attraction this layman's example has for us today, as Pierre combined sanctity with joy, holiness with humor, and married love with a constant yet extraordinary life with God for over half a century. But can this man, who gave to all the example of meekness and mildness, be an example for blacks today? It is ironic that in his time, whites gave him their highest accolade by calling him "a Catholic Uncle Tom."[118] The question of Toussaint's "black consciousness" is best answered by a close examination of the letters written to him by blacks, both American and Haitian. His militancy was in the strength of character that enabled him not only to survive the racial prejudice of his day, of which there are several examples in his life, but to do so with grace and magnanimity. He was not overcome by the racism of his time. He refused to be constrained by the limitations imposed by others. He remained throughout his life his own man because in his fidelity he was God's.

The same year that Pierre Toussaint died, a black woman of New York, Harriet Thompson, wrote a letter to Pope Pius IX. She began:

Most Holy Father Visible Head of the Church of Jesus Christ,
　　I humbly write these lines to beseech your Holiness in the name of the same Saviour if you will provide for the salvation of the black race in the United States who is going astray from neglect on the part of those who have the care of souls. Now I would not dare to say anything disrespectful against the ministers of God but the reason of this neglect is, as it is well known to your Holiness, that most of the Bishops and priests in this

country is either Irish or descended from Irish and not being accustomed to the black race in Ireland they can't think enough of them to take charge of our souls. Hence it is a great mistake to say that the church watched with equal care over every race and color, for how can it be said they teach all nations when they will not let the black race mix with the white. We know that this teaching does not mean high learning but means a teaching of Holy Doctrine. But in this country the teaching of the word of God and learning is so closely connected together that he who receives the one receives the other. The Catholics teach the pure word of God and gave learning at the same time. The Protestants gave learning and teach the word of God adulterated. Now the Protestant rule in the city and county of New York is that all poor children in every district no matter what color they are must attend the state schools. A very good rule too, but the evil overshadows the good. Those are the evils: as soon as the teachers find any children in these schools to be Catholics they teach them directly to protest against the church of God. They tell them that the Blessed Eucharist is nothing but a wafer, that the priest drinks the wine himself and gives the bread to us, and that the Divine institution of confession is only to make money and that the Roman pontiff is Anti-Christ. This is what Catholic children are taught in Protestant Schools, but the church [can] remedy these evils for the white children by providing schools where they can learn the pure word of God and how to keep it. But the church do[es] leave the colored children a prey to the wolf. Now the Protestants well know that the Catholics do not like the black race with them neither in the churches nor schools. Hence they take the advantage of the opportunity.

Yes, Holy Father, this is precisely the conditions of the colored Catholics in most of the United States, but particularly in New York. If your Holiness's Nuncio were to condescend while he is here to inquire about the colored people he would find many families with the parents Catholics and the children Protestants, overwhelmed with the belief that the name of Catholic amongst the black race will in a few years pass away.[119]

Harriet Thompson continued in her letter telling the pope that the black Catholics in New York sent two delegates to the cathedral to talk with the vicar-general, Father Loughlin, to see if something could be done for the black children. The vicar-general inquired about the possibility of black children going to the school operated by the

Sisters of Charity. The sisters informed him that white children were not willing to attend class with blacks. Father Loughlin then informed the black delegation that there was nothing that he could do about it.

The letter went on to state that Archbishop Hughes "did not recognize the black race to be a part of his flock." She pointed out that when a proposal for a school for black children at St. Vincent de Paul's Church was drawn up, the archbishop refused to approve it. She added that "it is well known by both white and black that the Most Reverend Archbishop Hughes... [hates] the black race so much that he cannot bear them to come near him." In closing, she mentioned the name of four priests who did care for the blacks. They were Father McColgan, Father Anwander of Baltimore, Father Lafont, and Father Loughlin, who was to be consecrated bishop of Brooklyn on the morrow.[120] She closed her letter with the hope that "if it is the will of God for the black race to be saved something will soon take place for the better." The letter was signed by twenty-six persons besides Harriet Thompson.

The nuncio, who was on a visit to the United States from June 30, 1853, to February 4, 1854, was Archbishop Gaetano Bedini (1806–64), sent by Rome to assess the advisability of establishing a nunciature in the United States. Archbishop Hughes's attitude toward blacks was well known; he was indifferent if not hostile to African Americans. His lack of enthusiasm for the abolition of slavery was mentioned in chapter 2. A Catholic school for black children was indeed opened in 1846 in the basement of St. Vincent de Paul Church, but it was not in existence in 1853. The circumstances of its closing are not clear at this time.

New York City in the mid-nineteenth century was a cauldron of social unrest, with crowds of immigrants pouring into the city, many of whom were Irish and were subject to racial discrimination and economic exploitation. At the same time, more blacks were entering the city. Free blacks were in competition with the Irish for the bottom rung of the socioeconomic ladder. The Irish saw the blacks as labor scabs who as freed laborers would threaten their jobs. For blacks the Irish began to epitomize Catholicism. The black Catholics found themselves in the middle. This cauldron of discontent finally boiled over ten years after the posting of Harriet Thompson's letter. In the summer of 1863, mobs of whites — many of whom were Irish — attacked and killed blacks in the bloody riots in the city of New York as a result of the anger unleashed by Lincoln's signature of the first military draft.[121]

She did not know it, but Harriet Thompson had set the course for black Catholics in the United States for the next century. In a sense the twenty-six signers of the letter that Harriet Thompson wrote expressed the sentiments of future black Catholics with a precision that was also prophetic. For the first time but not for the last, black lay Catholics had spoken out for themselves expressing both loyalty and love for the church and anger and dismay at the racist practices of those within the church. That twin characteristic of strong Catholic loyalty and angry denunciation at a lack of Christian justice will appear again at the end of the century with the black Catholic congress movement, at the time of the First World War with the Federated Colored Catholics, and in the 1960s with the formation of the black Catholic Clergy Caucus. For the most part, it will be black laypersons who lead the struggle. It will finally be to Rome that the appeal will be made. Harriet Thompson may never have known what happened to her letter. There is no record of a response. If Hughes was contacted, there may have been no movement on his part. Real apostolic work among black Catholics in New York City did not begin until after the Civil War. Still, the pattern of appeal to Rome regarding the plight of black Catholics, both on the part of blacks themselves and on the part of those who labored among them, will eventually result in a Roman response that will change the American church decisively.

Chapter 4

BUILDERS OF FAITH: BLACK RELIGIOUS WOMEN BEFORE AND AFTER THE CIVIL WAR

Religious life among black Catholics began in Kentucky in 1824 with a community of three black free women whom Father Charles Nerinckx brought together as an auxiliary group affiliated with the Sisters of Loretto. Charles Nerinckx (1761–1824) was a Belgian priest who came to the United States in 1804 in the aftermath of the French Revolution. Bishop Carroll sent him to the Kentucky missions the following year. At that time there was already a colony of Catholics who had migrated from Maryland and settled in what was Nelson County and adjacent territory. Many of these Catholics had brought with them slaves, who were also Catholics for the most part.

Nerinckx was indefatigable. Among his works was the foundation in 1812 of a religious community of women, the Friends of Mary at the Foot of the Cross, soon called the Sisters of Loretto. The sisters had begun by establishing a girls' school. He had encouraged them to take some black girls. In 1824 he had encouraged three of the black girls to become postulants in a special community with a habit and a rule slightly different from that of the Sisters of Loretto. Shortly after this, Father Nerinckx was forced to leave Kentucky. He had many critics among the clergy in Bardstown, who considered him to be too strict in his government. Leaving Kentucky, he went to Missouri, where he died. The foundation of black sisters did not survive his departure. Unfortunately, the documentation regarding the foundation he names of the young women did not survive either. From all accounts those who succeeded Nerinckx saw no need for black sisters, and the foundation was abandoned.[1]

I

The first successful foundation of black sisters took place five years later in Baltimore. It was the work of a French priest and four women of color, all of whom were part of the Haitian refugee colony in Baltimore. These Haitians worshiped each Sunday in the lower chapel of St. Mary's Seminary on Paca Street. In August 1827 a Sulpician priest, Jacques Hector Nicolas Joubert de la Muraille, had been asked to take over the pastoral charge of the chapel.[2] Joubert was born in 1777 at St-Jean d'Angély in western France. He had served as a government official in Haiti until the revolution. He eventually arrived in the United States by way of Cuba. In 1805 he began studies for the priesthood at St. Mary's Seminary, was ordained in 1810, and became a Sulpician.[3] Joubert soon discovered that it was difficult for the Haitian children to learn their catechism because they were unable to read. Making the acquaintance of two young Haitian women who had already begun a free school in their own home and who had already considered the idea of a life consecrated to God, Joubert began to think of founding a religious community.[4] The two young women added a third to their number, and in June 1828 they had a house with eleven girls as boarders and nine as day students. At the same time the young women began their religious life.

The leader of the group and the first superior was Elizabeth Lange, who had been born in Cuba of Haitian parents. She apparently came to the States by way of the Carolinas around 1817. Shortly thereafter she arrived in Baltimore, probably settling in the region of Fell's Point, where many black Haitians lived.[5] Five years later, Elizabeth Lange received a settlement of some $1,400 that she donated to the community, with the understanding that her mother could join the community later, which in fact she did.[6] The second and third members of the group were Marie Madeleine Balas and Rosine Boegue, who were also Haitians, about whom little is known before their entrance into the community. The fourth member was Almeide Duchemin Maxis, a young girl of nineteen who had lived with them for several years. Her mother, who had fled Haiti as a young girl and had lived with the Duchemin family, was named Maxis. Later she also joined the community; Almeide's father was an English military officer named Howard.[7]

It seems that the news of a black religious foundation initially raised some opposition in Baltimore. Joubert, however, had the full support of Archbishop Whitfield, the ordinary of Baltimore. The archbishop told him that he had the power to found a religious community in his diocese: "It is not lightly but with reflection that I approved your project. I knew and saw the finger of God; let us not oppose His holy will."[8] On July 2, 1829, the four women made their profession. Evidently, it was Joubert who decided to name the new congregation the Oblate Sisters of Providence. The spirituality given to the young community was essentially the French spirituality of the nineteenth century. The Blessed Virgin was the principal patron of the community. The patronal feast was that of the Visitation, which was July 2 in the liturgical calendar at that time. On that day the sisters renewed their vows each year. It was not until later that the sisters made perpetual vows. On the first anniversary of the young community, Father Tessier (1758–1840), the Sulpician superior, who gave frequent conferences to the sisters, enrolled the sisters in the Association of the Holy Slavery of the Mother of God. As a sign of this act of piety, each sister received a small chain. It was decided that in the future each sister would be enrolled and receive the chain at the time of her investiture with the habit.[9]

There is perhaps a symbolic connection with the African origin of the sisters and slavery and the sign of slavery, the chain. It is also possible that the Association of the Holy Slavery of the Mother of God is related to the devotion preached by St. Louis-Marie Grignion de Montfort (1673–1716),[10] a French priest who stressed handing over to Mary the disposition of one's merits and graces. The metaphor used was that of slavery. De Montfort's teaching was not the first to use the term "holy slavery," but his form of the devotion became the most popular and best known.[11] It is not clear whether Tessier introduced the sisters to the de Montfort form of the devotion. One difficulty is that modern research has shown that the manuscript written by St. Louis-Marie Grignion de Montfort, "True Devotion to the Blessed Virgin," remained relatively unknown until it was rediscovered and published in 1842.

St. Frances of Rome (1384–1440) became one of the secondary patrons of the community because she was the founder of a community of religious women who were not cloistered and who renewed their vows each year and were engaged in external works in the Trastevere section of the city of Rome.[12] Frances was heavily influenced by the Olivetan Congregation of Benedictine monks. The Oblate Sisters of Providence identified with the community begun by Frances, and a union of prayers was established with them.[13] The African element in the spirituality of the sisters was made evident, however, by their devotion to St. Benedict the Moor.[14] Benedict, who died in 1589, had been canonized in 1807 as a statement of opposition to the slave trade. The sisters took him as one of the secondary patrons of the community and celebrated his feast day on the Sunday within the Octave of the Ascension.[15]

With the advice and encouragement of Joubert, the sisters were able to combine the activities of the school and the devotional life of a religious community. In 1831 they were approved by Pope Gregory XVI. On that occasion they received several spiritual privileges and favors that Joubert had requested. The archbishop granted them permission to reserve the Blessed Sacrament in their convent.[16]

The habit of the first Oblate Sisters had been a black dress with white collar and a large white bonnet. A black bonnet was substituted for the white, and a black cape was worn when they left the convent. Only in 1906 did the sisters begin to wear a veil and a white linen guimpe.[17] From the beginning the school for girls was very successful. The examinations were often oral recitations, at which the Sulpicians assisted. A school for boys was finally opened by the sisters in 1852.[18]

On August 26, 1832, a request was made that four of the sisters might nurse the indigent sick with cholera, a disease that had reached epidemic proportions. It was Father Joubert who was approached by the city official for the poor. The Sisters of Charity had been asked for eight sisters, and they had sent only four. The officials were told that there was a convent of black religious. Hence, the request. Joubert informed them that "the Sisters of Charity were by the spirit of their institute obliged to look after the sick." He explained that the vocation of the Sisters of Providence was education of black children. He went on to say that he "hoped that they would not have less charity than the daughters of St. Vincent de Paul." In fact, when he asked for volunteers, all stood up. Father Joubert chose the four to go, one of whom had not yet made vows, so permission was given that she might make vows at Mass in the morning before they went to the hospital.[19]

Joubert spoke to the sisters at Mass the next morning. His words give us some idea of the spiritual climate in the community during what might be called the "heroic" period of their history.

> I addressed a few words to them on the good work they were about to undertake, on the merits attached to the sacrifice they were making to God of the life He had given them. I pointed out to them the dangers to which they were obliged to expose

themselves in thus devoting themselves to the service of the sick poor... I told them that if God permitted that they should be victims of their zeal, they would die martyrs of charity.[20]

A few days later the director of the almshouse expressed his "admiration of the goodness and promptness with which the Colored Sisters repaired to the beds of the sick."[21] A month later another heroic service was asked of the sisters again. Sister Anthony, the mother of Sister Therese Duchemin Maxis, was asked to nurse the archbishop's housekeeper, who was ill with cholera. A few weeks before, Sister Anthony had nursed the archbishop during the same malady. This time Sister Anthony contracted the disease, and within twenty-four hours she was dead.[22]

In 1835 the sisters were asked to supply two sisters to take over housekeeping in the seminary. The sisters felt obliged to respond in the affirmative because of the kindness that the Sulpicians had shown them. They felt constrained to request that certain safeguards be established so that the sisters in that service could maintain their rule. It is interesting to note that the question of race was not absent from the deliberations.

We do not conceal the difficulty of our situation as persons of color and religious at the same time, and we wish to conciliate these two qualities in such a manner as not to appear too arrogant on the one hand and on the other, not to miss the respect which is due to the state we have embraced and the holy habit which we have the honor to wear. Our intention in consenting to your request is not to neglect the religious profession which we have embraced.[23]

On November 5, 1843, Father Joubert died. His death left a void in the life of the sisters because he had been not only the director and the chaplain for the community but also the protector and spokesperson for the sisters. Louis Deluol, S.S. (1787–1858), the superior of the Sulpicians, acted as consultant, but he did not replace Joubert. He celebrated Mass occasionally for the community, but there was no longer anyone to say Mass daily for them or to give spiritual direction. It seems clear that the Sulpicians deliberately began to distance themselves from all pastoral involvement with the community. It has been suggested that the reason for this change was the desire of the Sulpician authorities in France to limit the ministry of the Sulpicians to their main apostolate of training men for the priesthood.[24] Another reason, no doubt, was the lack of enthusiasm of many in Baltimore for the existence of a convent of black religious women. It is during this period of practical abandonment of the sisters that the archbishop of Baltimore, Samuel Eccleston, is reported to have suggested that there was no need for black religious and that they might do well to disband and become domestics.[25]

Help came to the sisters in the person of a young Bavarian Redemptorist priest, Thaddeus Anwander (1823–93), who joined the Redemptorist Congregation in Germany and later came to the missions in America as a young cleric in 1845. Ordained a priest in 1846, he was appointed pastor to a German parish. Anwander became interested in the Oblate Sisters through the intervention of St. John Neumann (1811–60), the Redemptorist superior and pastor of the parish where the Oblate Sisters' convent was located. In 1852 Neumann became bishop of Philadelphia. Anwander made the decision to become the spiritual director of the sisters, went to the archbishop, and got down on his knees to beg his permission for authorization to work with the community. In fact, Anwander became a second founder for the Oblate Sisters of Providence.[26] In October 1847 he began his tenure as chaplain, while remaining a busy pastor. At the same time many of the black Catholics in Baltimore began to attend Mass regularly and to receive the sacraments at the chapel of the Oblate Sisters on Richmond Street.

Anwander's ministry was both dedicated and joyous. The following is an extract of the convent chronicle for Christmas 1849.

> We had today the happiness of having Mass in our chapel at 3½ o'clock said by our Rev. Director, at 3 o'clock he baptised Mr. Watts, who took the name of Alphonse,[27] he before made his profession of faith, in a distinct, composed voice which denoted that the words came from the heart, after which, the ordinary ceremony of Baptism was performed, then Mass commenced...truly happy Daughters of Providence, for that Providential hand always supplies...unexpectedly at 3 o' clock in the evening [Anwander] came and gave Benediction of the Blessed Sacrament. He brought a dove which was given to him as a present for the season, he gave [it to the] community wishing us according to St. Francis de Sales to practice some virtues that are applied to the dove.[28]

When Anwander could not come, he was at times replaced by the Redemptorist superior, St. John Neumann. On April 7, 1850, Archbishop Eccleston, evidently convinced of the community's viability, came to the house and confirmed both adults and children, fifty to sixty in all.[29]

In 1863 the community made its first foundation outside of Baltimore. A school for black children and a night school for black women was begun in Philadelphia during the Civil War. At first the school was very successful, but in 1867 it had to be closed. In 1864 a free school for black girls and women was opened in Baltimore. Many of the students were the children of freed slaves or orphans. In 1865 an orphanage was established, in part for the children of the war — many of whom were abandoned black children living in the streets of Baltimore. The sisters also briefly operated an orphanage in New Orleans from 1867 to 1872.[30]

Indirectly the Oblate Sisters of Providence were responsible for one of the largest communities of religious women in the United States today. Sister Therese Duchemin Maxis, the fourth member of the founding group, served as superior from 1841 to 1844, during the years of crisis. Although the circumstances are not clear, it seems that Sister Therese had her own plans as to how the community could best surmount the crisis. The plans included a change of name for the community and new constitutions. It was hoped that the Carroll family of Maryland would become benefactors of the community. This did not occur, and in December 1844, Sister Therese was not reelected superior.[31]

At this time Father Louis Gillet, C.SS.R. (1813–92), a native of Antwerp, entered the Redemptorist novitiate at St-Trond in 1833 and was ordained a priest in Liège in 1838. He came to the United States as a missionary in 1843. Eventually Gillet became part of a contingent of Redemptorists that established a foundation in the diocese of Detroit. Before that, Gillet served in Baltimore, where he met the young superior of the oblate house, Sister Therese Duchemin Maxis. Father Gillet interested her in the mission that the Redemptorists were establishing in Monroe, Michigan.[32] On September 9, 1845, the community chronicle stated that Sister Mary Therese left the community for "reasons unknown . . . only that she wished to serve Almighty God as a true religious."[33] Another oblate, Sister Ann Constance, soon joined Therese Maxis. In 1847 Gillet was peremptorily dismissed as superior. He left Monroe and returned to the East. In 1850 he received a dispensation from his vows as a Redemptorist, eventually entering the abbey of Sénanque in France as a Cistercian monk.[34]

Sister Therese Duchemin also suffered rejection and dismissal. As superior she was responsible for the foundations that the sisters made in Pennsylvania. At the same time there was misunderstanding between herself and the bishop of Detroit, Peter Paul Lefevere, C.M. (1804–69), who had given his approval to the foundation in Monroe. In the course of this misunderstanding, Bishop Lefevere reached the conclusion that Sister Therese was insubordinate. He came personally to the convent on April 1, 1859, and relieved her of her rank as superior. Later she and Sister Ann Constance were sent to the foundation at Susquehanna. Lefevere referred to the race of both Sister Therese and Sister Ann Constance in a letter to the auxiliary bishop of Philadelphia, James Wood.[35] Sister Therese tried to return to her convent in Monroe, Michigan, but Lefevere never permitted her return; she was also unable to go back to the community of I.H.M. sisters in Pennsylvania. Eventually, she was made welcome by the Grey Nuns in Ottawa, Canada, and lived with them from 1869 to 1885. In 1885 she was finally permitted to return to the I.H.M. convent in West Chester, Pennsylvania; and it was there that she died in 1892.[36]

II

New Orleans was the home for the second black religious order of women. Here again it was French-speaking African Americans who began the community, and here also the new community faced bigotry and harshness from the beginning. The milieu of New Orleans, however, was different from that of Baltimore. The people of mixed African and white ancestry, the free people of color, formed a wedge midway between the white population and the black population. Concubinage between white men and women of color was accepted and recognized. It was into this world of ambivalent values and confused racial boundaries that Henriette Delille was born in 1813.

Henriette was the illegitimate daughter of Jean-Baptiste Delille-Sarpy and Pouponne Dias.[37] She was the youngest of three children. As an adolescent, she made the acquaintance of a member of a French nursing order who had come out alone from France, Soeur Ste-Marthe Fontier. She engaged in social work among the black population of New Orleans, and Henriette began to work with her. They opened a school for young girls, daughters of the free people of color, who were educated by day, while slaves received religious instruction by night. This separation was no doubt due to social distinctions and the demands of toil. Eventually Soeur Ste-Marthe returned to France. A proposed foundation of religious women, black and white, never materialized.

Juliette Gaudin, born in 1808 in Cuba, was the daughter of mulatto parents originally from Haiti who migrated to New Orleans, where Juliette grew up. As a young girl, she became a good friend of Henriette Delille. The two young women eventually came to the notice of another Frenchwoman, Marie-Jeanne Aliquot; born in France about 1783, she arrived in New Orleans in 1832. She already had two sisters in New Orleans, one an Ursuline and the other a lay teacher in the school for black children, the latter who died in 1832, a victim of the yellow fever epidemic. On her arrival, while disembarking from the ship, Mademoiselle Aliquot accidentally fell into the river. A black man dove into the water and saved her; in appreciation, Marie-Jeanne Aliquot determined to spend her life in the service of blacks. Aliquot took over the school opened by Soeur Ste-Marthe and located it in more commodious buildings. Eventually selling the school to the Ursuline nuns, Aliquot made an attempt in 1836 to begin a religious community with young women of color, among whom were Henriette and Juliette. Known as the Sisters of the Presentation, they worked among the poor blacks. The endeavor was stopped, however, because it violated the laws of segregation of the state.[38]

It was the intervention of a priest, the Abbé Rousselon, who finally helped Henriette and Juliette's dream become a possibility. Etienne Rousselon was born in Lyons, France, in 1800. He was ordained in 1827 and came to New Orleans ten years later. He became the vicar-general for Bishop Antoine Blanc and pastor of the newly constructed church of St. Augustine. He supported the plans of Henriette Delille and Juliette Gaudin for a religious community because he realized that they could be of help in ministering to the poor blacks in the parish. He obtained support from the bishop for this purpose. Marie-Jeanne Aliquot, being white, would not be able to belong to the community. She began her ministry to blacks in the rural areas and on the plantations.

The community was established on the Feast of the Presentation of the Blessed Virgin Mary, November 21, 1842, a very special feast for Henriette. Abbé Rousselon, however, insisted that the name of the small community should be the Holy Family. In the beginning the two women took care of the destitute black poor, both men and women, in rented lodgings. Then they were able to buy a house in what is now the French Quarter of New Orleans, living first on St. Bernard Street and then on Bayou Road. The next year another woman joined them, Josephine Charles (1812–85), member of a prominent family among the New Orleans Creoles. Josephine Charles is considered as one of the founders and would succeed Henriette as leader of the community. In 1847 the new community saw the necessity of becoming legally incorporated. In order to make this possible a group of men and women, free people of color, formed the Association of the Holy Family so the community could find legal support and moral and financial help. The association was able to purchase a home for destitute blacks that served as a hospice. The sisters provided food and clothing to those who came to them for help.[39] Their work was not only educational but also service to the poor. This would remain the pattern of their religious life during the nineteenth century and up to the present.

In 1852 Henriette Delille and Juliette Gaudin made a novitiate with the Religious of the Sacred Heart in a convent in St. James (civil) Parish.[40] In October of that same year the three women made their first canonical vows as religious. Under civil law, however, they were not recognized as religious.[41] In fact, it would seem that the civil authorities in this city of slavery tolerated the existence of the sisters because of the work they did in nursing the sick poor among the black population. The sisters visited the sick in their homes; established an orphanage, the Asylum of the Children of the Holy Family; and in addition continued to operate a school for girls, established in 1850, and to teach the children catechism in two New Orleans parishes.[42]

During the epidemic of yellow fever in the summer of 1853, the sisters nursed many of the ill at great cost in physical hardship to themselves. It was this service that finally won them public recognition as Sisters of the Holy Family.[43] By 1860 there were six sisters in the small community. One of them, Sister Suzanne Navarre (1821–87), came all the way from Boston to join them. She was an expert seamstress and helped support the community by sewing garments for the well-to-do.[44] The epidemic strained the physical and spiritual resources of the community. No one, however, was taxed more than the superior, Henriette Delille, whose health was never the best. She continued her activity despite her ill health, even during the troubled time of the Civil War. In April 1862 New Orleans was captured by Union troops. In October of that year, Henriette fell ill with pleurisy. On November 17, 1862, she died at the age of fifty.[45]

In 1866 Abbé Rousselon died as a result of a fall suffered on shipboard on his trans-Atlantic voyage from France. He had promised to bring with him the pattern for a religious habit for the fledgling community. Up to this time, the sisters wore a blue cotton dress of the period with a black bonnet. Only in 1872 did the Sisters of the Holy Family finally obtain the right to wear the habit publicly in New Orleans. It is part of the unwritten history of the community that when the sisters finally designed a religious habit that was approved and accepted, Mother Josephine Charles sent a novice clad in the new habit to see Archbishop Perché. The archbishop at first mistook the novice for a religious from a white community and was very upset to realize that she was a sister of the Holy Family. He ordered her to take off the habit with the words, "Who do you think you are?...You are proud, too proud!"[46] Permission was eventually granted for the adoption of the new habit, once the archbishop was approached through the good offices of the vicar-general, the Reverend Gilbert Raymond, who had succeeded Abbé Rousselon as chaplain and director for the sisters.[47] It was the period of Reconstruction. The Civil War and slavery had passed, but the status of blacks, even that of black religious, evolved with hesitation and pain.

Like the spirituality of the Oblate Sisters of Providence, that of the Sisters of the Holy Family seems to have been very much influenced by nineteenth-century French spirituality. Father Rousselon had drawn up the rule and constitutions of the community. The rule was based on the Rule of St. Augustine, and St. Augustine was considered one of the chief patrons.[48] The conventual life was moderately severe. The sisters arose at 4:30 in the morning, and they retired at 8:45 in the evening. At 5:00 A.M. there was morning prayers, with a half hour of meditation followed by Mass. They recited fifteen decades of the rosary divided up into three portions during the day. The meals were in silence with reading. Individual spiritual reading in French or English preceded supper. There were two periods of community recreation each day. In 1893 the sisters began the daily recitation of the Little Office of the Blessed Virgin in choir.[49] Their spirituality was based upon the imitation of the life of the Holy Family at Nazareth. Devotion to the Sacred Heart of Jesus was seen as the source for the community's mutual charity. Unlike the Oblate Sisters, there was no overt indication of an African American theme in their spirituality. This is not surprising inasmuch as the cultural milieu from which the community arose was that of the free people of color, who were more French than African in inspiration.[50]

The Sisters of the Holy Family were a diocesan congregation during the entire nineteenth century. Archbishop Janssens (archbishop of New Orleans from 1888 to 1897) intended to seek approval of the congregation from the Holy See. He died, however, on the way to Rome. Only in 1949 did the Holy Family Sisters receive canonical recognition as a religious congregation of pontifical rite.[51]

Josephine Charles died in 1885, and Juliette Gaudin in 1887. In 1873 the first foundation outside of New Orleans was made in

Opelousas, Louisiana. In 1881 a school was opened in Baton Rouge, but it was closed after a year. In 1885 another foundation was made in Donaldsonville, Louisiana. In 1881 the community purchased the historic Orleans Ballroom on Orleans Street in New Orleans. It was an edifice that had once played an important role in the history of the city. It had been the scene of the fabulous quadroon balls at which the wealthy white men danced with the beautiful women of color. In 1881 it became a school and convent, the ballroom itself becoming a chapel. This convent was relinquished in 1955 with the construction of a new motherhouse. The building itself was sold only in 1964.

An invitation to begin a school had been extended to the Holy Family community by the archbishop of St. Louis, Peter Kenrick. The superior of the community, Mother Magdalen Alpaugh (1882– 88), did not believe that she could accept the invitation to make a foundation at St. Louis at that time. Three of the sisters, however, who had been stationed at the Holy Family convent on Bayou Street made the decision to go to St. Louis. A foundation in St. Louis became impossible, however, when the archbishop discovered that the superior in New Orleans withheld authorization. The three sisters returned to Louisiana but not to New Orleans. Instead they began a convent at St. Michael's near the town of Convent in St. James Parish. They chose the Franciscan way of life and spirit. They ceased being Holy Family sisters and formed a new diocesan congregation. From all indications, their desire was a more contemplative form of life.

Archbishop Blenk (archbishop from 1906 to 1917) suppressed the community at the time of the death of the superior, Sister Theresa, shortly after the turn of the century. At the time of the suppression, two of the community rejoined the Holy Family Sisters, and a third, Mother Theodore Williams, as will be seen subsequently, was to become the founder of another community of African American sisters, the Franciscan Handmaids of Mary.[52] In the *Catholic Directory* for the period, the community is listed as being at St. Michael's Parish, with the post office at Convent. The name of the community was given as Sisters of the Third Order of St. Francis (Colored). There is no indication as to whether they taught in the school for black children or as to the size of the community.[53]

One of the most bizarre histories of a foundation of African American nuns in New Orleans is that of the Sisters of Our Lady of Lourdes. It was founded as a diocesan community by Archbishop Perché in 1883. Three young girls of the people of color had become students at a white Catholic school in Kentucky. A visitor from New Orleans evidently recognized them and informed the school administration that the young women were not white. They were dismissed and returned to New Orleans in their own minds disgraced; without hope of marriage, their only recourse was to take the veil. In the judgment of these young women, the Holy Family Sisters were not light-skinned enough, while the white communities rejected them as black. Archbishop Perché accepted them as a diocesan community and received their vows. They transformed a large dwelling on Chartres Street that belonged to one of the three into a convent, and the title of Our Lady of Lourdes was given to the house and the community.

For a while the community attempted to conduct a school, but the attempt was never successful. They did needlework and embroidery and practiced manual skills such as making artificial flowers. From all appearances they had little resources except the support of people in the neighborhood. By 1896 they numbered seven. In the end they were only two.[54]

III

At the end of the last century in Savannah, Georgia, a black community of Franciscan sisters was established by an extraordinary woman, Mother Mathilda Beasley. She was born about 1833 in New Orleans; her mother was a Creole of color, and her father an Indian. In the 1850s she married a free black man in Savannah, Georgia, named Abram Beasley. Evidently, this was his second marriage. Abram Beasley was fairly wealthy, owning a restaurant and a general store as well as land; his business seemingly included at times the sale of slaves. After the Civil War he continued to prosper and was the owner of several racehorses and a great deal of property. Mathilda Beasley is said to have risked imprisonment by instructing black children, slave and free, in antebellum Savannah.[55]

Her husband died in 1878. We know that she gave some land to the church of Savannah. A letter from the Benedictine Oswald Moosmueller to Mother Mathilda Beasley gives some idea of her financial help to him in the erection of Sacred Heart Church as a parish in 1880.[56] She either donated or lent $350. At the same time, Mathilda Beasley had evidently donated the house of Abram Beasley to Father Oswald.[57] Mathilda went to England to become a religious. In his letter Father Oswald notes that in 1885 he sent her on two occasions a money order for $50. Some time after that date Mother Mathilda Beasley returned from England and began a community of Franciscan Sisters in Georgia. It is not certain whether she herself had made profession in the community in England. According to the *Catholic Directory* for that period, Mother Mathilda's convent and orphanage are mentioned for the first time in 1891 in Washington, Wilkes County, Georgia, which is midway between Athens and Augusta. In the same city the Sisters of St. Joseph had a school for black children. The entry mentions only the Colored Orphan Asylum, run by Sisters of the Third Order of St. Francis.[58] The following year the description is more complete. "Colored Orphan Asylum. Sisters of the Third Order of St. Francis. Mother Mathilda, Supr. 3 sisters (colored). 19 girls."[59] By 1894 the directory lists five sisters and the same number of girls. By 1896 the convent was located in Savannah with five sisters and nineteen girls.

On October 2, 1889, the bishop of Savannah, Thomas Becker, wrote to Father Bonaventure Frey, O.F.M. Cap., in New York City concerning this community. By this date, the community had already been established in the diocese. Becker wrote for advice concerning some kind of rule "for the pious colored women of the third Order of St. Francis under a certain matron, Mathilda Beasley, black in color, desirous to live in a sort of community." He described the community of sisters as "not many in numbers, few of them capable of reading and hardly are they capable of doing anything in the spiritual life."[60] Becker's estimation of the abilities of blacks tended always to be very low, so his description of the sisters must be qualified somewhat. What is important is that he sought some sort of affiliation with the Franciscans but seemingly was unsuccessful. It is interesting to note that Father Bonaventure Frey was a Capuchin friar, not a Franciscan of the Order of Friars Minor, as he addressed him in his letter. On the other hand, Becker spoke of Mother Mathilda Beasley as someone who "deserved great praise."[61]

It is possible that between 1885 and 1889, Mother Mathilda had become a religious in England. One could also speculate that she received authorization to return to the United States and make a foundation for black sisters. We simply do not know. What we do know is that the life of the small community was extremely hard and that Mother Mathilda struggled with very little encouragement. One gets a sense of this in reading the small collection of her letters. In 1893 she wrote Cardinal Gibbons thanking him for his support and begging him for further help if possible, "for my community is so very small. If your Eminence can send me a few subjects, it will be one of the greatest help for this Mission. Then we could work and help ourselves."[62]

That same year Mother Mathilda Beasley entered into protracted negotiations with the newly established Sisters of the Blessed Sacrament for Indians and Colored People, a religious congregation established in 1890 by Blessed Katherine Drexel, a Philadelphia heiress, who used her wealth to aid in the evangelization of both Native Americans and African Americans.[63] A note taken from the Annals of the Sisters of the Blessed Sacrament for 1893 indicates that Mother Mathilda Beasley and a companion visited the motherhouse of the Blessed Sacrament Sisters just outside Philadelphia in Bensalem, Pennsylvania. They requested aid in the spiritual formation of the small community. Consideration was given to the possibility of transporting the entire community from Georgia to Pennsylvania. In the end, the proposition was considered unfeasible because of racial feeling and the fear of mutual antagonism. Consideration of the two black religious communities of women already in existence also influenced the negative decision.[64]

The archives of the Blessed Sacrament Sisters has six letters from Mother Mathilda Beasley to Blessed Katherine Drexel from 1893 to 1895. At present there seems to be no explanation as to why the *Catholic Directory* lists the convent of Franciscan Sisters as located at Washington, Georgia, while all the letters have the home address as St. Francis Home, Savannah, Georgia. In many respects the letters are painful to read because Mother Mathilda needed both financial assistance and moral support. Mother Katherine supplied some financial assistance. She sent $150 to cover the travel expenses of some of the female orphans to the care of the Good Shepherd nuns in the North.[65] Evidently these were older girls who would be trained by the nuns.[66] There were two groups of girls. One group went to Philadelphia; the other to Baltimore.

The following year, in 1894, Mother Mathilda wrote Blessed Katherine, alluding to a second visit to see her. Evidently Mother Mathilda had received the loan of a construction plan for the building of an orphanage and convent. It seems that the community in Savannah desperately needed lodgings, and some funding had been promised by Mother Katherine Drexel. The letters are plaintive. Explaining that the plans supplied by Mother Katherine were considered unsatisfactory by the architect, Mother Mathilda wrote, "The architect told me to give him a sketch of just what we could manage to get along with . . . I will send them to you by express. Dear Mother if they should please you, then everything will be right . . . I cannot say satisfied. For that is not the word. All we desire is to please you."[67]

Two months later the desperation of Mother Mathilda is more clearly revealed in a letter to Blessed Katherine. "Do please pardon me for troubling you with another letter. My anxiety is so very great that I could no longer refrain from begging you to please be so kind as to favor me with a letter."[68] In less than a week she wrote again, explaining that the bishop, Thomas Becker (bishop from 1886 to 1899), was away but that they needed lodging so badly that she had decided to build the "centre and one wing, the one with the kitchen, that is if you will approve of it."[69] The last two letters reveal that Blessed Katherine Drexel did write Mother Mathilda, but seemingly she sent or promised to send the money to Bishop Becker, who was in Rome. Mother Mathilda explained that they would not commence the building until his return in June (at that time it was March). In the meantime the community was evidently in need of money for the short term.[70]

The only other direct source of information about the fate of Mother Mathilda's community is three short letters addressed to Father John Slattery, S.S.J., the superior general of the Josephite Congregation in Baltimore. By this time Father Slattery had become the unofficial Catholic supervisor of all African American Catholic work in the United States.[71] A year after her last correspondence with Blessed Katherine, Mother Mathilda wrote Slattery. Three letters in all have been preserved in the archives. In November 1896 a brief note asked him to send them books or anything else that might be done "for God's glory."[72] In the following summer, Mother Mathilda wrote Slattery again, saying that the bishop had suggested that Slattery might help them get more vocations for the community. She spoke of the slow growth of the community and the need they had for more sisters. Slattery had penned a notation for his secretary on the letter saying that he would do what he could for the community.[73]

The last letter was about a year later in May. It was to announce that the bishop was suppressing the community. She explained that "my health has failed me and I can no longer carry on the work and have not been able to raise a community." She went on to say that the bishop had been able to get sisters from Rome and that they would take a black sister but that the youngest sister in her community would try to find another convent. The two oldest might stay. For herself, "I am going out in the cold world to be alone until I pass, for I see plain that I can't stay with them so I will leave as soon as I get permission from the Right Rev. Bishop." She intimated that it was better to go before she was made to do so.[74]

In the end, the Missionary Franciscan Sisters of the Immaculate Conception, who had already established a convent and a school in Augusta, Georgia, took over the convent and orphanage in Savannah.[75] This congregation of sisters was one of the first to have an African American novice. Miss Frederica Law, a pupil in the Franciscan sisters' school in Augusta, was received as a novice into the community and took the name Sister Benedict of the Angels. She entered the novitiate in Rome, and there she died in 1883, making her profession as a sister in the order on her deathbed.[76]

Mathilda Beasley remained in Savannah. She lived alone in a small house near Sacred Heart Church, which Father Oswald Moosmueller had built for the black Catholics. There she engaged in sewing and devoted her earnings to charity. She was cared for by the parishioners. When she did not come to the early Mass on Sunday morning, December 20, 1903, she was found dead in her home in an attitude of prayer before a statue of the Virgin. Her shroud was found in the room, and on her clothes was found her will. She had made funeral arrangements beforehand. At the funeral Mass in the packed church, no eulogy was given, according to her wishes.[77] By all accounts the work of Mother Mathilda Beasley was a failure. Her foundation did not succeed. Yet the witness of her life, the effort made on behalf of the orphans, the memory that she left in Savannah, and the quiet dignity of her last letter to Father Slattery leave one with the impression that here was a woman of extraordinary faith. She has earned an honored position in the history of African American religious women.

The history of black sisters in the nineteenth century is a pivotal chapter in the history of African American Catholicism, for three reasons. First, black religious women were present at the very beginning of the history of Catholic nuns in the United States. Among the religious sisterhoods, they made a unique contribution by their ministry to neglected African Americans; and they were uniquely American, although the white community often withheld recognition.

Second, the African American religious communities witness to the existence of a vigorous black Catholic community even prior to the Civil War. Vocations come from a community, from a milieu in which a faith is shared and spiritual values are passed on. Black women experienced the call to organize religious communities according to particular charisms and gifts. They were joined by other black women who had experienced the call to respond to the needs of the church in her broken and most neglected members, the slaves, the former slaves, the free African American community relegated to the margins of society. Yet these black women would not have responded had there not been black Catholic parents, sisters and brothers, aunts and uncles, who served as a support and an inspiration. The African American sisters reflected and called forth the spiritual values of African American Catholics who gave their daughters and their sisters in service to God and to the challenge of the gospel.

Third, the African American religious sisterhoods helped lay the faith foundation of the black Catholic community. No one would contest the fact that white sisters and priests carried out remarkable work in the evangelization of the African American population. Catholicism exists in many areas among the black community because of their work. Nevertheless, the pioneers in black ministry were the followers of Elizabeth Lange, Henriette Delille, and even Mathilda Beasley. As pioneers, they often worked without encouragement or support and too often in the face of indifference and antipathy. Without them the black Catholic community would not be what it is today.

The documentation of the history of the black Catholic religious communities, on the other hand, still needs to be developed. There is no adequate history of any of the black Catholic sisterhoods. There are no adequate biographies of the founders. What is desperately needed is the compilation of a list of the members of the two major communities, going back to the beginning. With a list of names and as much pertinent information as is available — such as date and place of birth, baptism, parents' names, social background (slave or free), and early education — one can continue the task of identifying the black Catholic community by name and place.

Finally, a more detailed examination of the spirituality and the type of education of the black religious sisterhoods during the nineteenth century will go a long way in understanding the spiritual and cultural framework within the black Catholic community today. There is every reason to believe that more careful research may reveal that the influence of black sisters within the community was far greater than that of their white counterparts in their respective ethnic communities precisely because the black religious were at home, whereas the white priests and sisters were not.

Chapter 5

A GOLDEN OPPORTUNITY
FOR A HARVEST OF SOULS:
THE SECOND PLENARY
COUNCIL OF BALTIMORE, 1866

Halfway through the Civil War, when the tide had turned in favor of the Union forces, the agent of the Holy See in New York, Henry Binsse, reported to the Congregation of the Propaganda that by the end of the war the slavery question would be definitively decided. He also noted that in his opinion it would no longer be possible for the church in the United States to maintain "a political policy of reticence and abstention." He pointed out that the "laws which regulate slavery are a violation... of marital rights, of the natural rights of the family, and that religion made little progress in the Slave states."[1]

I

Three years later and one year after the end of the war, the episcopate of the United States was no longer faced with the moral question of slavery. Rather it was faced with the necessity of working out a policy on the national level for ministry and evangelization of the former slaves. In the end no coherent policy was forthcoming. This failure is one of the tragedies of American church history.

The agent of the Papal States was correct in speaking of the "reticence" of the American bishops regarding slavery. In the seven provincial councils of Baltimore (1829–49), neither slaves nor African

116

Americans in general were mentioned. Peter Guilday, one of the most important American church historians, in speaking of the First Plenary Council of Baltimore, held in 1852, had nothing but praise for this silence of the American bishops.

> When, therefore, as the Council proceeded, it became evident that the attending prelates had decided to keep silence on the question... Catholics realized more acutely than ever the real meaning of the church's place in American life, and non-Catholics appreciated the fact that here was a body of American spiritual leaders who meant to bring to the disturbed condition of the times the one asset the country needed: peace and calm... By their silence our prelates divorced this burning political question from church affairs.[2]

History since that time has taught us that no one can remain silent in periods of great social turmoil and still retain any moral authority. It has also taught that there is no such thing as a political issue without moral consequences. From today's vantage point, it can be said that the American bishops in the period of slavery made a bad choice. At the end of the Civil War, they were given a chance to rectify it.

Martin J. Spalding (1810–72) had become archbishop of Baltimore in 1864. Previously, from 1850 to 1864, he had been bishop of Louisville. Born into a slaveholding family in Kentucky, his sentiments during the Civil War had been for the Confederacy. In a memorial written to the Congregation of the Propaganda in 1863, he set forth the background and the causes of the Civil War. His work, entitled "Dissertation on the American Civil War," was thorough in its treatment but not unbiased. He admitted that "slavery is a great social evil," for which he blamed the British. He believed that emancipation of the slaves would result in "ruining the country and causing injury to the poor slaves themselves." He wrote, "Our experience... shows us... that those who are... liberated ordinarily become miserable vagabonds, drunkards, and thieves... Such emancipated ones are lost in body and soul."[3]

Even with such views, Spalding had a genuine concern for the religious welfare of the African American population. Hence, not only did he see the necessity for a plenary council right after the war, but one of the major items, in his opinion, should be the religious care of the freed slaves. As a result Spalding wrote Cardinal Barnabò,[4] the prefect of the Congregation of the Propaganda, in regard to a second plenary council. Among the reasons he gave for calling one at this time was the religious situation of the newly emancipated slaves.[5] He received from Cardinal Barnabò approval for the council and particularly for measures furthering the apostolate to American blacks. He received less than enthusiastic support from his fellow bishops. In a letter to Archbishop McCloskey of New York, Spalding spoke about the objective of the forthcoming council in dealing with the question of African Americans. "I think it precisely the most urgent duty of all to discuss the future status of the negro. Four million of these unfortunates are thrown on our Charity... It is a golden opportunity for reaping a harvest of souls, which neglected may not return."[6]

Among the many questions that Spalding, who had been named the apostolic delegate for the plenary council, wanted treated at the council was the preliminary schema "Title 10, On the Care of Souls," as well as the schema known as "Title 13, no. 4," regarding the appointment of a prefect apostolic for the spiritual care of African Americans. In the former, the proposals considered special churches for African Americans, African American priests, and missionary endeavors among blacks. The latter dealt with the creation of new dioceses and candidates for the episcopacy, and with the advisability of creating a prefect apostolic to oversee the spiritual work on behalf of African Americans on a national level.[7] Rome had given final approval of this agenda in the same papal brief that named Spalding as the leader of the council. Of the topics that were to be covered in the council, the eighth and last dealt with the evangelization of the African Americans. It was this last measure that would create so much difficulty.[8]

The council opened on October 7, 1866. Discussion regarding the question of a prefect apostolic for the spiritual care of the African Americans did not take place until after the council was officially over. Because of the immense amount of work, the council fathers were unable to accomplish it all. It was finally suggested that certain matters be dealt with in an extraordinary session to be held after the plenary council had officially closed.[9]

The extraordinary session opened on Monday, October 22, at 9:00 A.M. In the acts of this session, the Latin text laconically relates that "the Apostolic Delegate offered certain things to be considered by the Fathers... earnestly exhorting them that, accommodating themselves to the wishes of the Sacred Congregation of the Propaganda, they might decide what would seem most profitable in the Lord for the salvation of the black people. For a long time this was discussed among the Fathers."[10] The discussion was long and bitter. Spalding never admitted that the idea of an ecclesiastical coordinator on a national level or prefect apostolic was originally his.[11] In the original wording of the schema as approved by Rome, it was suggested that an "ecclesiastical man, residing in Baltimore," should be responsible for coordinating efforts for the spiritual care of the African Americans. It was also suggested that perhaps the pope might wish to make him a bishop.[12] It was this last proposition that raised the ire of the bishops.

Archbishop Odin of New Orleans expressed his feeling that "just as in the past so also in the future he would do everything for these people as he did for others...Now he would increase the number of missionaries [but] nothing more must be innovated."[13] Augustin Verot, the bishop of Savannah, did not agree, "especially in view of the hopeless situation of the blacks." He had brought French sisters into his diocese to work with the blacks, although they were still struggling with the language. He strongly urged the establishment of an "ecclesiastical man" who would take charge of the salvation of the African Americans. It is interesting to note that before the Civil War Verot had preached in defense of slavery; after the war, however, he did all in his power to aid the former slaves and to combat the sentiment against them, going as far as to write a pastoral letter to his people urging them "to put away all prejudice...against their former servants."[14] Verot was among the few at the council who wholeheartedly supported Rome's plan for a national coordinator of evangelization for blacks.

The bishops brought up many objections. Bishop McGill of Richmond noted that there were many African Americans in the city of Richmond but few Catholics. Before the war the Daughters of Charity had cared for them as much as they could. He did not understand why Rome was acting in this way toward the bishops.[15] Even when Archbishop Spalding pointed out the desires of Propaganda regarding the care of blacks and the necessity of yielding to this directive, the bishop of Richmond asserted again that "the Sacred Congregation had not well understood the situation in our region, they had been badly advised by someone."[16] Peter Kenrick, the archbishop of St. Louis, who had been in very bad humor throughout the council, "asserted that he would accept no such prefect; if one were forced upon him, he would renounce the episcopacy."[17] He spoke about the evils of a divided administration.

Bishop Verot came out in favor of the plan again by pointing out that there was no reason to worry about the jurisdictional question. At this point the bishop of Richmond wanted to know if anything was to be done for white people: "Behold so strong was the desire for promoting the salvation of the blacks as if they alone were derelict and neglected."[18] Verot countered that the question under consideration was about blacks, and "according to the mind of the Sacred Congregation something special for blacks was to be done."[19] When Spalding suggested that the bishops should encourage their priests to work among blacks, Kenrick angrily replied that if something new were established, it would seem as if the bishops had been previously remiss. He added, with some bitterness it would seem, "Bishops are placed by the Holy Spirit to rule the church of God not to receive those things which have been sanctioned by Propaganda into law." The secretary added in parentheses in English, "not to know the Instructions of Propaganda."[20]

In the end the council fathers rejected the notion of an ecclesiastical coordinator or prefect apostolic. In fact, nothing new was created to deal with the situation on a nationwide scale. It was decided that each bishop who had blacks in his diocese should decide what was best and work in concert with others in the provincial synods.[21]

In the published decrees of the council, the same ambivalence regarding ministry to blacks was revealed. All agreed on the need for pastoral care, especially since the Protestants were laboring with so much success; but the bishops were divided on the question of separate churches for blacks or the worship of blacks in the parish churches, where normally they were relegated to a segregated area.[22] The council decreed that it should "gravely weigh on our conscience that all might have access to draw near to Christ; that all who administer the sacraments might be present to all who seek them; and in every way a place might be provided in which all who wish might be able to be present on Sundays and Feastdays for the tremendous Sacrifice of the Mass."[23] If "through some stupidity" it should happen that this is not the case, "one will merit the greatest opprobrium, who forgetful of his office, shall not offer the means of salvation to all who seek, whether black or other and who on account of this lack of care should perish [spiritually]."[24] Whether many blacks perished spiritually is one question that cannot be answered; that many black Catholics would be turned away from "the means of salvation" is a fact.

The bishops sought missionaries from Europe to work among the black population. They begged and pleaded for priests "through the bowels of mercy of... God that as many as could would devote their strength, their time, and their whole being" to the ministry of blacks. They especially pleaded for schools for black children and for religious to take care of orphans. They closed with the hope that "from all of these things the most efficacious and best method for promoting the salvation of the blacks... might be arrived at in the provincial councils."[25]

The bishops did not bring credit to themselves in their failure to work for a unified and practical way to meet the crisis caused by the emancipation of the slaves. The large influx of European immigrants at this time can scarcely be sufficient reason for the lack of a national plan on behalf of the African Americans. Men like Spalding and Verot appreciated the gravity of the situation. Many of the other bishops, however, perhaps sharing too much in the resentment many felt toward the freed slaves after the Civil War, could not understand the concern for blacks.

The fact that certain bishops were suspicious of the motives of the Congregation of the Propaganda is less a statement about the independence of the nineteenth-century American bishops than it is a tribute to the Roman Curia. From this point on, the history of African American Catholics would have a new factor in the racial equation in the American church. Rome will intervene on behalf of black Americans. Like all bureaucracies, the Roman Curia had a long memory — the advantage of a rich archives. The Curia, innately conservative or cautious, like all bureaucracies, would not forget the question of a national ordinary for American black Catholics, nor would it forget the issue of pastoral care for African American Catholics. These two themes recur in different guises in the story of black Catholicism.

In the pastoral letter issued in the name of the plenary council of 1866, the bishops expressed a less than enthusiastic response to the emancipation of the slaves.

> We must all feel, beloved Brethren, that in some manner a new and most extensive field of charity and devotedness has been opened to us, by the emancipation of the immense slave population of the South. We could have wished, that in accordance with the action of the Catholic Church in past ages, in regard to the serfs of Europe, a more gradual system of emancipation could have been adopted, so that they might have been in some measure prepared to make a better use of their freedom, than they are likely to do now. Still the evils which must necessarily attend upon the sudden liberation of so large a multitude, with their peculiar dispositions and habits, only make the appeal to our Christian charity and zeal, presented by their forlorn condition, the more forcible and imperative.[26]

Unfortunately, this passage represents in an official way the feelings of the American hierarchy on the occasion of the emancipation of the slaves. The sentiments were scarcely magnanimous or generous. The allusion to medieval serfdom had no historical justification. The reference to "peculiar dispositions and habits" concealed a racial bias that was ill becoming the pastoral office. The sentiments do reveal, however, the sort of barriers that black Catholics had to face within their own church for the rest of the century.

II

Some bishops continued to work for the evangelization and ministry of the blacks in their dioceses. A bishop like Spalding went even further. While he was in Rome in 1867, Spalding sought help from the Congregation of the Propaganda in obtaining from Pope Pius IX a mandate that certain of the religious orders — notably the Jesuits, Dominicans, Redemptorists, and Vincentians — cooperate with the bishops in evangelizing African Americans in the United States. The Congregation accepted the idea that the pope should send a letter to the American bishops on this matter. It seems, however, that such a letter was never sent, nor was any pressure brought to bear on the religious orders.[27]

Archbishop Spalding called a provincial council of his suffragan bishops in 1868. This was the Tenth Provincial Council of Baltimore, which met the last week of April 1869. In keeping with his deep concern for blacks, Spalding included the question of the African American apostolate in the topics for discussion. One of the recommendations made was the establishment of separate churches for blacks. Moreover, it was urged that missions be held for the black Catholic people, that special instructions be organized for them, and that separate parish organizations and confraternities be organized. Finally, there was the suggestion that richer dioceses should take up special collections to further the African American apostolate in the poorer dioceses of the province.[28]

Augustin Verot, the bishop of St. Augustine, took his responsibility for the blacks in his diocese very seriously. In 1865 he visited Le Puy, which was his birthplace, and persuaded the superior of the Sisters of St. Joseph at the motherhouse in that city to send eight volunteers to work among the blacks in the city of St. Augustine. They arrived in 1866. The next year they had opened a school for black children.[29]

In Savannah Bishop William Gross, C.SS.R., brought two Bene-

dictine monks to his diocese in 1874. The year before he had succeeded Bishop Ignatius Persico as the ordinary of the diocese.[30] Gross
was seriously interested in the religious welfare of the blacks in his
diocese. He had contacted the abbot-general of the Congregation of
the Primitive Observance (commonly known as the Congregation of
Subiaco) for monks to work among the blacks. Abbot Raphael Testa,
O.S.B., the abbot-general, sent Father Raphael Wissel of the abbey
of Subiaco in Italy and Father Gabriel Bergier, O.S.B., of the abbey
of La Pierre-qui-Vire in France. They established a black parish in
Savannah, but their hope was to establish a monastery that would be
a center of evangelization of the African Americans. Father Gabriel
decided to establish his monastery at the Isle of Hope, a small spit of
land on the coast some six miles from Savannah. The community had
to struggle against many odds, not the least of which was an epidemic
of yellow fever. In the fall of 1876, the superior, Father Gabriel, and
three other members of the community succumbed to the disease.
Father Raphael Wissel left Savannah and went to Oklahoma.[31]

Abbot Boniface Wimmer of St. Vincent Abbey in Latrobe, Pennsylvania, sent two monks to Savannah the following year to establish
a school at the request of Bishop Gross.[32] It was hoped that eventually
a monastery of African American monks could be established. The
two monks of St. Vincent, Father Oswald Moosmueller and Father
Maurice Kaeder, decided against occupying the original monastery
on the Isle of Hope. Instead they established a school on Skidaway
Island, which was close by, on land given them by the bishop. In the
end Father Maurice was engaged in work elsewhere, and the task of
building and organization was left to Father Oswald.

The plan was to have a farm that would make the foundation self-
sufficient and to open a school for the black youths in the area. It
was to be an industrial school, where agriculture and the manual arts
would be taught. By 1878 a school had been opened, but the local
black community, which for the most part was Protestant, was not
so much in favor of an industrial school as of a regular school that
might prepare the youths for a professional career. At that time the
monastic community had seven members, including two blacks —
Siricius Palmer, a cleric, who was from Skidaway Island, and Brother
Rhaban Canonge, a monk of St. Vincent's, who was originally from
New Orleans. With the arrival of two more monks from St. Vincent,
the number rose to nine. At first the school seemed to be a success,
but the regime imposed upon the students was more monastic than
scholastic. A public school was established on the island, and Frater
Siricius became a teacher. Unfortunately, Frater Siricius did not per-

severe in the monastic life and was dispensed from his simple vows in 1882. Other monks came from St. Vincent's Abbey. Father Oswald became pastor of Sacred Heart Parish in Savannah, and it was here that Father Oswald came into contact with Mathilda Beasley.

By 1887 the monastery on Skidaway Island had been transferred to the jurisdiction of Belmont Abbey in North Carolina. It was the decision of Abbot Leo Haid of Belmont to close the monastery and the school after more than a decade of existence. The parish on the Isle of Hope was also abandoned for a while, although later the Benedictines returned.[33] Father Oswald went to Illinois in 1892, where he established another monastic community, which was named Cluny. In 1903 this community was moved to Saskatchewan in Canada, where it now exists as St. Peter's Abbey. Among the monks that accompanied Father Oswald to his new foundation in Wetaug, Illinois, was an African American, Brother Rhaban Canonge from New Orleans. When the community moved to Saskatchewan, Brother Rhaban was one of the founding members. He acted as cook for the monastic community until his death in 1920.[34]

Another black brother who was a monk for a time on Skidaway Island was Arthur Mason, who probably came there as Brother Albert in 1878. He left Skidaway in 1881 and apparently reentered St. Vincent's Abbey in that same year but did not persevere. He later took part in the first black Catholic lay congress in 1889 in Washington, D.C.[35] It is regrettable that the Benedictines were unsuccessful in their attempt to establish a monastery on Skidaway Island. It may be, as one historian has suggested, that little attempt was made to adapt the monastic life and the school to the culture and the needs of the African American community.[36] It may be also that patience was lacking. The presence of African American vocations suggests that in time a stable community would have developed.

An interesting sidelight to the failed venture of the Benedictines on Skidaway Island was the community of Poor Clare nuns that came to the island under Bishop Gross in 1885 just shortly before his transfer to the see of Oregon City. The community was composed of four nuns. The abbess, or superior, was Mother Dominic O'Neill, a professed nun from the Poor Clare convent in York, England. The other members of the community were seemingly not regularly professed.[37] From all indications this was not a regularly constituted community of cloistered Poor Clare nuns. In fact, it was understood that they were to organize a school for African American girls on the island along with an orphanage. The nuns, it seems, did not enjoy a good reputation. This was partly because of the unconventional way that they raised much-needed funds: they resorted to using a rowboat to visit the ships in the harbor to beg for money from the sailors. They also solicited funds in the taverns on the waterfront.[38] Thomas Becker, who succeeded Bishop Gross as bishop of Savannah in 1886, was particularly annoyed by the nuns, and in 1887 he dismissed them.[39] The nuns left, but they appealed to the Congregation of the Propaganda for compensation from the diocese. Cardinal Simeoni, prefect of the Congregation, sought the aid of Cardinal Gibbons to ascertain the validity of the sisters' claims. In a letter to Gibbons, Bishop Becker pointed out that the nuns not only had no claim for compensation but that they left owing a great deal of money to creditors.[40]

III

In 1871 the first four members of a missionary society in England arrived in Baltimore. They had come to do missionary work among the African Americans. Archbishop Spalding was delighted at their arrival. He had always been convinced that only a missionary congregation from Europe would be able to undertake the monumental task of the evangelization of black America. Unfortunately, Spalding died February 7, 1872.

The missionaries belonged to a newly founded group established by Herbert Vaughan (1832–1903) in 1866 on property he acquired just outside of London in a locality named Mill Hill. Vaughan was from an old English family that was traditionally Catholic and Royalist. Six of the eight sons in the family became priests, three of them bishops, and the five daughters all became nuns. His uncle William Vaughan (d. 1903) had been the Catholic bishop of Plymouth. Herbert Vaughan's vision of missionary labor was mingled with a vision of Great Britain as a worldwide empire. He wished for a Catholic missionary presence in this period of England's expansion, and his thoughts turned especially toward Africa. In 1871 Herbert Vaughan, seeking a field of missionary labor, was contacted by Michael O'Connor, S.J., who was on a visit to England. O'Connor arranged for the first group of Mill Hill Fathers to come to Baltimore and to accept St. Francis Xavier Parish.

The young society in America had a difficult beginning, first, because the one bishop who badly wanted them, Spalding, died before they could become solidly established. The second reason for their precarious beginnings was the fact that Herbert Vaughan, who was cold and aloof in manner, was physically removed from the day-today governing of the society, as he was made bishop of Salford in 1872, then archbishop of Westminster in 1892, and cardinal a year later, all the while retaining his position of superior general of Mill Hill.[41]

In 1875 Bishop Vaughan and an Anglo-Belgian, Canon Peter Benoit, who acted as superior of the society for Vaughan, came to Baltimore for the first general chapter of the society. After the meeting in Baltimore, Vaughan returned to England; Canon Benoit, however, who by this time had resigned his prebend in the cathedral chapter of Salford and had become a member of the society, stayed in America and made an extensive tour throughout the South to examine the situation of the African American population and the possibilities of evangelization. He was also to collect money for the work of the society. Benoit wrote down his observations in a lengthy journal so as to be able to make a detailed report to Bishop Vaughan. The journal is important because Benoit recorded the attitudes and mentality of the Catholic clergy of the time regarding black people and the prospect of their evangelization. At the same time some of the bias of Benoit himself is apparent.

Benoit was impressed by the black community at St. Francis Xavier Church in Baltimore, which the Jesuits after much discussion had turned over to the Mill Hill Fathers. In his journey to Washington, D.C., he noted that black Catholics occupied the gallery at St. Matthew's Church, not far from the White House. He noted the presence of two Italian priests, Father Barotti and Father San Martino, at Blessed Martin de Porres Chapel, which would later become the parish of St. Augustine, a church that was in the process of construction with money that had been partly raised with help from President Lincoln, who authorized the parishioners to hold a tea on the White House lawn.[42] While in Washington, Benoit visited the president of Georgetown University, Father Patrick Healy, S.J. Benoit made no mention of the fact that Healy was black. As will be pointed out in chapter 6, this fact was apparently not well known.

Benoit often noted the climate of racial prejudice as he traveled. In Washington, D.C., he observed that the "antipathy against the Negro is here what we found it in Baltimore." He was told by a priest that local feeling was so intense that the priest would not be able to sit beside a black person.[43] The riverboat captain on the Mississippi expressed this antipathy to Benoit as he was traveling from New Orleans to Natchez. When Benoit told him that he was in the States "to see the condition of the Negro with a view of working for him," the captain, a Kentuckian in his fifties, replied:

Your object is a most useless one, it is a sheer loss of time and money to attempt anything for the negro. I know him well, having been brought up among the blacks and even I like him: for he is simple and docile. But as for doing anything to raise him above what he is now, [it] is lost labor. God Almighty has made him what he is and you cannot change God's work. He has scarcely any brains, he is a thief, a liar and not virtuous, if left to himself he would go back to the most loathsome fetichism; he ought to have remained in Africa; he cannot compete with the white man and he will die out in time.[44]

Opposition to the evangelization of blacks on the part of the hierarchy was rarely openly expressed. It was usually couched in terms suggesting the uselessness of evangelizing the African American. Benoit wrote regarding the archbishop of Baltimore, James Roosevelt Bayley,[45] "that he had but little hope of any substantial good being done among the negroes in America, that you had to cut the head off first of those whom you wished to instruct: that the antipathy was ineradicable."[46]

James Gibbons, the future cardinal archbishop of Baltimore, whom Benoit met when he was bishop of Richmond, was open to the idea of the Mill Hill priests working among the blacks in his diocese. He showed Benoit land that he would give for an African American mission. Benoit had learned from the Little Sisters of the Poor that they would be "much pleased . . . to have to wait on old negro people." He urged Gibbons to open a wing of the Little Sisters' home for blacks. Gibbons also hoped to have sisters sent who would open a school for black children.[47]

Under Bishop Lynch,[48] Charleston had a Catholic church for blacks, St. Peter's, about which more will be said later. Lynch was interested in African American evangelization. He was more sanguine than others regarding the conversion of blacks to Catholicism. He told Benoit that Catholics would be more successful than the Methodists, "for though we have not the bellowing of the camp-meeters, we have . . . our beautiful ceremonial and Religious processions." On the other hand, reported Benoit, Lynch resented the efforts of Reconstruction; he felt "bitterly the humiliation of being ruled now by the negro and ruled so badly."[49]

Throughout his account, Benoit seemingly reflected the common attitude of his hosts to the political and social situation in the country after the Civil War. He seems more and more to have willingly adopted the viewpoint of the former slaveholders. His observations were not always flattering to the people for whom he was raising money, the African Americans themselves.

> The Negroes...were at their emancipation like a boy of nine who is told that he may do as he likes. The Carpet-baggers and the "hollerin" religious sects got hold of them. They are naturally peaceful but lazy. They look on labor as a curse and they rendered the curse as soft as possible by not working. Their laziness is the cause of their begging much less than the Irish. The men are barbers, waiters and many, I notice are labourers; the women are washerwomen, servants and nurses.[50]

In Georgia he noted that "the negro here retains the same respect for the whites as before and is not stuck-up, as many are in S. Carolina."[51] At the same time Benoit could not refrain from an example of jokes about blacks. "Poor darkie's simplicity is often a subject of jokes...A negro went to a clothier and said to him: Cannot I buy a pair of pants here now that we have the "swivel" (civil) rights bill?"[52] In Philadelphia, on the other hand, Benoit had a different judgment of blacks. "The Negro has 400 votes in Philadelphia. There are some Catholics among them. But the greater number have fallen away. The other are a noisy, stealing, lecherous set."[53]

Bishop Gross of Savannah welcomed the work of the Mill Hill Fathers. Quinlan in Mobile lectured Benoit on the Creole population.

> In Mobile a Creole means generally a Negro who was emancipated at the cession of Florida to the United States...These Creoles, as they are called at Mobile,...consider themselves much higher than the negro who has been a slave till the late war; and they have as great an antipathy against these than the Whites have. Hence an endless difficulty in church accommodation. They are not permitted to mix with the Whites and they won't mix with the recently emancipated slaves.[54]

From this comment Benoit concluded that the Mill Hill Society might not have a place in Mobile.

Polarization between whites and blacks was most intense in Louisiana. Benoit was instructed by one of the Redemptorists about the workings of slavery in Louisiana: "It was no wonder that the negroes grew up without any sense of morality. For among the non-Catholic Masters the virtue of a slave girl was ever at the mercy of her Master." And it was not any different with those who were Catholic. "Both

Catholic and acatholic Masters took care that their slaves received no education." The Catholics ignored any religious education for their slaves.[55]

Archbishop Perché of New Orleans gave little encouragement to Benoit. The latter was told that the diocesan clergy provided for the needs of black Catholics. Perhaps among the English-speaking population of blacks something could be done. Perché, however, precluded any immediate work by the Mill Hill Fathers because of his impending trip to Europe, which was in fact a begging tour. The archdiocese was in serious financial difficulties. Benoit described the situation as he saw it.

> The position of the negro here and that of the clergy towards him differs materially from that of most cities. In the French or old part of the city the negroes are in a great measure Catholics; they occupy pews on one of the aisles and the poorer ones kneel on the altar-steps; they are quite satisfied with their position. The French clergy would not like to have them withdrawn from their churches, because they are their chief support. The Creoles or real French are, I am sorry to say, as stingy here as in their own country...The negroes in the English portion of New Orleans are pretty much in the condition as they are in other cities. The best go to church. The nominal ones don't go...Hence the anxiety of the [Redemptorist] Fathers that we should come. They have a Negro school and they will gladly hand it over to us.[56]

At Natchez Bishop Elder was very anxious to do something for the evangelization of the freed slaves. Benoit visited the Catholic school for black children. There was one teacher for sixty children, twenty of whom were Catholic. The Catholic school was practically the only opportunity for schooling among the black children, since the black public school was open only four months of the year. Benoit noted that the history and geography lesson showed "that the colored children have as good a memory as the whites." He went on to add that "all agree...that colored children learn every thing as sharp as the white, but stop at a certain point, as their intellect is unmistakably inferior."[57]

This notion that the intellectual activity of black boys and girls simply closed down at the beginning of puberty was a commonly held theory accepted at the time. A professor of natural sciences at Harvard University wrote some nine years after Benoit's visit:

The passage from childhood to adult age brings in the negro a more marked and important change in the tone of the mind than it does in the white. In youth the black children are surprisingly quick, — their quickness can be appreciated only by those who have taught them; but in the pure blacks, with the maturing of the body the animal nature generally settles down like a cloud on that promise.[58]

This climate of public opinion that placed African Americans in a subordinate position in society because of their purported inherent inferiority would affect the work of evangelization. It would affect not only the perception of those who did the evangelizing but the public's attitude toward them. The Josephites and others would share the stigma attached to the black population in America.

In Little Rock, Bishop Fitzgerald encouraged the work of Mill Hill and was interested in giving them an entire strip of territory to evangelize.[59] In St. Louis Benoit had a different reception. Although Benoit did not mention the archbishop, Peter Richard Kenrick was not favorably disposed to the work of the Mill Hill Fathers. When Vaughan had visited St. Louis in 1872, Kenrick was pessimistic about the evangelization of African Americans and refused permission to collect money for the work.[60] On the whole it seemed that Kenrick was scarcely more than indifferent if not hostile to the black population. Despite this attitude, however, Kenrick permitted Father Ignatius Panken, S.J., to establish a church, St. Elizabeth's, as a parish for the black population of St. Louis. For a long period Father Panken served the black Catholics of the entire city and helped preserve the faith within that community. Father Benoit expressed regret at not being able to meet Panken and to obtain from him solid advice regarding the ministry to blacks.[61]

In Louisville the Mill Hill Fathers already had a black parish, St. Augustine's, which had been opened in 1870 through the efforts of John Lancaster Spalding, nephew of Archbishop Spalding and a future bishop himself. He served as secretary to Bishop McCloskey and took upon himself the task of opening a church for the black Catholics.[62] The younger Spalding did not stay very long as pastor of a black parish. By 1872 he had a leave of absence from Louisville to devote himself to writing the life of his uncle.[63]

Benoit met John Lancaster Spalding in New York at the end of his tour. Spalding was rather critical of the idea of an English society coming to the United States to work for the black community. He stated that Bishop Vaughan had "displeased many by running counter to the commonly received notions of social propriety by mixing familiarly with the negroes."[64] Spalding expressed the opinion that the African American would die out in the North and be found eventually only in the South.[65]

In Cincinnati Benoit visited the black parish of St. Ann, which the Jesuits had established at the request of black Catholics, who were not readily welcomed in the other Catholic churches in the city. In 1866 the church of St. Ann along with a school was opened for black Catholics in a building that had formerly been a public school. The money for the renovation had been raised in large part through the efforts of Father Francis Xavier Weninger, S.J., who obtained a personal donation of four thousand dollars from King Ludwig I of Bavaria through the Ludwig-Missionsverein. Other leading Catholics in Cincinnati donated funds. The efforts had the full support of Archbishop Purcell, who in 1868 made a contribution of one hundred dollars to the ongoing campaign organized by Father Weninger to keep the school in operation. Weninger, a famous preacher, moved from an interest in St. Ann and the black Catholics of Cincinnati to an interest in raising money on the national level for the cause of ministry to all blacks. He wanted to institute a national collection for the Indians and African Americans, and he received papal encouragement when Leo XIII granted a plenary indulgence to everyone who would contribute to a collection for Indians and blacks. In the end, the Third Plenary Council of Baltimore finally institutionalized this special collection.[66]

Father Benoit's trip took him through Detroit and Niagara Falls to New York City. He returned to England on May 29, 1875. He had been given the opportunity to see how much labor there was for the evangelization of the African American. The Mill Hill Fathers in America eventually separated from the English body under Cardinal Vaughan in 1893. It was particularly the first superior general, John R. Slattery, who set the American branch — the Society of St. Joseph of the Sacred Heart, or Josephites — firmly on its feet as an instrument of evangelization for African Americans. Slattery's work and the ministry of the Josephites will be discussed further below.

The Congregation of the Holy Ghost, or the Spiritans, had been originally founded for missionary work in Africa.[67] They too came officially to the United States in 1872 to Covington, Kentucky. Unfortunately, the first group could not stay in Kentucky but moved to Ohio. Later they set up their headquarters in Pittsburgh. The first opportunity to carry out the mission to African Americans came as early as 1878 in Arkansas, where Bishop Fitzgerald was willing to give them a parish and a whole territory where the black population was numerous. The superior, Joseph Strub, and his council were agreeable, recognizing that "the Congregation's primary purpose is the evangelization of the black race." They also noted that in the United States "almost nothing had been done so far by Catholic missionaries."[68]

The Holy Ghost Fathers envisioned the Arkansas mission as the starting point for what was to be an extensive Southern ministry. The proposed German parish in Little Rock, which was to be the financial base for their mission activity, did not materialize. Strub, however, had acquired over 312 square miles from the Little Rock and Fort Smith Railroad on which immigrants from Europe, especially Germans, were to settle. When it seemed unlikely that they would be able to have a black parish in Little Rock, Strub did accept the arrival of twenty black farmers in the colony near Conway and Morrilton. He also accepted black orphan boys in the orphanage run by the Spiritan Brothers. In 1879 they had received three young black men as postulants for the brotherhood. Michael McKnight of Memphis seemed not to have persevered. The second and third, a Brother Columbus from Louisiana and a George Henry from Natchez, remained with the brothers until the late 1880s. The Sisters of St. Joseph of Cluny opened a school a second time for black children in Conway in 1884, and a school for blacks and whites was opened in Morrilton in 1883 that lasted until 1898.[69]

IV

In the eighteen years since the Second Plenary Council, not a great deal was accomplished to encourage the evangelization of American blacks. There were many reasons, including a lack of personnel and a shortage of financial resources. Francis Xavier Weninger showed that it was possible to cover the financial aspect with planning and organization. The groundwork for this organization was the result of the Third Plenary Council of Baltimore in 1884.

The initiative for the Third Plenary Council came from Rome, not from the United States. The discussion regarding ministry to African Americans also came from the Curia and not from the American bishops as a whole. In the spring of 1883, Cardinal Simeoni, the prefect of Propaganda, invited the archbishops of the United States to a meeting in Rome in November of that year. Cardinal Franzelin, S.J. (1816–88), the noted theologian and member of the Congregation of the Propaganda, drew up a list of twelve subjects related to the United States that merited particular study. On the list was the "conversion of the Negroes." He gave a summary of the situation of the newly freed population. Reference was made to the instruction of Propaganda following the last plenary council. The arrival of the Mill Hill missionaries was also noted. Most important, he observed that little had been done.[70] It was in this report that the question of a special nationwide collection each year was first broached.

The metropolitans (at that time only the archbishops met annually) had their meeting for a month at the end of 1883. Among the items discussed was the question of an annual collection for African Americans to be taken up in all of the dioceses. At that meeting the decision was to take up the collection in the name of the Society for the Propagation of the Faith, but to inform the faithful that the money was destined for the black apostolate.[71]

The Third Plenary Council opened on November 9, 1884, and it closed on December 7, 1884. After much discussion the council decided that one collection would be taken up in all dioceses on the first Sunday of Lent for Indians and Negroes, the money to be sent to a special commission composed of the archbishop of Baltimore and two bishops who were to be appointed. Working with them was to be a priest-secretary, preferably a Sulpician.[72]

The council urged that seminary officials inspire the seminarians to work among African Americans. Religious orders were also urged to send missionaries for this work. The bishops advocated forming catechists, laypersons of both sexes, who would spread the gospel, "whereby the hard labor of the priest might bring forth richer fruit." Those bishops who would be recipients of financial aid for the missions among the Indians and the blacks were to make known to the commission the number of Indians and blacks in their respective dioceses, their spiritual condition, and any other pertinent information that would aid the commission in allocating funds.[73]

The sessions of the plenary council were closed to the public. In the evening, however, special services were held for the laypeople, at which sermons were given by various bishops. Archbishop Gibbons asked Bishop Gross of Savannah to speak on "The Missions for the Colored People."[74] The sermon was not long, but it was of sufficient length to insult enough people. Bishop Gross had taken a sincere interest in the spiritual well-being of the black members of his flock in Georgia. There is no reason to doubt his sincerity; but as was the case with so many of the Catholic clergy at that period, there was little respect for people of African descent, either for their history or for their humanity. The bishop stated, "We know the history of this people. In their native country, Africa, they were sunken from time immemorial in barbarism; and their religion, Fetichism, was the most depraved that the world has ever known."[75]

In an age that lacked any ecumenical openness, his attack on the black Protestant ministers was most unfortunate. "We know as a fact that at present the colored people know very little if anything of these great truths of holy faith, whence all morality must grow. As a general thing, their ministers are poor colored men, the vast majority of them uneducated, and they only make a travesty of religion — 'the blind leading the blind.'"

It must be added that the bishop did not treat whites any better: "The white ministers...are so disunited and divided on doctrines and dogma that they could not teach these fundamental truths were they to go among them...which...they do not, especially in the South."[76] This remark, no doubt made in the heat of oratory, was strange, since Catholic bishops had been lamenting the fact that the Protestant clergy were making inroads among the freed slaves. It was common knowledge, moreover, that the Protestants from the North were the ones who came south and opened schools on all levels for the education of the black population. Gross also made the usual remarks about the morality of the black population. "Man has a fallen nature, and it is not necessary for me to state that the poor colored people do not stand very high in the scale of morality."[77]

The one positive remark about African Americans that the bishop did make was a tribute to the Oblate Sisters of Providence and their work.

That the Catholic church can elevate the colored women is evidenced by the fact, that here in Baltimore, exists this wonderful institution of the Oblate Sisters of Providence, a colored convent where women make vows of perpetual virginity and rival their white sisters by going among their race to educate the young, to take in the poor little orphan and help the sick and dying.[78]

It is interesting to contrast this negative picture of the African American people and their religion with the very positive picture of the Native Americans in the sermon preached by Archbishop Seghers of Oregon City.[79] Gross would succeed Seghers in Oregon City the following year.

One is not surprised that the sermon was offensive to many African American Protestant ministers. As one clergyman pointed out, "[Gross] is connected with a church which for years before and since the war has failed to raise one hand to relieve the Negro of his ante-bellum embarrassments and his post-bellum afflictions."[80] In fact, the remarks of Gross caused a protest meeting of black ministers to be held in which the Catholic church came under sharp attack.

In the aftermath of the Third Plenary Council, one endeavor by a leading Catholic laywoman is worth special mention. Katherine Drexel, who was beatified in the fall of 1988, was a wealthy Philadelphia heiress who used her wealth to further evangelization among blacks and Native Americans. She was born in Philadelphia in 1858 into a banking family of Austrian and German origin.[81] Her father was Francis Anthony Drexel, and her mother was Hannah Langstroth. It was her paternal grandfather who had come from the Austrian Tyrol. He was first of all a painter and then became a banker, a very successful one, leaving a thriving business to his son. Katherine, one of three daughters, grew up in a comfortable home. In 1885 her father died leaving $14 million in trust to her and to her sisters, from which they would receive an annual income.[82] Almost immediately the three sisters became benefactors of many causes. Her younger sister, Louise Drexel Morrell, was especially interested in the needs of African Americans. She and her husband, Colonel Edward Morrell, continued their contributions to black Catholic causes until Louise Morrell died in 1943.

Katherine's interest first lay with the Native Americans. Almost from the time that the newspapers published accounts of the Drexel sisters' inheritance, requests for donations poured in. Katherine was contacted by two of the best-known Indian missionaries of the time, Bishop Martin Marty, O.S.B., vicar apostolic of the Dakota Territory, and Msgr. Joseph Stephan, who was to become director of the Catholic Bureau of Indian Missions.[83] Blessed Katherine Drexel would serve as benefactor of Native Americans for the rest of her life.

In January of 1887 Katherine had a private audience with Pope Leo XIII. At that time she had, it seems, a sudden inspiration to beg the pope to send priests to the Indian territory. The pope looked at her and asked her why she did not become a missionary.[84] The answer to this question finally came some two years later when, at the urging of her spiritual director, James O'Connor, bishop of Omaha,[85] she decided to begin a community of sisters whose mission would be service to both the Indians and African Americans. In 1889 she entered the novitiate of the Sisters of Mercy in Pittsburgh with the understanding that the novitiate was for her profession in a newly established religious community. Before her novitiate was ended, her friend and spiritual director, Bishop O'Connor, was dead.

It was Archbishop Ryan of Philadelphia who took over as guide and counselor for the young heiress. On February 12, 1891, in the chapel of the Mercy Sisters in Pittsburgh, Blessed Katherine Drexel made her profession as the first member of the Sisters of the Blessed Sacrament for Indians and Colored People.[86] By July 16, 1891, ten sisters were professed. The motherhouse was erected at Torresdale, Pennsylvania, the site of her parents' summer home. Blessed Katherine played a most important role in the church's institutional relationship with the black community. Both with personnel and with funds, she helped shape black Catholic America.

The history of the Catholic church's efforts to evangelize the black people of the United States in the period following the Civil War is not a very glorious one. One might note that the ethnic group that she had known the longest in this country, aside from the Indians, longer than any of the more recent immigrant groups in this country, was the group that she treated as stepchildren, the last considered and the first to be jettisoned when funds and personnel were scarce.

Still there were individuals like Cardinal Vaughan, Katherine Drexel, and also Archbishop Spalding and Bishop Verot who never dismissed black men and women in the United States as pathetic creatures without honor, without respect, and without resolve. Catholicism is the history of a people, and neither prelates nor priests nor councils tell the whole story.

Mother Mary Elizabeth Lange, founder of the Oblate Sisters of Providence. Courtesy of Josephite Archives.

The grave of Jean-Baptiste Pointe du Sable, trapper, trader, French-speaking black man, buried in St. Charles Cemetery, St. Charles, Missouri. Courtesy of Olmsted Family.

Page from the Baptismal Register for Blacks. Volume I. 1784–1793. St. Augustine in Florida. Courtesy of the Archives of the diocese of St. Augustine.

Mathilda Beasley as a young women.
Courtesy of the Georgia Historical
Society.

Augustus Tolton as a young seminarian.
Courtesy of A. Rankin.

LEFT: Daniel Rudd in 1889 at the age of thirty-five.
RIGHT: Frederica Law of Savannah, who became a novice as Sister Benedicta of the Angels in the Missionary Franciscan Sisters of the Immaculate Conception. She died in Rome in 1883. Courtesy of Frederick Foster.

Frontpage of *American Catholic Tribune*, black Catholic weekly newspaper published by Daniel Rudd. Courtesy of the Archdiocese of Philadelphia Archives and Historical Collections, Overbrook, Pennsylvania.

LEFT: William Henry Smith of Washington, D.C., librarian of the House of Representatives Library and leading member of the black Catholic lay congresses, shortly before his death in 1903. Courtesy: Archibald Grimké Papers, Moorland-Spingarn Research Center, Howard University.

RIGHT: Charles Butler of Washington, D.C., leading member of the black Catholic lay congresses. Courtesy of Charles B. Cobbs.

LEFT: William S. Lofton, dentist in Washington, D.C., important member of the black Catholic lay congresses. Courtesy: Archibald Grimké Papers, Moorland-Spingarn Research Center, Howard University.

RIGHT: Fredrick McGhee, prominent Minnesota attorney and important leader in the black Catholic lay congresses about the age of forty. Courtesy of Minnesota Historical Society.

Left to right: Father John Dorsey, S.S.J., Father Charles Uncles, S.S.J., and Father Joseph John, S.A.M., before St. Augustine's Church in Washington, D.C., in the early 1920s. Courtesy of Josephite Archives.

Brother Albert Mason, O.S.B., for a time a monk on Skidaway Island near Savannah, Georgia, about 1880. Courtesy of St. Vincent Archives.

LEFT: Father William Markoe, S.J. Courtesy of Jesuit Archives, Department of Special Collections and University Archives, Marquette University.

RIGHT: Father John Albert, S.S.J. Courtesy of Josephite Archives.

Doctor Lena Edwards wearing the Medal of Freedom conferred by President Lyndon Johnson in 1964. Courtesy: Lena Edwards Collection, Moorland-Spingarn Research Center, Howard University.

Chapter 6

SHEPHERDS WITH BLACK SKINS: THE FIRST AFRICAN AMERICAN CATHOLIC PRIESTS

Pope Gregory XV (reigned 1621–23) created the Congregation for the Propagation of the Faith in January 1622. His successor, Pope Urban VIII (1623–44), established a seminary in 1627 under the direction of the Congregation, for the training of missionaries, that still bears his name — the Urban College.[1] The Congregation of the Propaganda owed its origin to the need for the Holy See to take the initiative in the missionary activity opened up by the explorations of the European countries at the beginning of the sixteenth century. Up to the seventeenth century the colonial nations like Spain and Portugal had taken charge of the missionary enterprise in their respective colonies and trading centers. This resulted in the church's granting the kings of Spain and Portugal the right to name candidates to all ecclesiastical offices in the new territories and to tailor church policies and methods of evangelization to the political needs of the respective states. As a result, evangelization became subordinate to the good of the state. From this point of view, it would be perfectly normal for the Council of the Indies in Spain to decide that no nonwhites should be ordained to the priesthood or admitted to religious life. This system was the *patronado*, or "the right of patronage," granted to the respective sovereigns by the popes.[2]

The Congregation for the Propagation of the Faith, known at the time as the Propaganda,[3] became from the beginning a center of innovation in the formulation of church policy in the missions. It is not surprising, then, that among the directions adopted from its inception by Francisco Ingoli, one principle remained constant in the mind of the Roman officials: the importance of establishing a native priesthood.[4] As a result in the modern period the ordination of Africans to the priesthood took place as early as the eighteenth century, and even earlier in the case of the son of Afonso the Good.[5]

In the United States, however, the notion of an indigenous African American clergy was generally unacceptable. When it was a question of blacks, the American hierarchy in the nineteenth century and even in the early part of the twentieth century did not share the views of the Congregation of the Propaganda on the importance of people having priests from their own ethnic background. Even before the Civil War, however, black Catholic men were ready to step forward to become priests. The story of their courage and persistence is a glorious and sometimes tragic page in the history of American Catholicism.

I

The first three black priests in the United States were three brothers, all of whom were born slaves to Michael Morris Healy, an Irishman. Healy came to the backwoods of Georgia about 1816. He had been born in County Roscommon in Ireland about 1796, had served in the British army during the War of 1812, and had joined a distant cousin in Georgia a few years later. Eventually, Michael Healy purchased almost four hundred acres of land a few miles to the north of Macon in central Georgia. With the help of slaves, he cleared the land and erected the buildings necessary for a plantation. By 1831 he had become a wealthy man with sixteen hundred acres of land and seventeen slaves. In 1829 he chose a light-skinned slave woman named Mary Eliza as his mistress. It was illegal for Healy to have married a woman who had become his slave, and it was likewise impossible for the church to bless such a marriage. Whether he considered her his wife is not known. It seems clear that theirs was a monogamous relationship and that she and Healy had ten children, all of whom, of course, were slaves.[6] Three of Michael Morris Healy's first four sons became the first African American Catholic priests in the United States. The eldest was James Augustine Healy, born in April 1830. The second was Hugh, tragically dead by his early twenties, born in 1832. Patrick Francis Healy, who became a Jesuit, was born in February 1834, and Alexander Sherwood Healy, born in 1836, became, as James did, a priest of the archdiocese of Boston.

Michael Healy did not rear his children as slaves, but it was practically impossible for him to make them legally free without action by the state legislature. It seems to have been his decision to send them to the North not only for an education but also to find the freedom that was denied them at home. In 1837 he took James Augustine north and enrolled him in Quaker schools, first on Long Island, and then in New Jersey. In subsequent years his three younger brothers followed him to the school on Long Island. All four brothers had been removed from their home and family before they were ten years old.[7]

Religion seems not to have been important in the life of Michael Morris Healy. There is no record of his children being baptized as infants. It was his friendship with the bishop of Boston, John Fitzpatrick, that changed the life of his sons. Michael Healy met John Fitzpatrick in 1844, when the latter was coadjutor bishop of Boston. Fitzpatrick persuaded Healy to send his four sons to study at the newly founded Holy Cross College in Worcester, Massachusetts. He also urged him to send his daughter, Martha Ann, to live in Boston, where she boarded with one of the bishop's relatives. As a result the four boys were enrolled in the Jesuit school in the summer of 1844, and in November of that year, the four were finally baptized. They found a home at Holy Cross, something they had not known since leaving Georgia. Except for Hugh, they were not to return when it was time to settle their father's estate.

James Augustine Healy entered the seminary in Montreal in the fall of 1849. His mother, Mary Eliza, died suddenly in May 1850, followed by the death of his father in August. This created a serious problem for the young seminarian. It was questionable whether the will would be followed, and whether the state would discover the slave status of the children, thereby hindering their inheritance of the property and its final disposition. Finally, the will was probated, and the property sold. Hugh, the second brother, risked his own safety to return to Georgia and bring back the three youngest children to live in New York. With the sale of the property the Healy children were assured of enough money to live on. After the slaves on the plantation had been hired out in accordance with the will, the proceeds were applied to the education of the Healy children.[8] In 1855 the fifty-seven slaves of the Healy estate were sold. It would not have been possible to free them because of the laws then in force, but it is an irony of history that the first black bishop in the United States and his brothers and sisters, themselves all of slave origin, had profited from the labor of slaves.[9]

After ordination to the subdiaconate in 1852, James transferred from the seminary in Montreal to the Sulpician Seminary at Issy-les-Molineaux outside of Paris. Before setting sail for Europe, James arranged that his brother Michael and his three sisters would attend school in Canada. There one of his sisters, Martha, became a member of the Congregation of Notre Dame of Montreal. Later she would be dispensed from her vows and return to Boston, where in time she married. His other two sisters, Josephine and Eliza, both became nuns in Montreal, the former becoming a member of a nursing order, the Religious Hospitallers at the Hospital of the Hôtel-Dieu in Montreal, and the other, a sister of the Congregation of Notre Dame in Montreal.[10] Two of his brothers followed James into the priesthood. Patrick Francis Healy entered the Society of Jesus, where he made vows in 1852. His first assignment was teaching at St. Joseph's College in Philadelphia. Alexander Sherwood Healy entered the Sulpician Seminary at Paris in the fall of 1852. Hugh had seen him off in New York and then had taken a boat out into the harbor. The boat capsized, and Hugh swallowed some of the polluted water; he contracted typhoid fever and died shortly thereafter on September 17, 1852.

James Augustine Healy was ordained a priest in the Cathedral of Notre Dame on June 10, 1854. He returned to Boston and became the personal secretary of Bishop Fitzpatrick, who had been for a long time his friend and protector. Later he was named chancellor of the diocese and eventually became vicar-general.

In the meantime, Sherwood transferred from the Sulpician Seminary in Paris to Rome, where he studied at the Institute of the Apollinaris, the Faculty of Canon Law at the Lateran University. He was ordained a priest in Rome on December 15, 1858, and two years later he received a doctorate in canon law. He returned to Boston in 1860 and served for a while as chancellor while James was on an extended vacation because of ill health. Upon the return of his brother James in 1864, Sherwood was named to the faculty of the newly established provincial seminary in Troy, New York. When Bishop Fitzpatrick died in 1866, John Williams, the pastor of St. James Church in Boston, became the next bishop. Bishop Williams was especially close to Sherwood Healy and chose him as his theologian at the Second Plenary Council of Baltimore in 1866. He again chose Sherwood Healy to be his personal theologian at the First Vatican Council in Rome in 1870. After the council it was apparent that Sherwood's health was not strong enough to permit him to continue his work in the seminary. But in the five years of life left to him, Sherwood was busier than ever. He was named rector of the almost-completed new cathedral, a job that entailed exhausting fund-raising to defray the debt. He was a well-known, popular preacher and was active as a canon lawyer. In the midst of this unremitting labor and activity, his health became more and more precarious, and he died on October 21, 1875.[11]

Alexander Sherwood Healy was a remarkable man who crammed a great deal into his thirty-nine years of life. Like his brothers, he was both gifted and talented. Shortly after his ordination in 1858 the North American College was established in Rome as a seminary for American students, and the bishops had to choose a priest to act as rector for the new institution. Bishop Fitzpatrick mentioned his name in a letter to John Hughes, the archbishop of New York. After stating that he really was at a loss regarding the qualifications of the persons suggested, he proceeded to write, "There is a third man who in my opinion is admirably qualified for the office. But he is very young, just ordained, and wholly unknown to any of our prelates, except myself. That man is Alexander S. Healy, the brother of my present secretary."[12] Fitzpatrick pointed out Sherwood's intellectual qualifications, stating that "he has had the advantage of a most complete education... at St. Sulpice, Paris where he was *facile princeps* in studies." Fitzpatrick admitted, however, that "it would be useless to recommend him even were he known to the other bishops as well as to myself." The reason, of course, was the fact that Sherwood was much too young for the position, having been just ordained. Then the bishop adds: "There is also another objection which though in reason less substantial, would in fact be quite as stubborn. He has african blood and it shews distinctly in his exterior. This, in a large number of american youths might lessen the respect they ought to feel for the first superior in a house."[13]

This letter of Bishop Fitzpatrick is important for two reasons. It says something about the honesty of Fitzpatrick and the high qualities of Sherwood Healy that the bishop would consider him the best candidate he knew for what was an important ecclesiastical charge. It reveals that in the case of Sherwood and (from other sources) in the case of James, the Healy brothers were clearly seen as being black.

In 1875 James Augustine Healy was named the second bishop of Portland, Maine. The diocese covered the entire states of Maine and New Hampshire. From all reports, Healy was an exemplary bishop — hard working, industrious, and cautious. He presided over the "brick-and-mortar" stage of the diocese's growth. In 1884 the diocese of Manchester was created for the state of New Hampshire, an indication of Healy's achievement.

Healy was a short, unprepossessing man who, some felt, did not look like a bishop. Still, he was an excellent preacher: "Portland had one of the best preachers in New England during the last quarter of the nineteenth century."[14]

Healy was a cautious, careful administrator, with a reputation for close attention to details. Early in his career he had a violent altercation with an irremovable pastor, who went all the way to Rome and won his case.[15] He had a row with the superior of the Sisters of Mercy from which he did not emerge unscathed.[16]

Even before his promotion to the see of Portland, Healy had had to endure the hostility of a pastor who denounced Healy from the pulpit as one who was coming from the outside and interfering with his pastoral duties. This charge was caused by the fact that Healy, who always got along well with children, had rehearsed the catechism lessons with them on his vacation with a family in Maine. This annoyed the pastor, who proceeded to refer to Healy's "indelicate blood" in his denunciation.[17] The pastor tendered his resignation when Healy was named bishop, but Healy refused it. Apparently, the people of Healy's diocese accepted him as a black man with few if any objections. The real racial tensions were between the Irish and the French-Canadians, whose numbers increased dramatically during his tenure.[18] Another important ethnic group was the Native Americans, specifically the Abnaki, Penobscot, and Passamaquoddy tribes. There were very few blacks and even fewer Catholics. One estimate is that there were some three hundred black Catholics.[19] Bishop Healy took part in the Third Plenary Council of Baltimore in 1884. To the discussions regarding African Americans and their status and condition, he seems to have made no contribution. Still he was a member of the subcommittee on Negro and Indian Missions preliminary to the council, and he was part of the Commission on Negro and Indian Missions that the Third Plenary Council established. One cannot say whether his appointment to the commission was in virtue of his ancestry or because of the Indian Missions in his diocese.

Healy was the first black Catholic bishop in the history of the United States. He did not exploit this fact, nor did he speak out on behalf of African Americans. One might wonder why he never addressed the issue of racial inequities in this period of growing tension. In the last decade of his episcopate, black Catholics began to make their voices heard within the church. Healy, however, never accepted the invitations made by the leaders of the black Catholic congress to address their meetings or even to be present at them. On one occasion he cited Colossians 3:11 ("There cannot be Greek and Jew, circumcised and uncircumcised, barbarian, Scythian ... "). Presumably blacks must not seek special identification and recognition within the church, something that every other ethnic group passionately sought and diligently worked for in the nineteenth century.[20] Similarly, Healy seemed to discourage any identification of himself, his slave mother, or his racial background; even his younger brothers and sisters were unaware of the family's origins.[21]

The third Healy brother, Patrick Francis, also made a brilliant career in the church as a member of the Society of Jesus. After teaching both at St. Joseph College in Philadelphia and at Holy Cross College, his alma mater, Patrick was sent to Georgetown College in the District of Columbia, where he began studies in philosophy. In 1858 Patrick went to Rome to continue his studies. After a few months, for reasons of health, he transferred to the University of Louvain in Belgium. He was ordained a priest in 1864 in Liège and spent one more year at the university to receive a doctorate in philosophy.

In 1866 Patrick began teaching philosophy at Georgetown. Three years later he became vice-president of the college and, in 1873, with the sudden death of the president, Patrick Healy became vice-rector and, in 1874, president.

Healy's dream was to make Georgetown into an American version of Louvain. To this end he engaged in a fund-raising campaign for a massive central building that would house classrooms, science laboratories, dormitories, and meeting rooms. He transformed the liberal arts college into a university by increasing the departments, notably in the natural sciences. He upgraded and reorganized the medical school and the law school. The cost of the new building placed the university in debt, so Healy began an alumni organization to provide donations. Seeking funds became his major preoccupation and a major source of anxiety. As a consequence, his health suffered, and in 1882 he was forced to retire. The new building, the heart of the university, still bears his name. It is, again, one of the ironies of history that this university — which owed so much to a former slave who became known as its second founder — did not admit African American students until the middle of the twentieth century, and then only as a result of the civil rights movement. From 1882 until his death in 1910, Patrick Healy, broken in health, lived in retirement. When his brother the bishop died on August 5, 1900, Patrick was not present, although he was in Maine. He was able, however, to oversee the disposition of James Augustine Healy's papers, which were deposited in the archives of Holy Cross College. Patrick Healy died a decade later on January 10, 1910.[22]

In the history of black Catholics in the United States, the Healy brothers unquestionably take pride of place. Yet this position, in spite of everything, leaves many questions unanswered. Patrick Healy concealed his African origins for much of his career, while James and Sherwood did not. Doubtless, their origins were overlooked not because the atmosphere was one of tolerance for blacks but because the brothers were seen as exceptions; doubtless, too, it was because the brothers did not enter into solidarity with either the African American community as such or even the black Catholic community. At a time when racial bigotry was rife, when blacks were being systematically stripped of their rights, and when in the South violence against blacks was becoming normal, no word of concern, no sentiment of outrage, no reminder of justice escaped their lips. They never used their position to champion the cause of their fellow blacks. Nor did they ever give their fellow blacks the opportunity to bask in the reflected glory of their own noteworthy achievements. One may not judge the intentions and the unexpressed sentiments of another or apply the sensitivities and the awareness of a later historical period to an earlier time, yet one may still wonder how these good and upright men judged themselves in the silence of their own hearts.[23]

The biographer of James Augustine Healy, Albert Foley, investigated not only the origins of America's first black bishop but the subsequent history of their collateral descendants. Many of them were able to pass successfully into the white race. This came about, no doubt, because the details regarding the slave children of Eliza and Michael Morris Healy were never passed on to subsequent generations. It is interesting to note that the family prospered socially and economically. Michael Healy (1839–1904), the younger brother in the family and namesake of the father, joined the merchant marine and eventually became an officer in the United States Revenue Marine Service. A colorful figure, he became famous in his own right.[24]

II

The first black American priest whom all knew and recognized as black was Augustus Tolton, born a slave in Ralls County, Missouri, in 1854, the year James Augustine Healy was ordained a priest.[25] His mother, Martha Jane Chisley, had been a slave on the Manning plantation in Mead County, Kentucky. She came to Missouri in 1849 as part of the dowry when the slaveowner's daughter, Susan Manning, married Stephen Elliott, owner of a plantation in Ralls County, northeastern Missouri. In 1851 Martha Chisley married Peter Paul Tolton, a slave on the Hagar plantation adjacent to the Elliott's land.

Both Martha and Peter Paul were Catholics. Peter Paul and Martha were married before a Catholic priest in the small parish church of St. Peter's at Brush Creek, near Hannibal. They had three children; Augustus was the second child and was also baptized at St. Peter's.

In 1861, at the outbreak of the Civil War, Peter Paul Tolton escaped slavery and went to St. Louis, where he became attached to the Union army. Missouri was a slave state that did not secede from the Union; however, it was sharply divided between antislavery and proslavery factions. The latter in turn were divided between unionists and rebels. Lincoln's administration had every reason to persuade the proslavery unionists to stay within the union. Hence, nothing was to be done to belie the assurance that all property rights, including slave ownership, would be respected. As a result, the slaves feared that the loyal slaveholders might continue to hold slaves despite the war and its outcome.

In the summer of 1861, General John C. Frémont became commander of the Department of the West, with his headquarters in St. Louis. Frémont was ardently opposed to slavery. With the declaration of martial law, the slaves of pro-Confederates were confiscated and set free. Proponents of the antislavery forces were favored and encouraged by Frémont. It is probably in this historical context that Peter Paul Tolton decided to flee his owners and make his way to St. Louis. It is probably also in this context that Martha would make her courageous flight to freedom as well. The first black regiments began to be formed in Missouri in 1863. It is not certain whether Peter Paul Tolton was still alive then or whether he remained as one of the numerous refugees who had gathered around every camp of Union soldiers in the divided state of Missouri.[26]

In the midst of this uncertainty Martha Tolton decided to leave the Elliott plantation with her three children for the free state of Illinois. When she arrived at Hannibal on the Mississippi, she narrowly escaped arrest by the slave catchers through the intervention of Union soldiers. At this time the Union soldiers, contrary to military orders, took the side of the slaves and aided their escape.[27] Martha Tolton rowed across the Mississippi River to the Illinois side with her children. There she made her way to Quincy, a city at that time crowded with refugee slaves.

Martha Tolton raised her family in the midst of poverty and virulent racism. She was a fervent Catholic, so she wished to enroll her children in a Catholic school. Here she met rebuff and rejection. Not all Catholics welcomed blacks, even black Catholics, into the parochial schools. Martha Tolton was persistent, and eventually they were accepted in another Catholic school. Augustus was limited, however, in the times during which he could attend school. Poverty forced him and his sister to work in a tobacco factory during most of the year. (His elder brother died in 1863.) It is in these circumstances that the young boy first made known his desire to become a priest. It appears that his pastor at the parish where he attended school may have first broached the subject, and for Augustus it became a dream that he clung to with a passion. The two pastors in Quincy worked together to find a seminary in the United States that would accept him, but since no seminary would receive him, he had to receive private tutoring from various priests. From the spring of 1873 to the fall of 1875, the curate at St. Boniface Church in Quincy, Theodore Wegmann, taught Tolton and two German students Latin, Greek, German, English, ancient and modern European History, American history, and geography. In a letter written much later Wegmann stated that Tolton read and spoke German fluently.[28]

Finally, after another series of priest tutors, Tolton was admitted to studies in Quincy College, an institution recently founded by the Franciscans. He was registered as a special student in 1878 and probably remained so until 1880. This meant that he was the only student in the course, apparently because he had to accommodate his studies to his hours of work. During this time Tolton acted as a teacher in the Sunday school that was opened for black children in Quincy. One of the Franciscan friars, Michael Richardt, O.F.M., who taught philosophy to Tolton at Quincy College, was responsible for this mission to the blacks in the city, where Tolton became the leading worker. One of the School Sisters of Notre Dame, Sister Herlinda, became the teacher in the school, which began in the early part of 1878.

Despite the rejection, the disappointment, and the repeated refusals, Tolton persevered in the desire to become a priest, and his dream became reality in a rather dramatic way. Father Michael wrote the minister general of the Franciscan Order in Rome, Father Bernardino dal Vago da Portogruaro,[29] who was influential with the Congregation of the Propaganda. Incredibly, the former slave who had faced rejection after rejection found acceptance in the Urban College, attached to the Congregation of the Propaganda in Rome.

As mentioned earlier, the Urban College had been established to prepare young men for the work of evangelization and to promote indigenous vocations. Augustus registered in the college in March 1880, when he was twenty-five years old. At that time there were 142 students from various nations enrolled in the school. Three were Africans from Central Africa. Apparently, Tolton's stay at the Urban

College was uneventful and without problems. He was described in a letter to the bishop at the close of his academic career as "truly a man to be trusted on account of his industry and obedience." He was considered to be pious and diligent. It was noted that he "did not possess a great deal of intuition," but with adequate direction he would be able "to find his bearings." In the same letter it was also noted that since he did not have sufficient funds to make the trip back to the States, the funds were to be lent to him and the college reimbursed.[30]

The original understanding was that Tolton was not to study for the diocese of Alton (today the diocese of Springfield, Illinois) but that he was to go to Africa as a missionary. In the end this did not happen. Many years later Tolton described in a speech at the first black Catholic congress in Washington in 1889 how it was changed.

> I heard the words of St. John "prepare the ways of the Lord" and God gave me strength to persevere, for Rome had heard that no one of us could be found here to preach the Gospel. I rejoyced [*sic*] when I heard that I was [to] be sent to America. God is over us all, and he has many blessings for men of every race. When on the eve of going to St. John Lateran to be ordained, the word came expressing doubt whether I would be sent here. It was said that I would be the only priest of my race in America and would not be likely to succeed. All at once Cardinal Simoni [*sic*] said, "America has been called the most enlightened nation; we will see if it deserves that honor. If America has never seen a black priest, it has to see one now."[31]

Tolton was ordained on April 24, 1886, Holy Saturday, in the basilica of St. John Lateran in Rome. He was thirty-two years of age.

The bishop of Alton, Peter Joseph Baltes,[32] had been willing to accept Augustus Tolton into his diocese. According to a letter from Father Michael Richardt, O.F.M., to the unknown author of an article on Father Tolton that appeared in the *St. Joseph Advocate* the year after Tolton's ordination, the bishop of Alton sought to gain admittance for Tolton into the Urban College but was unsuccessful.[33] Unfortunately, Baltes died in February 1886, two months before Tolton's ordination. When the rector of the Urban College wrote the diocese of Alton, Rev. John Janssen replied as the administrator of the diocese. He informed the Congregation that Tolton "had celebrated solemn Mass before an immense multitude of people in the city of Quincy."[34]

In fact, Tolton's return to the United States from Rome was like a triumphal march. He arrived in New York on July 6, 1886, and celebrated his first Mass in the United States the next day in Hoboken, New Jersey, at St. Mary's Hospital. The next Sunday, July 11, Tolton sang his first Solemn Mass in New York City in the newly established black parish church of St. Benedict the Moor on Bleeker Street. The deacon at the Mass was the pastor of the church, Father John Burke, who would later become the first director of the Catholic Board of Negro Missions and who was an important figure in the ministry to blacks on behalf of the hierarchy. The sermon was preached by Richard Burtsell, rector of Epiphany Church.[35] St. Benedict the Moor Church was filled to capacity with black Catholics from all over the city and beyond. For them this was a major event for the race, the first Solemn Mass of America's first black Catholic priest.

Even more triumphant was the celebration the next Sunday, July 18, in Quincy, Illinois. The Mass was at St. Boniface, the German parish. It was reported that the crowd in attendance was the largest in the history of the church. In glowing terms, Tolton described the event in a lengthy letter to Cardinal Simeoni. He reported that a crowd of a thousand whites and five hundred blacks, mostly Protestant, were in attendance. "All cried out: Long live the Propaganda!"[36]

Sad to say, the exhilaration of those first days did not last. Tolton was made the pastor of a black church, St. Joseph, but the number of black Catholics in the parish was minimal. The number of conversions from the black community was also small. In 1887 he wrote Cardinal Simeoni to say that he had had only six conversions up to that point. He pointed out that he received a lot of support from the German and Irish Catholics in the city. In that letter there is the first suggestion of trouble with a priest in Quincy.[37]

A large part of the problem apparently arose from the fact that many white Catholics came to Father Tolton's parish and received the sacraments from him, to the annoyance of other priests in the city, especially a neighboring German priest. Tolton described the trouble in a letter to James Gibbons, the archbishop of Baltimore, dated July 24, 1888. He speaks of the thirty-one blacks in the parish, "mostly women," and of the fact that sometimes as many as two hundred whites attend regularly. Observing that this "causes a little jealous feelings among other neighboring brother priests," who wonder why their white parishioners wish to go to the "nigger priest," Tolton admitted that these remarks had caused resentments in the black community. He stressed the fact that "the white people in this little Gem City of Quincy, Illinois, are really good-hearted, charitable, and non-prejudicial, no feelings of bitterness at all against a man on account of complexion."[38]

In that same letter to Gibbons, Tolton revealed what had been and would continue to be perhaps his greatest trial — his loneliness. He wrote: "I must say, Most dear Cardinal, that I have never found a companion of my color since I have returned from Rome consequently I don't think there is a second colored priest yet...I would be but too proud if a second [priest] could be found in America." Tolton evidently knew nothing about the two Healy brothers in New England, Sherwood Healy having died by this date. Tolton did rejoice that another black seminarian was then in Rome. Tolton had no support, it seems, from his fellow priests in the city. He wrote in the same letter, "The priests here rejoiced at my arrival, now they wish I were away because too many white people come down to my church from other parishes."[39]

The situation did not improve. Tolton became discouraged, and he began to think of moving to another diocese. This he could not do, however, without the permission of the Congregation of the Propaganda. He made inquiries of the archdiocese of St. Paul, where John Ireland, already by this time a staunch friend of African Americans, was archbishop.[40] In 1888 Father John Slattery, the former provincial of the American province of the Mill Hill Fathers, who had just begun a seminary for the training of American priests of the mission society in Baltimore, received a letter from Father James Byrne, secretary to Archbishop Ireland, informing him that Tolton had applied to the archbishop for a place in his diocese. "The poor fellow is sent from post to pillar...and no one appears to help him or give him a guiding hand." Father Byrne, at the instruction of Ireland, was writing to Slattery to find a "place where he might do good and where a Bishop could be found to take an interest in his work."[41]

In July 1889 Tolton wrote in detail to Cardinal Simeoni describing his untenable situation in Quincy. He spoke of the German priest who had turned against him and had written the bishop that he should be moved. He pointed out that this priest had a great hatred of blacks. The priest was Father Michael Weiss, the pastor of St. Boniface Parish, who seemingly resented the fact that so many of his parishioners went to Mass at Father Tolton's church of St. Joseph. Tolton reported that the new bishop, James Ryan (bishop from 1888 to 1923), was also of the opinion that he should find another diocese.[42] He then pointed out that the bishop of Galveston had asked him to come to his diocese.

It is perhaps difficult to understand why Tolton allowed this Father Weiss to disturb him so much. It seems to be more than the usual desire to please and to maintain harmony that was so typical of Tolton. Rather, Tolton gives the impression of a person obsessed with a physical fear of a formidable opponent. In writing to Slattery after he had been received into the archdiocese of Chicago, he stated that "if any jealousies arise here among the priests...like in Quincy, I will put all of my books in the trunk and come right there to Baltimore." He adds that he would give himself to Father Leeson, the provincial of the American province of Mill Hill at the time; and then he adds the curious remark: "then I know that I will be protected here in America."[43] A little later he added, "I am safe now, thanks be to God." Tolton was physically afraid, justifiably so or not; but even more, Tolton lacked a sense of security and a sense of self-worth. He was desperately lonely. In that period of time, the only friends a priest could safely have were to be found among other priests. Tolton was without friends and the kind of peers among the Catholic clergy who would support him, reach out to him, and make him feel that he had accomplished something. Cardinal Simeoni was a friend, but not a peer. He was in a superior position, one who had to judge, and Tolton's own bishop in Alton had all but abandoned him.

The following October Tolton made known to Cardinal Simeoni that Archbishop Feehan of Chicago had invited him to that city and that Bishop Ryan had given permission for him to go. He spoke again of the "persecution" of Father Weiss. He also announced that the nineteen black converts he had made were planning to accompany him to Chicago.[44] In the meantime, the Congregation of the Propaganda made judicious inquiries with Bishop Ryan to try to ascertain the nature of the difficulty that Father Tolton was having. In a letter to the ordinary of the diocese, dated August 5, the cardinal prefect pointed out Tolton's request for a transfer. Then he rather testily remarked that the bishop had written not long before, indicating that young Tolton worked zealously in the diocese, and now the cardinal would like to know the reasons behind Tolton's sudden request.[45] Bishop Ryan replied on August 20.[46] Tolton was described as a zealous laborer, very pious. And then the bishop rather disingenuously added that "he was in no way able to form a congregation of blacks in Quincy, which I would understand was the special mission designated by the Propaganda." He went on to write that the impossibility of forming such a congregation arose from the small number of blacks in Quincy and the difficulty of "stable conversion." He concluded by saying that Tolton had a good name with both Catholics and non-Catholics and that he left everywhere a favorable impression.[47] What the bishop omitted to mention was the abuse of which Tolton was a victim. The bishop also carefully omitted to say that little aid or support was given Tolton to carry out "the special mission designated by the Propaganda."

Tolton went to Chicago in December 1889, after receiving the permission of the Congregation of the Propaganda. In fact, it was pointed out that since the two dioceses were in the same province, it was not necessary for any other permission be granted as long as the two ordinaries were in agreement.[48] Tolton left Quincy believing that he had been a failure. He acknowledged in his letter to Cardinal Simeoni that nineteen of his converts were going to Chicago with him. Looking back on his work in Quincy during two and a half years, it seems amazing that he had made nineteen converts who were willing to leave their homes and follow him to Chicago. By all accounts this would not indicate a mission that had failed.

Black Catholics in Chicago had been worshiping in the basement of St. Mary's Church since 1881. They had formed a congregation that was named St. Augustine's. This was to be the "Negro parish" where Tolton began his labors in the winter of 1889. With the encouragement of Archbishop Feehan,[49] a site for a black parish was secured at 35th and Dearborn streets. The construction of the new parish church began in 1891. By 1893 the church, although unfinished, was opened for worship. Because of lack of funds the building was never completed. Still the parish, dedicated to St. Monica, was the scene of Tolton's labors for the last four years of his life.[50]

Tolton spent much of his energy trying to raise money for the church. We have the letters that he wrote to Blessed Katherine Drexel begging for funds. His letters to her, conserved in the archives of the Blessed Sacrament Sisters, reveal more of his character. He wrote with a certain diffidence. Yet he also revealed the extent of his ministry and his enthusiasm.

> I have together 260 souls to render an account of before God's majesty. There [are] altogether 500 souls but they have become like unto the dead limbs on a tree and without moisture because no one had taken care of them: just Sunday night last I was called to the death bed of a colored woman who had been 9 years away from her duties because she was hurled out of a white church and even cursed at by the Irish members, very bad indeed! She sent for me and thanked God that she had one [a black priest] to send for.[51]

He constantly excused himself for "vexing" Mother Katherine for his request for money. "I for one cannot tell how to conduct myself when

I see one person at least showing their love for the colored race."
He told her that it had taken the Catholic church a hundred years
for generosity such as hers: "In the whole History of the church in
America we can't find one person that has sworn to lay out their
treasury for the sole benefit of the colored and Indians." He then
added, "As I stand alone as the first Negro priest of America, so you
Mother Catherine [*sic*] stand alone as the first one to make such a
sacrifice for the...downtrodden race."[52] Mother Katherine sent over
thirty thousand dollars to Father Tolton before his death. Through
the St. Augustine's Society, which had been formed when the first
congregation was begun at St. Mary's Church, his parishioners also
raised funds, and he received funds through the Commission for the
Negro and Indian Missions.

Father Tolton shared in the poverty of his people. His mother
lived with him and served as housekeeper. His reputation, however,
had spread far beyond Chicago. In a sense he was the priest for all
African Americans. In a letter to Father Slattery that began, "My
dearest friend and Father Slattery," he wrote, "I wish at this moment
that there were 27 Father Toltons or colored priests at any rate who
could supply the demands." At that time he had "27 letters...asking
me to come and lecture, come and give my assistance." In that same
letter he spoke of "what a grand thing it would be if I were only a
travelling missionary to go to all of the places that have called for
me." He even talked of "what a grand thing if I were a Josephite
belonging to your rank of missionaries."[53] It was a passing thought
perhaps, but it revealed the sense of mission that possessed him. Perhaps it also revealed his sense of being pulled in more than one
direction.

Tolton's health was not good. No doubt the stress of financial wor-
ries and the work of building up a parish contributed to his health
problems. We have a letter from a certain Mary C. Elmer, who worked
with the Visitation and Aid Society in Chicago. In the letter, Miss
Elmer (who signed herself as Sister Angela de Merici, O.S.F.) gave
her impressions of Father Tolton.

> Poor father — it seems strange after all the "*gush*" we read from
> week to week in the papers about the "*dear negro*" he is left
> to struggle on almost alone; in poverty and humility grappling
> with the giant task of founding a church and congregation in
> Chicago. We who come in contact with him in our labors, and
> are the witnesses of his ardent charity and self-denying zeal feel
> ourselves privileged to bow the knee for his saintly blessing.[54]

Mary Elmer mentioned in the same letter that Father Tolton complained of "feeling so ill." Augustus Tolton worked for seven years in Chicago, alone, suffering from ill health, and perhaps suffering even more from a sense of inadequacy. He died on July 9, 1897. He had just spent a few days in retreat at Kankakee and had emerged from the railway station to walk back to his rectory. The temperature was over a hundred degrees. He was overcome by heat exhaustion, collapsed, and was rushed to the hospital, where he expired later that day. Augustus Tolton was forty-three years old.[55] Following his desire, he was buried in St. Peter's Catholic cemetery in Quincy. A large cross surmounts his grave and that of another priest buried in the same place some years later.

Tolton felt himself to be a man alone, and at the same time a man who was constantly under surveillance. He mentioned in a letter to Blessed Katherine Drexel that he stood alone as the first Negro priest in America. In that same letter he referred to the fact that everyone was watching him: "They watch us, just the same as the Pharisees did our Lord."[56] For another person, in another set of circumstances, this might seem a little paranoid. As a black priest who was both a curiosity and an anomaly in a segregated society and as the sole visible example of what black Catholics could aspire to, Tolton could not escape scrutiny. This did not change his sense of duty as one chosen for a task. He wrote in the same letter, "I really feel that there will be a stirr [sic] all over the United States when I begin my church; I shall work and pull at it as long as God gives me life, for I see that I have principalities to resist anywhere and everywhere I go."

He remained a man of simplicity and faith. He never forgot what he was taught, that a priest should be obedient to his superiors. He expressed himself to Slattery as one who loved Archbishop Feehan, his ordinary. He told Cardinal Simeoni that he loved Bishop Ryan, the bishop of Alton.[57] He treated Cardinal Simeoni in his letters as a father. He began his letters to him with the Italian words "Carissimo Eminenza" (Dearest Eminence). He wrote to Slattery using such expressions as "you are our man and Priest" at the end of a letter in which he stated that Slattery was the only priest "that cares for us."[58]

If Tolton were to be faulted, it would be that he was not aggressive enough. This certainly seemed to have been the opinion of men like Slattery, who despite Tolton's appreciation, in reality did not think highly of Tolton. It also was true of Archbishop Ireland, the pugnacious leader, who knew how to fight hard and well. In a letter to Slattery, Archbishop Ireland inquired about a prospective black student, James Brooks of Baltimore. He wanted a recommendation from

Slattery. Ireland stated that he would like to have a black seminarian "for the purpose of a solemn protest against color prejudice." He wanted a black candidate in the seminary who was "solidly good, and intelligent, fit to be a leader of his people. I want no Toltons."[59]

In a letter written a few months before Tolton's death, Slattery wrote Walter Elliott, the editor of the *Catholic World*, concerning the question of Native American and African American priests. Slattery saw the need for black priests and fought hard for it. But he could not help a passing reference to Tolton and to Father Charles Uncles, S.S.J., who in 1891 had been the first black Josephite ordained a priest. "Alas, there is fresh opposition to negro priests. The two already ordained have not been conspicuous successes; one of them lost his health just as a bishop of the Diocese he lives in, had had his impaired. The other gave a little trouble some years ago, nothing serious but enough to justify a hue and cry against negro priests."[60] The problem with Father Uncles was the latter's disagreement with Slattery regarding mission work in the South.[61] The reference to Tolton was a suggestion that he had suffered a nervous breakdown just as Bishop James Duggan, installed in Chicago in 1859, had succumbed to mental illness and was hospitalized permanently in 1869. Although Tolton had become ill in 1895, it is not certain whether it was an emotional crisis rather than a physical one. In any case, Slattery had a low opinion of him.

Today we can look back at the priestly career of Augustus Tolton and recognize the courage and the faith of a man who persevered in his vocation despite insuperable obstacles and opposition. Neither brilliant nor clever, America's first black priest whom all could recognize as black was a man with whom all African Americans could identify. He was a pastor, first and last, and justly merits the title of father of all the African American priests who would come after him. More than he realized, he was the inspiration for the remarkable movement of faith and evangelization among the African American Catholic laity in the last decade of the nineteenth century.

Chapter 7

"A HUMBLE EXPERIMENT...
AN ENTERING WEDGE":
THE EMERGENCE OF
THE BLACK CATHOLIC LAITY

On a winter afternoon in January 1889, a group of almost a hundred men, all African Americans, made their way through the streets of Washington, D.C., to the White House to be ushered into the presence of President Grover Cleveland. It was a unique occasion. Cleveland was in the last days of his first term as president, and blacks were not frequent guests in the White House. What was more significant, however, was that this body of men were both blacks and Catholics from all parts of the nation and that this was the first time in the Catholic church's history in the United States that blacks had come together as a body, consciously aware of themselves as a group. President Cleveland told them that good religious people were a powerful help to the government and administration of a nation. This comment was in response to the opening address of the delegates, who thanked the president for what he had done for the black race.

The date was January 4, 1889, and the occasion was the last day of the four-day meeting of what was the first black Catholic lay congress in the nation's history. This visit to the White House and reception by the president was the climax of what had been a triumphant meeting of black Catholics, where as a body they deliberated, voiced their opinions, and made decisions regarding their church and their place within it. The visit to the White House was surpassed only by the cablegram from Pope Leo XIII's secretary of state, Cardinal Rampolla,

which made known to the delegates of the congress that the pope had
sent them his apostolic blessing. Less than a quarter of a century after
the end of slavery, a Roman pontiff had given his approbation and
blessing to a nationwide assembly of black Catholic men. Thus a new
age for the black Catholic community had emerged.[1]

I

The one individual responsible for this new development among
black Catholics was Daniel Rudd, a figure that for a long time was
not well known in American church history.[2] And yet at the end of
the nineteenth century, Rudd — newspaperman, lecturer, publisher,
publicist, and "leading Catholic representative of the Negro race" —
had made himself very well known to members of the hierarchy and
to Catholic laymen, as well as to one French cardinal.

Daniel Rudd was born on August 7, 1854, in Bardstown, Kentucky. His parents were Robert and Elizabeth Rudd. His father was
a slave on the Rudd estate near Bardstown, and his mother a slave
of the Hayden family in Bardstown.[3] Both parents were Catholics.[4]
Daniel was one of twelve children.

After the Civil War, Daniel Rudd moved to Springfield, Ohio
(where his elder brother, Robert Rudd, was living), in order to get
a secondary-school education. There in 1886 he began a black newspaper that was called the *Ohio State Tribune*.[5] That same year Rudd
changed the focus of this weekly newspaper and gave it a new name,
American Catholic Tribune. He announced the change with the words:
"We will do what no other paper published by colored men has dared
to do — give the great Catholic Church a hearing and show that it is
worthy of at least a fair consideration at the hands of our race, being
as it is the only place on this Continent where rich and poor, white
and black, must drop prejudice at the threshold and go hand in hand
to the altar."[6] The newspaper proudly stated on the editorial page,
"The only Catholic Journal owned and published by Colored Men."
The masthead indicated that the weekly newspaper was published
with the approval of "Cardinal Gibbons, archbishop of Baltimore,
Md., the most Reverend Archbishops of Cincinnati and Philadelphia,
and the Right Reverend Bishops of Covington, Ky, Columbus, O,
Richmond, Va, Vincennes, Ind, and Wilmington, Del."[7]

Most of the issues of the newspaper were four pages, although for
a short time it ran to eight pages. On occasion certain articles were
repeated, suggesting that Rudd ran out of material for a given week.

Other articles were copied from other newspapers, both secular and Catholic, a frequent practice for small newspapers at the time. By 1887 the newspaper was being published in Cincinnati. Rudd, moreover, had the services of correspondents who also doubled as agents for the newspaper's distribution. Isaac Moten, a native of Fort Wayne and Indianapolis, was a correspondent for the Midwest. Lincoln Vallé, originally from St. Louis and originally a journalist for another black newspaper, the *St. Louis Advance*, reported from various parts of the country. Robert L. Ruffin for a time was correspondent for New England. Rudd also had a Rome correspondent for a while, a black seminarian at the Urban College.[8]

Many news stories dealt with matters of particular interest to African Americans — for example, the article by Frederick Douglass in which the former minister to Haiti explained the circumstances of his resignation.[9] News of the black community in Cincinnati appeared under the byline of John R. Rudd, Daniel Rudd's nephew, who had the title of city editor. At other times local news of the black community in Chicago, Baltimore, and Louisville/Bardstown as well as other cities appeared. There were also the usual space fillers, such as anecdotes, jokes, and always a serialized version of a novel or short story.

The feature unique to the newspaper was Rudd's thoroughgoing commitment to Catholicism as a church and as a cause. This partisanship in an African American setting was unprecedented. It was expressed especially in Rudd's editorial comments and in the feature articles. It could be reduced to one simple thesis: the Catholic church is the great hope for black people in the United States. Or as he wrote: "There is an awakening among some people to the fact that the Catholic Church is not only a warm and true friend to the Colored people but is absolutely impartial in recognizing them as the equals of all and any of the other nations and races of men before her altars. Whether priest or laymen they are equals, all within the fold."[10] In a more forceful way the same idea was repeated a few years later:

> The Negro of this country ostracised [*sic*], abused, downtrodden and contemned, needs all the forces which may be brought to bear in his behalf to elevate him to that plane of equality which would give him the status he needs as "a man among men." ... We need assistance and should obtain help whenever and wherever it can be given. The Holy Roman Catholic Church offers to the oppressed Negro a material as well as spiritual

refuge, superior to all the inducements of other organizations combined...

...We need the church, the church wants us. Investigate, brethren! See, comprehend for yourselves and we are satisfied as to what will be the answer.[11]

Rudd could put the same message more succinctly, as he did when he wrote, "The Catholic Church alone can break the color line. Our people should help her to do it."[12] Or as he wrote a few months later, "We believe there is no leadership quite so capable as that of the Catholic Church, because she has up to this time, been the only successful leader of men of all the other races."[13] The message of Rudd was simple and easily understood. It was written in the triumphalist spirit of American Catholicism of the nineteenth century. The only difference was its perspective — a black person's point of view.

However, Rudd's loyalty was not uncritical. In his editorial columns he took issue with the comments and opinions of other Catholic newspapers regarding questions of race and racial segregation. Also as a consequence of his racial background, Rudd was interested in the church's social teaching. In 1891 his newspaper published the translation of Pope Leo XIII's encyclical on labor, *Rerum Novarum*, in six installments.

We have noticed in many of the papers published by Colored men, statements that the Catholic Church is not and has not been the Negro's friend. Of course, any one with a grain of sense either knows better or is unwilling to learn better, but for the information of both these classes we call attention to the encyclical letter of our Holy Father, Pope Leo XIII, which for some weeks has had the run of the columns of the AMERICAN CATHOLIC TRIBUNE. In its treatment of the rights of rich and poor it has not been equaled by any writer upon this subject, besides it comes with the authority of the teaching Church.

Then he adds, "In this day of strikes and the oppression that causes them, of the injustice of man to man, of prejudice, of murder and of violence, this great paper... is as refreshing as a summer shower and as strong as everlasting truth."[14]

Rudd went as far as to compare the encyclical of Pope Leo XIII to the efforts of the abolitionists in the United States. In fact, he estimates that such men as Lincoln, Sumner, and Garrison "were not the first abolitionists," for the Catholic church's teachings "have at last in this our own century gathered such force as to sweep slavery from the face of the earth; and this last letter from the successor of St. Peter gathers the tangled threads of difference between men and sends forth the law that should govern the rights of men."[15] He saw that the encyclical must apply particularly to the plight of poor black people in America in his time.

Rudd was most outspoken regarding the situation of blacks within the United States. The last decade of the nineteenth century, sometimes referred to as "the Gay Nineties," was in fact, the nadir of African American history. Violence against blacks increased with impunity throughout the South; lynchings doubled tragically each year. The volume of segregation laws swelled as the decade progressed. Rudd publicized the growth of lynching.[16] He published articles and editorials regarding the spread of racial segregation. He particularly opposed such laws when attempts were made to introduce them in the state of Ohio.[17] Rudd made his newspaper columns available to militant black journalists such as T. Thomas Fortune, the editor of the prestigious black newspaper *New York Age*.[18]

If Rudd was outspoken in regard to civil rights for African Americans, he was particularly anxious to promote what was called at the time "race pride." In some respects, this was one of the purposes of the newspaper. Rudd published the portraits of important black leaders and featured them in the news. In 1887 he ran an illustration of Father Augustus Tolton with the caption "The most conspicuous man in America."[19] A Republican in politics, Rudd featured black political leaders as well, such as George H. Jackson, a member of the Ohio State legislature.[20] Another portrait was that of John Mitchell, Jr., editor of the *Planet* of Richmond, Virginia. Mitchell was president of the Negro Press Association, in which Rudd was an active participant. Through his efforts, the organization met in Cincinnati in 1891. He believed that the black press was a source of potential power for black people in this country. In commenting on the success of the Negro Press Convention and the good it would do for black people, he added, "One hundred and sixty newspapers is not a very large showing for seven or eight millions of people, yet taking into consideration the length of time these papers have had to develop, they are marvels of beauty, information and strength."[21] Rudd not only played a part in the Afro-American press association, he also maintained a connection with the Catholic Press Association.[22]

Rudd was also a lecturer of some renown. His newspaper reported on his lectures, which in fact served to augment the readership of the *American Catholic Tribune*. Traveling over much of the Midwest, the South, and parts of the East Coast, he addressed white and black audiences on the topic "The Catholic Church and the Negro." For example, Rudd published in the *Tribune* the report that appeared in the *Louisville Courier Journal* on May 29, 1887, about his lecture at Jackson Hall in Lexington, Kentucky, entitled "The New Civilization." He was quoted as saying:

> To keep pace with his fairer-hued brother, [the Negro] must be grounded in truth and fairness... and enter every field where the genius of man avails to conquer. As a means to this end I feel it my duty... to dispel some of the misinformation that exists among a portion of my race concerning the Roman Catholic Church... I want to show him that today, greater than ever before, Holy Mother Church is striving to educate and build up the unfortunate of every race and tribe.[23]

Rudd had delivered this same lecture in Fort Wayne, Indiana, earlier in the year at the Catholic Library Hall. He continued to speak in other areas around the country, places as widely separated as Lewiston, Maine, and Natchez, Mississippi. Rudd spoke German, and he even lectured on this subject in German in the areas around Cincinnati.[24]

From all indications, Rudd's lectures were optimistic and hopeful, stressing the improvement of the race in a clear and simple message. Early in his career, in June 1888, when he was about thirty-three years old, Rudd addressed the Catholic Young Men's National Union in Cincinnati. Later his talk was summarized in the *Catholic World*.[25]

> I hardly expected when a little boy, in the State of Kentucky, that at this early day of my life — and I am a young man yet — I would be standing before a Catholic convention of the Union, to lift my voice in the interest of my race and of my church; but such is the case.
>
> This is the third time that it has been my pleasure to meet Catholics of this country in national convention assembled; the first time was in Toledo, in 1886; the second, in 1887, at Chicago; and now, in this year of our Lord, 1888.

He proceeded to acquaint his listeners with the relevant facts concerning black Catholics. Rudd claimed that black Catholics numbered 200,000 out of a black population of 7 million. He chided his audience with the assertion that "this race [African Americans] is increasing more rapidly than yours . . . by the middle of the next century [it] will outnumber your race." He described the purpose of his journalism. "We have been led to believe that the church was inimical to the negro race . . . I owe it to myself, my God, and my country to refute the slander." He then unveiled for the first time his great project. "We are publishing a weekly newspaper; whatever it is, it is the best we can do in this work. A meeting of our people will be held somewhere; the time and place has not yet been fixed, but I am here, gentlemen, to ask your assistance, to ask your kindness, and you have shown it to me to-day." The talk concluded with characteristic optimism: "I believe that within ten years, if the work goes on as it has been going on, there will be awakened a latent force in this country."

In the summer of 1889 Rudd was sent to Europe, where he met Cardinal Lavigerie.[26] The cardinal had organized an antislavery conference that was to be held that summer in Lucerne. The exact circumstances regarding the origin and the funding of Rudd's trip are not completely clear. Some indication is given, however, by a newspaper column that originally appeared in a Philadelphia newspaper. In the July 6 issue of the *American Catholic Tribune* for that year, a column appeared entitled "Catholics in Boston" under the byline of a certain J. Gordon Street. Street informed the readers that Cardinal Lavigerie was arranging a conference against slavery to be held in Lucerne and that he had appealed to "prominent colored men in the United States asking them to take an interest in the matter." Black Catholics in Boston had responded to the appeal, and Robert L. Ruffin, a prominent black Catholic and a collaborator with Rudd on the *Tribune*, had been chosen to represent Boston at the conference in Lucerne. Street's article went on to say that John Boyle O'Reilly, the editor of Boston's Catholic paper, the *Pilot*, had begun a campaign to raise funds for Ruffin's passage.[27] In the same article, Street wrote, "There is another black man . . . that the colored Catholics must see that he goes to Lucerne — I mean Daniel A. Rudd of Cincinnati."

Ruffin wrote an obituary notice of Cardinal Lavigerie at the time of his death in 1892, which appeared in the *AME Church Review*. Ruffin noted that he had met the cardinal "through the kindness of His Grace, Archbishop Williams of Boston, and the late John Boyle O'Reilly." He indicated in the same article that he was "accompanied by Mr. Daniel A. Rudd, who was sent by His Grace, Archbishop Elder of Cincinnati, to represent the younger and growing section of America."[28] It seems very likely, then, that Rudd's expenses were paid at least in part by Archbishop Elder.

Rudd remarked in an editorial that appeared a week after the publication of J. Gordon Street's article that "the Catholics of the United States seem to be the only class of... citizens... taking proper interest in the great International Anti-Slavery Congress."[29] Rudd complained in the same editorial that American blacks did not seem to be interested in this project to end the slave trade. Rudd set sail for Hamburg from New York, according to the *Tribune* article, with "his French Secretary, Mr. Henry L. Jones, of New Orleans and Mr. Robert L. Ruffin — and probably Father Tolton."[30] In actual fact, there is no indication from subsequent reports that either Tolton or Jones made the trip. Rudd wrote reports of his travels for publication in the newspaper.[31] It was not until his arrival in Hamburg that Rudd learned that the international congress was postponed. In fact, it would be held the next year in 1890 in Brussels. Rudd described his visit with Lavigerie in a letter to Archbishop Elder. "The reception extended us was royal, for His Eminence kissed us like a father. So overjoyed was Africa's great Apostle when he read our letters and credentials that he said our very presence there would give him new life and new zeal for a race that was so full of gratitude."[32]

Rudd wrote this letter from the residence of Cardinal Manning in London, where he and Robert Ruffin stayed on their way home from Switzerland. Lavigerie had given Rudd a letter of introduction to the cardinal of Westminster. Rudd stayed there over a week. Cardinal Manning invited him "to address a large meeting at St. George's Cathedral Hall." In concluding his letter to Archbishop Elder, Rudd informed the archbishop that Lavigerie had made him his representative in the United States for "his work for the African Slaves." Cardinal Lavigerie made a great impression on Rudd. After the cardinal's death, November 26, 1892, Rudd ran a lengthy obituary notice on the front page of the *Tribune*, along with a picture of the cardinal. More than once Rudd would refer in his articles to his meeting with Cardinal Lavigerie.

In 1894 Rudd moved his paper from Cincinnati to Detroit. In fact, the *Tribune* of December 1893 was published in Detroit. The issue of February 1, 1894, however, was published in Cincinnati. A week later the paper had the dateline February 8, Detroit, and John R. Rudd was listed as city editor. The Detroit city directory listed the address of Rudd and his nephew until 1897.[33] It would seem that the paper did not flourish in the new surroundings. Judging from the numbering of the issues, it appeared somewhat irregularly. The last extant issue is dated September 4, 1894.

II

Even if Daniel Rudd had never published a black Catholic newspaper, he still would have left his mark on the history of black Catholics in the United States. It was he who had the idea to call together a national congress of African American Catholics. In the summer of 1888, Rudd wrote Archbishop Elder about a proposed national convention. Elder replied, giving his approval.[34] Earlier that year, Rudd had submitted a detailed plan for the congress to Rev. John Slattery, S.S.J. He asked him for a meeting, telling him that "we know you will agree with us and lend us your invaluable aid." No doubt to reassure him, he added, "Our experience in state and interstate meetings will aid us much in this. Rest assured that we are not going in blind."[35] Finally, in the fall of 1888, Rudd wrote Cardinal Gibbons, asking for permission to hold the meeting in Washington, D.C.[36]

Rudd first broached the idea of a national congress in the columns of the *Tribune* in May 1888, about the same time that he wrote Slattery.[37] Under the title "Congress of Colored Catholics," Rudd wrote: "Among the Colored people, none are so desirous for their advancement in every sphere as the Catholics of the race . . . The Catholics of the Colored race should be the leaven, which would raise up their people not only in the eye of God but before men."

After speaking in general about unity and the ideal of unity among African Americans, Rudd continued: "First then, Colored Catholics ought to unite. Let the leading Colored Catholics gather together from every city in the Union in some suitable place, where under the blessing of Holy Mother Church, they may get to know one another and take up the cause of the race." In response to the question, Why should there be such a congress? Rudd gave this answer in the same article:

First of all: To have our people realize the Church's extent among them. We are hidden away, as it were. Let us stand forth and look at one another . . .

Every Colored Catholic must, at times, feel that his Colored brethren look upon him as an alien, and may, even be told so. Our Protestant friends have false notions of us. At the hearing of a gathering of Colored Catholics, almost the first thoughts in their minds will be: Will the Church allow Catholics to meet? What will they do in their assembly? Who will be there? It will be a wonder to them.

Rudd proceeded to point out the precedent of the Germans and Belgians meeting in lay congresses. But Rudd saw another desirable effect of a black Catholic congress, namely, the forging of bonds of community.

A far more desirable boon is that in such an assembly Colored representative Catholics would get to know one another, and also respect one another and one another's views. There are many able men among our Catholic brethren; but they have never come in contact. Gather them and let them exchange views on questions affecting their race; then uniting on a course of action, behind which would stand the majestic Church of Christ, they must inevitably become — what has already been said they should be — the bearer of their race.

Finally, a month later Rudd added another reason for a national meeting of black Catholics — the question of pride. "We had watched for years the tendency on the part of some people to ignore the Negro as a man and citizen in the United States ... We thought that if we would turn the attention of our people to the moral truths ... taught by Holy Mother Church ... our Lord would lift us ... from oppression, doubt, ignorance."[38]

Hence, the necessity of marshaling the forces of the black Catholic community. It was necessary to know the strength of the black Catholic population, as Rudd pointed out in the same editorial: "The best way to turn the attention of our race to [the] Church was first [to] find out how many Catholics we would have to start with and then put that force to work." Thus as Rudd's lecturing took him all over the country, so he came in contact with many black Catholics. "We not only found thousands of scholarly and wealthy Negro Catholics who stood ready to work for the race and church but we have been able to enlist the zeal of that matchless army of Christian workers — the bishops and clergy of the Church." Ignoring Rudd's characteristic hyperbole regarding the number of wealthy black Catholics, we should note that Rudd did discover a population that had never before been contacted or consulted. Thanks to Rudd, the black Catholic community found a place on the American Catholic scene.

Each black parish and black Catholic society was to elect delegates to the congress. Although the procedure was spelled out in the *Tribune*, it is not at all clear how the election was carried out in local situations. According to the newspaper, Catholic societies and organizations were to have the right to one delegate for each five hundred persons or portion thereof. In addition, each black parish had the right to one delegate.[39]

This first black Catholic lay congress took place January 1–4, 1889, and was a tremendous success. The *Catholic Mirror* of Baltimore gave a detailed description of the opening of the congress and the sermon delivered by Cardinal Gibbons at the opening Mass, which was celebrated by Father Augustus Tolton. The newspaper stated that two hundred delegates were present at the opening.[40] The account of the proceedings published later by Daniel Rudd lists the names of about eighty.[41] Both Cardinal Gibbons and Archbishop Elder addressed the congress. At the congress, Daniel Rudd was elected president, and he gave a short address in which he spelled out for the delegates the work they had to do. He suggested the need for schools, the need for training in labor skills, and the need for family virtues.[42] All American bishops had been invited. Bishop Healy of Portland acknowledged the invitation and added, "My uncertain health hinders me from accepting any invitation to distant places."[43] Other addresses to the congress were given by Rev. P. A. McDermott, C.SS.P., of Pittsburgh, John Slattery, S.S.J., and Archbishop Elder. Perhaps the most stirring was that delivered by Augustus Tolton on the first evening.[44]

Most important was the statement to their fellow Catholics drawn up by the congress participants at the end of their session. "We delegates of the Colored Catholics of the United States, deem it proper, at the close of the deliberations, to address our Fellow Catholic citizens of this country, and to put before them a summary of the work we have accomplished." One can sense the feeling of euphoria and excitement as the statement continued:

> In this meeting...to consider in a public manner and for the first time in our history the needs and claims of our race, it was natural to feel that a herculean task awaited us. But, relying on the assistance of the Holy Ghost, whose inspiration, we have no doubt prompted the call of this assembly...we congratulate ourselves upon the results at which we have arrived.
>
> Although, we did not, at the outset, presume to think that this Congress could be other than an humble experiment — although we do not, even still, presume to claim that its results be other than an entering wedge in the breaking of the mighty wall of difficulties lifted up for centuries against us and a mere preliminary step in the progressive march and final regeneration of our people — yet we feel that we can safely present these results

to the entire world, assured that they will mark the dawn of a
new and brighter era in the history of our race.

Nevertheless, the congress members recognized that "the sacred
rights of justice and of humanity are still sadly wounded." As a result they mentioned the areas in which change must occur. First was
education. "We pledge ourselves to aid in establishing... Catholic
schools." They singled out the need for trade schools, "where the hand
of our youth may be trained, as well as the mind and heart." They
called for literary societies "as a means of completing our young men's
training and attainments." They urged the practice of temperance
"either individually or in the societies already existing in connection
with the church." They made an "appeal to all labor organizations,
trade unions, etc., to admit Colored men within their ranks... We
appeal... to all factory owners and operators, telegraph and railroad
companies, store and shopkeepers, to give employment to Colored
people... without discrimination, and on the merit of their individual capacity." They spoke of the children and the indigent and the
"need of orphanages, hospitals and asylums."
    They condemned "in the most emphatic terms the custom of rent-
ing to our people, or constructing for... them poorly lighted, poorly
ventilated and roughly planned tenement houses... hot beds of vice
and... a standing menace to morality." They underscored "the discrimination practiced by real estate owners and agents against respectable Colored people in refusing to rent them desirable property
because of their color." They praised the religious orders of the church
for "the admirable and remarkable efforts thus far accomplished for
the benefit of the African race, either in this country or on the African
continent." Finally, they endorsed Rudd's newspaper, the *Tribune*,
concluding with the hope "that our Catholic brethren throughout the
land will generously help us by their sympathy and fellowship in the
great and noble work which we have inaugurated for the welfare... of
our entire people."[45]
    The statement summed up the feelings of the congress members
and of the clergy who had encouraged the event. The mood was
joyful and optimistic. In giving his approval, Archbishop Elder had
cautioned Rudd that the congress must proceed with "wisdom and
discretion."[46] Moreover, Cardinal Gibbons in his sermon at the opening Mass had admonished them, "Remember the eye of the whole
country is upon you. It is not the eye of friendship, but... criticism."[47]
The deliberations had been very discreet; nothing was said that was
too disturbing.

Later that year Rudd took part in what is considered to be the first lay Catholic congress in the United States, which was held in Baltimore on November 11–12, 1889, to commemorate the centenary of the American hierarchy. Rudd was a member of the committee on organization along with such prominent figures as William J. Onahan and Henry F. Brownson.[48] It was desired that Rudd deliver a paper on Cardinal Lavigerie and his work, but Rudd demurred because of lack of time.[49] He did not hesitate, however, to make demands regarding the place of blacks in the program. In a letter to Slattery, the secretary of Archbishop Ireland wrote about Rudd's insistence that black Catholics not be treated in a special category but as part of the whole. The secretary betrayed his opinion of Rudd by closing the letter with the hope "that that 'nigger may never die' except with colors flying."[50]

Subsequent black Catholic congresses were held after 1889. In a way, these congresses were more significant as the congress members began to treat of more substantive issues. The members also began to think in terms of cohesive action and a permanent organization. In a sense, a certain radicalization began to take place; on the other hand, there emerged what can only be called, for want of a better term, a black Catholic theological consciousness. In all of this, the role of Rudd began to lessen in influence and the activity of other black leaders began to emerge.

The congress held in Cincinnati on July 8–10, 1890, was not as euphoric as that of the previous year, but it was more practical in its approach. Meetings were held in the cathedral hall. In writing up the proceedings of the congress, Father Slattery estimated the number of delegates as 125.[51] The account in the *Cleveland Gazette*, Ohio's leading black newspaper, gave the number in attendance as 48, which seems nearer the truth.[52]

Two noteworthy addresses were made to the congress. The first was by Dr. William S. Lofton, a prominent Washington, D.C., dentist, one of the first graduates of the Dental School at Howard University. Born in Arkansas in 1862, he was converted to the Catholic faith as an adolescent in Washington, D.C. He was at the time a trustee of St. Augustine's Parish. Lofton spoke to the issue of education, affirming, "I dare today to insist upon the education, manual, industrial and intellectual of our down-trodden race." Discussing these three types of education, Lofton spoke of the necessity of creating schools for black youth in all three areas. His point was that most trade unions were closed to blacks and apprenticeship in a trade was therefore practically inaccessible. Schools of the manual arts might be the only way to open up certain trades to black workers. The same held true for what Lofton termed "industrial schools," where business or commercial and other types of nonacademic courses were offered. Lofton deplored the fact that the Catholic church provided few schools for black children. "The Church teaches that we must send our children to Catholic schools. We value our religion and Catholic training; we marvel that the Divines of the Church do not support their teaching by having Catholic colleges and schools open their doors to at least those of our Colored children who are well behaved and able to pay."[53] Since this is the state of affairs, he went on to say, "it behooves us for the love of God, our race and children, to establish schools of a high order ourselves." Lofton's proposal was acted upon, and a committee was set up to seek congressional appropriation for a Catholic industrial school for blacks in Washington, D.C.

A paper in the same vein was read to the congress by another black Catholic leader from St. Augustine's Parish in Washington. Charles H. Butler was a clerk in the Treasury Department, the Division of Appointments. For an African American to work for the Federal government was a notable achievement. Butler had an established reputation as a speaker. The cause of education for black Catholic youth was extremely important to him. Essentially he restated many of the same points made by Lofton.

> I am prepared to say without fear of contradiction that a mighty host of Colored Catholics are being yearly lost to the Church because of the non-existence of Catholic schools and especially for Colored youth... There is not a single Catholic school in the city of Washington whose doors are open to the Colored youth after they reach the age of twelve years. Hence, they are deprived of an education unless they seek it in a public school, possibly at the loss of their religion. The establishment of a Catholic National High School at the city of Washington will in my judgment remedy a great injustice and secure to our Holy Mother many of her children.

Butler was convinced that the great need for black youth at this time was an education in the trades. "Industrial education is the great need for our boys; it will give them the most complete control of their faculties, will make them alert, accurate, ready physically as well as mentally for the performance of the duties of life."[54]

At the close of this second congress a set of resolutions was voted on. These called for the establishment of night schools, for all Catholics to have access to a religious education, for all cities to guarantee both the moral and civil rights of all their citizens, for access by black members of a union to all conferences and union benefits, and for storekeepers to hire blacks as clerks. The congress called for an end to the slave trade and aid to black orphans. The delegates promised support for religious vocations among blacks and filial obedience to the Catholic church. They voted a resolution to express gratitude to Archbishop Ireland as "a champion of the race."

It is important to note that at this period of African American history, Booker T. Washington (1856–1915), an educator, community leader, and African American spokesperson in the eyes of many, had transformed his Tuskegee Institute from a normal school to a mechanical and agricultural school in Alabama to provide black students with an agricultural and industrial education. In fact, by 1892 Washington had become well known as the proponent of vocational training for African American youth.[55] Washington did not oppose academic education as much as he believed that too many blacks sought to enter the professions when they would have been better off economically by striving to become farmers, laborers, mechanics, and industrial workers. The large majority of black Americans tended to agree with him. It is this majority that the congress members seemed to reflect when they called for vocational training for African American youths.

On May 23, 1891, the executive committee of the Colored Catholic Congress met at St. Peter Claver House in Philadelphia.[56] The committee was composed of Washington Parker, Willis J. Smith, J. T. Maxwell, P. J. Augustin, Daniel Rudd, Charles H. Butler, and Dr. William S. Lofton. Six members were absent. The committee wished to call on Archbishop Ryan of Philadelphia but were unable to obtain an appointment. As a result they sent him a letter, asking his permission to convene the third congress in Philadelphia. The permission was subsequently granted. Plans were made for speakers at the congress. The decision was also made to attract more representation at the future congress from New Orleans and other parts of the South. Charles H. Butler of Washington, D.C., announced in a written memorandum that efforts to establish an industrial school in Washington had met with little success. "Distinguished prelates admit the necessity of such a school, but they fear no community will take hold of the work." It is not clear what was meant by a community. The memorandum did suggest that there was some indication that Mother Katherine Drexel was considering the prospect of such a school.

The president of the executive committee was a political leader from New York City, Washington Parker (1839–1915). For most of his life he was an employee in one capacity or other of the New York City government. More important was his political activity on behalf of the Republican party.[57] Parker was one of several congress members who was especially active in local politics. The congress member from Philadelphia who contacted the archbishop of Philadelphia for his consent to the upcoming meeting was a prominent black Catholic in the city, Peter Jerome Augustin (1828–92). Augustin's father, a native of Haiti, had established himself in Philadelphia and had become a caterer, a business that his son continued. At the time of his death the catering business had made Peter Jerome Augustin a fairly wealthy man.[58]

The third black Catholic lay congress opened in Philadelphia on January 5, 1892, with about fifty delegates. The opening Mass was celebrated by Augustus Tolton at the newly refurbished St. Peter Claver Church. The church had formerly been used by a Presbyterian congregation, and with the help of wealthy benefactors the building was purchased and remodeled. The church building was blessed for public worship by Archbishop Ryan two days before the opening of the third congress. The parish community of black Catholics in Philadelphia had been formed as early as 1886, when they received permission to have a Mass each Sunday at Holy Trinity Church, a German parish in the city. The St. Peter Claver Union was formed, which became the nucleus for St. Peter Claver Parish in 1892. With the help of Blessed Katherine Drexel, the community of St. Peter Claver was taken over in 1889 by the Holy Ghost Fathers, or Spiritans, in the person of Patrick McDermott, C.S.Sp. Father McDermott was present at the first black Catholic congress.[59]

Two matters dominated the third congress: the question of education, particularly industrial or vocational schools, and the establishment of a permanent organization, one aspect of which would be the examination of grievances. Daniel Rudd delivered a talk entitled "Our Catholic Young Men." He spoke about the absence of young Catholic men "battling for themselves and the Church." "We have a large number of educated young men, who are Catholics more in name than in action." The reason is that "having lost the benefits of Catholic education during the formative period, they become lukewarm or drift away from the safe guidance of the Church."

Rudd wanted Catholic schools that would be open to these youths and the creation of a society that would encourage martial bearing and self-reliance. They should "be encouraged to learn some trade suitable to [their] strength,... condition and...locality." He then attacked the trade unions that forbid "the acceptance of men because of their complexion." He also criticized the use of prison labor. "Hundreds of our young men are gathered in for minor offences; sentenced to prison for long term of years, they are at last turned loose upon the community branded criminals and having lost their manhood — they form an eating cancer." He then set forth a challenge that typified his lifelong message. "One of the first ideas I had in mind when seeking to organize these Congresses, was that our Catholic young men should stand up for the faith that is in them . . . Get close together, young men, fling personal ambition to the winds, work for the general good and all will be well."[60]

A delegate from the South, William Edgar Easton, delivered a stirring address on behalf of Catholic schools. He called for a moratorium on Catholic churches for blacks and the construction of more schools. "Although the importance and necessity of establishing churches are apparent, the greatest need of Colored Catholics at present, is more schools and better educational facilities . . . While these are being secured the building of churches could for a time be stopped." He pointed out that black Catholic parents in the South had no colleges other than church-related colleges to which to send their children. He called for the establishment in Texas of "a Catholic academy or college, which will comprehend in its course of study the education of the head, hand and heart of the youth of the race . . . a school whose departments will include the sewing room for girls, and the skilled mechanics, arts for our boys." In his peroration he said:

> Let the Catholic Church, which has always been first in extending a helping hand to the needy, in raising up the humble and rebuking the proud; the Church that to-day is so actively engaged in taking the gyves and shackles from the neck and limbs of the poor benighted African; the Church that has a deeper and a more sublime breadth of humanity than all other churches combined, whose dogmas are truth, whose worship of God comprehends the essence of faith, love and charity, let that Church but take the initiative in this great southern work, in the very heart of the South, and gratitude the strongest characteristic of a down-trodden people will make the people knock at her doors for admission.[61]

William Edgar Easton was from Galveston, Texas, and was very active at this time in the Republican politics of Texas. He was the protégé of the black Republican leader, Norris Wright Cuney, who was a political force in Galveston at this time. Easton had a position in the United States Customhouse in Galveston, where Cuney was collector of customs for the Port of Galveston. At the same time Easton was secretary of the Executive Committee of the Republican party in Texas.[62]

One of the most important talks was given by Fredrick McGhee, entitled "Our National Institutions." This was the first congress that McGhee, a recent convert, attended. He was to become one of the most important members of subsequent congresses. Fredrick McGhee was born a slave in Mississippi in 1861. After the Civil War, his family moved to Tennessee, where he studied at Knoxville College. McGhee studied law in Chicago and obtained his degree in 1885. With his wife (who was from Louisville, Kentucky) and family, McGhee moved to St. Paul in 1889, where he was the first black to be admitted to the bar in the upper Midwest. He became well known as a trial lawyer and was very active in local Democratic politics. He was a friend of Booker T. Washington but subsequently became a follower of W. E. B. Du Bois. He was associated with the latter in the Niagara movement and in the establishment of the NAACP. McGhee was head of the legal department of the Niagara movement and in that position played a seminal role in the development of the legal arm of the NAACP. He was converted to the Catholic faith in 1891 partly in response to the forthright stand of Archbishop Ireland on behalf of African Americans.[63]

Using his exceptional oratorical skills, McGhee called for racial integration in the education of black youth. "We proclaim that all Americans are equal, but the common equality of man is but like the enchanted palace...and this system of separate schools for whites and blacks is the strong, hungry glaring lion." McGhee believed that there were enormous advantages in black students' studying with whites. He, unlike the other speakers, was concerned mainly with the public school system. "Away with the evil of caste school...We cannot hope that our country's institutions will remain safe when in the public school we foster and keep alive the very thing that threatens our Government most." In taking this position, he was faithful to the convictions expressed by his own beloved Archbishop Ireland.[64]

McGhee's greatest contribution to the third congress was not his address, however, but his proposal for a permanent organization of the congress movement. This organization would be the source of an ongoing implementation of the designs set forth in the congresses. It would also be an umbrella organization covering the activities of the various parish societies that had sent delegates to the congresses.

McGhee wanted an executive board of fifteen members who would choose among themselves an executive council. Each society would pay a tax into the executive council based on its membership. Finally, McGhee envisaged a fund for the building of churches and institutions to be known as a Catholic Building and Loan Association of Colored People. A board of directors would be appointed by the congress.[65] The congress passed several resolutions, one of which was to set in motion the permanent organization suggested by McGhee. The other was introduced by Charles H. Butler to call attention "to the unjust discrimination made against Colored children by reason of their color." Robert N. Wood of New York City moved the resolution that a committee be formed "to investigate the discrimination against colored children in the Catholic schools and institutions." The committee was established, and Wood was named chairman.[66]

The congress ended on January 7, 1892, with an address to the Catholic fellow citizens of America. Although lacking some of the eloquence and emotion of the other addresses, this address renewed the convention's fidelity to the teachings of the Catholic church and then quoted from the letter that Archbishop Ireland had sent to the congress in response to its invitation, which he could not accept. Ireland had endeared himself to all black Catholics by the public stand that he had taken against racism, especially in a sermon delivered in St. Augustine's Church in Washington, D.C., on May 4, 1890, in which he called for an end to the "Color Line." Ireland denounced racism within the Catholic church and called for it to end.[67] The address also included the words of Archbishop Ryan that he had addressed earlier to the congress, "[The church] preaches one origin for all mankind, and, therefore, all are brothers and sisters." The congress concluded:

> Bending humbly before the decisions of the Church, loving our country next to our God, willing to sacrifice our lives and whatever earthly goods we may possess for advancement in right lines of Catholic truth and American equality, knowing, as we do, that the sublime courage of the Negro American, which is matchless in the world's history, will be patient enough with the Church and country to bear us through any shade of disappointment that may fall athwart the pathway of our progress,... we humbly submit ... our declarations of the duties, the rights, the privileges, the hopes and the aspirations of this Congress and those it represents.[68]

III

The fourth black Catholic congress, held in Chicago in 1893 in conjunction with the Columbian Exposition, was the highpoint of the black Catholic congress movement. Also in conjunction with the Columbian Exposition was held the second lay Catholic congress in the United States, also known as the Columbian Catholic Congress. This congress had been organized by many of the same men who had worked to bring about the 1889 congress. The Congress of Colored (Negro) Catholics, as it was described in the program, met from Monday, September 4, to Friday, September 8, in Columbus Hall. At certain of these sessions women were present. Thus it seems likely that many of the sessions were open to the general public. On Tuesday morning, there was a joint meeting of the Columbian Catholic Congress, essentially white, and the black Catholic congress.

In the spring of 1892 Father Slattery, superior of the Josephite Seminary and the unofficial authority on black Catholic matters, answered a letter from William Onahan of Chicago relative to a black man's speaking at the Columbian Catholic Congress. The choices, according to Slattery, were limited. "It seems to me," he wrote, "that it is an excellent thought to have a colored man plead for his people at the coming Congress. And I quite agree with you that neither Father Tolton nor Rudd would answer." He went on to say that probably the best under the circumstances was Charles Butler, clerk in the Treasury Department in Washington. He also suggested James C. Spencer of Charleston. "But he is very poor and could hardly bear the expenses of the trip." He concluded by saying that Robert C. Ruffin of Boston, "who undoubtedly would make the best effort," had a "bad name (confidential) among the Clergy of New England."[69] It is not clear what was the cause of Ruffin's reputation among the New England clergy. It is not clear, either, why Tolton and Rudd would be unacceptable. Because of historical circumstances, we have some of the thoughts and feelings of contemporary white Catholic leaders but almost no indication of how the black Catholic leaders felt among themselves. Slattery at times made known his feelings about certain of the black Catholic leaders.[70]

Charles H. Butler addressed a joint session of the two congresses, giving a talk entitled "The Condition and Future of the Negro Race in the United States."[71] When it was announced that the black Catholic congress had prepared an address to their fellow Catholics, a resolution was passed to invite the black congress to come to the Columbian Catholic Congress. At that point Archbishop Ireland exulted, "I beg leave to express the utmost delight of my heart that a proposition was made to invite here the members of the Catholic Colored Congress... I have but one regret — that they are not one hundred fold more numerous."[72]

Butler's address began with a brief history of the African American from the time of slavery through Reconstruction and the gradual exodus of blacks from the South, which was a current issue then. The talk was conciliatory and calculated not to offend. Nevertheless, in speaking of the Catholic church, he had the following to say:

> It is to be regretted that the Catholic Church did not take earlier steps in the missionary work among the emancipated slaves of the South... The reputation of the church for civilizing and educating nations is established in history. It seems, however, to have been left for the Plenary Council of Baltimore to issue the mandate... The Protestant Church is greatly in advance of us, for their colleges and industrial schools, supported by white philanthropists of the North, are dotted all over the Southland.

Butler then proceeded to speak of "social equality" and "civil equality."

> There is one subject upon which the negro has been greatly misunderstood by his friends, and purposely so by his enemies — they have made the clear and definite term "civil equality" synonymous with that other definite term of entirely different significance, "social equality." If civil equality and social equality had the same application there would be room for complaint, and justly so, but upon a calm and dispassionate thought it must be apparent to all intelligent men that such a thing would be as distasteful to the negro as to the white man.

By civil equality, Butler meant no discrimination in public facilities and equal access to jobs and other opportunities. Three years later in Atlanta, Booker T. Washington would make his famous speech in which he called for opportunities for blacks in the educational and economic area but made no mention of social equality, dramatically holding out his hand with the words, "In all things that are purely social we can be as separate as the fingers, yet one as the hand in all things essential to mutual progress."[73] Butler had not gone that far, but like many blacks in this period, he was allied more with Washington's views than with the militant stance of Du Bois, Washington's great antagonist.

Still, neither Butler nor the members of the black Catholic congress were appeasers in the question of discrimination. It is especially in regard to prejudice within the church that Butler took a forthright stand: "I cannot dismiss this consideration without saying a word to those who would carry their prejudices into the sacred confines of God's holy church, and relegate the negro to an obscure corner of the church...How long, oh Lord, are we to endure this hardship in the house of our friends?" He asked his audience "to assist us to strike down that hybrid monster, color prejudice, which is unworthy of this glorious Republic."

Father Slattery addressed the Columbian Catholic Congress at a later time on the topic "The Negro Race: Its Condition, Present and Future." Both his ardent championship of the cause of the African American and his paternalistic conception of their lack of moral fiber, which he blamed on the institution of slavery, were evident in his talk. Nevertheless, just as Butler did, he pointed out the enormous effort that Protestants had made for the education of American blacks in contrast to the slight efforts of American Catholics. "Is not the Catholic church in America to be blamed for lack of zeal? I answer with an unhesitating Yes. After all, Protestantism has done something to Christianize the blacks; but we have done, I may say, nothing." He pointed out that the Protestant churches had expended $35 million in their evangelization efforts. "Add to that immense sum, the hundred and thirty higher institutions, with twenty-five thousand scholars, of whom one thousand are preparing for the Protestant ministry."

Catholics in America, he went on to say, have a role to play chiefly in providing blacks with moral training. "In the formation of his character, which is his weak spot, chief stress should be laid on moral training and education...Neither by nature nor by traditional training can the colored people, taken as a body, stand as yet upon the same footing of moral independence as their white brethren." He also called upon Catholics to open up the labor unions to blacks. "We [Catholics] are a large proportion, if not a majority, in many labor organizations." Catholics should use their influence on behalf of blacks. Catholic schools should be open to them. If Catholics continue to exclude blacks, "then the name 'Catholic' would be a misnomer when applied to the American Church, and we should sink into the position of a sect." He concluded with a list of the religious communities and the number of priests in the black apostolate, plus the number of churches and schools that were devoted to the service of black Catholics.[74]

Dr. William S. Lofton at some point also had the opportunity to address the Columbian Catholic Congress in a talk entitled "Wider Fields for Negro Employment."[75] For Lofton a dangerous situation was arising as the number of educated blacks increased, but the opportunities open to them remained relatively small because of "the spectre of prejudice." It was this exclusion of qualified and educated blacks on all levels of opportunity that created a climate of frustration. "Such people must become anything but good citizens. With nothing but their wits they become a prey on the community; a constant menace to the individual and the Nation." Lofton suggested the remedy: "Give to the black man a chance to earn the bread by the sweat of his brow. A chance to use those talents given him by a common Father... Why are you to prefer the expense of importing turbulent foreigners for the work that we can do? Why do you lessen the mechanical output of the country by denying us the privilege of working at trades for which we have demonstrated a fitness?"

The man who presided over the sessions of the fourth black Catholic congress was James Alexander Spencer (1849–1911). Among the congress movement leaders, he was one of the oldest and the most respected. Spencer had been a free black before the Civil War. He belonged to the free black community in Charleston, S.C., which had enjoyed some status and prominence before the war. Spencer had been a member of the Reconstruction legislature in South Carolina for the term of 1874–76.[76] For a time in his youth, he had been a schoolteacher. In 1867, shortly after the Civil War, Bishop Lynch of Charleston established St. Peter's as a black parish for the black Catholics in Charleston. Spencer served as secretary to the board of trustees. Canon Benoit mentioned Spencer in the diary of his journey through the South undertaken in the first half of 1875. He was introduced to him in a visit to the state legislature in Columbia. Benoit described him as "a sincere Catholic." Spencer told Benoit that his father had been "a zealous leader in the Catholic cause of Charleston." Benoit gave his assessment of Spencer as "one of the advanced Civil Rights-men... [who] looks with an Evil eye on any exclusive works for the Negroes since he wants all: blacks and whites, to stand on an equal footing, at least in the churches, if it cannot be done anywhere else."[77]

To show how independent black Catholics in Charleston were and how convinced they were of the equality of all members of the church, the following example is most illuminating. In his capacity as secretary to the board of trustees, Spencer had written a letter to Bishop Northrop regarding access of white Catholics to services in the black church. This letter was the result of a prior letter that had been sent to all the Catholic churches in Charleston, informing the people that all whites were to attend Mass in their own churches and not interfere with the black people of St. Peter's. The members of St. Peter's Parish wanted to know whether the letter meant "that no white Catholics whether living in the parish of St. Peter's or not shall attend Holy Mass at this church?" Did the circular also mean that blacks living at a distance, some of whom were aged and infirm, were constrained to attend Mass only at St. Peter's? Were the black Catholics at St. Peter's still free to attend Mass at other churches? These questions were submitted to the bishop by the trustees "in order that we may know something of our future position and obligations in the church to which we are firmly united."[78] The letter was signed by James A. Spencer, secretary of the meeting and by eighteen trustees.

Bishop Northrop would not reply in writing, but he invited them to come and see him so that he might discuss the matter "as brethren should do or as a father (though most unworthy) with his children."[79] It is not known what the outcome was. What is most interesting is that this black parish not only had a board of trustees but that a major concern was that the church not be a totally segregated church and that blacks should have access to other churches.

It is precisely this question of separate churches for blacks that Spencer, who served as president for the fourth congress, addressed in his lengthy talk to the congress. He spoke of the reason why the church established parishes for people of different nationalities. The reason was that all should have access to the church but also the church should be open to the needs and wishes of each. Thus the bishops establish national parishes in order to encourage diverse national groups. It is for this same reason that parishes should be established for her black children. Spencer underscored the enormous advance that African Americans had made in terms of education and prosperity since slavery. He stated that the American blacks had shown that they were worthy of the consideration and aid of the church. Separate churches for blacks, however, should not become a pretext for discrimination and segregation. Black churches should be on the same footing as German or Polish churches. He admitted, however, that separate churches for blacks had not been without detriment to the race in some places. Expressing his own opinion in the matter, Spencer suggested that the time had come when perhaps Catholic schools for blacks were more important than the establishment of more separate churches for African Americans.[80]

The most important document of the fourth congress, however, was the final address to their fellow Catholics. This document was drawn up by a committee of eight, with William Edgar Easton as chairman. The others were Lincoln Vallé, Fredrick McGhee, W. N. Woods of New York, Charles H. Butler, Daniel Rudd, Willis J. Smith of Washington, D.C., and S. K. Govern of Philadelphia. Govern's name appears on the printed text in the *Boston Pilot* but not on the typewritten text in the University of Notre Dame Archives.[81]

The document begins: "The colored Catholics of the United States, through their representatives to their 4th congress, in convention assembled in the city of Chicago, with the approbation of his Grace, Archbishop Feehan, invoke the blessing of God, the prayers of the holy church, and the good will of mankind in issuing their 4th address for the kind consideration of those interested in spreading the faith among our people." One important feature of the address is the balance between expressions of loyalty to the church and rejection of racism within the church. "The Catholic Church, guided by the spirit of truth, must always preserve inviolate the deposit of faith, and thus she cannot err in proclaiming the rights of man." Unfortunately, members of the church have not lived up to the church's mission "to raise up the downtrodden, and to rebuke the proud ... to proclaim to the ends of the earth that we all have stamped on our immortal souls the image of God." Because of an intense desire to spread the faith to other members of the black race, there is an obligation "to the Church and to God that we draw attention of every member of the learned Roman hierarchy to such deviations from Catholic law and Catholic practice."

At this point the address referred to the committee of grievances that had been set up in the third congress. The fourth congress as a committee of the whole had examined this report.

> The voluminous report was carefully sifted. The evidence, oral and written, fairly showed that though no children of the world are more docile to their superiors than the children of Christ's true Church, yet owing to the frailty of human nature, if we would have our rights, we must needs demand them.
>
> Whatever action is taken to thwart the racist practices of some members of the Church, it is done by those who both love and take pride in the Church.

A distinguished lady of color who is not a Catholic asserts that the Catholic Church of all Christian churches comes nearest practicing the doctrines of the rights of man. We know that the Roman Church, as she is One and Apostolic, is also Catholic and Holy. With thorough confidence in the rectitude of our course, in the enduring love of Mother Church and the consciousness of our priesthood, we show our devotion to the Church, our jealousy of her glory, and our love for her history in that we respectfully call the attention of the Catholic world, and in particular of the clergy, to those wrong practices which mark the conduct of those of the clergy who have yielded to the popular prejudice... Those who have departed from the teaching of the Church, we would see reclaimed and those of our own people who have not yet had their eyes opened to the light of God, we would see converted.

Pride is expressed in being Catholic, in the charitable works of the church, in the history of the church, and especially in the African history of the church and in the recent history of the church in regard to black Americans. "Above all things, we rejoice that our Church, the Church of our love, the Church of our faith, has not failed to stand by its historic record. For did not Holy Church canonize Augustine and Monica, Benedict the Moor and Cyprian, Cyril, Perpetua and Felicity?" No matter what might be the prejudice of others, the church has entrusted the priesthood to black men.

Public opinion has moulded the sentiment that a negro could not be a priest of the Roman Catholic Church. The Catholic Church has rebuked this sentiment by ordaining the Reverend Father A. Tolton, the first negro priest in America, and the Rev. C. R. Uncles to the exalted estate of Catholic priesthood.[82] We desire to say every encouragement, every fraternal greeting extended the priests of our race are in our opinion so many more proofs of the divine truth of Catholic religion.

The address ended perhaps a little tamely with the promise of a mass conversion of blacks if the clergy would do away with external signs of racial prejudice. "The day will yet come when the whole colored race of the United States will be knocking at her doors for admittance, anxious to be of that faith which teaches and practices the sublime essence of human rights, in the sight of God and our fellow man." Mass conversion was a favorite theme of Rudd that had passed on into the language of the black Catholic congress.

This address of the fourth congress gives a glimpse of what might be called an incipient black Catholic theology of church. First of all, the church preserves the deposit of faith because it teaches the doctrine of the equality of all peoples before God. The mission of the church is to announce love in place of hate, to raise up the downtrodden, and to proclaim the essential value of all men and women. In a word, these black Catholics at the end of the nineteenth century made the social implications of Catholicism one of the most important features of the Catholic church. In this period of church history this approach was unconventional in American Catholicism. It is also most interesting that these African American Catholics spoke about the "rights of man," a term associated with the French Revolution. In this black Catholic text, the church's concern for such rights is the same, it would seem, as the present-day ideal of "human rights," an unusual approach for the time.

Another aspect of this black Catholic theology is the moral imperative to denounce racism within the church because it goes contrary to authentic Catholic belief and morality. They do not see themselves as rebels or even as a loyal opposition. Rather they are eminently loyal and faithful to the church that they love and are proud of. One phrase in this document is very obscure. The address states: "With thorough confidence in the rectitude of our course in the enduring love of Mother Church, and the consciousness of our priesthood, we show our devotion to the Church, our jealousy of her glory and our love for her history." Very few lay Catholics at the end of the nineteenth century would have spoken of their "priesthood." The notion of the "priesthood of the faithful" is very much a part of Catholic tradition, but at this time it was not widely used. Did the congress members mean by "their priesthood" the theological concept that all baptized Christians share in the priesthood of Christ? If they did, whence came their acquaintance with this idea? For these men to have a consciousness of their priesthood was to have a very profound sense of the Catholic teaching on the sacraments and grace.

Equally profound is the historical awareness of the black Catholic congress. Historical references to Africa were not at all uncommon in these congresses. In this document we see that blacks appropriated for themselves a Catholic history. Where other ethnic groups looked to their European ancestors for their Catholic roots, the black Catholics in America looked to the early church in North Africa for theirs. Sts. Augustine, Monica, Cyprian, Cyril of Alexandria, Perpetua, and Felicity are saints of North Africa (Cyril was an Egyptian). Only Benedict the Moor, mentioned in the previous chapters, was a descendant of black slaves from sub-Saharan Africa, and he was a Sicilian. As a result, black Catholics had fashioned for themselves a rootedness in Christian antiquity that neither the Irish nor the Germans possessed; and they had made a link with Africa that no black Baptist or AME church member could ever forge. They had a ready-made history that the average American Catholic lacked. They had seized the opportunity for acquiring a sense of pride. In doing all this, they were quite in line with the romantic historical writing of the period.

IV

On Friday, June 29, 1894, a letter appeared in the *New York Sun* entitled "The Treatment of Colored Catholics by the Church." The letter, in the form of an article, was written by Robert N. Wood, chairman of the Committee on Grievances among Colored Catholics. Wood described how the committee had been formed in the third congress in Philadelphia in 1892 and a report was made in the fourth congress in Chicago in 1893. It was then decided that another report should be made in the fifth congress, which was to be held in Baltimore in 1894. The letter gave several examples of discrimination in Catholic churches in the South. Wood explained that he had received sixty-seven letters from the American bishops, "some good, some not." Wood stated that he planned to take these grievances to Rome to Pope Leo XIII.

Robert N. Wood was a Democratic politician in New York. For many years he headed the black political club known as the United Colored Democracy, which was aligned with Tammany Hall. He had a colorful career as a political leader. In his obituary notice in the *New York Times*, he was credited with having organized the first black regiment of the New York National Guard. His son, Robert N. Wood, Jr., who owned a printing establishment, would publish W. E. B. Du Bois's periodical, the *Crisis*.[83] Robert Wood as chairman of the grievance committee had sent letters to each American bishop inquiring about the treatment of blacks in his diocese. He reports in his letter in the *New York Sun* that he had received sixty-seven responses. There were eighty-two dioceses and four vicariates in the United States in 1893, which means that more than two-thirds of the bishops answered the letter. A copy of this letter and a covering letter were sent to Archbishop Francesco Satolli, the apostolic delegate, who had assumed the position that year.

The covering letter, written by Wood, requested an audience with the delegate at his earliest convenience. "While your humble suppliant is a most unworthy person, the cause he represents is one which interests not only the Colored people, but the country in general and the entire Catholic Church."[84] Enclosed with this letter was a copy of the circular that had been sent to all of the United States bishops. The first paragraph explained the circumstances of the letter's writing — namely, "complaints of the humiliating discriminations imposed by the different Catholic churches and Institutions . . . so numerous that a committee was appointed to investigate these complaints." The letter went on to explain that "in order that we may ascertain the exact status of the Colored Catholics in this country, the following questions are respectfully submitted to every Bishop in the United States." The questions asked whether rules imposing segregation were found in the churches and institutions of the diocese, whether blacks enjoyed the same freedom as white Catholics, whether black children attended the same parochial schools and Catholic colleges as whites, whether blacks were admitted into the hospital, and whether blacks were seated in the rear of the church or in the gallery. If there was racial discrimination, who would the bishop say is to blame?[85]

The circular letter was signed by Mr. Pinckney of Florida, Charles Butler of Washington, D.C., and R. N. Wood, chairman, of New York. The *Church News* reported that the bishops in general replied that black Catholics were not discriminated against "by any rule of the diocese." They agreed that there was some discrimination by individual churches, which they deplored.[86]

On September 20, 1894, Dr. Lofton wrote the apostolic delegate, Archbishop Francesco Satolli, asking him to attend the fifth congress, which was to meet in Baltimore October 8–10. Satolli, in fact, did not attend the meeting, but he did write a letter that was read at the congress by Lofton. The apostolic delegation file contains several drafts of the letter that the archbishop toiled over. In the file are two rough drafts in Italian and then over four drafts in English. Satolli declared that he had great sympathy "for the colored race." He acknowledged, "I cannot dissimulate that in my opinion if from the happy day of their liberation from the yoke of slavery, the civilizing action of Catholics had been exercized widely and efficaciously, to-day their condition would be better than it is." He was under the impression that many blacks were not civilized: "I have heard that it is difficult to describe the degree of degradation." Satolli spent a great deal of time on the notion of duty and rights regarding the African Americans. One has the impression that he wanted to stress the idea that blacks must be aware of their duties at the same time that they demanded their rights. He praised the congress and stated that he wanted to give "words of encouragement and felicitation, that not only may wise and practical resolutions be taken, but that Congress may lead to other conventions to maintain and increase the same action to the end, which I have mentioned above." In his draft Satolli had crossed out the word "congresses" and substituted "conventions." This may be significant inasmuch as the fifth congress was the last to be held until 1987.[87]

The *Church News* stated that there were thirty-eight delegates and nineteen alternates who assembled for the fifth congress, which was held at St. Peter Claver Hall in Baltimore. Father Slattery's sermon to the congress at the opening Mass was summarized in the newspaper. He noted that "the colored man needs encouragement to well-doing, to ambition, to rise above the degrading circumstances." He went on to repeat what he had said at the Columbian Catholic Congress, namely, that blacks were not on the same moral footing of independence as whites. "They need the whites and the whites need them." He spoke about the needs for a better family life and the need for religion — "not a religion which puts holiness and sanctification in the whirl and excitement of a camp-meeting or a revival."

Slattery in his sermon seems to have cautioned against too much activism on the part of the congress members when he said, "Two powerful factors, whose influence for good can never be realized, are working in favor of the colored race. They are Time and Silence." He stated that blacks must "get along with their neighbors...that they have everything to gain by patient forbearance, and much to lose by hurry and temper." In this address, it could be said that the paternalistic tendencies of Slattery were somewhat more evident.[88]

There were other addresses at the congress. Butler's talk was entitled "The Humane Element of the Catholic Church." The matter of the complaints of discrimination received by the grievance committee was discussed at length. It was decided that Robert N. Wood of New York and S. K. Govern of Philadelphia should go to Philadelphia and lay before the archbishops, meeting in Philadelphia, the complaints that were received by the grievance committee. It is not recorded what response, if any, the archbishops made at their meeting. The question of the creation of an industrial school was taken up again. Plans were made to try to buy land owned by the Bureau of Catholic Indian Missions near Washington, D.C., and to contact Father Stephan, the head of the bureau.[89]

The fifth congress was the last to be held in the nineteenth century. Was this because the congresses had become more active and thereby perhaps more militant? Or was it because Rome itself became more wary of the activities of lay Catholic congresses in general?[90] In a letter to Father Slattery in 1900, McGhee and Lofton wrote that they regretted being unable to see him when they were in Baltimore. They wished to discuss with him the possibility of another congress to be held in Baltimore. "Such a meeting will be the means of arousing our people and bringing together forces that will mean much in the interest of Holy Mother Church." They went on to say that "we are not forgetful of some mistake[s] of the last meeting, yet a good cause should not be allowed to die because of a few mistakes and hot heads, neither should all be held responsible for the shortcoming of others." The two men deplored the fact that "the Catholic Church is looked upon by most non-Catholic[s] of our race as distinctly White." They felt that many of the most intelligent black Catholics were abandoning the church and that something had to be done.[91] There is no record of a reply.

The black lay Catholic congresses were not a failure. In fact, they achieved what Rudd set out to do in calling the first congress. They demonstrated beyond a doubt not only that a black Catholic community existed but that it was active, devoted, articulate, and proud. It also demonstrated that given the opportunity, there was real leadership within the black Catholic community. Other ethnic groups had their clergy who could speak on their behalf. Black Catholics lacked a body of black priests who commanded respect on a national scale. From the beginning a black laity had to take charge. Strong lay leadership would remain a constant characteristic of African American Catholicism. Furthermore, this leadership involved men who were authentic leaders within the black community and men who were also strong Catholics despite many rebuffs.

These congresses were a success also because they created a movement that was intellectual as well as social. Theirs was a rhetoric that unlocked the doors of certain key ideas — namely, the mass conversion of blacks and the power of the church to change racism within this country. The further careers of such men like Rudd, Vallé, and McGhee, which we will note in the following chapter, indicate that the congress movement did bear fruit in the realm of faith. The congresses also laid the foundation for future black Catholic movements, including those of very recent times. One last point often overlooked is that the black Catholic congresses were more of a sign of lay involvement than any similar movement in the American church as a whole. There were never more than two general lay Catholic congresses. Black Catholics had five in the nineteenth century. Finally, the congresses made their impact on Roman authorities. The extent of this impact will be better known as more documents from the Vatican Archives become available. In the next chapter, however, we shall see how Rome reacted to the plight of the black Catholic community, a community that had articulated its hopes and its dreams so well in the congresses.

Chapter 8

BLACK AND CATHOLIC: A TESTIMONY OF FAITH

In January 1904 Archbishop Diomede Falconio, O.F.M.,[1] the apostolic delegate of the newly elected Pope St. Pius X, received a letter from the cardinal prefect of the Congregation of the Propaganda, Girolamo Maria Gotti, O.D.C.,[2] which marked a renewal of interest on the part of the Holy See in black Catholics in the United States. Gotti noted, "It has been referred to this Sacred Congregation that in some of the dioceses of the United States the condition of the Catholic negroes, not only in respect to the other faithful but also in respect to their pastors and bishops, is very humiliating and entirely different from that of the whites."[3] The letter went on to point out that such actions were "not in conformity with the spirit of Christianity, which proclaims the equality of all men before God." Alluding to the fact that these actions militated against charity and the work of evangelization, the cardinal prefect insisted that Cardinal Gibbons should confer with the archbishops of the country "to procure that this diversity of treatment may be lessened and thus little by little entirely removed."[4]

In 1904 the United States was still subject to the Congregation of the Propaganda. Hence, the situation of black Catholics was the concern of Cardinal Gotti. The tone of the letter is somewhat surprising, for it is blunt and not diplomatic. There is no judicious inquiry as to the existence of the "humiliating conditions." There are no discreet questions or politely phrased suggestions. There is simply a peremptory command to correct the situation because it is, in a word, unchristian. As to when the sacred congregation became aware of the situation, there is no specific information in the files of the apostolic delegation, although it seems safe to assume that Rome was made aware by firsthand reports from the United States. One need only recall the investigation of the Committee of Grievances, which gave its report at the fourth black Catholic lay congress in Chicago in 1893. These allegations were to be made known to the Holy See.[5]

I

There is one copy of a document in the delegation files that had certainly reached Rome only the year before. This document was a red-bound, printed booklet of forty-six pages, addressed *Ad Sanctissimam Sedem*. The text was in Latin, and it was published in 1903 at Namur in Belgium. The booklet is found in the delegation files with a handwritten dedication "to the most excellent and most gracious Apostolic Delegate, D. Falconio, D.D. with the hope of benevolence for the black people."[6] The cover has stamped on it in gold lettering, *confidentiale*. The title of the booklet was *The Miserable Condition of Black Catholics in America*. The author was Joseph Anciaux, S.S.J., who had been born in Belgium in 1860 and had entered the Josephites in 1904.[7] Anciaux had sufficient influence to see that his little work was introduced into the highest circles.

Anciaux spelled out the civil disabilities and the social inequities that oppressed African Americans. He spoke of the injustices in the legal system that resulted in a black man's always being punished with the severest penalty. And he quoted the adage "The law for whites differs from the law for blacks." Referring to the evils of lynching, he pointed out that this meant that in many cases, blacks could be put to death without a trial by private citizens. He indicated that lynching was a daily occurrence in the United States and that three thousand lynchings had occurred in a period of ten years. He spoke of the evils of segregation, which reduced all African Americans to the status of outcasts in American society. He cited instances of these social inequities from his personal experience.

> Nearly all priests (even the most pious) fear the reproach of white citizens so much that they scarcely dare to make the slightest effort on behalf of blacks; others are so imbued with prejudice that they say: "The care of blacks is not my concern, they do not belong to my flock."

> A certain priest said to me: "One wastes time and money in ministering to blacks"; and another said to me: "What reason can there be that you are so solicitous for the Negro?"[8]

He described the segregation of blacks in Catholic churches, the humiliation of being relegated to the gallery or the side aisles. He went on to speak of the refusal to admit blacks to schools in the South or to any Catholic college or university in the country, with the possible exception, he noted, in most recent times of certain Cuban or Filipino students. He stated that the bishops desired that souls be saved, "but one cannot deny that they suffer something of human [frailty]." Making exception for certain of the bishops such as Ireland of St. Paul, Durier of Natchitoches, and Janssens of New Orleans, he knew of no one "who had the boldness to protect or defend openly the rights of blacks."

Anciaux then went on to cite specific cases of racism among the American prelates. He cited the speech of Bishop Keiley of Savannah,[9] who publicly criticized President Theodore Roosevelt for inviting Booker T. Washington to dinner at the White House. On another occasion when visiting with the vicar-general of New Orleans, the conversation turned to the question of American blacks.[10] This prelate gave as his opinion that "in America no black man should be ordained. Just as illegitimate sons are declared irregular by Canon Law . . . so blacks can be declared irregular because they are held in such contempt by whites." While noting that this opinion was foreign to the mind of the church and that the prelate had made clear that it was his private opinion, Anciaux remarked that such a sentiment was held by many priests in America.

He also quoted the words of a bishop whom he much admired, Theophile Meerschaert, who had done much for the Native Americans and blacks in his diocese,[11] "It is best for blacks to labor, but let them be mindful of their condition and stay in their place like the good blacks of former times." Anciaux noted that such a statement ignored the times and the spirit of progress. The Protestants had opened innumerable schools and colleges for African Americans, as had also the American government. Books and newspapers daily encouraged blacks to civil progress, ambition, and pride. He considered it "most imprudent that priests should impose upon them that they not think about a higher status, that they cast aside all hope of future civic equality, and that they remain in a lowly condition." He added that this was the greatest error "of holy prelates of a former time." He concluded by wondering how such statements would have been received in the Europe of that day if the clergy had told the workers to remain satisfied with their inferior condition.

Anciaux suggested a twofold solution to these problems. First, bring to the United States the religious and the sisters who had been expelled from France by the anticlerical governments and turn their zeal to the conversion of the African Americans.[12] Second, attach to the apostolic delegation in Washington a prelate who would have the pastoral responsibility for the ministry and evangelization of the black community.

II

The result of Cardinal Gotti's letter, no matter who or what prompted its origin, was not a concerted effort to end racial segregation in the churches or to end the rejection of blacks from educational institutions. What the bishops did was create another agency, in 1907 establishing the Catholic Board of Negro Missions, with the Reverend John E. Burke, a diocesan priest from New York, as the first director.[13]

The Roman Curia, on the other hand, did not simply confine itself to a single recommendation made to the American hierarchy. In fact, for the period between 1912 and 1921, the files of the apostolic delegation reveal a great deal of interest on the part of the prefect of the Consistorial Congregation, Cardinal Gaetano De Lai,[14] and the prefect of the Congregation of the Propaganda, Cardinal Willem van Rossum.[15] In a series of communications with the apostolic delegate of the time, Archbishop Giovanni Bonzano,[16] these two prelates undertook a series of initiatives seeking to provide for the spiritual welfare of black Catholics and to further the evangelization of American blacks as a whole. These initiatives were threefold and were based on three presuppositions: (1) an effective program for evangelizing the black community must be devised, (2) a corps of missionaries provided with resources and incentive must be found for this purpose, and (3) discrimination against blacks in Catholic institutions of higher learning and in seminaries must be brought to an end. The presuppositions were that little was being done by the American church for the evangelization of blacks, that a nationwide ordinariate or an autonomous episcopal jurisdiction would be most effective for coordinating evangelization efforts, and that the creation of an indigenous clergy was fundamental for effective ministry to blacks.

Cardinal De Lai diligently sought out details regarding population, religious facilities, and mission efforts established for the black apostolate. Inquiries were sent to the Census Bureau by both Archbishops Falconio and Bonzano requesting population figures for blacks in each state. The apostolic delegate was requested to find and send a publication of the United States Government Printing Office on higher education among Negroes.[17] This interest on the part of the Roman Curia extended for more than a decade, but most of the activity occurred about 1911–12 and the years 1919–21. Examples of this solicitude were two reports that Cardinal De Lai forwarded to Archbishop Bonzano. Both documents were drawn up in French by two French-speaking missionaries who had worked in Africa. Both had recently visited the Southern part of the United States and had made known to the Roman Curia their observations on the mission work among the blacks. Both documents were unsigned, and both offered solutions based on the authors' African experience.

The first document was four pages, entitled *Nègres*, sent by Cardinal De Lai with a cover letter in June 1912. Bonzano was to examine the report very carefully, as it was "questione tanto importante." He was to consult with others and then send in a report in triplicate to the Consistorial Congregation in preparation for a full-scale discussion of the religious situation of blacks in the United States.[18] The writer of the report had visited the South, and it is evident that he had garnered some information but had received other impressions that in the main were superficial. Recognizing the profound prejudice against blacks that existed in the country, he noted the rapid increase in the black population as compared to the relatively small number of black Catholics. It was his opinion that little effort was made for the conversion of blacks to Catholics. Not only was there little enthusiasm for ministry to blacks, but those who engaged in it were despised by the white population.

Convinced that success in such a ministry demanded religious dedicated to that work, he called attention to the apostolate of the Holy Ghost Congregation and the Society of the African Missions. Without mentioning their name, he referred to the work of the Josephites, suggesting that they did good work but noting that it was insufficient. Their seminarians were described as more pious than intelligent. There were few black priests, and he foresaw only a slow increase in their number. The work of the black sisters, however, was praised. On the other hand, the writer was under the impression that missionary activity in the South was potentially more fruitful because, unlike Africa, there was no institution of polygamy, the black population had a great desire for schooling, the missionaries had less need to occupy their time with the material construction of their missions, American blacks had greater material resources to contribute, and, not the least, the physical conditions that shortened the life of many African missionaries did not exist in the American South.

Bonzano took this report, which was certainly far from adequate in its analysis of the situation, and submitted it to Father John E. Burke, the New York priest who had organized the Catholic Board for Negro Missions. Bonzano wrote Burke in October of that same year, asking him for statistics on the black population and the black Catholic community according to dioceses. He sought information regarding the number of churches, converts, and such activities as parish missions. Finally, he requested his opinion on the best means of attracting blacks to the Catholic faith as well as any other pertinent information that he might have.[19]

Burke's response to these questions was not made until the following spring. When it finally came, it was a thoroughgoing analysis of the situation of black Catholics in the United States at that time.[20] Burke apologized for being unable to give anything other than approximate figures for the number of black Catholics in the country. He pointed out the lack of hard data and the amount of guesswork often used to arrive at the figures. He acknowledged that the highest number of black Catholics were to be found in the states of Louisiana and Maryland and the coastal areas along the Gulf of Mexico; however, the large cities in other states had their share. Unfortunately, in the wake of the Civil War, several thousand blacks had left the church in Louisiana.

The pattern of racial segregation within the churches in the South was described in detail. If the number of black Catholics in a given locality was large, they were relegated to a side aisle; smaller numbers were confined to a section in the rear of the church or to a place in the gallery. Burke ironically pointed out that the significant numbers of black Catholics who abandoned the church in the period following the Civil War was clear evidence that blacks had "never been spoiled by too much care."

Burke listed the missions for black Catholics established by the three religious communities — the Josephites, the Society for African Missions, and the Society of the Divine Word. In his estimation, there were about a thousand conversions per year within the black population, not forgetting that probably the leakage from the church was greater than the increase. Finally, Burke noted that there was a gain in membership where separate churches for black Catholics had been established, but where white Catholics and black worshiped together, there was a loss precisely because of the humiliation of segregated seating and prejudicial treatment, which the younger generation of blacks would no longer accept.

Burke treated the subject of evangelization in two sections: (1) the obstacles to the conversion of the African American, and (2) the best means to reach out to non-Catholic African Americans. The obstacles were four: the lack of priests, the existence of secret societies, the lack of rapport, and low standards of morality. Burke placed the question of vocations squarely in the first place of obstacles. At a period when other professions and opportunities were being opened to blacks, there were only four black Catholic priests in the United States. Furthermore, white priests, even though they worked among blacks, failed to gain a sympathetic rapport with the people and thus never won their trust. Many blacks joined secret societies that were banned by the church for the insurance benefits attached to membership. Burke noted that many blacks had joined the secret societies long before the Catholic church had made any serious effort at their conversion. Finally, many blacks would be unable to comply with the marriage laws of the church. Burke blamed this in part on the "baneful and corrupt teaching of ignorant colored preachers." He noted that many marriages were invalid. At the same time, he observed, there were many more who lived in good and stable marriages than many would suppose.

In the list of means for gaining black converts to Catholicism, Burke gave first priority to the establishment of Catholic schools. In regard to the secret societies, Burke suggested that the ban regarding membership should be maintained for black Catholics, but permission should be obtained from the Holy See allowing prospective converts to retain their membership in such societies for the sake of the financial benefits. Burke noted that black secret societies did not present the same threat to Catholicism that the white societies did. He also urged that the church should create societies with similar financial benefits for black Catholics.

In order to attract more African Americans to Catholicism, Burke advocated separate churches for blacks, especially in the area of Texas, Louisiana, and the Gulf coast. Finally, he came back to the question of black vocations to the priesthood. He insisted that an indigenous priesthood was the church's traditional method of missionary activity: raise the converted people's "sons to the ministry, until finally a complete body of clergy of their own flesh and blood was established." Consequently, Burke urged the establishment of a separate college and seminary as soon as possible for the training of black candidates for

the priesthood. It was important that the students learn to create a
social life of their own, "thus doing away with a delicate situation."
Burke was referring to the question of social contacts between blacks
and whites. It was of paramount importance that the black priest not
expect social equality with white priests.

Burke, moreover, went on to express the belief that once the number of black clergy had grown to sufficient numbers, a black bishop
should be consecrated. He was convinced that only through black
priests and sisters would the black race be converted. "We live next
door to the negro and yet he is like a sealed book. His lips are closed
to the white man. It is only a colored priest who could know all about
him. The Catholic Church will never gain the colored race until she
has a colored priesthood." Burke added one more suggestion in his
report regarding the role of the church's pageantry and ceremonies
in the conversion of blacks. "As the negro is naturally of a sentimen-
tal temperament, greater results can be obtained by appealing to this
sentiment." Along with "good practical instruction," there should be
provided "plenty of missions, processions with banners and regalia,
in a word apply the truth of the church in as concrete a manner as
possible."

Burke concluded his report with the summation of an article that
had appeared in a Southern periodical, the *South Atlantic Monthly*.
A professor in a Southern theological seminary gave his students the
task of writing an essay on the subject, "What will become of the
American Negro?" His students, all coming from Mississippi, Tennessee, Louisiana, Alabama, Georgia, Virginia, and Florida, were
from the leading families in the South, many of them students for
the ministry. Almost without exception, they were thoroughly convinced of the inferiority of blacks to whites, the uselessness and
even the harm of education for blacks, the inevitable position of
servitude that blacks must maintain toward whites, and the likeli-
hood that there would be a racial war between blacks and whites
in the United States. For Burke, it was important that the delegate
have some idea of the gravity of the racial situation in American
society and the importance of what the church was called upon to
do.[21] Burke's conclusion expressed his own assessment of African
Americans based upon thirty years of ministry in the black community. He pointed out that a large number of blacks belonged to no
church. "There are certainly about five millions of unbaptized negroes in the United States." He, like most of the Catholic clergy at
the time, had little esteem for the black Protestant churches. Yet, unlike most Catholic priests, Burke expressed a high regard for black

Protestants. He had nothing but praise, though, for the spirituality of black Catholics.

Burke's report is exceptional because of its fairness and thoroughness. Unlike many ecclesiastics writing at the time, Burke never spoke about blacks in a condescending and demeaning manner. He made no assumption of black inferiority and no complacent observations about black people's lax morality. The man who had devoted thirty years of his life to ministry in the black community was one who evinced a sincere respect for the people whom he served. Attached to Burke's report was another report entitled "How to Convert the Colored Race." It was unsigned, but a subsequent communication made a few months later identified the author as a Josephite priest, John Albert, at the time pastor of St. Peter's Church in Pine Bluff, Arkansas.[22]

Albert was convinced that only African American priests would be fully acceptable to black Catholics. He insisted that if one cannot encourage priestly vocations from the youth, then one cannot hope to convert the black population. He went on to point out that under the existing conditions it was impossible for black priests to be accepted into the general society. The solution lay in the creation of a totally separate jurisdiction. At first there should be a white bishop whose jurisdiction would extend wherever blacks were found. He would be in complete control of the recruitment and education of a black clergy. An education totally separate from white students was necessary, for the black students would have to learn from the beginning that they must form a social life on their own. Once there was a sufficiently large number of black clergy, the autonomous jurisdiction should have a black bishop at its head.

Albert rejected any notion that this would be simply the creation of a "Jim Crow Church." He did admit, however, that there would be resentment "to the idea of a separate church as much as...[to] the Jim Crow car." He labeled such conclusions as sentimentality. He was convinced that his was the only practical solution in a period of serious racial conflict and in the face of massive withdrawal from Catholicism, particularly by light-skinned blacks in Louisiana and the Gulf states. He believed that desperate times called for daring solutions. Albert followed up this addendum with another missive to the delegate in the fall. This time he wrote to the delegate directly and signed his name, indicating that he was the author of the anonymous addendum to Burke's report.[23] Albert proceeded to review the arguments for the necessity of a black clergy. He pointed out that during the past academic year there had been some fifteen or so applications for the Josephite seminary from black youths. All were refused. Albert stated that such could not be the will of God.[24] According to Albert, two bishops from the South had suggested their own solution to the question of black priests, namely, the creation of a religious community of black priests under the direction of a white abbot. Being religious, they would be separate from the diocesan clergy and not directly under the bishops. Thus, there would be little temptation for them to enter into social relations with whites. Albert claimed that the bishop of Little Rock, John B. Morris, had offered to fund the establishment of the motherhouse of such a community in his diocese.

Even more interesting in the light of the recent history of the church was Albert's suggestion that the office of the permanent diaconate as it existed in the early church be revived. This would mean that a white priest would be responsible for a number of churches in a certain area. Black married deacons would take charge of the individual churches, where the priest would offer Mass according to a regular cycle. On those Sundays when the priest would not offer Mass, the deacon would "exercise all of the functions allotted in primitive Catholicism except, perhaps, the giving of Holy Communion." He pointed out that the office of deacons that existed in the Protestant churches could serve as a model. These married deacons need not be so well educated that they could not relate to the people. It would be sufficient that they be men of "piety, zeal, and prudence with a thorough knowledge of the catechism." Albert acknowledged that this idea had been suggested to him "by a member of the hierarchy." He urged Bonzano to present this suggestion to Rome after consultation with the American hierarchy. John Albert's suggestion of married deacons is highly significant inasmuch as this innovation would be adopted by the church as a result of the Second Vatican Council.

Before Bonzano could make his report to the Curia, Cardinal De Lai sent him another report concerning the church in the South. De Lai also stated that copies had been sent to the archbishop of Baltimore and the archbishop of New Orleans.[25] The report was seven pages long and was also written in French without an author's name.[26] It was entitled "Evangelization in the States of the South in the United States of America." The author indicated that he was a vicar apostolic in Africa. (At that period a vicar apostolic was a bishop who served as the head of an ecclesiastical territory, usually in mission countries, that had not yet been formed into a regular diocese.) By his own admission he had visited only Louisiana and the neighboring states. Nevertheless, he saw these states as having the character of a mission country, with few priests, most of whom were not native to America. He considered that the black Catholic population was for the most part abandoned and that the priest for the whites was in general unable to minister to the blacks. To remedy the situation, the writer proposed that a cadre of priests specifically mandated for black ministry be formed in each diocese. In fact, if it were a religious community, it would be all the better, as it would assure greater continuity and homogeneity. A director general with all the powers of a vicar-general should be placed at the head in the respective dioceses. In each black community where no priest is available, a layman or laywoman would serve as a catechist who would take charge of the education, lead the Sunday worship, baptize when necessary, nurse the sick, and represent the church.

The writer gave several recommendations concerning the financial aspect of the missions. The people themselves should contribute to the needs of the parish along with the diocese. The author noted that the Southern dioceses lacked a steady supply of priests from their own population. He suggested the creation of "apostolic schools" along with a theological seminary. In Europe the "apostolic schools" were high school seminaries. He believed that the Southern dioceses should use the example of the Josephinum in Columbus, Ohio, to create a seminary for the special needs of the South. There is no indication of how Bonzano reacted to this second report dealing with the question of evangelization of African Americans in the South. The suggestion of catechists as a means of evangelization was not entirely new. John R. Slattery, who had become the first superior of the Josephite Society, opened a school for black catechists in Alabama. It was begun as a result of the initiatives of Slattery and was established as St. Joseph's College for Negro Catechists, near Montgomery, Alabama.[27] In fact, Slattery hoped that it would be not only a training center for catechists but also a preparatory seminary for future black seminarians. Ultimately, it did not succeed in any of these endeavors and became a sort of high school. By 1921 it was closed.[28]

In May 1914 Bonzano made his report to Cardinal De Lai.[29] He acknowledged that he had gathered the information from Burke and other sources. His report contained information regarding the number of clergy, both secular and religious, that ministered to the black Catholic community; also an explanation of the pattern of segregation in the churches, which he said was decreed by law in the Southern states; and the devotions and services such as missions that were regularly held in the black parishes. It was acknowledged that in mixed parishes the pastor often favored the needs of whites over those of the black parishioners. As a result each year there was a loss of blacks to the church. He estimated that every year in the whole of the United States there were about a thousand African American converts but that the number of those leaving was probably greater.

Among the reasons given for the loss of so many black Catholics and the obstacles to their conversion, Bonzano mentioned in the first place the dearth of priests dedicated to the apostolate of blacks. It was true that there were few advantages in such a mission. It was also true, he noted, that some did not appreciate or understand the particular conditions and needs of their black parishioners. In the very dioceses in which blacks were most numerous, however, the number of priests for even the white parishes was the most limited, leaving, of course, the blacks even more abandoned. Just as the clergy were not numerous, so too there were few parochial schools for black children. Many black Catholic children were forced to attend public schools in which their faith was threatened. Bonzano brought up the question of the societies to which many blacks belonged. Like most Europeans Bonzano saw these secret societies as reflections of the Freemasons in one form or another. Last of all, Bonzano spoke of the natural disposition of the Negro, for blacks had "a proclivity to material pleasures, and [as] the level of morality is rather low, they cannot but find a serious difficulty in the sanctity of Catholic morality."

The means to evangelize African Americans, according to Archbishop Bonzano, came down essentially to one factor — that there be a sufficient supply of priests dedicated to that mission. He pointed out the presence of the Josephites and of other religious communities, such as the Holy Ghost Fathers, the Society of African Missions, and the Society of the Divine Word. Bonzano did not support the idea of a special jurisdiction or semiautonomous administration in a given diocese for the pastoral care of black Catholics. He believed that each bishop should have responsibility for the spiritual welfare of the blacks just as he had for the whites in his diocese. Bonzano did not agree with Burke that some means should be provided so that those black members of the secret societies who might wish to enter the Catholic church could retain passive membership with its financial benefits and still become Catholics. Bonzano was skeptical about the possibility of a purely passive membership.

Concerning a native clergy, Bonzano took an entirely different view from that of Burke. Bonzano did not favor the ordination of black men to the priesthood, because he was convinced that it was a "fact confirmed by experience" that blacks preferred white priests who were considered to be "from a superior race and hence had greater trust placed in them." Bonzano repeated again his assertions regarding the nature of blacks, their low moral standing, and their limited intelligence. He based his decision on his own personal experience as former rector of the Urban College attached to the Congregation of the Propaganda in Rome, the seminary from which Augustus Tolton had graduated. Bonzano had had occasion to render a decision regarding the fitness for ordination of two African students of the Zulu tribe. He voted against their ordination but was overruled. A few days after their ordination, one was placed in a hospital for the mentally ill, and the other was suspended from his priestly functions. He added that two other Zulu priests had faced a similar fate.

About two weeks later, Cardinal De Lai acknowledged the receipt of Bonzano's report. In the middle of the summer De Lai reported to Bonzano the result of the deliberations by the Consistorial Congregation regarding the reports that they had received on the religious situation of American blacks.[30] The letter was carefully worded so as to give sufficient credit to the American bishops, pointing out that "they had truly done as much as was in their power to lead to the Catholic Faith and to the practice of the Christian life that numerous population" and expressing admiration for the zeal and abnegation of many religious congregations in the work. Nevertheless there is expressed disappointment and a barely concealed criticism that the "harvest is indeed too small when comparing the number of converts to the number of missions." The cardinal noted that it is "far from the minds" of the members of the consistorial congregation to wish "to attribute a lack of diligence and care to the episcopate and the clergy, both secular and religious of the United States." This disavowal suggests that it had not been far from the minds of others who had reported to the Holy See.

What is most striking in De Lai's response to Bonzano's report is that after acknowledging the efforts made and the meager results, the cardinal proceeded to give specific recommendations as to how such evangelization could be improved. First, catechists were to be encouraged and developed, schools were to be increased, and hospitals and "diverse associations even of an economic nature" must be established for the needs "exclusively of the people of color." At the same time, in reference to some of the suggestions, the cardinal insisted that all the efforts were to be "under the oversight and the exclusive direction and surveillance of the ordinaries." It is interesting to note that the Roman Curia saw the evangelization efforts regarding blacks to include much more than worship and catechetics — it was to include concern for the health care and financial needs of a people whom they described as being "especially in a difficult situation."

III

One bishop in the South who did make a concerted effort to stem the leakage from the church was Francis Janssens, archbishop of New Orleans from 1888 to 1897.[31] As early as 1887, Janssens wrote an article in the *Catholic World* in which he analyzed the position of blacks in the Catholic church.[32] In asking the question as to how the Catholic church would reach the African American, Janssens answered by stating that it would only be through a clergy that was African American. It was his observation that "the colored race... mistrusts anything carried on for their benefit by the whites, unless the colored men are themselves allowed to act the principal parts." He then asked, "Why should not a colored boy who receives a special religious training obtain the grace from God to lead a pure life?" He urged that part of the collection for the Negro and Indian Missions be used to establish a school for black youths where the training would include Latin and where potential priestly vocations might be encouraged.

Francis Janssens was a daring, innovative man who, unlike many other bishops in the South, took a very active interest in the pastoral care of blacks. Noting that most blacks in the rural areas of Louisiana had little opportunity to share in the religious life of the Catholic parishes, where whites were in the majority, and that they were merely passive participants at the Sunday Mass, he believed that, if given the opportunity, many black Catholics would prefer a church of their own. There they could belong to the parish societies, have their own choirs, and generally play an active role in parish activities. As a result he was determined to establish a black parish as an experiment. Black Catholics were to have an option of belonging to the parish, but they would remain free to attend, if they so wished, the territorial parish.[33]

Janssens received opposition to his plans from some of the French priests in his archdiocese. Although white pastors in the French-speaking areas generally gave little if any pastoral care to their black parishioners, they did not wish to lose the financial contributions of the blacks. In some areas the blacks were more generous than the white parishioners. On the other hand, many blacks saw the proposal as another act of discrimination against them. This was especially true in the city of New Orleans, where many of the free people of color had a long-standing position of privilege.

Janssens brought the Assumptionists, a French-based religious community, into Louisiana to work exclusively among the black Catholic population. Although unable to create a black parish because of opposition from the Creoles and the French pastors, the Assumptionists were given a parish at Klotzville near Paincourtville in Assumption (civil) Parish in 1895. That same year, the archbishop did create a black parish in the city of New Orleans, with financial assistance from Mother Katherine Drexel. The Vincentians had relinquished St. Joseph Church, and Janssens prevailed upon them to reopen it as a black parish for non-French-speaking blacks. Janssens made it clear that the new parish, renamed St. Katherine's in gratitude for the financial support of Mother Katherine Drexel, was to be like a national parish to which no one was forced to belong.[34]

Eventually Archbishop Janssens entered into agreement with the Josephites to open churches for black Catholics in the rural areas of Louisiana. The Josephites were especially interested in work among the non-Catholic black population rather than in maintaining regular parishes. The first Josephite parish in Louisiana was opened in 1897 at Petite Prairie under a pastor who was a native of the area and an enthusiastic, energetic missioner. He became so well known and so beloved that his name was eventually given to the locality's first post office. His name was Pierre LeBeau, and he served at what is now LeBeau in St. Landry (civil) Parish until 1909. While Janssens sincerely believed that black Catholics were spiritually better off in a parish where their own wishes and desires could be fulfilled, he believed that memberships in such parishes should be optional. Later, however, under the administration of James Hubert Blenk, S.M., who was archbishop of New Orleans from 1906 to 1917, many more black parishes were established in the city and in the rural areas. By this time it was understood that black Catholics had no choice; they belonged to the black parish and not to the territorial parish.[35]

In more than one instance, black Catholics kept their Catholic faith alive without a pastor or the regular administration of the sacraments. The best-known example is the settlement at what is now known as Catholic Hill in Collerton County in the diocese of Charleston, South Carolina. A church dedicated to St. James the Greater was established in 1833 in this area by Bishop John England for the several Catholic families who had plantations and slaves. In 1856 the church of St. James burned to the ground. Within the decade the Civil War broke out, the church was not rebuilt, and the slaveholding families moved away, leaving only a small nucleus of Catholics among the blacks in the area that had come to be known as Catholic

Crossroads and is known today as Catholic Hill in Ritter, South Carolina. Without priest, church, or sacraments the Catholic faith was kept alive over a period of forty years through the efforts of a certain Vincent de Paul Davis, former slave and storeowner, who instructed the children.

In 1897 a priest attached to the cathedral in Charleston, Father Daniel Berberich, discovered this community of "lost" Catholics. Eventually the church of St. James the Greater was rebuilt, and Father Berberich became a regular pastoral visitor until 1909. Following him, other priests came from other towns to serve the community. But always there was a core of laymen and laywomen who taught and led the community in worship during the periods when a priest was absent. In 1935 a new church was built and the school remodeled. Over the high altar still hangs the painting of St. Peter Claver painted by a French artist, Emmanuel Dite, contemporary of Jacques David, which was in the original edifice of 1897. This painting, the church, the school, the cemetery, and the present congregation remain a visible monument to the tenacious faith of a community of black Catholics.[36] It is also another reminder of the fact that the preservation and the spread of Catholicism among the African American population has very often been the work of black laymen and laywomen.[37]

Some of the laymen who articulated this faith so well in the course of the black Catholic lay congresses of the 1890s gave a practical witness to it in the period following. Lincoln Charles Vallé is a striking example of a congress member turned apostle. In the summer of 1908, Vallé and his wife, Julia, arrived in Milwaukee from Chicago. Vallé went to Milwaukee with the avowed purpose of preaching to the blacks in Milwaukee. Sebastian Messmer,[38] the archbishop of Milwaukee, encouraged Vallé in his work of evangelization. There is no indication as to why Vallé chose Milwaukee as a place to bring Catholicism to the black community.

In 1900 there were fewer black Catholics in the city than at an earlier period.[39] Vallé, a journalist, had been active in Tolton's parish at St. Monica's in Chicago. After Tolton's death in 1897, Vallé wrote two years later to Slattery, asking him to let Charles Uncles come to Chicago and succeed Tolton as pastor. At the time he indicated that he had been very active in the parish.[40] At the end of the nineteenth century, Vallé served as editor of the *Conservator*, a Chicago black newspaper, which represented the viewpoint of a rising black middle class. It seems that he did not hold the post very long.[41] By the time Vallé went to Milwaukee, he had married a woman named Julia Yoular.

Vallé began by holding public meetings at a Catholic school on the edge of the black neighborhood, where he gave explanations concerning Catholicism. A short time later Vallé was able to rent a storefront building for the meetings. The neighboring black Methodist congregation lent them chairs through the kindness of the deacon. This became the St. Benedict the Moor Mission. By the next year the mission had moved from the storefront to a frame building on State Street. A chapel was installed, the School Sisters of Notre Dame began a course of religious instruction, and Mass was celebrated. In the period of a year and a half, some thirteen people entered the church.[42] Among the priests who came on an irregular basis to the mission were the Capuchin friars.

In 1911 the mission was confided to the care of the Capuchin friars by Archbishop Messmer. In the summer of 1910 Lincoln Vallé wrote to Father Justin McCarthy, S.S.J., the superior of the Josephites, inquiring as to the number of blacks who might be studying for the priesthood. Vallé went on to talk about his own work in Milwaukee: "Our work is moving along nicely, here. In fact the success of this work, through my own efforts, as a layman has startled this part of the country." He described how much was being accomplished "without a Pastor and without the regular attention of a Priest." Vallé stated that he had persuaded the Capuchins to "volunteer their services" and that he had the "full endorsement" of the archbishop.[43] The letterhead gave the name of Capt. L. C. Vallé as manager and editor of "The Catholic Truth." No editions of such a publication seem to be extant. It was probably a type of newsletter giving information about the mission and soliciting donations. The printed letterhead also indicated that the mission had a free employment service "where colored help can be furnished. Cooks, porters, coachmen and waiters." This aspect of the mission would change with the permanent arrival of the Capuchins.

The Capuchins brought regularity and stability to the mission. The number of baptisms of adult converts increased. Mass was celebrated regularly. A choir and a band were established. Regular instructions were instituted, and a new house was purchased by the Capuchins for the mission. In July 1913 Father Stephen Eckert, O.F.M. Cap., became the first permanent pastor. But with the establishment of the Capuchins as owners and directors of the mission, the position of Lincoln Vallé became more and more ambiguous. The relationship between Vallé and the Capuchin friars finally broke down completely just before Eckert became pastor. The house chronicle of St. Benedict the Moor Parish described the wife of Lincoln Vallé as an officious, gossiping woman who was not well liked by the black community. The chronicle criticized Mrs. Vallé for hiring a maid to help with the housekeeping at the mission. In the author's estimation she was lazy and unwilling to work.[44] Misunderstanding arose also with Lincoln Vallé himself. The notion of a "lay apostle" was not current at the time. The notion of a black being a professional man was also an unfamiliar concept. Vallé was considered a janitor and was to be paid a janitor's salary. His work as a journalist, editing an apologetic tract, was scarcely appreciated.[45] The chronicle reported that Vallé often drank to excess and suggested that not all money donated to him for the mission was given to the fathers, and Vallé was quoted as saying that the agreement called for these monies to be used to defray the expenses for the free distribution of "The Catholic Truth."[46]

Doubtless, the seeds of discontent and misunderstanding were sown when neither the Vallés nor the friars were asked to formalize their respective responsibilities. The question of race, however, was not entirely absent inasmuch as the friars combined great generosity with little trust in the people. Vallé was dismissed with the remark that the publication of "The Catholic Truth" was a financial failure, as the fathers received no funds from it. It was stated that had "a white, reliable man . . . been at head, with a little business understanding and tactics," the publication would not have failed.[47] Perhaps it would be more correct to say that without the zeal of the Vallés, the evangelization of Milwaukee's black community would not have taken place at the time or in the manner that it did. It seems less than magnanimous that they were simply dismissed without a word of gratitude or appreciation for their endeavors as Catholic lay leaders.

In the aftermath the Vallés returned to Chicago. Although Lincoln Vallé continued to write for various black newspapers,[48] not much information is available. In 1914 Stephen Eckert wrote Father Edward Hoban, the chancellor of the archdiocese of Chicago, regarding the appointment of Lincoln Vallé to a committee preparing for the fiftieth anniversary of the death of Abraham Lincoln. Eckert felt that Vallé was unworthy to represent Catholics and reiterated the charges of excessive drinking and misappropriation of funds.[49]

The last known communication from Lincoln Vallé was an article in 1924 entitled "The Catholic Church and the Negro," in *America* magazine.[50] In this article, written when Vallé was close to seventy, he gave his assessment of the relationship between black Americans in the South and the Catholic church. His basic thesis was that the Catholic church lost the opportunity to win the allegiance of the American Negro in the period following the Civil War because it did not invest people, time, and resources in the education and well-being of the freed slaves as did the Protestant churches. "The Catholic Church which possesses the deposit of Divine Faith is the only organism capable of producing, developing and maintaining in the race an adequate, moral basis, necessary for any noteworthy success."[51]

Vallé emphasized that the African Americans themselves must be the catalytic agent for the conversion of the blacks in this country. This will be done when the church begins to try in earnest to reach the educated portion of the black race. When Vallé wrote the article, he was an old man, one who had "as a Negro Catholic, ... spent the earlier part of my life in building up a healthy public opinion in favor of the Catholic Church among my people."[52] He may have felt that he had labored in vain when he observed at the end of the article: "What a gain, not only to the Negroes themselves, but also to our country, if very large numbers of the race had been led into the Catholic Church!"[53] He might have had some regrets; but the article showed that despite the unfortunate incidents in his relations with the clergy, he had remained steadfast in his faith and in his conviction regarding the place of the African American within it.[54]

Daniel Rudd, who could be called the father of the congress movement, continued his active participation on behalf of the black community. After moving his newspaper, the *American Catholic Tribune*, to Detroit in 1894, Rudd resided in that city until about 1899. It appears that the newspaper ceased publication about this time, although there are no extant copies after 1894. In 1910 the census data reveal that he was living in Bolivar County, northwestern Mississippi, where he was the manager of a lumber mill and where he boarded with a black family on their farm.[55] Some time before 1919, Rudd moved to Madison, Arkansas, and began working as an accountant for Scott Bond, a well-to-do black farmer, and his two sons. He coauthored a life of Scott Bond with his elder son, Theo Bond.[56] By the next year Rudd was working for another well-to-do black farmer, John Gammon, who operated a feed store on his farm in Marion, Arkansas, not far from Madison and the outskirts of Memphis, Tennessee.[57]

Rudd corresponded with Bishop Morris of Little Rock in 1919, using stationery bearing the heading "Scott Bond and Sons, General Merchandise and Cotton Buyers, Madison, Arkansas." Later he wrote on stationery with the letterhead "John Gammon, Merchant and Planter, Marion, Arkansas." Rudd introduced himself to the bishop and sought his backing to represent the diocese at a meeting of the NAACP in Cleveland in June 1919. He also sought a monetary advance. Bishop Morris would not accept him as representative of the diocese; but acknowledging that he had "great personal confidence" in him and because he wished "at all times to assist the colored race," he sent him a check for sixty dollars to defray his expenses.[58]

In an undated letter written about 1920, Rudd again sought authorization to attend an unnamed conference of laymen to be held in Washington, D.C. In that letter Rudd mentioned his past achievements and his accomplishments on behalf of his race.[59] When the bishop was ready to close down the black Catholic hospital in Pine Bluff, Rudd, who was far removed from the black Catholic center in Pine Bluff, offered his services as mediator. The bishop did not accept Rudd's help.[60] Finally, in a letter dated July 12, 1926, Rudd thanked the bishop for having appointed him as a representative of the black Catholics of the Little Rock Diocese at the Eucharistic Congress held in Chicago that year. Unfortunately, Rudd did not attend because his appointment came too late.[61]

It seems that Rudd continued to live in Arkansas until 1932. It is not at all clear what his later activity was in Arkansas. In 1932 he returned to Bardstown, having suffered a stroke.[62] He died on December 3, 1933. at the age of seventy-nine. He was laid to rest in St. Joseph's Cemetery.[63] With him ended one of the most important influences in the history of black Catholicism in this country. Most of his accomplishments belonged to the pre–World War I period, but his vision and his dreams of what the church could be for blacks and what blacks could be within the church would still be an expression of hope and challenge in the contemporary period.

IV

The man who became the founder of a second black Catholic movement was a university professor from the farmlands of southern Maryland. Thomas Wyatt Turner was born in 1877 in Charles County, Maryland, an area rich in the heritage of black Catholic history. His parents were Catholics and sharecroppers. Baptized a Catholic as an infant, Turner took his secondary schooling at a black Episcopalian school. He had the opportunity to receive a scholarship for his college education on the condition that he convert to the Episcopal church. On the advice of a Quaker friend who told him that if he loved God and his church, he should stay where he was and all things would work out, he went on to study at Howard University in Washington, D.C., preparing himself to become a teacher of biology.[64] Graduating from Howard in 1901, Turner attended classes at Catholic University in the same city. It was a time when the doors of Catholic University were still open to black students. Unable to stay at Catholic University because of lack of funds, he began a career of teaching, first at Tuskegee Institute in Alabama, then in high schools in Baltimore and St. Louis. He continued postgraduate study at several schools, eventually receiving a master's degree in biology from Howard University and a doctorate from Cornell in 1921. In 1913 Turner became professor of biology at Howard University. About this time Turner began to write articles regarding Catholic education and black youth, and he proceeded to call attention to the policy of racial segregation in church affairs.

During the First World War services and aid were given to the members of the armed forces according to religion and race. White Protestant soldiers were cared for by the white branch of the YMCA, and black Protestant soldiers by the YMCA, black section. White Catholic soldiers were cared for by the Knights of Columbus, an all-white organization at this period. Black Catholic soldiers were cared for by no one, so Turner brought together a group of laymen, five in all, who contacted the pastor of St. Augustine, Father Alonzo J. Olds.[65] The decision was made to go as a group to Cardinal Gibbons, who encouraged them and referred them to the National Catholic War Council, the central organization that coordinated the public services of the church during the First World War; in this way the needs of black Catholic servicemen were soon met.[66] The broader needs and desires of the entire black Catholic community, the greater problems of racial discrimination, and the massive indifference within the American church became the issues that would engage the attention of Thomas Wyatt Turner and his close collaborators for the next four decades or so. What began as a small group became a national body that would provide a focus for black Catholic leadership and a pressure group for the black Catholic laity.

It was the summer of 1919, "called by James Weldon Johnson the 'Red Summer,' that ushered in the greatest period of interracial strife the nation had ever witnessed."[67] It was the year that saw the demobilization of black soldiers who had fought in the First World War, and who had seen their companions die for a country in which they often could not live in human dignity. In that year, beginning with June, seventy-five lynchings of black men took place. Beginning in April there were twenty-five race riots in the United States. Two of the worst took place in Washington, D.C., and in Chicago, but the riots in Elaine, Arkansas, were the bloodiest, with over two hundred blacks killed.[68]

Also in 1919 there took place a full meeting of the American hierarchy at Catholic University in the nation's capital. It would become an annual event. In 1919 this first meeting was important because it also launched the establishment of the first permanent organization of the hierarchy on the national level, the National Catholic Welfare Conference.[69] From the viewpoint of the black community, however, one event had to be on everyone's agenda: the racial strife and violence throughout the United States.

Rome viewed the rioting and killing of the year 1919 as a matter of grave concern. On September 12 Cardinal Gasparri, the secretary of state to Pope Benedict XV (reigned 1914–22), sent a cablegram to Msgr. Aluigi Cossio, secretary at the apostolic delegation, requesting him to urge certain members of the hierarchy that "it would be opportune that in the imminent meeting of the episcopate there be treated the problems of the black population and that there be deplored the recent killings."[70] Cossio at the same time wrote to Archbishop (later Cardinal) Mundelein of Chicago in a letter marked "confidentiale," asking that Mundelein personally find a way of introducing the subject of the racial problem and the recent violence before the assembled bishops. It was observed that Mundelein's diocese had been the scene of much of the killing.[71] Cossio made known to Mundelein that the rioting was "a subject that was taken to heart by the Holy See."[72] The apostolic delegation files reveal that someone from the delegation, more than likely Bonzano, went to see Cardinal Gibbons in Baltimore to impress upon him the importance that the Holy See placed on the "black people, their needs, their grievances, their dying, etc."[73] The cardinal replied that the "Negro Problem was always very delicate and difficult," but the topic would be taken up. It is important to note that Gibbons gave definite assurance that the matter would be treated. Bonzano, however, wrote Gasparri a month later to say that despite all the messages, personal interviews, and special missives, the bishops assembled in Washington did *not* address the issue of blacks dying in the streets. Bonzano assured the secretary of state that in November the question of racism would be discussed in a special committee meeting.[74]

As one looks back in time, it is evident that Pope Benedict XV had a more profound pastoral sense of what the church should deem important and to what the church should respond in regard to the unfortunate and the downtrodden than those who were its pastors in a land where the streets ran with blood. Ironically, the document in the file next to Bonzano's letter is a printed letter addressed to the United States Congress from nine African Methodist Episcopal churchmen concerning the race riots of 1919.[75]

The Pastoral Letter of 1919 was the result of this first assembly of the American hierarchy. In two places "the Negro question" was referred to.

> In the name of justice and charity, we deprecate most earnestly all attempts at stirring up racial hatred; for this, while it hinders the progress of all our people, and especially of the Negro, in the sphere of temporal welfare, places serious obstacles to the advance of religion among them. We concur in the belief that education is the practical means of bettering their condition; and we emphasize the need of combining moral and religious training with the instruction that is given them in other branches of knowledge. Let them learn from the example and word of their teachers the lesson of Christian virtue: it will help them more effectually than any skill in the arts of industry, to solve their problems.[76]

In one other place there was an allusion to the question of racial conflict. "At no period in our history, not even at the outbreak of the war, has the need of unity been more imperative. There should be neither time nor place for sectional division, for racial hatred, for strife among classes, for pure partisan conflict imperilling the country's welfare."[77] As we view this letter today, it can be said that the failure to speak plainly, emphatically, and in detail about the racial strife of 1919 was a serious omission. Even worse was the patronizing and gratuitous reference to blacks' learning from "their teachers the lesson of Christian virtue."

In November 1919 Thomas Wyatt Turner wrote Archbishop Bonzano, enclosing a copy of the statement sent to the bishops at their first annual meeting. Bonzano was asked to give assistance "that the Catholic colored laymen may enjoy the benefits of the church and grow in grace."[78] Turner wrote as the chairman for the Committee for the Advancement of Colored Catholics. The original action group of a few years before now numbered almost twenty-five members. In his letter to Bonzano, Turner remarked that black Catholics were "without voice anywhere in the Church." He asked Bonzano's help in opposing acts of discrimination carried out by Catholics against fellow Catholics who were black. He wanted Bonzano to be fully aware of the "pressing need of more colored priests to aid in the work of bringing the colored people into the church." He called attention to the Josephites' failure to educate more black students for the priesthood, the policy of the Catholic University to reject the applications of blacks, and the neglect of Catholic education for black children. Matters were made worse in that the black sisters who staffed many of the schools could not get their further training because Catholic University would not permit them to attend summer school education courses. These were normally frequented by teaching sisters at that time because they were not allowed to attend secular schools. Finally, Bonzano was asked to see that there be representation by blacks "on all the Boards of the Church that have to do with their welfare." "We do not feel that adequate judgment of the needs and necessities of the Negro can be had from any one except the Negro himself."

The statement (or, as Turner referred to it, the brief) was almost twenty typewritten pages. Addressed to the "Venerable Hierarchy of the United States," the Committee for the Advancement of Colored Catholics identified itself as having come into existence in 1916; it "has for its purpose... the collection of data concerning colored Catholics, the protection of their interests, promotion of their welfare, and the propagation of the Faith among colored people.[79] It was composed of "Catholic colored laymen... all persons of superior training and judgment... among its membership [are] teachers, doctors, lawyers, government employees and others." The statement went on to give the background for its conclusions.

> The Committee is expressing no individual opinion, but the crystallized point of view of the intelligent Catholic colored laity. We are hoping through our statistical studies to become a real asset to the Church, and thereby render a genuine service. If at any stage we may seem a bit over-zealous... in discussing these matters, we beg you to consider it in the light of our profound feelings that methods and policies which heretofore kept us an isolated group have served also to keep us a backward group.

The brief brought up five points: (1) education, (2) Catholic organizations, (3) Catholic University, (4) black priests, and (5) racism within the church. Regarding education, it was simply pointed out that the Catholic church's investment in some 6,000 parish schools, 600 high schools for boys and some 570 for girls, 87 colleges, 10 of them universities, all with a budget of nearly $20 million, is "a great showing, but the Catholic colored child has been well-nigh excluded from these benefits as though he were not a Catholic or... not expected to share in the Church's blessings." It was requested that blacks not be placed under the same bureaucratic control as Indians, who were separated onto reservations and not considered citizens. The point was also made that too often the issues relating to blacks were discussed without any contribution from the people themselves. A case in point was the Richmond, Virginia, meeting in 1918 of Catholic educators and priests who formed the National Catholic Association for the Advancement of Colored People.[80] The brief continued, "There was not...a single colored man present...It can be readily seen that effective work can be done among no people when it leaves that people out of the conferences and off the advisory boards which make plans for them."[81]

The fact that blacks were not part of the Knights of Columbus meant that black Catholics "received very scant and grudging consideration" in the welfare work for servicemen during the war. There was a plea again that black Catholics have a greater participation in the organizations that touch their concerns. In this regard it was noted with a certain poignancy that "at present we are neither a part of the colored world (Protestant), nor are we generally treated as full-fledged Catholics."

The policy of the Catholic University of America, it was pointed out, was a change from its original acceptance of black students. A copy of a letter to a black applicant from the registrar of the university was included that informed the applicant that it was not possible for blacks to be accepted: "It was tried once with exceeding unhappy results, and the policy had to be adopted otherwise."[82] The brief pointed out that "most all large non-Catholic Universities now take colored students." Such a policy on the part of the Catholic University risked doing harm to the very notion of catholicity.

A great deal of space was devoted to the question of a black clergy. This was an issue that would become a major source of contention for Turner and the movement that he headed. Several quotations from popes and American churchmen calling for the ordination of black men to the priesthood were set forth. The brief called attention to the policy of the Josephites. "In our quest for facts as to why colored candidates for the priesthood have been so few in late years, we found much circumstantial but convincing data." The brief laid the blame on the present and former superiors of the Josephites and detailed some of the conditions imposed on black candidates for the priesthood, which practically cut off any further ordinations of black men.[83]

Finally, the brief treated the matter of racial discrimination within the Catholic church. It warned of the serious problem of the presence of a "dessicating [*sic*] race prejudice at every stage of our religious observance." This racism, it went on to say, had "passed up the aisles and found its way through the railing to the Sacristy." The brief declared that "race prejudice was the outstanding sin of the present age." The members of the committee called for a campaign from the pulpit and the Catholic press against this sin, and for public lectures "to inculcate the spirit of the Church's Catholicity." Included with the brief was a copy of the goals and objectives of the Committee for the Advancement of Colored Catholics. They were pledged to work for "better feeling and closer union among all Catholics," and to work to remove all hindrances that keep black men and women from all the "temporal and spiritual graces" of the Catholic church. They were to work to advance the condition of black Catholics and to keep a record of discriminatory actions within the church and present them to the proper ecclesiastical authorities. They would endeavor to secure all of the spiritual advantages of Catholicism for black Catholics through contact with the various pastors of black parishes.

In 1924 the Committee for the Advancement of Colored Catholics developed into the organization known as the Federated Colored Catholics. The purpose of the organization was to unite black Catholics in a closer bond, to increase the possibility of Catholic education in the black community, to raise the overall position of black Catholics within the church, and to bring about a greater participation of black Catholics in the cause of racial justice. In short, the organization was to be an action group led by black Catholics and for black Catholics that would ensure that the black Catholic community take a responsible and leadership role in American Catholicism and American society.[84]

Archbishop Curley of Baltimore addressed the first national convention in Washington, D.C., in December 1925.[85] As president, Turner presented the federation as "a voice of the Catholic Negro in America." One of their first goals was the increased opportunity for Catholic education for blacks.[86] In the following year in November the organization wrote the first of its annual letters to the American bishops assembled for their annual meeting. The letter covered much of the same material treated in the letter of 1919. It expressed satisfaction at the establishment of a seminary for black candidates for the priesthood at Bay St. Louis in Mississippi, which opened in 1920. It noted the continuing need for more extensive Catholic education on all levels for black students, while expressing appreciation for the foundation of the Cardinal Gibbons Institute, an agricultural school for black youth modeled on Tuskegee Institute. Other points treated were the question of black parishes in the North and the policy of the Josephites toward the admittance of black students in their seminary.[87]

The Federated Colored Catholics met in 1927 in New York, the following year in Cincinnati, in Baltimore in 1929, in Detroit in 1930, and in St. Louis in 1931. The program included not only the official liturgies, where the ordinary of the diocese was usually present and welcomed the delegates, but also leading authorities in a wide variety of areas that were of importance to black Americans: labor relations; economic and business issues as they affected blacks; social conditions, including the question of public health; and interracial relations. There was not always harmony in the discussions at the conventions. At times there were sharp exchanges between the black laity and the white clergy, most notably at Baltimore in 1929, when the Josephites played a part in the proceedings.[88]

The disagreement that eventually resulted in a split took place following the New York convention in 1932. The split was caused by a misunderstanding about the basic purposes of the federation and its future direction. It involved Turner and two Jesuit priests who were well known for their dedication to the cause of racial justice and for their own service to black Catholics. One of the two Jesuits was John LaFarge, who had collaborated with Turner practically from the beginning of the federation, and the other was William Markoe, the pastor of a black parish in St. Louis, who began his collaboration with the federation in 1929. The rupture began with a basic misunderstanding regarding goals and objectives, and became a bitter and acrimonious quarrel centering on the ultimate control of the organization as a national body of black Catholics.

V

William Markoe, S.J., was a charismatic, courageous, and resourceful man. He had a gift for organization and a gift for motivating others to do what seemed like the impossible. Coming as he did from a background of privilege and prestige, he had little fear of failure and very little sense that something could not necessarily be done once one had determined that it should be. In fact, life for him was an adventure more than a struggle. This perspective did give him at times the air of being brash and even arrogant — and in fact to a certain extent he was. Having an unlimited supply of self-confidence, he was convinced of his own wisdom and knowledge. He loved black people, and he delighted in ministering to blacks — even to the point, it could be said, of wanting to be black, or almost black, himself. He sincerely wished to give his life, total and entire, for the black race. What he could not do was accept the position of trusting in the resourcefulness of blacks themselves, of recognizing the leadership qualities of blacks. Because of this blind spot a clash with Thomas Wyatt Turner was inevitable.

Markoe was born in 1892 in St. Paul, Minnesota. He belonged to a family that had originally been landowners in the Virgin Islands. At the time of the Revolutionary War, the Markoe family had already been established in Philadelphia, and one of William Markoe's great-grandfathers, Abram Markoe, had founded the Philadelphia City Cavalry in 1774 and helped originate the design that would develop into the present American flag.[89] Markoe studied one year at St. Louis University in 1912. The next year he entered the Jesuit novitiate just north of the city at Florissant. While he was a seminarian, Markoe, who had never had previous contacts with black people, became acquainted with the many blacks that lived in the areas known as Anglum and Sandtown in the Missouri River bottoms. Within a short period of time, he had interested some of the other Jesuit scholastics in the black population. Clothing and religious instruction were dispensed. By 1917 Markoe had brought about the construction of two churches, one at Anglum and the other at Sandtown, and made thirty converts.[90]

William Markoe's older brother, John (1890–1967), entered the Jesuit novitiate at the time when William was still a scholastic. John had been a cadet at West Point, served in Arizona as officer with the Tenth Cavalry, a black regiment, and was cashiered out of the army because of public drunkenness; he then served honorably as a captain in the Minnesota National Guard on the Mexican border, and finally in 1917 he entered the Jesuit novitiate. John Markoe never quite forgave himself for his dismissal from the army. He always believed that he had let down his fellow classmates. Universally admired, he was, unlike his brother, modest and unassuming. In his own way, he was as equally devoted to the cause of blacks and to their ministry as was his brother William. John Markoe played a major behind-the-scenes role in the desegregation of St. Louis University in the late 1940s. He spent the last years of his life working in the black community of Omaha and died in 1967, universally acclaimed and loved.[91]

Under the leadership of William Markoe, his brother, John, and two other Jesuit scholastics, Austin Bork and Horace Frommelt, a pledge was made "to give and dedicate our whole lives and all our energies, as far as we are able and it is not contrary to a pure spirit of perfect indifference and obedience, for the work of the salvation of the Negroes in the United States."[92] They made this pledge before a statue of the Virgin on the Feast of the Assumption, August 15, 1917. They resolved to repeat the words of the pledge daily. As a student in theology at St. Louis University, William Markoe set out to acquaint himself with the black population of St. Louis. It was a population that had little contact with the church. Thanks to Markoe and his fellow Jesuits, almost every section of the teeming black ghetto, with its alley dwellings and tenements, with its population of all sorts and ages, became known to the young Jesuits, and the church became known to them. According to Markoe, many blacks never realized that they could become Catholics.[93]

It was typical of Markoe's innate ability to instill enthusiasm and to take on any challenge that he and his fellow scholastics baptized over two hundred adult and children converts and opened a Catholic school in a converted warehouse. Although neither Markoe nor his fellow scholastics were yet ordained or had any official position in the archdiocese, not to speak of any official approval from their local superiors, he set up a full-scale catechetical service, and he personally contacted Blessed Katherine Drexel and got the services of two of her sisters to staff a school in a building that they rented, personally renovated, and furnished with funds that they had to beg or borrow. On his own, Markoe was able to persuade four black laywomen to be hired immediately to supplement the two sisters. One of these teachers was Minnie Bardeaux, the mother-in-law of Roy Wilkins, director of the NAACP during the 1960s. This kind of initiative and ability to take charge, this willingness to act first and to ask afterward, was a quality that made Markoe's ministry a success; it also, unfortunately, made teamwork and collaboration almost impossible for him.

In 1926 Markoe was ordained, and his first assignment was St. Elizabeth's Parish, the original old Jesuit parish that had served St. Louis's black Catholics since the nineteenth century. In 1928 the old church was badly damaged by a tornado, and the decision was made to rebuild and relocate. Throwing himself and his collaborators into a fund-raising campaign, Markoe raised enough money to purchase property in an area of St. Louis that was still largely white but into which blacks were moving. As soon as it became known that Archbishop Glennon had finally consented to the purchase of the property outside of the black area,[94] Markoe ran into opposition from the business and real estate leaders of the city. Those opposed to the construction of a black Catholic church within an all-white area called a meeting at the Catholic Church of the Visitation. Markoe described his strategy in his autobiography.

> The next skirmish in this battle had to do with a protest meeting held in the Visitation Parish Hall, with Father Collins, Father Douglas, and other neighboring pastors on the speakers' platform. This meeting was under the auspices of the Protective Association. . . . Of course we heard about this forthcoming meeting. It was time to call in some extra troops. I telephoned my brother John and asked him to get Mr. Laurence Barry, S.J., both Scholastics at the University, and to come to our rectory. We held a council of war. My brother being a West Pointer and an old army man was a good strategist. He had also played football on the same squad with Ike Eisenhower. We decided we should cover the un-Catholic anti-Negro meeting to be held at the Visitation. I was known to the enemy. My brother and Mr. Barry were not.[95]

Markoe's brother and Barry attended the meeting without clerical garb and were able to take down the speeches and statements of the leaders so that they could be published the next morning in the *Catholic Herald*, an independent newspaper. The result was more than satisfactory for Markoe's strategy. "Speakers at the meeting in the presence of pastors of churches not only lambasted me as a fool and a liar, but fortunately they also took the Archbishop apart. A digest of each speech was duly typed out within quotation marks. The general story of the meeting, its purpose, the participants, speakers, and pastors on the platform were all told."[96] By Sunday the newspaper was on sale in all of the churches. The news of the meeting and what transpired was publicized, and the pastor of the church where the meeting was held "left the city for an extended vacation."[97] This was the sort of coup that delighted Markoe. His brother began the publication of the *St. Elizabeth's Chronicle*, a parish newspaper. Realizing its potential, Markoe began "featuring articles on behalf of interracial justice directed towards white readers with the hope of enlightening them in matters of race relations."

Markoe attended his first meeting of the Federated Colored Catholics in Baltimore in 1929. Almost from the beginning he began to have his own ideas on what was wrong with the group and how it could be improved. For Markoe, segregation of any sort was a great evil. Integration or interracial unity was the ideal. For him the Federated Colored Catholics was a segregated, Jim Crow organization. At the first convention that he attended, Markoe offered *St. Elizabeth's Chronicle* as an official publication for the group. The offer was accepted, and Markoe became the editor. In his autobiography, Markoe described this event as his "infiltrating the organization, because I was a white man. We didn't like the self-imposed segregation that we saw ... like a good infiltrator I innocently suggested that they might like to use the St. Elizabeth Chronicle as their official organ."[98]

In 1932, as preparations were made for the convention meeting in New York that September, Markoe was able to gather support for his notion that the federation should change from a black organization to an interracial one. To this end he had the support of John LaFarge, his fellow Jesuit, who had been with the organization almost from the beginning. Even prior to the September meeting Turner confronted Markoe regarding this change in direction. Markoe wrote later:

> Dr. Turner seemed to disagree with me that the objective of the Federation was to promote better race relations. Rather he seemed to think that the purpose of the Federation was to fight for Negroes' rights within the church by fighting the whites in the church. This idea was the opposite of promoting better race relations as a means of attaining for the Negro what was due him within the church in keeping with the basic meaning of Catholicism and justice.[99]

In the September issue of the *Chronicle*, Markoe wrote an editorial in which he asked whether there was a place for the Federated Colored Catholics. His answer was that what was needed was for the federation to become "a National Catholic Interracial Federation."[100] Markoe was afforded the opportunity to steer the federation in this direction through the new constitution that was drawn up at the New York convention. LaFarge himself wished to broaden what he felt was a narrow focus on the rights of blacks within the church. The broader focus should be, he believed, the education of the Catholic public regarding racial relations, which would lead to the elimination of racial injustice.[101]

VI

John LaFarge was one of the giants of American Catholic thought in the mid-twentieth century. He was born in 1880 in Newport, Rhode

Island, the scion of a distinguished Catholic family, which on his mother's side numbered Benjamin Franklin among its ancestors. His father was a descendant of the Binsse family of New York, Louis F. Binsse having been a friend of Pierre Toussaint. John LaFarge's father was a celebrated artist; his mother's grandfather was Commodore Perry, who opened Japan to the influence of the West. LaFarge studied at Harvard and was ordained a priest in Innsbruck in 1905. Later that year he entered the novitiate of the Society of Jesus.

LaFarge's delicate health prompted his superiors to assign him to pastoral ministry rather than to the pursuit of an advanced degree. As a result, shortly after the completion of his formation, LaFarge began to do pastoral work in the Jesuit parishes of southern Maryland. This was historic Jesuit country, and it was also traditional black Catholic country. It was the homeland of Thomas Wyatt Turner; it was the land of the descendants of Jesuit slaves. From 1911 to 1926, a period of fifteen years, LaFarge worked as a country pastor among whites and blacks in the rural area. During this period he was able to bring about many improvements for the people. At the same time he came to appreciate the history of black Catholics in southern Maryland and the pride of these people in their past. He became aware for the first time of the enormous injustice visited upon black people not only in southern Maryland but elsewhere. He began to ponder the problem of change in the area of racial injustice. He realized that both blacks and whites had to be educated. Blacks needed education to equip them for a better social condition; whites needed education in the rudiments of justice based on Christian principles.

LaFarge was an intellectual with a broad sympathy for many people, but he remained a patrician, always a little removed from daily conflict. He did become involved, however, in the education needs of his parishioners, both black and white, in southern Maryland. In this regard, his work in establishing the Cardinal Gibbons Institute at Ridge, Maryland, in 1924 was a significant achievement and a tragic failure. It was to be an agricultural school for blacks, and LaFarge often referred to it as a "Catholic Tuskegee," for he had a great respect for Booker T. Washington.[102] A black principal, Victor Daniel, and his wife became the head of the school, and it had a black faculty. The school faced enormous problems; Victor Daniel and his wife were not always in agreement with LaFarge and other white members of the governing board; and there was little support for the school from Catholics, black or white, in the national population.[103] The school soon acquired a large debt. Because Archbishop Curley, the ordinary of the diocese and head of the board of trustees, was unwilling to remain connected with the institute until the debt was liquidated, the Cardinal Gibbons Institute was forced to close in 1933.[104]

LaFarge and Markoe were very different in character and temperament, although in a sense they came from the same background and were distantly related.[105] LaFarge had become convinced that the Federated Colored Catholics had to have interracial understanding and collaboration as its primary goal. It should provide, in his opinion, a forum for the best minds of both races to discuss and get acquainted with each other. It would be a source of education for the white race and would go beyond narrow-based racial concerns. The 1932 convention in New York was the arena in which Markoe's and LaFarge's new vision of the federation would be made into a reality through the revision of the constitution. There was a suggestion that the name of the organization be changed to the National Catholic Federation for the Promotion of Better Race Relations. Father Markoe also changed the name of the *Chronicle* to the *Interracial Review*.

This change had the full support of LaFarge, but it did not have the support of Turner. In fact, Turner had become very disturbed by what he felt was a takeover of the organization by Markoe and a fundamental shift in its goals. There were many black members of the federation, it must be admitted, who supported the ideas of Markoe and LaFarge. The main opposition came from Turner and his supporters, many of whom had been the original founders of the federation. In the fall of 1932 a meeting was held in Chicago, and Turner was ousted as president. The account of the controversy within the federation was reported in the black press. Some of the newspapers openly supported Turner against what was considered an attempt by whites to control a black organization.

Despite his removal by a section of the federation leadership, Turner and the leaders in Washington and the East Coast rejected the action. The result was a split in the organization.[106] The midwestern branch became known as the National Interracial Federation, which in a few years became inactive. Turner's organization remained as the Federated Colored Catholics but was drastically weakened. Markoe became disinterested in the organization altogether, and the *Interracial Review* was transferred to New York and to the responsibility of LaFarge, who had already established the Catholic Interracial Council of New York, an organization that would later branch out into other cities. It became exactly what LaFarge had always envisioned — an organization of black and white leaders who would meet, discuss, and try to influence others through its publicizing Catholic social teaching on racial justice.

In her excellent analysis of the career and efforts of Thomas Wyatt Turner, William Markoe, and John LaFarge, Marilyn Nickels remarked that the quarrel that pitted Turner against Markoe and La-Farge was more than simply a question of strategy.[107] The differences lay in the perceptions that each one had regarding the question of being black in a hostile society and belonging to a church that was both universal in self-concept but very racist on the local level. Markoe has been aptly described as a maverick.[108] William Markoe, S.J., is one of the best examples of a distinctive pastoral phenomenon in the first half of the twentieth century: the white priest-pastor in the black community. The majority of these men lived lives of extraordinary sacrifice and toil. They found themselves often discriminated against by their superiors. The normal access to funds and likely donors was frequently unavailable to them. Most of them found themselves in the position of independently finding help, searching for funds, and using any and every means to help their parish and their people receive a fair hearing in the public life of the time. Hence, they learned to be resourceful, to get along without priestly support, to work outside of ordinary channels, and to be tenacious and to fight with all their strength for their own people. And most of them identified with the black community while maintaining ties with the white world. Had they done otherwise, black Catholics would have been even more neglected.

William Markoe was a great man; he had also a complex personality. His name is justly revered to this day in the black Catholic community of St. Louis, although he left the pastorate of St. Elizabeth's Church in 1942. From 1942 until his death in 1969 in Milwaukee, Markoe continued to work, write, and speak on behalf of blacks and the cause of interracial justice. In his long and rich life perhaps his one serious mistake was the role that he took in the destruction of the Federation of Colored Catholics.[109]

LaFarge, on the other hand, was an intellectual leader whose contribution to understanding the racial question was fundamental. In a sense, LaFarge saved the honor of Roman Catholicism in America by being the persistent voice of reason and justice in a time of apathy and racism. He did so especially during his long years of service on the editorial staff and then as editor of *America*, the Jesuit weekly of opinion.[110] LaFarge was neither petty nor vindictive. He was perhaps an elitist; no doubt unconsciously, he related less well to an educated black person than to the rural black Catholics of southern Maryland with their simplicity and deeply grounded faith. He did not wish to interfere in the direction of the federation, but it was very difficult for him not to do so. He did not wish to abandon Turner, but it was difficult for him to allow Turner to lead. LaFarge's fundamental mistake was to think that racism could be combatted by good manners and reasonableness. He did not realize that in the face of racial injustice, violence and a social revolution were inevitable. And he did not understand that in it the church would have to confront her own soul.

Thomas Wyatt Turner was not as well known as the two priests, but he was every bit as intelligent as LaFarge and as determined as Markoe. He represented the generation of American blacks that came to maturity after the First World War. These men were the first university-trained generation among blacks. They were proud, independent, and determined that the Negro should be the equal of any white man or woman. They were the generation of black professionals and of the Harlem Renaissance. Hence, for Turner and those who were closest to him, it was important that the federation remain black in its leadership and problem-oriented in its purpose. The problem was not primarily relations between whites and blacks, but the discriminatory actions that prevented blacks from becoming mature and responsible members of the church. In this regard, Turner and his followers were in the long line of black protest leaders. They were also heirs of the black Catholic congress movement of the 1890s and forerunners of the civil rights movement and the black Catholic movement that evolved from it in the 1960s. They were also part of the tradition of lay leadership that characterized the history of the black Catholic community. When Turner died in 1978, a little over a year after receiving an honorary degree from the Catholic University of America, it was apparent that the position of black Catholics in the United States at the time owed more to the decisive actions of protest carried on by Turner than to the interracial movements supported by Markoe and LaFarge.

VII

The education of more black clergy was a major issue for Turner and the Federated Colored Catholics. It was also a preoccupation for curial officials in Rome. At the end of 1920, Cardinal De Lai began another series of letters with the apostolic delegate, Archbishop Bonzano, on the subject of black priests. In November of that year, Cardinal De Lai wrote Bonzano about a concern he shared with Cardinal van Rossum, the prefect of the Congregation of the Propaganda, regarding the situation of the 10 million or more blacks who were deprived of all religion or who were members of the Protestant churches. De Lai expressed concern about the attitudes of the American bishops to this situation and especially the case of the bishop of Savannah, Benjamin Keiley, and Ignatius Lissner of the Society of African Missions. De Lai wanted advice concerning the work of the Society of African Missions in other parts of the United States.[111] The copy of the letter of van Rossum to De Lai, dated October 30, 1920, was included with his letter.

The Dutch cardinal criticized the amount of spiritual care given to blacks by the American bishops and the inaccessibility of seminary education to young black men. As for spiritual care, van Rossum was of the opinion that the movement of conversion among blacks in the South was "rather difficult from the fact that the bishops very often are disinterested in their care." The proof of this attitude was seen in the fact that often the work of evangelization was confided to "the unequal strength of one sole priest." The Dutch cardinal was also disturbed by the fact that many American bishops refused to receive a black man into their seminary or to ordain black men as priests. He pointed out the lack of a seminary for the training of black priests and of a bishop who would take on the responsibility of the formation of an indigenous clergy. He went on to say that black Catholics found themselves in an inferior position in comparison with black Protestants, who had their own numerous clergy. The formation of a black clergy would be "a potent factor in the conversion of tens of million of this race living in the United States."[112]

Behind this correspondence between De Lai, van Rossum, and the apostolic delegate lay a situation that had developed in the diocese of Savannah, between the bishop, Benjamin Joseph Keiley, and the man who had been appointed superior of the mission for black Catholics, Ignatius Lissner, S.A.M.[113] In 1908 Bishop Keiley had turned over to the Society of African Missions all ministry to blacks in the state of Georgia.[114] At the beginning of 1920, Keiley was surprised to receive from the prefect of the Sacred Congregation of the Propaganda a letter proposing that one of the members of the Society of African Missions be made vicar-general for black Catholics and raised to the dignity of a bishop. Cardinal van Rossum stressed the need for a bishop for the blacks because a special solicitude was needed for them, particularly because the Protestants were zealously drawing them to their own teaching (the cardinal speaks of "their errors"), and he said that only the Catholics lacked a special bishop for the African American people. The cardinal went on to say that a bishop was needed who would "strive for the institution of an indigenous clergy, who would carry out the sacred rites, who would perform the administration of the sacraments with solemn ceremony, who would see to the collection of money for the blacks."[115]

Immediately Bishop Keiley wrote to Cardinal Gibbons enclosing a copy of the letter from van Rossum. He described the situation as a sort of "African Cahenslyism."[116] He pointed to the provincial of the Society of African Missions, Ignatius Lissner, as the one chiefly responsible. He rather snidely referred to Lissner's "Jewish ancestry" and his having "many of the qualities of the 'Chosen people.'" He added, "I need not tell you what that would mean to us in the South." He went on to say that his consultors at their meeting had unanimously condemned the idea, and he asked Gibbons to write to Rome because "it is hard to get Rome to understand conditions here."[117]

Gibbons replied that he would "regard the establishment of such a seminary as desirable." He advised Keiley not to oppose it, adding that they might convert the African American more readily "if we had a trained clergy of colored priests, presuming of course men of ability and zeal." He did state, however, regarding the place of the seminary, that if it is not suitable that it be in the South, then another location should be chosen and suggested that "perhaps room might be found at the Catholic University." Finally, regarding the question of a bishop for black Catholics, he thought it "entirely premature," mainly because the number of black Catholics in the United States at the time was about 200,000. He concluded by saying that Keiley might do better to write to Rome himself, "saying, if you wish, that you have consulted me in the matter."[118]

Gibbons's response was typical of his cautiousness, and his letter shows that he did not wish to become too involved. It also shows, however, that the thinking on the matter of a black clergy had begun to evolve.[119] Certainly, one of the reasons for the change in climate was the action of Pope Benedict XV, who in 1919 published an encyclical on the missions, *Maximum Illud*, in which he particularly called for the preparation of a native clergy to minister to their own people. Gibbons's response to Keiley also indicated that the suggestion made by van Rossum for a special bishop for blacks in the diocese of Savannah was being considered in terms of a bishop for all black Catholics everywhere. Seemingly for Gibbons, the question was not outside the realm of possibility.

The following month Keiley wrote a brief note to van Rossum explaining that the proposal to create a bishop for the blacks would be "a disaster," explaining that there were twenty thousand white

Catholics in his diocese and only eleven hundred black Catholics, who were ministered to by seven priests of the Society of African Missions. He made no mention of the seminary for black priests.[120]

The matter, however, did not remain closed. As is clear from the communication sent to Archbishop Bonzano by Cardinal De Lai mentioned above, the concern regarding black Catholics and their spiritual care was taken up by the Consistorial Congregation. A few days after he wrote Bonzano, Cardinal De Lai wrote Keiley. From all appearances the terse letter indicated that the cardinal was not pleased. Briefly, De Lai pointed out that since every effort must be made on behalf "of the unfortunate [blacks]," the creation of a vicar-general who would have the dignity of bishop would seem to be the "clearer and easier way" to carry out their evangelization. Keiley was invited to explain what the difficulties were.[121]

A handwritten copy of Keiley's response to De Lai is also found in the Savannah archives but is undated. Keiley defended himself by stating that he was against racial injustice and prejudice. He pointed out the virulent anti-Catholicism that existed in the state of Georgia and noted that the priests of the African Missions who worked among the blacks did not, with two exceptions, speak English well.[122] Gibbons also was prevailed upon to write Cardinal De Lai, pointing out the racial tensions that existed in the country at that time and suggesting that the time was not ripe for a bishop exclusively for blacks. Gibbons gently suggested that the local situation was not well understood in Rome.[123] Finally, Keiley wrote to Archbishop Bonaventure Cerretti,[124] mentioning again that Lissner was of Jewish ancestry, "and the traits of that race are very evident," and pointing out that in the diocese he was little liked. Again the reason against making Lissner bishop for the care of the blacks was based on "the fanatical bigotry of Georgia against the church, and the intolerance against the negro."[125]

In the end Keiley was successful in blocking the creation of a bishop. Lissner was eventually removed from Georgia, and Keiley resigned his see in 1922. Keiley did not believe himself to be prejudiced against blacks. He even attacked racial prejudice on occasion. It is evident, however, that he was unable to escape the emotional and intellectual climate of the South and his own milieu.

The Lissner/Keiley affair provided Cardinal van Rossum and Cardinal De Lai the opportunity to question Archbishop Bonzano regarding the status of blacks in the American church. A few months after the Savannah incident, van Rossum wrote Bonzano on the plight of black Catholics in America. The cardinal spoke of "the racial distinctions...that seemed to overlie and overcome every principle of Christian charity." He asserted that "given the strong opposition of the episcopacy to the creation of an Ordinary for the blacks," the idea would be abandoned for the present. Cardinal van Rossum added caustically that he failed to see why the Protestants could provide for the needs of blacks by having black bishops but that the Catholic church could not. The delegate was asked to encourage the American bishops to do their utmost to do away with the obstacles that prevent the reception of blacks into the seminaries and the Catholic University. He also wished to express the good wishes of the Holy See toward those bishops who "courageously" admitted blacks into their seminaries.[126]

Bonzano sought in his response to defend his record regarding support for the ministry to the blacks. There had been progress in the past decade; he added, however, that one must not forget the havoc wrought by the Civil War. It was unfortunate that there was not more missionary work among blacks, but in American dioceses there was not an overabundance of priests. In the end, however, Bonzano did pledge himself to work for the ordination of black men to the priesthood with the words: "I shall seek to encourage and to favor the progress of the formation of an indigenous clergy."[127]

This letter to van Rossum had been preceded by a lengthy report to Cardinal De Lai on the situation of blacks in the United States. Evidently, the letter of the prefect of the Congregation of the Propaganda had been a response. In the report to De Lai, Bonzano had mentioned the increase of churches and (primary) schools for blacks, and he explained why the United States bishops persisted in rejecting the notion of a national ordinary for black Catholics. He said that it would be wrong to divide dioceses and that the result of the creation of an ordinary for blacks would allow the other bishops to become less interested in the cause of blacks. It is not bishops who are needed but more priests. At the same time he brought forth some objections to Lissner himself. A foreign-born bishop, in his opinion, would have less influence in the United States church. Perhaps even more to the point, there were other religious congregations working among blacks, such as the Josephites, the Spiritans, and the Society of the Divine Word, who might have a better claim for one of their number to be chosen as bishop.

He then broached the subject of black priests. He admitted that some bishops were favorable to the idea of ordaining black men but that the majority of them — especially the Southern bishops — were opposed. He stated that this was not so much out of principle but because of local conditions. It was a social question. The gap between whites and blacks, especially in the South, was too great, and in some places, the law prohibited too much mingling of the races. Then Bonzano returned to one of his favorite themes: the relationship between whites and blacks was one of dependence on the part of blacks. Realizing that this situation could not be considered as very Christian, he confessed that this was the factual situation. And then sounding his favorite historical theme, he blamed the Civil War and its aftermath for the present state of affairs.

He also related that the three or four black priests who had been ordained in the United States had not given full satisfaction and that the Josephites had not ordained anyone for themselves in recent times, although it seemed that now they have changed.[128] Returning again to a favorite theme, Bonzano pointed out that for the bishops there was always the worry of a public scandal on the part of black priests because of their inferior intelligence and moral sense, "especially concerning celibacy." Nevertheless, he added, the idea of a "clergy of color is now discussed and has begun to make headway." He then mentioned the fact that there were two black students in the seminary at St. Paul and that the Society of the Divine Word was establishing a seminary for blacks.[129] It is interesting to note that Bonzano had to admit in his letter to a certain embarrassment in the face of the criticism leveled by Thomas Wyatt Turner and the Committee for the Advancement of Colored Catholics. He really did not know how to respond to the criticism that blacks were denied admittance to the Knights of Columbus, the Catholic University of America, and the seminaries.[130] He did point out that the Knights of Columbus was not a Catholic association in the official sense and that the bishops did not have direct control over their internal affairs. He also believed that if Catholic University and other Catholic colleges admitted blacks, the white students would leave the schools. At any rate, the numbers of blacks seeking admission was not large.

Certainly the establishment of a seminary for black students by the members of the Society of the Divine Word was one of the most important events in the history of black Catholics during the first part of the twentieth century.[131] In November 1921 the provincial of the Society of the Divine Word, Peter Janser, wrote Archbishop Bonzano informing him that the seminary for black students had been established first at Greenville, Mississippi, and then moved to Bay St. Louis. This was the same letter that was addressed to all members of the American hierarchy acquainting them with the developments. Janser made it clear that this seminary had the support and the full blessing of Rome, specifically Pope Benedict XV. This was necessary because not all American bishops were convinced of the wisdom of ordaining black men to the priesthood, whatever their status as either religious or members of the diocesan clergy. The provincial, however, asked in closing for any advice that the respective prelates might have to give.[132] Janser sent a covering letter to the apostolic delegate, informing him of his visit with curial officials in Rome and of the visit of the procurator general of the society with Pope Benedict XV, all of whom gave full support to the proposed seminary.[133] Janser thereupon asked for a word of recommendation from Bonzano to the Congregation of Religious regarding the establishment of the seminary of an autonomous province of the Society of the Divine Word that was being established for blacks.

Bonzano replied a few weeks later, again revealing his ambivalence over a black clergy. He told Janser that he was glad that the Divine Word Fathers had begun the experiment. He went on to explain that the term "experiment" was deliberately chosen because it was only a trial and required "prudence and forethought in order to have any chance of success." He counseled extreme caution and careful, slow development because if there was a mistake, there would be no lasting results. The unspoken supposition seemed to have been that it would most likely fail.[134] Later history would prove him wrong.

An important movement among black Catholics was begun in 1909 through the initiative of several Josephite pastors in the South. Conrad Rebesher, S.S.J., pastor of the Church of the Most Pure Heart of Mary, in Mobile, Alabama, wrote the superior general of the Josephites, Justin MacCarthy:

> I mentioned to you, that it was my intention to organize, a national association for the Colored men, along the same lines as the Knights of Columbus. The necessity and great need of such an organization, was clear to my mind, but I feared to undertake such a big task on my own initiative. Father Kelly, Van Baast, and myself had several meetings bearing on this matter, but did not arrive at any satisfactory conclusion.

Rebesher went on to explain that eventually they decided to go on with the idea of a fraternal organization because of the religious attitude of many men in their parishes who had "little interest...in church matters" and because many were joining secret organizations, namely the fraternal organizations open to blacks at the time, such as the Masons and the Elks. Rebesher announced that on September 15, 1909, over thirty men participated in a meeting at his church. Encouraged by their enthusiasm, Rebesher drew up the constitution, following that of the Knights of Columbus for an organization to be called "The Knights of Peter Claver."[135]

The Knights of Peter Claver was to be both a fraternal and a benevolent organization, supplying insurance for the welfare of each member's family on his death. The members were to be mobilized for charitable work and for assistance in programs on the diocesan level. It began in Mobile, then included a council on Mon Luis Island and Chastang. From Alabama the organization moved to Scranton, Mississippi, in 1910. By the end of that year, Conrad Rebesher was writing to the general:

> The Knights are doing well. Norfolk, Va. has applied for [a] council. Nashville, Tenn. has also applied. Bay St. Louis, Miss. and Pass Christian will be instituted about February. Pensacola, Fl. has taken the matter up and will make application soon. Richmond Council is making splendid progress, and will have another initiative soon. Neither gold, nor silver, nor position, nor influence, of any amount or any kind, could give me greater joy, than the Knights of Peter Claver.[136]

The three priests mentioned in Rebesher's letter (Samuel Kelly, Joseph Van Baast, and Conrad Rebesher himself) were joined by another Josephite priest, John H. Dorsey, and three laymen (Gilbert Faustina, Frank Collins, and Frank Trenier) as cofounders. Father Dorsey and the three laymen were black. Gilbert Faustina from Mobile served as head of the knights for the first seventeen years.

In 1922 the Ladies Auxiliary of Peter Claver was instituted, and a "junior knights" was organized in 1917 and "junior daughters" in 1930.[137] The Knights of Peter Claver spread throughout much of the South in the first twenty-five years of its existence, and it became a very important element in the religious life of black Catholics. It was for a long time their main social organization. The spread northward was more gradual. The first national convention held outside of the old Confederacy was in 1930 in Okmulgee, Oklahoma; in 1940 it was held in Louisville, Kentucky, and in 1946 in Chicago. By the end of the Second World War, the Knights and Ladies of Peter Claver had become a national black Catholic organization. By that time also the headquarters had moved from Mobile to New Orleans. These groups grew out of the early tutelage of the clergy, became more thoroughly middle class in structure and tone, and finally moved from a more conservative position on issues of race to a supporting role for civil rights organizations, like the NAACP and the National Urban League.

Chapter 9

COMING OF AGE: BLACK CATHOLICS IN THE MID-TWENTIETH CENTURY

The period between the two world wars was transitional for American society. From the euphoria and prosperity following the First World War to the depression and the New Deal on the eve of the Second World War, the nation underwent a social and cultural transformation. The change was accelerated and solidified by the Second World War and its aftermath.

For American Catholicism the period between the two wars was also a period of transition and development. The immigrant church became an American church as Catholics consolidated their resources with the building of new churches, parochial schools, colleges, and universities. Ecclesiastical leaders, Roman educated and Roman trained, arrived on the scene and wielded power, influence, and authority. The numbers of priests and religious grew steadily; Catholic laymen of immigrant backgrounds achieved prestige and political power. It was a church whose unity, stability, and wealth enabled it to withstand anti-Catholic bigotry. It was no longer a minority institution but a force to be considered, depending mainly on its own resources and its European-based traditions.[1] Despite its monolithic strength and grandeur, however, the American church too would undergo its own transformation during this period.

The African American community also passed through a massive transformation in the period between the two world wars, finally attaining a new position of freedom in the course of the Second World War and its aftermath. A tremendous migration of blacks from the

238

rural South to the urban, industrialized North created new tensions, problems, and opportunities. The return of African American soldiers after the First World War generated a new militancy, a new determination, and a new class of upwardly mobile blacks. It also began a new cultural awakening that has been labeled "the Harlem Renaissance," though it was not confined to New York or restricted to one generation. Finally, it saw the beginning of a new political alignment that overturned the old alliances and old dependencies that had characterized American society since the days of Reconstruction. It ultimately bore fruit in the civil rights revolution following the Second World War.

Black Catholics were part of the gradual transformation of both the American Catholic church and African American society. They also slowly emerged from mission status as recipients and dependents to a community that not only began to find its voice, as Thomas Wyatt Turner had hoped, but also began to make itself heard and heeded in the social and cultural revolution following the Second World War. Blacks also increased in numbers; they too made their presence recognized in the monolithic structure of American Catholicism, even when their demands generated cracks and fissures in the solid front of what some labeled as a "white, Euro-American church." In fact, the black Catholic community, more than any other ethnic group, brought about the Catholicization that made the American church "Catholic" in the full historical meaning of that word.

I

Black Catholics began moving northward even before the First World War. In 1889 the bishop of Leavenworth complained that "if we could keep all our Negroes that were converted, we would have a large number; but owing to their removing to other regions, we have not much of an increase to show."[2] After the war the numbers increased. In Chicago, St. Monica's Parish was merged with St. Elizabeth's, formerly an Irish parish that was given to the Society of the Divine Word in 1924. St. Elizabeth's became the center for black Catholic activity for an ever-increasing black population on the South Side of Chicago. The parish had a black Catholic elementary school and high school as early as 1922. In New York the traditional black Catholic parish was St. Benedict the Moor in lower Manhattan on West 53rd Street. In 1925, as Harlem had become the center of a growing black population, the church of St. Charles Borromeo became a thriving black parish. In 1912 the Spiritans took over St. Mark's Parish in Harlem as a black parish.[3]

In 1922 a community of black sisters moved from Georgia to New York. It was a community that had been founded in 1916 in Savannah by Ignatius Lissner.[4] At that time legislation had been introduced in the Georgia legislature that would prohibit the teaching of black pupils by white teachers. Such legislation would have seriously imperiled parochial schools for blacks, for all were staffed by white sisters. In order to prevent their closing, Lissner proposed the foundation of a community of black sisters. In the end, the law was never passed, but by that time the community known as the Handmaids of Mary had been established.

Bishop Keiley gave his full support to the establishment of the new sisters. He wrote Lissner:

> Your project of founding a community of colored women for the purpose of the Christian education of the children of that race is a most excellent one, and in view of the possibility of legislative interference with the work of white sisters...a necessary one...
>
>   Christ died for all — white and colored; and Christ's words are for the colored child as well.[5]

Later that year, Keiley wrote Lissner that he "was glad to hear that a beginning has been made on your plans to have a congregation of colored women to teach the children of their own race here." Keiley urged that the black sisters "should do everything in their power to encourage vocations among the colored girls."[6] Moreover, Keiley desired that they "should work in Georgia for their own."

The early history of the Handmaids of Mary tells a heroic story. Their foundation was the work of Ignatius Lissner, but the woman whom he persuaded to begin the work was a black woman of extraordinary strength and character. Her name was Elizabeth Barbara Williams, born in 1868 in Baton Rouge, Louisiana. When she was nineteen, she entered the Franciscan sisters at Convent, Louisiana. This was the community of black sisters who had formerly been members of the Sisters of the Holy Family in New Orleans. As mentioned in chapter 4, a group of Holy Family sisters withdrew from that congregation in 1887 to establish a more contemplative house that followed the Rule of St. Francis. When this convent was suppressed at the beginning of the century, Elizabeth Williams had to leave. She spent some time as a member of the Oblate Sisters of Providence,[7] although the extent of time is uncertain. It seems, however, that there was mutual agreement that Elizabeth Williams had a religious vocation but that it was not to be an Oblate Sister of Providence. Sometime after leaving the Oblate Sisters, Elizabeth Williams found a position as receptionist at Trinity College near Catholic University in Washington, D.C. Lissner had gone to Catholic University to visit a friend, who put him in touch with her. According to the sisters' chronicle, Lissner and Williams talked for an entire afternoon. At the end Elizabeth Williams agreed to become the foundress of a religious community; she became the first member and took the name Theodore.

The beginnings of most religious communities are difficult. This was true for the small community on East Gordon Street in Savannah, as it experienced extreme hardship. One early member who joined the community at the age of sixteen, when the community numbered five members, described the hunger that characterized those days of poverty. Unfortunately for the Handmaids of Mary, the anti-Catholic legislation outlawing white teachers in black schools was not enacted. As a result, the white sisters continued their work of teaching, while the Handmaids were without a mission. Lissner was often absent, and following his rift with Bishop Keiley, he was no longer stationed in Georgia. Most of the task of formation fell on the shoulders of Mother Theodore Williams. She was described by the sisters who had known her personally as a woman of courage, strong faith, and an ability to bear many trials without discouragement.[8] As time went on, the influence of Lissner ceased almost entirely. It was apparently Mother Theodore who made the decision that the Handmaids of Mary should leave Savannah and go to New York. There was little prospect for a viable future for the young community in Georgia.

In 1922 the community moved to Harlem at the invitation of Cardinal Hayes. The year before a few of the sisters had begun St. Benedict's Day Nursery in Harlem. It was near there that the convent was established. Again, the first years were very difficult. The sisters had charge of small children who were left by their parents — many of them single parents — as early as 5:00 A.M. Many were unable to pay very much. Financial aid came from Catholic Charities and the Christ Child Guild. A soup kitchen was established and is still in operation today. A kindergarten was part of the nursery. The children who were homeless found there a home.

In 1929 Mother Theodore affiliated the Handmaids of Mary to the Franciscan Third Order, hence their present title: the Franciscan Handmaids of the Most Pure Heart of Mary. The Franciscan

Fathers became their spiritual directors. Their spirituality was defined as service of "their neighbor with the same care, diligence, charity, religious zeal and love with which Mary served her Son... the sisters ought, in imitation of Mary, to glorify Our Lord by the practice of all the Christian virtues, especially humility, charity, simplicity of heart, cheerfulness, and friendliness."[9]

Despite the poverty of their beginnings, the community eventually flourished. They numbered sixteen by 1925. The sisters came not only from the United States but, soon after the removal to New York City, included black sisters from the West Indies and the Virgin Islands. In 1926 the sisters took over the parochial school attached to St. Benedict the Moor parish in lower Manhattan. Later the sisters staffed the grammar school in St. Aloysius Parish in Harlem.[10] In 1929 a separate novitiate was established on Staten Island, and in Harlem a home for working girls. Mother Theodore Williams died in October 1931 at the age of sixty-three. As always she had carried the major burden of the work for the black poor in Harlem during the preceding winter. At the time of her death, the congregation numbered twenty members. Although the community has spread to other parts of the United States and the West Indies, the Franciscan Handmaids of Mary have remained an integral part of Harlem.

Blacks had moved into Harlem by the beginning of the First World War. By 1920 Harlem had become a city within a city, a "black metropolis," as some called it. Others called it a "Mecca" for African Americans. Marcus Garvey (1887–1940), a Jamaican, came to Harlem in 1916 and began a black nationalist movement that had a major effect on the thinking of black people during much of the 1920s. Garvey's Universal Negro Improvement Association had its headquarters in Harlem. Garvey was deported in 1927.[11]

Harlem became a cultural center for artists, writers, poets, and dramatists in the early 1920s. Within its confines Harlem became a center for what Alain Locke, philosopher and social critic, called the "New Negro" — part of a new movement and a new artistic expression of a younger generation of American Negroes. "In Harlem," he wrote, "Negro life is seizing upon its first changes for group expression and self-determination."[12] This was the Harlem Renaissance, a bursting forth of talent and productivity. Black writers and black poets, like James Weldon Johnson (1871–1938), Langston Hughes (1902–67), Countee Cullen (1903–46), Sterling Brown (1901–), Claude McKay (1890–1948), and many others, gave a new meaning and dignity to African American culture and art. In this haven for writers, artists, philosophers, and politicians, black Catholics were not generally conspicuous, but two names associated with the black literary world are part of the history of Catholicism.

Ellen Tarry was born in Birmingham, Alabama, in 1906. She became a Catholic while a student at Rock Castle Academy in Virginia, operated by the Sisters of the Blessed Sacrament, the community founded by Mother Katherine Drexel. Ellen Tarry took with her from the school a profound attachment to the Catholic faith and a firm dedication to her vocation to be a writer. She arrived in Harlem in 1929 and eventually met some of the well-known black literary figures of the time when she was introduced to the Negro Writers' Guild. It was also in Harlem that she came in contact with the Baroness Catherine de Hueck and Friendship House across from St. Mark's Church.[13]

Catherine de Hueck was born in White Russia in 1900, lost everything at the time of the Bolshevik Revolution, fled to the West, became a Catholic convert, moved to Canada, and began a community settlement house in 1930 in Toronto. In 1938 the baroness came to Harlem. "Why had I chosen Harlem as my field of action? Here poverty, misery, race discrimination bring much hardship and sorrow. Here Communists find fertile ground for their claims that they the godless, have the only solution of the Race problem."[14]

The baroness was a very strong-minded person, able to motivate the young and the fervent. The young people, mostly white, and other more mature adults, some of whom were black, joined together in communities, depending upon the voluntary contributions of others and imbued with the ideas of Catholic action and racial justice, and convinced that Catholic teaching could supply answers to life's problems. The baroness and the members of Friendship House lived in the neighborhood, shared in the misery, experienced the same poverty, and spoke out bluntly about the evils of racism in American society and in the hearts of white Catholics. They had discussion groups and lectures, but they were also practical in their exercise of charity and social service. Ellen Tarry started working with the staff of Friendship House and began writing for Catholic periodicals. At the insistence of the Baroness de Hueck, she went to Chicago to help found the Chicago Friendship House in 1942; there she met the auxiliary bishop of Chicago, Bernard J. Sheil.

Among the people who encouraged Ellen Tarry in her desire to write was a proud, independent, and at times irascible writer and poet named Claude McKay. He was one of the black literary figures that helped launch the Harlem Renaissance. McKay was born in Jamaica on September 15, 1890, the youngest of eleven children, son of a prosperous farmer. After a short stint in the local constabulary and a few months of farming, McKay decided to go to the United States to study agronomy at Tuskegee Institute. He arrived in the United States in 1912, stayed a few weeks at Tuskegee, then transferred to Kansas State College in Manhattan, Kansas, where he remained for two years, leaving Kansas for New York in 1914 without a degree.[15]

In Jamaica, McKay had begun to write poetry, mostly in the Jamaican dialect. McKay arrived in New York, married a young Jamaican, and eventually took ownership of a restaurant. After a few months, he lost the restaurant, and his wife returned to Jamaica, pregnant with a daughter whom Claude McKay would never see.

During the First World War and the period afterward, McKay developed two all-encompassing interests while he worked at numerous jobs, the longest being service as a railroad dining-car waiter. He began to write poetry, no longer in dialect, but in language and rhythm that was rich and lyrical, European in form and structure. He became involved politically. The harsh racist structure of American society at that time was unlike what he had known in Jamaica. And in the period following World War I, when the bitter resentment of blacks began to explode, McKay, like many young blacks, became attracted to Marxism. As the situation became more violent and as blacks increasingly became more victimized, his poetry became more militant — yet always lyrical. His most popular poem, the sonnet "If We Must Die," was published in the summer of 1919 in the *Liberator*, a leftist periodical edited by a faithful friend of McKay, Max Eastman.[16]

In 1919 McKay went to England. Although already close to many Communists and Socialists from his experience in New York, it was in England that he studied Marx seriously and broadened his acquaintance with Socialist ideas and leaders. In 1921 he returned to New York and Harlem, and was for a while one of the editors of the *Liberator*. At this time, with the publication of his poems in the collection known as *Harlem Shadows*,[17] he came into his own as a recognized black poet, ranking with James Weldon Johnson, Countee Cullen, and Langston Hughes.

In September 1922 McKay went abroad again, this time to Russia. He did not know it, but he would not return to the States for another dozen years. He arrived in Russia in time to be an observer at the Fourth Congress of the Third International and soon became a sort of unofficial spokesperson on the question of blacks and the Communist party in the United States.[18] In Russia, McKay was a celebrity. He met Leon Trotsky, who arranged a tour for him to lecture on the issues facing blacks in America, in the West Indies, and in colonial Africa. McKay would later insist that he was never officially a Communist, and in fact, he had a long-standing quarrel with the American Communist party that was never resolved. But he did join the party in Russia. Leaving Russia in 1923, McKay lived the next several years on the Mediterranean coast of France at Toulon, Marseilles, and Nice, and then later in Barcelona; his longest stay was in Tangier, Morocco. It was in these port cities that he came to know the life and situation of the sailors, dockers, and prostitutes, many of whom were blacks from Africa, the West Indies, and even the United States. These experiences were drawn upon in the novels he wrote at this time, novels that many criticized for their frank portrayal of life on the docks.

Claude McKay returned to the United States in 1934, then in his mid-forties. While in Europe, he had developed several physical problems, including high blood pressure, which would create the problems that ended his life in a little more than a decade. In the midst of the depression he came back to a Harlem that was not ready to give him a hero's welcome. In fact, he faced much criticism for his prolonged absence. He also faced hostility from the American Communist party, which at the time was gaining sympathy among young black intellectuals. McKay had grown to hate the Stalinist regime; he also hated the American Communist party's subservience to Stalinism and the exploitation of African Americans by the American party.

In 1944 Claude McKay wrote his friend Max Eastman that he had been baptized a Catholic on October 11. He stated that he had always wanted to belong to some religion, "now ... I have chosen the one that meets my needs." He went on to say that choosing a religion was something "like falling in love with a woman. You love her ... for her Beauty, which cannot be defined."[19]

In the period following his return to Harlem, McKay was never really able to feel accepted. He found it difficult to get his writings published. All of his projects failed.[20] In the end his health deteriorated. In 1942 he became very ill with influenza, which was complicated by high blood pressure and heart disease. It was Ellen Tarry who described how she discovered him "alone and ill in a rented room. Claude needed medical attention and nursing care and I had no one to appeal to but my friends at Friendship House. Claude was fiercely proud and it was not easy, but the girls took turns nursing him."[21] It was in this way that McKay came to know the Baroness de Hueck and Friendship House.

While working in a shipyard as a riveter in the summer of 1943, he suffered a stroke. He would never really recover from this last

illness. Through friends whom he had known in New York and who
had moved to Chicago, he received an invitation from Bishop Sheil
to come to Chicago and work in the Catholic Youth Organization,
which the bishop had established.[22] In 1944 he moved to Chicago. It
was there that he renewed contact with Dorothy Day and the Catholic
Worker Organization.[23] In December of that year he made a retreat
at the Catholic Worker Farm in Easton, Pennsylvania, and he also
published some of his poetry in the *Catholic Worker.*

McKay never really recovered his health. He was able to do some
teaching at the Sheil School of Social Studies attached to the CYO.
He also worked with Friendship House and did some lecturing at
Catholic schools. He wrote articles for Catholic publications; one entitled "Right Turn to Catholicism," which was never published,[24] is
his very personal explanation of why he became a Catholic. He explained that he had fallen in love with the "Catholic way of life" in
Spain and that he had always had an "intellectual sympathy" with
Catholicism; that before he actually joined the church, he had spent
many hours reading in the New York Public Library about the history
of the church, especially in the patristic period. He believed that the
Catholic church had room for everyone who believed in Christ. It
was the Catholic church that was the true international organization
where all people were a family.[25]

In the summer of 1945 McKay spent two weeks at St. Meinrad's
Abbey, a Benedictine monastery in southern Indiana. He sent a post-
card to his daughter, Hope, whom he had never seen. Earlier he had
begun correspondence with her. For the next three years he was in
and out of hospitals, still working at times with the CYO. Finally,
just when he was planning to meet his daughter for the first time, he
had to return to the Alexian Brothers Hospital in Chicago, where he
died on May 22, 1948, at the age of fifty-seven.

Black Catholics in the United States have not preserved the memory of Claude McKay, perhaps because he was not readily associated
with church causes. McKay, nevertheless, deserves better. It is not
just because he wrote some of the most passionate poetry in American literature, or because he was a perceptive writer who celebrated
and critiqued the role of blacks all over the world, or even because
he was a renowned black who converted to Catholicism; but rather
because he was a man who had never lost pride in his culture and his
people, never surrendered in his fight for justice and truth, and found
it finally fulfilled in the teaching and the tradition of the church.

Many of McKay's friends and supporters, companions in the struggle of the American Left against oppression and racism, found it im-

possible to accept his conversion. Others, more objectively, knowing the details of his life, his difficult temperament, his sexual excesses, his turning away from wife and child, his willingness to exploit his friends, find it impossible to credit the sincerity of his conversion. His biographer, Wayne Cooper, suggests that at the end of his life, lonely and without resources, he turned to the Catholic church as a last possible benefactor.

> In any event, however, he convinced himself and insisted to others that he had in fact become a Christian and a Catholic. All the while, of course, he never lost sight of the fact that for both himself and for the church, his conversion had practical benefits...
>
> In a real sense, the Roman Catholic church became the last and greatest of his patrons. In its bosom he found the means not only to live awhile longer but to die with some solace, dignity, and assurance that he had not labored wholly in vain...As difficult, tortured, and ambivalent as it was, he viewed his conversion as genuine, and that perhaps was what mattered most.[26]

No one can read the heart of another, and motivations are rarely unmixed. Yet it is difficult to imagine that he allowed himself to be deluded into an act of faith that was somehow superficial. In an undated letter to a friend after his baptism, McKay pointed out that not many people understood how profoundly he had changed. He went on to say that others made their judgment from the outside, and then he quoted the gospel, "The kingdom of heaven is within you." He ended expressing the desire that he receive the sacrament of confirmation.[27] Conversion, in the end, is a change; and faith, a leap.

> And so to God I go to make my peace,
> Where black nor white can follow to betray.
> My pent-up heart to Him I will release
> And surely He will show the perfect way
> of life. For He will lead me and no man
> Can violate or circumvent His plan.[28]

McKay was not the only black who discovered a home in the Catholic church in the middle period of the twentieth century. Few, however, were as well known as he. At least two left an account of their faith journey. Others, motivated by their faith, dedicated themselves to service for others, especially for the poor. Their story is a significant contribution to the social consciousness of the church in that period.

About the same time that Claude McKay was discovering the Catholic church, a young black woman in Los Angeles recorded the story of her conversion to Catholicism.[29] Born in Santa Barbara, California, in 1909, Elizabeth Laura Adams was reared in a very strict, middle-class black family.[30] She became interested in the Catholic church when in her teens and became a Catholic in 1928. Lack of financial resources after the death of her father forced her to leave college and work as a domestic. Despite constant ill health and the need to provide for her mother, she began to publish articles and poetry, mostly in Catholic publications. She wrote a moving account of her spiritual journey both before and after her conversion; very much part of that experience was being a black woman in a racist society. She recounts with sensitivity and serenity what this meant in terms of her relationship with God. Her story is significant because it is an example of the kind of journey more than a few African Americans were making in the mid-twentieth century.

Helen Caldwell Day took the same spiritual path as a young black woman in Mississippi and Tennessee. She wrote about her conversion and postconversion experience in an autobiography, entitled *Color, Ebony*. In a sequel she described her ministry to the poor, which came as a result of her conversion experience.[31] Helen Day was born in Marshall, Texas, where her father was an instructor at Bishop College, a small black school. The family moved about a great deal until her father finally got an appointment at another black college, in Holly Springs, Mississippi. When she was twelve her parents were separated and later divorced. Her mother went to live in Memphis, and her father remained in Holly Springs.

During the Second World War, she studied nursing at Harlem Hospital. In New York she was received into the Catholic church, entered into an unfortunate marriage and gave birth to a son. While still in nursing school, she became ill with tuberculosis and had to go to a sanatorium. At the same period, her infant son, who was living with her mother in Memphis, contracted polio.

Helen Day had been for a time a volunteer at the Catholic Worker House on Mott Street in lower Manhattan. When she recovered from her illness, she returned to Memphis, and there with the collaboration of some other Catholics, both black and white, she began planning a house of hospitality. The bishop of Nashville, William Adrian, gave his approval to the house in 1950,[32] and in the next year Blessed Martin House was established as an interracial venture in Memphis.

Despite hardships and misunderstandings, the house lasted for some five years. During that time Dorothy Day came and spoke, giving moral and financial help, but the house was closed in 1956. Helen Caldwell Day (her name by a second marriage was Riley), like Elizabeth Laura Adams, wrote the story of her spiritual life in the context of a black woman's journey to God.

Practical charity, the translation into concrete action of the gospel injunction to love one's neighbor and to forgive one's enemy, the living out in practice of the Sermon on the Mount and the parable of the Shepherd-King has been a characteristic of black Catholic holiness, as witnessed by such lives as those of Pierre Toussaint, Mathilda Beasley, and Mother Theodore Williams. It is not surprising that public service has been a major characteristic of black Catholic endeavor also in the mid-twentieth century.

It was Dorothy Day's life and example that prompted the extraordinary work and mission of an ordinary black man with an ordinary clerical job in the United States government in Washington, D.C. Llewellyn Scott was born in Washington, D.C., in 1892 and spent part of his boyhood in Charlottesville, Virginia. His mother was a masseuse; his father a day laborer. As a boy Scott suffered from rickets and was so crippled that he was unable to walk. Fortunately for him, his mother revealed the condition of her infant son to one of her clients, the wife of retired army surgeon-general, Brigadier General John A. Moore. General and Mrs. Moore offered to make a home for young Llewellyn and were eventually able to find medical help for him. Finally, when he was ten years old, Llewellyn Scott was able to walk. Mrs. Moore was a Catholic; as a result Llewellyn was enrolled in the parochial school and soon developed an interest in the Catholic church. He became a Catholic at St. Augustine's in Washington, D.C. Remarkably the young boy was able to make up the studies he had missed because of his illness, and he was ready to graduate from high school with his contemporaries. He volunteered as a soldier in the First World War, serving in France. After the war, he enrolled in the liberal arts faculty at Howard University and later did graduate work at the Catholic University in sociology.

Llewellyn Scott began his life's work during the Depression. It was Dorothy Day who gave him his first contribution to begin a hospice for indigent black men. In the beginning he rented space; later he used his savings to buy two adjoining houses, which he renovated and named Blessed Martin de Porres Hospice. He worked as a government clerk during the day and took care of the house in the evening, devoting his entire salary to the work. A quiet, unassuming man who never married, he not only provided food and shelter but listened to the men and counseled them. A devout Catholic, he went to daily Mass, provided a chapel in his hospice, but never forced religious duties on the men to whom he gave shelter. He also provided an unofficial employment service. After his work was established, he received donations from many sources, including the district government and the archbishop of Washington, Patrick A. O'Boyle.[33] He also had volunteer help from seminarians at the Catholic University.

Llewellyn Scott took an active part in church affairs in the District of Columbia. He belonged to the Catholic Interracial Council of Washington, and he served a term as president. He was enabled to make three visits to Rome, was introduced to three popes, and attended the canonization of St. Martin de Porres in 1962. He marched with Martin Luther King, Jr., in Memphis in 1968. One who worked with him closely for many years described him as a quiet resistant in the cause of civil rights. A Franciscan tertiary, his spirituality was inspired by the life of St. Francis of Assisi, namely, the love of poverty and the acceptance of all things with "perfect joy."[34] Scott died of leukemia on December 17, 1978, at the age of eighty-six.

Other black Catholic laypeople served God in serving others. Mrs. Emma Lewis, who was known simply as Mother Lewis, was one of these. Mother Lewis was born in Galvalease, Ohio, in 1868. She left Ohio at the beginning of the century and went first to Pittsburgh and then to Philadelphia. On her own she began catechetical work among the black children in North Philadelphia and then among the adults. She was honored by Archbishop Ryan of Philadelphia with the gift of a crucifix from Pope St. Pius X.[35] In response to a request of the archbishop and with financial assistance from Blessed Katherine Drexel, she began a mission, Our Lady of the Blessed Sacrament, which later developed into a parish. Her work continued when she moved to Atlantic City and began in 1916 another mission in the black community, which was named in honor of St. Monica. The Augustinian friars took charge of the parochial needs the following year. Mother Lewis continued her work until her death in 1921.[36]

The last example of uniquely black spirituality, also inspired by the example of St. Francis, was Lena Edwards, born in Washington, D.C., in 1901, the third of four children in a middle-class black Catholic family. Her father, Thomas Edwards, was a dentist and professor of dentistry in the Howard University Dental School; her mother, Marie Coakley, the daughter of one of the founders of St. Augustine's Church in Washington, D.C., provided a home of culture and refinement. It also produced a determined, no-nonsense woman who graduated from Howard University in 1921 and from the Howard University Medical School in 1924. That same year she married a fellow classmate, Dr. Keith Madison. Lena Edwards would continue throughout her professional life to use her maiden name.

The next year the couple moved to Jersey City, where each opened up a practice and where Lena Edwards eventually became a member of the staff of the Margaret Hague Maternity Hospital. By this time her specialty had become obstetrics and gynecology. Dr. Edwards soon learned that she had two obstacles to overcome: she was black, and she was a woman. In her career as a physician, she overcame both because she was tenacious and hard working. Not only was she successful in her professional career, but she also raised a family of six children.

Dr. Edwards worked as a physician for almost thirty years in Jersey City. After most of her children were grown, she decided to return to Howard University in 1954. By this time she had a national reputation and was the recipient of many honors. She was a devout Catholic who attended Mass every day and was an active member of the Franciscan Third Order. She had a love for St. Francis of Assisi and a devotion to the ideal of poverty. She became an active member of the Catholic Interracial Council in Washington, as she had been in Jersey City. As a Catholic obstetrician, she was very much opposed to abortion and sterilization. She was also a firm believer that the good physician must be concerned with the total welfare of the patients, including social as well as medical needs.

It was this concern about the social dimensions of medical care that prompted her to embark upon a mission to the poorest people in the country. One of her sons, Martin Madison, had been ordained a priest in the Society of the Atonement, a branch of the Franciscan family. Another Atonement friar had begun a mission for the Mexican-American migrant workers in Hereford, Deaf Smith County, Texas. Giving up the position at Howard University Medical School, Dr. Edwards went to Hereford in 1961, where she shared the poverty of the workers, living and working among them. She contributed her own life savings and raised additional funds for the construction of a maternity hospital for workers. This hospital was constructed by the migrant workers themselves. She also trained the volunteer staff and established a credit union. In 1964 President Lyndon Johnson awarded her the Medal of Freedom, the highest award given to an American civilian, at the same ceremony that honored Theodore Hesburgh, C.S.C., the president of Notre Dame, and two other famous African Americans: opera singer

Leontyne Price and labor leader A. Philip Randolph. In 1965 Lena Edwards was forced to leave the mission and return to Washington, D.C. Her activities on behalf of poor children and the needy did not cease, however. Her interest in medicine and disease prevention continued. She lectured, served on committees, and received further honors. She also continued to use her own funds to pay for the education of needy students on the college and professional level, finally establishing a scholarship program for women at the Howard University Medical School. She was untiring in her service and in her dedication to God.[37] She died on December 3, 1986.

II

The middle years of the twentieth century saw the conversion of many blacks to the Catholic church, but the church itself did not play a leading role on the national level in the struggle of blacks against discrimination and segregation until the period of the Second World War. In 1931 Thomas Wyatt Turner addressed a letter to the American hierarchy asking them to see that "none of the doors of our schools, colleges, universities, or seminaries will be closed to us because of the color of our skin."[38] The following year he seems to have addressed another letter asking for more direct action against racial segregation in the church, "that every bishop shall see to it that no Catholic institution in his diocese, school, hospital, protectory, orphanage, college, university or seminary, shall be closed to colored Catholics." The letter went on to ask the bishops to apply sanctions to those in the church who bar black Catholics from activities in their respective dioceses to which other Catholics have access. The bishops were asked to speak out against lynching and the "driving out of the colored residents from a town."[39]

In 1939 Turner wrote again in the name of the Federated Colored Catholics of the United States, noting that some changes for the better had occurred but that not enough had been done. The letter closed with the statement: "We are conscious of the fact that attitudes may not immediately be changed by a fiat, but we believe that an authoritative word from Your Excellencies concerning this question, which is so deeply rooted in justice and morals, will go far toward stimulating a larger number of the clergy to become aware of the changed conditions in the progress and life of the Negro."[40]

The change in the American church came about in a large degree because of the activities of white clergy and religious, working alongside of African Americans and at times working independently. Despite the rift between LaFarge and Turner regarding strategy and basic philosophy of interracial cooperation, the Catholic Interracial Councils provided an arena for change. LaFarge in a private communication to Archbishop (later cardinal) Spellman,[41] who had just been named to the see of New York, spelled out the activities of the Catholic Interracial Council in his archdiocese. He outlined the scope of the works accomplished: publication of the *Interracial Review*, a speakers' bureau that addressed parish organizations like the Holy Name Society and college students in various Catholic colleges and universities, and the organizing of allied groups such as the Clergy Conference on Negro Welfare, the Catholic Laymen's Union, and the De Porres Interracial Center in New York City.[42]

One of the outstanding leaders in the struggle for racial justice in the middle years of this century was a white layman, George K. Hunton, whose maternal grandparents had been close friends of Bishop James Augustine Healy. George Hunton, who was born in New Hampshire in 1888, became associated with LaFarge in 1931 and the Laymen's Union, an organization of black Catholic laymen who were professional and business men, who met for an annual retreat and bimonthly Mass and communion breakfast. It was this organization that helped form the first Catholic Interracial Council in 1934. Hunton became editor of the *Interracial Review* and was LaFarge's right-hand man in interracial affairs; Hunton devoted himself to this cause with heart and soul. He was a worker and a fighter. He became a force in the Catholic Interracial Council and enabled it to take what was then considered radical positions regarding the passage of antilynching laws, support for the young black men in the famous Scottsboro Trial of 1934, and the Fair Employment Practices Committee.[43] Hunton was perhaps most important in that he formed close alliances with the black leaders of the time, such as Roy Wilkins of the NAACP. Hunton died in 1967.

The Catholic church in mid-twentieth-century America acquired a reputation for racial fairness among African Americans (a reputation often compromised at the local level). A dramatic incident on the part of a Catholic priest or religious often made an impression. Such an incident occurred at Manhattanville College, a liberal arts college for women operated by the Religious of the Sacred Heart.[44] The college was a Catholic counterpart of Smith or Vassar. It was at Manhattanville that George K. Hunton spoke on several questions of racial justice and Catholic teaching. At Manhattanville in 1938 the president of the college, Mother Grace Dammann, accepted a young black woman into the freshman class for the following year. Mother Grace was confronted by a wave of opposition from some alumnae. On Class Day at the end of the school year, she addressed the alumnae on the topic "Principles versus Prejudices."[45] She acknowledged that "for some years we have known that the racial problem in Catholic education would have to be met by us not in theory only but in practice"; and the student body had been prepared through education for this fact. She explained that the applicant in question had met all of the requirements, that the college was not lowering its standards — in fact, the college was seeking to live up to the teachings of the church. "A Catholic colored girl who meets the requirements of a Catholic college and applies for a Catholic education has a right to it and in consequence the college has a duty to give it to her."[46] She concluded with words that were prophetic. "The day has gone by when we can blithely live as compartmental Catholics, with our political, business, intellectual, social activities in air-tight compartments functioning separately like parts of a well-behaved machine. Catholicism is nothing if it is not a *life*, unified, coordinated to its end."[47]

In the middle years of this century, Mother Katherine Drexel continued the work discussed in earlier chapters for the evangelization of blacks. Not only did the Sisters of the Blessed Sacrament continue to open schools for the education of blacks, but Blessed Katherine continued to disburse funds for church and school building in the black community. What is not well known is the financial contribution that she and her sister, Louise Drexel Morrell, made to the NAACP and to the campaign for congressional legislation to curb lynching in the South. In 1934 she encouraged many of the Blessed Sacrament Sisters in responsible positions to write letters to President Roosevelt in support of antilynching legislation pending in Congress.[48]

The most significant action of Blessed Katherine was the establishment of the only black Catholic institution of higher learning in the United States: Xavier University of Louisiana at New Orleans. In 1915 a high school was opened for black students in New Orleans by the Sisters of the Blessed Sacrament at the request of Archbishop Blenk of New Orleans,[49] with the idea of an eventual college. In 1925 a teachers' college and a college of liberal arts was added. In 1931 the new complex of buildings was dedicated as Xavier University. Two years later a graduate school was established.[50]

III

After the Second World War the United States confronted once again the issue of racial segregation. This time, however, things were different. American society was now forced to confront a new determination and resolve among black Americans. This confrontation now took place in a world in which colonialism was dying and new nations were arising amid wars of liberation. In America it was the beginning of a social revolution that would have enormous — indeed revolutionary — consequences in all sectors of American society. The story of this revolution has been often told, so the present book will discuss it primarily in its Catholic dimension.

In 1955 the blacks of Montgomery, Alabama, began a boycott of buses because of segregated seating. A young black Baptist clergyman, Rev. Martin Luther King, Jr., became the leader of the movement. The boycott was successful, and the African American community was galvanized across the nation. Three years later, in 1958, the American bishops addressed racism as a moral issue and finally took an unequivocal stand. They stated for the first time that racial discrimination was immoral and unjust.

> The heart of the race question is moral and religious. It concerns the rights of man and our attitude toward our fellow man. If our attitude is governed by the great Christian law of love of neighbor and respect for his rights, then we can work out harmoniously the techniques for making legal, educational, economic, and social adjustments. But if our hearts are poisoned by hatred, or even by indifference toward the welfare and rights of our fellow men, then our nation faces a grave internal crisis.[51]

They went on to point out that "discrimination based on the accidental fact of race or color...cannot be reconciled with the truth that God has created all men with equal rights and equal dignity."[52] Furthermore, they went on to say, from the Christian point of view segregation can in no way be justified. But they injected a note of timid caution by seeking to create a balance between what they saw as "a gradualism that is merely a cloak for inaction" and a "rash impetuosity that would sacrifice the achievements of decades in ill-timed and ill-considered ventures."[53] What the bishops did not know was that the situation had reached a point that a deliberate and well thought out series of measures was no longer possible.

It is often stated that the bishops made powerful statements but that little was done to change the situation on the local level. Maybe forgotten is the fact that the task of bishops is to preach and to teach and to recall the principles and the teachings of the gospel in order to create a climate where concerted action is possible. Of course, some bishops were more directly insistent that the church's teachings on racial justice be implemented on the local level. Joseph Ritter, the archbishop of St. Louis,[54] ended racial segregation in the city's Catholic schools in 1947, despite loud protestations from many of the city's white Catholics. The archbishop of Washington, Patrick O'Boyle, did the same shortly after he was named to the see of Washington in 1947. Vincent Waters, bishop of Raleigh,[55] ended segregation in the parishes and other church institutions in his diocese in 1954. The courageous action of these bishops took place before judicial decisions had overturned the pattern of racial segregation in the public schools or the Congress had been prodded into the enactment of civil rights legislation.

By and large Catholics, either black or white, were not in the forefront of the civil rights movement or among the leadership of the protest organizations. Black priests, unlike many black Protestant clergymen, were not in the vanguard of grass-roots leadership that supported and followed King on the local level. One reason for this, of course, was that few black priests were in leadership positions of any kind in the early sixties. In general, they were neither pastors nor religious superiors. Moreover, the notion that it was unseemly for either clergy or religious to engage in public spectacles like demonstrations was especially strong among Catholics in general. The massive demonstration by whites and blacks at the Lincoln Memorial in Washington, D.C., on August 28, 1963, did, however, include some Catholics of diverse backgrounds as well as some Catholic organizations, including religious communities. Archbishop O'Boyle was on the platform with civil rights leaders and delivered the invocation just before Martin Luther King began his famous "I Have a Dream" speech. For the first time, the Catholic church was significantly present at a massive public demonstration under the leadership of black civil rights leaders. But this was a demonstration with official, governmental support.

The real change in Catholic attitudes came with the clarion call by Martin Luther King, Jr., to all of the nation's clergy to come to Selma, Alabama, in March 1965. The response of white Catholic priests and sisters was enormous, despite the disapproval of the bishop of Mobile-Birmingham.[56] That same year Harold Perry, S.V.D., provincial of the southern province of the Divine Word Missionaries, was named auxiliary bishop of New Orleans by Pope Paul VI, the second black Catholic bishop in American history.[57] By the mid-sixties the nonviolent stance of Martin Luther King yielded in some places to violence in response to the growth of desperation among blacks, displayed in riots and burning, and in response to the new sense of black nationalism represented by the cry of "Black Power!" In 1965 Malcolm X was assassinated in New York City. Three years later, on April 4, 1968, Martin Luther King was assassinated in Memphis, Tennessee. The black community erupted in fury, frustration, and despair. Riots broke out in areas already ravaged by fire and in areas never before touched by black frustration.

The Catholic Clergy Conference on the Interracial Apostolate had its scheduled meeting in Detroit at the Sheraton-Cadillac Hotel, April 16–18. Before the meeting, Father Herman Porter, black priest of the diocese of Rockford, Illinois,[58] and vice-president of the organization, circulated a letter to all black priests in the country inviting them to a special caucus. The invitation was in response to the police order of Chicago's mayor Richard J. Daly "to shoot to kill" all those engaged in looting. The caucus took place on April 16, with the program for the Catholic Clergy Conference to begin that same evening. While many of the white clergy were registering for the conference, whose theme that year was "Black Power and the White Church: The Christian Ministry in the Ghetto and the Suburb," some sixty or more black priests were meeting as a group for the first time in American history. In that meeting, which went on through that day and night, black priests of all ages and backgrounds dealt with the question of their personal and corporate responsibility in a time of racial crisis. In order to determine such responsibility, the individual priests had to look at their respective sense of racial identity. Ultimately, this meant a look by each one at his own personal history as an African American cleric in the American Catholic church. For many it was a time of painful discovery and sometimes bitter revelation. For all it was either a time of anger or of deep-seated unease.

The discussions eventually settled upon certain objectives. Very clearly the ad hoc caucus wished to form itself into a permanent organization of black priests that would include permanent deacons and religious Brothers. For the immediate future the decision was made to deliver a statement to the American bishops, to let them know the seriousness of the situation facing the church in the black community. The result was a lengthy statement with some highly charged phrases critical of the American church. The wording of the statement was adopted after prolonged discussion and argument. The participants were pulled between a real sense of loyalty to the church and a sense of responsibility to the black community in a time of struggle and increasing militancy.[59]

The statement began with a confrontational assertion. "The Catholic Church in the United States, primarily a white racist institution, has addressed itself primarily to white society and is definitely a part of that society."[60] The statement called for the church to heed the new spirit that was sweeping through the black community in the wake of the civil rights movement and the Black Power movement. It called for the church to look again at the issue of militancy in the matter of rights for black Americans. It called for greater control by blacks themselves of the Catholic institutions in the black community, and warned that the church "is rapidly dying in the black community . . . In many areas there is a serious defection . . . on the part of black Catholic youth . . . The black community no longer looks to the Catholic church with hope." The caucus then made nine demands of the American bishops.[61]

The demands were that black priests be placed in decision-making positions in their dioceses and in the black community; that black priests be given the opportunity to work directly within the black community; that in areas where black priests were nonexistent, efforts be made to bring them in or that white priests who were "black thinking" be chosen for ministry; that greater efforts "to recruit black men for the priesthood" be made; that formation in black ministry be established for white priests chosen to work within the black community; that a department be established in the United States Catholic Conference under black leadership for the affairs of African Americans; that black religious also be employed in the foregoing positions; that black men, including married men, be chosen for the permanent diaconate; and that each diocese set aside funds on a permanent basis for leadership training of black laypersons.[62]

The calling of the Black Catholic Clergy Caucus was a milestone in the history of the black Catholic community. It created a solidarity among the black Catholic clergy that had never previously existed. It was a return to the tradition of black Catholic initiative that had marked the black Catholic lay congresses and the Federated Colored Catholics. The one significant change was that this time it was the clergy that had seized the initiative. The demands of the clergy became a program that was implemented or has been in the process of implementation. It was, finally, the beginning of a change of direction on the part of the American Catholic church. No matter how one may view the assertion that the Catholic church in the United

States was "a white racist institution," it is remarkable that the church as an institution opened itself with a minimum of resistance to the needs of its black members in most areas. How this was done and the part that black Catholics themselves played in the American Catholic church in the second half of this century must be the subject of another historical study.

IV

We can, however, draw some conclusions as we look back over the history of the black Catholic presence in the United States for the last three hundred years. First of all, it is clear that the Catholic church in the United States has never been a white European church. The African presence has influenced the Catholic church in every period of its history. More than this, the Catholic church was as much affected by the issue of slavery and its aftermath as any other American institution. The issue of slavery affected the American episcopate in its own understanding of what freedom, justice, and human dignity really mean; the issue of slavery and the evangelization of the African American affected the relationship between the American episcopate and the Roman Curia.

Too often black Catholics have been ignored in conventional assessments of American Catholicism. In the light of history, they cannot be ignored. They add another essential perspective to the meaning of the word "Catholic" and to the understanding of the American Catholic church.

The story of African American Catholicism is the story of a people who obstinately clung to a faith that gave them sustenance, even when it did not always make them welcome. Like many others, blacks had to fight for their faith; but their fight was often with members of their own household. Too long have black Catholics been anonymous. It is now clear that they can be identified, that their presence has made an impact, and that their contributions have made Catholicism a unique and stronger religious body.

POSTSCRIPT

As we have seen, the last three decades of the twentieth century witnessed a momentous period of change within the black Catholic community. The number of black Catholics has grown to approximately 1.5 million, with the major centers still being southern Louisiana and the metropolitan areas of New York, Chicago, Washington, D.C., Miami, and Los Angeles. In 1979 the American hierarchy addressed the issue of racism in a pastoral letter, "Brothers and Sisters to Us." Five years later, in 1984, ten black bishops (thirteen by 1988) issued a pastoral letter on evangelization and African American Catholics, "What We Have Seen and Heard." In 1987 the first black Catholic congress in the twentieth century was held in Washington, D.C.; and in the fall of the same year, Pope John Paul II gave a special audience to black Catholic leaders in New Orleans. That same year there was created the Black Secretariat in the service of the National Council of Catholic Bishops. Also in 1988, Eugene Marino, the auxiliary bishop of Washington, D.C., was transferred to the see of Atlanta, becoming the first black archbishop in the history of the nation.

As a result of the National Black Catholic Congress of 1987, a national program for evangelization in the black community was drawn up and adopted by the American bishops in 1989. It was a commitment to the African American community and a pledge of support to the zeal of black Catholics. In that same year, a charismatic black priest of the Washington, D.C., archdiocese, George Stallings, launched a call for a separate, semiautonomous status for black Catholics through the formation of an African American Rite, or more precisely, an African American ecclesiastical jurisdiction. Disciplined by his ordinary because of the formation of an unauthorized parish, the Imani Temple, George Stallings (who subsequently severed his ties with Rome) and his popular following may well present a challenge and an opportunity to the American church that will be another turning point in its history.

CHRONOLOGY

1565   Establishment of St. Augustine in Florida by Spain. Inhabitants both white and black.

1639   Death of St. Martin de Porres in Lima, Peru.

1738   Establishment of free black town of Santa Teresa de Mose in Florida for freed slaves converted to Catholicism.

1781   Settlement of Los Angeles by blacks and Indians from Mexico.

1793   Arrival of Haitian refugees at Fells' Point, near Baltimore.

1824   Unsuccessful foundation of a community of black women religious by Charles Nerinckx in Loretto, Kentucky.

1829   Elizabeth Lange, Marie Balas, Rosine Boegue, and Almeide Duchemin Maxis began religious life in Baltimore as the Oblate Sisters of Providence. First black religious congregation of women in the United States.

1839   Condemnation of the slave trade by Pope Gregory XVI in the bull *In Supremo Apostolatus.*

1842   Henriette Delille and Juliette Gaudin began the Sisters of the Holy Family in New Orleans.

1843   Formation of the Society of the Holy Family in Baltimore. First known black Catholic society of lay persons.

1853   Death of Pierre Toussaint in New York.

1854   Ordination of James Augustine Healy in Paris. Ordinations of Alexander Sherwood Healy in Rome (1858) and Francis Patrick Healy, S.J., in Liège (1864).

1871   Arrival of Mill Hill Fathers (Josephites) in Baltimore.

1874   Francis Patrick Healy named president of Georgetown University in Washington, D.C.

1875   James Augustine Healy consecrated second bishop of Portland, Maine. First black bishop in the States.

1886   Ordination of Augustus Tolton in Rome.

1889   First black Catholic lay congress, in Washington, D.C. Other congresses held in Cincinnati (1890), Philadelphia (1892), Chicago (1893), and Baltimore (1894).

1891   Ordination of Charles Uncles, S.S.J., in Baltimore. First black priest ordained in the United States. Foundation of the Sisters of the Blessed Sacrament for Indians and Colored People by Blessed Katherine Drexel.

1897   Death of Augustus Tolton in Chicago.

1908   Lincoln Vallé opened Catholic mission for the black community in Milwaukee.

1913   Thomas Wyatt Turner organized a committee on behalf of black Catholic servicemen.

1916   Mother Theodore Williams and Father Ignatius Lissner began the Handmaids of Mary in Savannah, Georgia.

1920   First seminary for black candidates for the priesthood begun by the Society of the Divine Word in Greenville, Mississippi, later moved to Bay St. Louis (1923).

1924   Founding of the Federated Colored Catholics of the United States.

1934   Organization of the first Catholic Interracial Council in New York City, by John LaFarge, S.J.

1966   Episcopal ordination of Harold Perry, S.V.D., as the auxiliary bishop of New Orleans. Second black bishop in the history of the United States.

1968   Formation of the National Black Catholic Clergy Caucus in Detroit, resulted in the subsequent development of the National Black Sisters' Conference (1968) and the National Black Catholic Seminarians Association.

NOTES

Preface

1. See "Epistula XI seu Epistula Ferrandi Diaconi ad Sanctum Fulgentium Episcopum de Salute Aethiopis Moribundi" and "Epistula XII seu Sancti Fulgentii Episcopi Rescriptum ad Ferrandum Diaconum," in *Sancti Fulgentii Episcopi Ruspensis Opera*, ed. J. Fraipont, *Corpus Christianorum, Series Latina*, 91:359–78.

2. John T. Gillard, *The Catholic Church and the American Negro* (Baltimore: St. Joseph's Society Press, 1929), and *Colored Catholics in the United States* (Baltimore: Josephite Press, 1941).

3. Albert Foley, *God's Men of Color* (New York: Farrar, Straus, 1955), and *Bishop Healy: Beloved Outcaste* (New York: Farrar, Straus, and Young, 1954).

4. Marilyn Wenzke Nickels, *Black Catholic Protest and the Federated Colored Catholics: 1917–1933. Three Perspectives on Racial Justice* (New York: Garland Publishing, 1988), and Stephen Ochs, *Desegregating the Altar: The Josephites and the Struggle for Black Priests, 1871–1960* (Baton Rouge: Louisiana State University Press, 1990).

5. Maria Caravaglios, *The American Catholic Church and the Negro Problem in the XVIII–XIX Centuries* (Charleston, S.C.: Caravaglios, 1974).

Chapter 1: African Roots

1. In its address to the clergy and laity of the Catholic church in America in Chicago in 1893, the fourth black Catholic lay congress spoke in glowing terms of the historic record of the church and then referred by name to Augustine, Monica, Benedict the Moor, Cyprian, Cyril, and Perpetua and Felicity. This address appears in the William Onahan Papers in the University of Notre Dame Archives. See chapter 7 for a fuller discussion of this remarkable address.

2. Origen, *The Song of Songs: Commentary and Homilies*, trans. R. P. Lawson (Westminster, Md.: Newman Press, 1957), 98.

3. Ibid., 98–99.

4. In the Book of Numbers, chapter 12, Miriam and Aaron were punished for criticizing the Kushite woman whom Moses married. Normally in Hebrew the words "Kushite" and "Kush" referred to sub-Saharan Africa, particularly Nubia. Most Scripture scholars today, however, would not consider the wife of Moses as coming from Kush, properly so called. The Greek word for Kush was "Ethiopia" (*aethiops* meant "burnt face," that is, those who are black).

Ebed-melech in Jeremiah 38 and 39 was a royal slave and a Kushite and was quite obviously a black African, probably from Nubia. For Origen he too was a symbol of the church. See Jacques Chênevert, *L'Église dans le commentaire d'Origène sur le Cantique des Cantiques* (Brussels: Desclée de Brouwer, 1969), 148. For a more recent study of blacks in Scripture from an African American perspective, see Cain Hope Felder, *Troubling Biblical Waters: Race, Class and Family* (Maryknoll, N.Y.: Orbis Books, 1989), 5–48.

5. For information regarding ancient Nubia, see William Y. Adams, *Nubia: Corridor to Africa* (Princeton, N.J.: Princeton University Press, 1984). See also S. Adam and J. Vercoutter "The Importance of Nubia: A Link between Central Africa and the Mediterranean," chap. 8; N. M. Sherif, "Nubia before Napata, −3100 to −750," chap. 9; and J. Leclant, "The Empire of Kush: Napata and Meroe," chap. 10, all in *General History of Africa*, vol. 2, *Ancient Civilizations of Africa* (Berkeley: University of California Press, UNESCO, 1981), 2:226–95.

6. See Adams, *Nubia*, 260, and *General History of Africa* 2:302–4.

7. See Paul de Meester, "'Philippe et l'eunuque éthiopien' ou 'Le baptême d'un pèlerin de Nubie'?" *Nouvelle Revue Théologique* 103 (1981): 360–74, and Clarice Martin, "A Chamberlain's Journey and the Challenge of Interpretation for Liberation," *Semeia: An Experimental Journal for Biblical Criticism* 47 (1989): 105–35.

8. See K. Michalowski, "The Spreading of Christianity in Nubia," chap. 12 in *General History of Africa* 2:326–40. For the Melkite presence, see p. 332. For information regarding Christian Nubia, the classic work remains Ugo Monneret de Villard, *Storia della Nubia Christiana* (Rome: Pont. Institutum Orientalium Studiorum, 1938). See also Adams, *Nubia*, 459–507.

The discovery of the treasures of Christian Nubia has taken place only since 1960. Much excavation had to be done hurriedly to save many of the treasures, as the northern part of ancient Nubia was eventually flooded through the construction of the Aswan Dam. Much was saved, but much was also lost. For a description of the excavations, see John Vantini, *The Excavations at Faras: A Contribution to the History of Christian Nubia* (Bologna: Editrice Nigrizia, 1970). For photographs of the excavation and massive removal of archaeological remains, see "Victory in Nubia: The Greatest Archaeological Rescue Operation of all Time," *UNESCO Courier*, February–March, 1980. Finally, as a summary of recent discoveries in Christian Nubia, see William Frend, "Recently Discovered Materials for Writing the History of Christian Nubia," in *The Materials, Sources, and Methods of Ec-*

clesiastical History, ed. Derek Baker (New York: Barnes and Noble, 1975), 19–30.

9. Adams, *Nubia,* 472.

10. William Frend, "Nubia as an Outpost of Byzantine Cultural Influence," in *Religion Popular and Unpopular in the Early Christian Centuries* (London: Variorum Reprints, 1976), sec. 12, 319–26, and "Coptic, Greek, and Nubian at Q'asr Ibrim," in ibid., sec. 22, 224–29. See S. Jakobielski, "Christian Nubia at the Height of Its Civilization," chap. 8 in *General History of Africa,* 3:194–223, and, for the plan of a Nubian monastery, see p. 205, fig. 8.4. For more details regarding Nubian monasticism, see Adams, *Nubia,* 478–80.

11. Frend, "Recently Discovered Materials," 25–26.

12. Adams, *Nubia,* 542–43.

13. See H. de Contenson, "Pre-Aksumite Culture," chap. 13 in *General History of Africa* 2:341–59.

14. See F. Anfray, "The Civilization of Aksum from the First to the Seventh Century," chap. 14; and Y. M. Kobishanov, "Aksum: Political System, Economics and Culture, First to Fourth Century," chap. 15, both in *General History of Africa* 2:362–400.

15. See Tekle Tsadik Mekouria, "Christian Axum," chap. 16 in *General History of Africa* 2:401–20. See also *Dictionnaire d'histoire et de géographie écclésiastiques,* s.v. "Edesius et Frumentius."

16. See *General History of Africa,* 2:413–15. See also *Dictionnaire d'histoire et de géographie écclésiastiques,* s.v. "Elesbaan."

17. See Tesfazghi Uqbit, *Current Christological Positions of Ethiopian Orthodox Theologians* (Rome: Pont. Institutum Studiorum Orientalium, 1973), on the question of doctrinal differences that exist today. For more information regarding the development of the Ethiopian church, see Steven Kaplan, *The Monastic Holy Man and the Christianization of Early Solomonic Ethiopia* (Wiesbaden: Franz Steiner Verlag, 1984).

18. For information regarding Palladius and his famous monastic history, see Joannes Quasten, *The Golden Age of Greek Patristic Literature,* vol. 3 of *Patrology* (Westminster, Md.: Christian Classics, 1986), 176–79. Palladius composed his work about the year 420, dedicating it to Lausus, the chamberlain at the court of Emperor Theodosius II.

19. *Palladius: The Lausiac History,* ed. and trans. Robert T. Meyer (Westminster, Md.: Newman Press, 1965), 67–70.

20. For the *apophthegmata* related to St. Moses the Black, see the translation by Sister Benedicta Ward, *The Desert Christian: The Sayings of the Desert Fathers: The Alphabetical Collection* (New York: Macmillan Publishing, 1980), 17–18, 138–43, 224.

21. Cassian's *Conferences* are found in Latin in Migne, *Patrologiae,* series latina, 49:481–558. The first conference is concerned with the purpose of the monastic life; the second is on discretion. The latest English translation is *John Cassian: Conferences,* trans. Colm Luibheid (New York: Paulist Press,

1985), 37–80. For biographical details on the life of Moses, see *Catholicisme*, s.v. "Moïse l'Éthiopien," and *Bibliotheca Sanctorum*, s.v. "Mosè di Scete."

22. For an example, see a passage in the *Historia Monachorum*, ed. A.-J. Festugière, in *Historia Monachorum in Aegypto: Édition critique du texte grec et traduction annotée* (Brussels: Société des Bollandistes, 1971), 60–61, lines 226–29. The Greek text seems to indicate that the "Ethiopians" were among the monks. In the most recent English translation by Norman Russell, *The Lives of the Desert Fathers* (Kalamazoo, Mich.: Cistercian Publications, 1980), 75, the translator renders the text: "One could also see negroes at that place practising *ascesis* with the monks. Many of them excelled in the virtues." The Greek text as given by Festugière says: "One was able to see also Ethiopians in that place with the monks practicing asceticism and surpassing many in the virtues."

23. For a discussion of the racial makeup of ancient Egypt, see Cheikh Anta Diop, "Origin of the Ancient Egyptians," chap. 1 in *General History of Africa* 2:27–51, and the following discussion, "Annex to Chapter 1: Report of the Symposium on 'The Peopling of Ancient Egypt and the Deciphering of the Meroitic Script,' Cairo, 28 January–3 February 1974," 58–82. Alexandria was founded by Alexander the Great in 331 B.C. An idea of the diverse population both in Alexandria and in Hellenistic Egypt is given by Frank Snowden, Jr., *Before Color Prejudice: The Ancient View of Blacks* (Cambridge: Harvard University Press, 1983), 88–90.

24. See J. Desanges, "The Proto-Berbers," chap. 17 in *General History of Africa* 2:423–28.

25. W. H. C. Frend, "Blandina and Perpetua: Two Early Christian Heroines," in *Town and Country in the Early Christian Centuries* (London: Variorum Reprints, 1980), sec. 15, 167–75. An English translation of the *Passio* of Sts. Perpetua and Felicitas is found in H. Musurillo, *Acts of the Christian Martyrs* (Oxford: Clarendon Press, 1972), 106–31.

26. See Frend, "Blandina and Perpetua," 170.

27. See Morris Rosenblum, *Luxorius: A Latin Poet among the Vandals* (New York: Columbia University Press, 1961), 150–52 and 230–32. Luxorius praised the prowess and the beauty of this black athlete who engaged in hand to hand combat with wild beasts. Blacks often acted as gladiators, charioteers, boxers, and wrestlers in the spectacles held in every large city of the Roman Empire. At the same time, they acted in the theater and worked as jugglers, acrobats, and musicians (See page 115, where Luxorius writes a poem about another animal wrestler who was black.) For blacks as entertainers in the Roman world, see Frank Snowden, Jr., *Blacks in Antiquity: Ethiopians in the Greco-Roman Experience* (Cambridge: Harvard University Press, Belknap Press, 1970), 156–68.

28. See Peter Brown, *Augustine of Hippo* (Berkeley: University of California Press, 1967). For a description of Augustine's background, see the opening chapters in the book.

29. The translation in the New Oxford Bible is: "Thou didst crush the

heads of Leviathan, thou didst give him as food for the creatures of the wilderness" (Ps. 74:14). In Augustine's Old Latin version "creatures of the wilderness" was translated "Ethiopian peoples."

30. St. Augustine, *Enarrationes in Psalmos*, in *Corpus Christianorum, Series Latina*, 39:1014. The translation is my own. Augustine quotes Scripture from the Latin translation of the Septuagint of his own time.

31. See *Dictionnaire de théologie catholique*, s.v. "Victor Ier (saint)."

32. See *Catholicisme*, s.v. "Melchiade ou Miltiade."

33. See *Dictionnaire d'histoire et de géographie écclésiastiques*, s.v. "Gélase [er]." P. Nautin, author of the article, rejects the notion that Gelasius was an African.

34. See L. Duchesne, ed., *Le Liber Pontificalis: Texte, introduction et commentaire*, 3 vols (Paris: E. de Broccard, 1955–57). 1:xxxvi–xliii, which gives information regarding the historical accuracy of the text; 137–38; 168–69; and 255–57 give the biographical text for the respective pontiffs.

35. It would not be surprising that he had been a slave. Pope St. Callistus I (d. ca. 222) is the first pope we know of who had been a slave before entering the ranks of the clergy.

36. The Blemmyes were a black African tribe in Upper Egypt and Nubia. They were especially fierce.

37. Eusebius, *The Life of the Blessed Emperor Constantine*, vol. 1 of *The Greek Ecclesiastical Historians of the First Six Centuries of the Christian Era, in Six Volumes* (London: Samuel Bagster and Sons, 1845), 182–83.

38. See *Dictionnaire de théologie catholique*, s.v. "Zénon de Vérone."

39. For information on St. Maurice and the Theban Legion, see *Catholicisme*, s.v. "Maurice (saint)," and *Dictionnaire d'archéologie chrétienne et de liturgie*, s.v. "Maurice d'Agaune (saint)." For Maurice and the Theban Legion in art, see *The Image of the Black in Western Art*, vol. 2, *From the Early Christian Era to the Age of Discovery*, part 1, *From the Demonic Threat to the Incarnation of Sainthood*, ed. Jean Devisse (New York: William Morrow, 1979).

40. For more information about the black king among the Magi, see *Bibliotheca Sanctorum*, s.v. "Magi, adoratori de Gesù, santi." See especially pages 509–18 and the section that follows in the same volume, s.v. "Iconographia." See also Devisse, *From the Demonic Threat to the Incarnation of Sainthood,*. 131–39.

41. *Correspondance de Dom Afonso, roi du Congo, 1506–1543*, ed. Louis Jadin and Mireille Dicorato (Brussels, 1974).

42. "Le vicaire Rui de Aguiar au Roi Dom Manuel, Banza Congo, le 25 mai 1516," in *Correspondance de Dom Afonso*, 116–18.

43. "Dom Afonso au Roi Dom Manuel, Banza Congo, le 5 octobre 1514," in *Correspondance de Dom Afonso*, 82–83.

44. Ibid., 86–87, 95–96.

45. For the question of African forms of slavery, see Suzanne Miers and Igor Kopytoff, eds., *Slavery in Africa: Historical and Anthropological Per-*

spectives (Madison: University of Wisconsin Press, 1977). For a comparative study of the historical phenomenon of slavery, see Orlando Patterson, *Slavery and Social Death. A Comparative Study* (Cambridge: Harvard University Press, 1982).

46. "Dom João III au Roi Dom Afonso," in *Correspondance de Dom Afonso*, 176.

47. "Léon X au Roi Dom Manuel, Rome le 3 mai 1518"; "Promotion de Dom Henrique au siège épiscopale d'Utique. Rome, le 5 mai 1518"; "Léon X au Prince Henrique, évèque d'Utique. Rome, le 8 mai 1518" "Léon X au Prince Henrique, évèque d'Utique. Rome, le 22 mai 1518," in *Correspondance de Dom Afonso*, 130–33.

48. "Clément VII, pape, à Diogo Ortiz de Villegas, doyen de la chapelle royale de Dom João III, roi de Portugal et Algarve. Rome, le 17 novembre 1531," in *Correspondance de Dom Afonso*, 189–90.

49. For more information, see W. G. L. Randles, *L'ancien royaume du Congo des origines à la fin du XIXᵉ siècle* (Paris: Mouton, 1968), 87–104. See also Basil Davidson, *The African Slave Trade* (Boston: Little, Brown, 1980).

50. Charles Verlinden, *L'esclavage dans l'Europe médiévale*, vol. 1, *Péninsule ibérique, France* (Brugge: De Tempel, 1955), 212–13.

51. Ibid., 226.

52. Ibid., 358–62.

53. For confraternities or confreries, see *Dictionnaire de spiritualité*, s.v. "Confréries."

54. Charles Verlinden, "L'esclavage dans la péninsule ibérique au XIVᵉ siècle," *Anuario de estudios medievales* 7 (1970–71): 577–91. See especially pp. 588–89.

55. See *Bibliotheca Sanctorum*, s.v. "Benedetto il Moro, santo," and *New Catholic Encyclopedia*, s.v. "Benedict the Moor, St."

56. For a brief survey of the Catholic church's attitude toward slavery, see John Maxwell, *Slavery and the Catholic Church* (Chichester: Barry Rose Publishers, 1975).

57. For a thorough discussion of slavery as a universal phenomenon, see Patterson, *Slavery and Social Death*. Historians are divided over the issue as to whether slavery in Latin America was more benign than that found in Protestant North America. The reason given for the former is the ameliorating action of the Catholic church. In Latin America the slave was a person because he or she was baptized and therefore the possessor of a certain dignity and certain rights. The slave in the United States had no rights. See Frank Tannenbaum, *Slave and Citizen. The Negro in the Americas* (New York: Alfred A. Knopf, 1946). For another view, see David Brion Davis, *The Problem of Slavery in Western Culture* (Ithaca, N.Y.: Cornell University Press, 1966), 224–27.

58. See Marcel Bataillon, "The *Clerigo* Casas, Colonist and Colonial Reformer," in *Bartolomé de Las Casas in History: Toward an Understanding of the Man and His Work*, ed. Juan Friede and Benjamin Keen (DeKalb: North-

ern Illinois University Press, 1971), 353–440. De Las Casas and black slavery are discussed in an appendix, 415–18.

59. Ibid., 416.

60. See Angel Losada, "The Controversy between Sepúlveda and Las Casas in the Junta of Valladolid," in *Bartolomé de Las Casas in History*, ed. Juan Friede and Benjamin Keen (DeKalb: Northern Illinois University Press, 1971), 279–306. See also Lewis Hanke, *All Mankind Is One: A Study of the Disputation between Bartolomé de Las Casas and Juan Ginés de Sepúlveda in 1550 on the Intellectual and Religious Capacity of the American Indians* (DeKalb: Northern Illinois University Press, 1974).

61. Philip D. Curtin, *The Atlantic Slave Trade* (Madison: University of Wisconsin Press, 1969). There is much discussion regarding the statistics for the importation of slaves during the eighteenth and nineteenth centuries. Not all accept Curtin's figures.

62. The Portuguese baptized the Africans before embarkation but often repeated it later. See Katia M. de Queiros Mattoso, *To Be a Slave in Brazil, 1550–1888*, trans. Arthur Goldhammer (New Brunswick, N.J.: Rutgers University Press, 1986), 31–32. The Spaniards baptized at the port of arrival, as is seen in the ministry of St. Peter Claver.

63. See *Bibliotheca Sanctorum*, s.v. "Pietro Claver, santo."

64. Frederick P. Bowser, *The African Slave in Colonial Peru, 1524–1650* (Stanford, Calif.: Stanford University Press, 1974), 223.

65. See Alonso de Sandoval, *De instauranda Aethiopum salute: El mundo de la esclavitud negra en América*, ed. Angel Valtierra (Bogota, 1956). See also the many references to Sandoval in Bowser, *African Slave in Colonial Peru*.

66. For Portugal and Brazil, see A. J. R. Russell-Word, *Fidalgos and Philanthropists: The Santa Casa da Misericordia of Bahia, 1550–1755* (Berkeley: University of California Press, 1968). See also " 'Children of God's Fire': A Seventeenth-Century Jesuit Finds Benefits in Slavery but Chastizes Masters for Their Brutality in a Sermon to the Black Brotherhood of Our Lady of the Rosary," in *Children of God's Fire. A Documentary History of Black Slavery in Brazil*, ed. Robert Edgar Conrad (Princeton, N.J.: Princeton University Press, 1983), 163–74, and "The Black Brotherhood of Our Lady of the Rosary in Recife in the Eighteenth Century," in ibid., 178–80.

For fuller information regarding the origin and development of the confraternities in the Middle Ages, see E. Delaruelle, E.-R. Labande, and Paul Ourliac, "Les confréries," chap. 3 of *L'Église au temps du Grand Schisme et de la Crise Conciliaire (1378–1449)*, vol. 14 of *Histoire de l'Église depuis les origines jusqu'a nos jours*, ed. Augustin Fliche and Victor Martin (Paris: Bloud and Gay, 1962), 666–93.

67. Russell-Word, *Fidalgos and Philanthropists*, 142. See also 142–45 and 216–23.

68. Bowser, *African Slave in Colonial Peru*, 247–51.

69. Ibid., 250–51.

70. See C. R. Boxer, "The Problem of the Native Clergy in the Por-

tuguese and Spanish Empires from the Sixteenth to Eighteenth Centuries," in *The Mission of the Church and the Propagation of the Faith*, ed. C. J. Cuming (Cambridge: Cambridge University Press, 1970), 85–105.

71. There is an enormous literature on St. Martin de Porres. What is lacking is a well-documented life of the saint that would meet the exigencies of scientific history. Martin needs to be put into the context of the society, both ecclesiastical and lay, of the time. See Ruben Vargas Ugarte, *El santo de los pobres* (Lima: Ediciones Paulinas, 1986), and *Bibliotheca Sanctorum*, s.v. "Martino di Porres, santo."

Chapter 2:
Catholic Settlers and Catholic Slaves: A Church in Chains

1. Frederick W. Hodge, ed., "The Narrative of Alvar Núñez Cabeça de Vaca," in *Spanish Explorers in the Southern United States, 1528–1543* (New York: Charles Scribner's Sons, 1907), 12–126.

2. For example, Jack D. Forbes, "Black Pioneers: The Spanish-Speaking Afroamericans of the Southwest," *Phylon* 27 (1966): 233–46.

3. Fray Marcos de Niza (d. 1558) was born at an undetermined date in Nice in what was then the Duchy of Savoy. He had served in Central America and Peru before coming to New Spain (Mexico) in 1537. See Cleve Hallenbeck, *The Journey of Fray Marcos de Niza* (Dallas: Southern Methodist University Press, 1987), 97. In the introduction David Weber discusses the work of Hallenbeck and the controversy regarding the veracity of Fray Marcos's account of his journey. Weber also discusses Fray Marcos and Estéban. Regarding the latter, he corrected Hallenbeck's assertion that Estéban was not truly black.

4. Frederick W. Hodge, ed., "The Narrative of the Expedition of Coronado, by Pedro de Castañeda," in *Spanish Explorers in the Southern United States, 1528–1543* (New York: Charles Scribner's Sons, 1907), 281–387.

5. Ibid., 288–90.

6. Ibid., 333, 364.

7. John Jay TePaske, *The Governorship of Spanish Florida, 1700–1763* (Durham, N.C.: Duke University Press, 1964).

8. Ibid., 5–6.

9. Ibid., 140–44. See Jane Landers, "Gracia Real de Santa Teresa de Mose: A Free Black Town in Spanish Colonial Florida," *American Historical Review* 95 (1990): 9–30. Information regarding the *palenques* in general as a part of African American history in the New World can be found in Richard Price, ed., *Maroon Societies. Rebel Slave Communities in the Americas*, 2d ed. (Baltimore: Johns Hopkins University Press, 1979), especially Francisco Pérez de la Riva, "Cuban Palenques," 49–59.

10. In 1768 there arrived a colony of Greeks, Italians, and Minorcans under the authoritarian leadership of a Scotsman, Andrew Turnbull. Over a

thousand came to settle at first in a colony named New Smyrna. They were Catholics and they settled as indentured servants. Despite great poverty, they also owned black slaves. Eventually, the Minorcans abandoned New Smyrna and moved as a group to St. Augustine in 1777. See E. P. Panagopoulos, *New Smyrna: An Eighteenth Century Greek Odyssey* (Gainesville: University of Florida Press, 1966).

11. Michael W. Gannon, *The Cross in the Sand* (Gainesville: University of Florida Press, 1967), 98.

12. Ibid., 96–98.

13. Brought into New Spain, or Mexico, as slaves from the beginning of the sixteenth century, this African population, as in most of Latin America, blended gradually into the general population of Mexico. For a study of black slaves in Mexico, see Colin Palmer, *Slaves of the White God: Blacks in Mexico, 1570–1650* (Cambridge: Harvard University Press, 1976).

14. See Forbes, "Black Pioneers," 234–35.

15. For information regarding the settlement of Los Angeles, see the entire issue of the *Quarterly of the Historical Society of Southern California* 15 (1931–32), later entitled *Southern California Quarterly*. This is the commemorative issue for the 150th anniversary of the foundation of Los Angeles. See also Harry Kelsey, "A New Look at the Founding of Old Los Angeles," *California Historical Quarterly* 15 (1976): 326–39, for subsequent corrections to the earlier studies.

16. See Forbes, "Black Pioneers." 233–46.

17. The Jesuits were suppressed by Pope Clement XIV in 1773. The Jesuits found in the English colonies at the time formed themselves into a legal corporation, giving them the privilege to own real estate and to have the means to support themselves and their ministry.

18. Leonardo Antonelli played a very important role in the Roman Curia during the French Revolution.

19. Letter to Leonardo Antonelli in *The John Carroll Papers*, ed. Thomas Hanley (Notre Dame, Ind.: University of Notre Dame Press, 1976), 1:179–82. Affinity was a relationship that arose not from blood or by marriage but because of sexual relations — for example, marriage with the mother of a young woman with whom one had had sexual relations remained forbidden. Because the slaves often were not free to marry when they wished and as they wished, promiscuous relationships developed, some of which, according to canon law, would have prevented subsequent marriage. The canon law regarding affinity arising from previous sexual relations has been changed since the eighteenth century. See Francis X. Wahl, *The Matrimonial Impediments of Consanguinity and Affinity: An Historical Synopsis and Commentary*, Catholic University of America Canon Law Studies, no. 90 (Washington, D.C.: Catholic University of America, 1934), 57–92.

20. For some notion of the legal development of slavery and the absolute control slaveowners had over their slaves, see A. Leon Higginbotham, Jr.,

In the Matter of Color: Race and the American Legal Process: The Colonial Period (New York: Oxford University Press, 1978).

21. See Aubrey C. Land, *Colonial Maryland. A History* (Millwood, N.Y.: KTO Press, 1981), 165–67.

22. See Emmett Curran, " 'Splendid Poverty': Jesuit Slaveholding in Maryland, 1805–1838," in *Catholics in the Old South: Essays on Church and Culture,* ed. Randall M. Miller and Jon L. Wakelyn (Macon, Ga.: Mercer University Press, 1983), 125–46.

23. Ibid., 134–35.

24. Ibid., 142.

25. Eccleston, who was no friend of the Jesuits, was archbishop from 1834 to 1851. It seems that Eccleston denounced the action of the provincial, Thomas Mulledy, to Roothaan, the general of the Jesuits. See ibid., 142.

26. Ibid., 146.

27. Louis William DuBourg was bishop of New Orleans from 1815. A native of the French West Indies, he himself owned slaves. See note 56 below.

28. Stafford Poole, and Douglas Slawson, *Church and Slave in Perry County, Missouri: 1818–1865* (Lewiston, N.Y.: Edwin Mellen Press, 1986), 148–49.

29. Ibid., 150–51.

30. Ibid., 156–57.

31. Ibid., 158.

32. Ibid., 162.

33. Ibid., 164.

34. Ibid., 186.

35. Sister Frances Jerome Woods. "Congregations of Religious Women in the Old South," in *Catholics in the Old South,* ed. Randall M. Miller and Jon L. Wakelyn (Macon, Ga.: Mercer University Press, 1983), 99–123. Regarding the dowry, see page 112.

36. Charles Warren Currier, *Carmel in America. A Centennial History of the Discalced Carmelites in the United States* (1890; 200th anniversary ed., Darien, Ill.: Carmelite Press, 1989), 83. The recent canonization of Philippine Duchesne, the foundress of the Religious of the Sacred Heart in this country, raises the issue of her ambiguous relationship to slavery. Can sanctity — that is, heroic charity, be compatible with an uncritical acceptance of slavery, especially a slave system that stripped individuals of all human dignity and rights and even of the possibility of claiming them? St. Philippine Duchesne evidently possessed some slaves or at least hired them from others. Although very much concerned about the evangelization of the Indians, she seems strangely unmoved by the situation of the slaves. See Louise Callan, *Philippine Duchesne: Frontier Missionary of the Sacred Heart, 1769–1852* (Westminster, Md.: Newman Press, 1957), 596, 598, 614, 636, 733–37.

37. See, for instance Woods, "Congregations of Religious Women," 113–14. A French sister, member of the Daughters of the Cross, wrote disparagingly of one of her slaves who had taken the opportunity to escape from

slavery, taking one of the horses. It was impossible for her to comprehend that a man should desire freedom and might claim compensation for unpaid labor.

38. See Anna Blanche McGill, *The Sisters of Charity of Nazareth, Kentucky* (New York: Encyclopedia Press, 1917), 104–5, 141.

39. Camillus Maes, *The Life of Rev. Charles Nerinckx* (Cincinnati: Robert Clarke, 1880), 255.

40. The text and translation of Pope Gregory XVI's letter condemning the slave trade are found in the introduction to the "Letters to the Honorable John Forsyth on the Subject of Domestic Slavery," written by John England, bishop of Charleston, in his diocesan paper "The United States Catholic Miscellany," and found in *The Works of the Right Reverend John England* (Baltimore: John Murphy, 1849), 3:108–12. It is also found in translation in "A Roman Critique of the Pro-Slavery Views of Bishop Martin of Natchitoches, Louisiana," by Maria Genoino Caravaglios, in *Records of the American Catholic Historical Society* 83 (1972): 72–75.

41. England, *Works* 3:112.

42. The best study to date of Gregory XVI is found in Roger Aubert's article in *Dictionnaire d'histoire et de géographie écclésiastiques*, s.v. "Grégoire XVI, pape de 1831 à 1846."

43. *John Carroll Papers* 3:247.

44. Ibid., 371.

45. Bohemia Plantation Record, 1790–1815, Archdiocese of Baltimore Archives. The record is in John Carroll's handwriting.

46. Carroll to Arthur O'Leary, Baltimore, 1787, in *John Carroll Papers* 1:225. See also Carroll to P. J. Coghlan, June 13, 1787, in ibid., 254–55, for an expression of the same idea.

47. Carroll to the Trustees of the Clergy, September 1, 1801, in *John Carroll Papers* 1:361.

48. Carroll to Francis Neale, November 12, 1805, in *John Carroll Papers* 2:497.

49. Carroll to James Barry, July 21, 1806, in *John Carroll Papers* 2:521.

50. Carroll to John Thayer, July 15, 1794, in *John Carroll Papers* 2:123.

51. *Scritture Riferite nei Congressi* 3, fol. 466, Congregation of the Propaganda Fide Archives, University of Notre Dame Archives (hereafter UND Archives), microfilm. See Finbar Kenneally, *United States Documents in the Propaganda Fide Archives: A Calendar*, 1st ser. (Washington, D.C.: Academy of American Franciscan History, 1966), 1:36, no. 213.

52. *Scritture Riferite nei Congressi* 9, fol. 339rv, undated, and *Decisioni, cherichiede alla Sac. Congr' de Propaganda Fide: Il Vescovo d'alta Louisiana.* UND Archives, microfilm. See Kenneally, *Documents in the Propaganda* 1:178, no. 1092.

53. For the canonical aspect of marriage, see Vincent Paul Coburn, *Marriages of Conscience: An Historical Synopsis and Commentary*, Catholic Uni-

versity of America Canon Law Studies, no. 191 (Washington, D.C.: Catholic University of America Press, 1944).

54. There is no record of a reply to the questions posed by Bishop DuBourg. Nevertheless, there is a record of a reply addressed to Bishop Rosati from the Congregation of the Propaganda on October 25, 1828. Rosati is addressed as bishop of St. Louis and administrator of New Orleans. Rosati had written on May 31, 1828, asking whether marriages contracted by Catholic slaves without the knowledge and consent of their respective owners can be considered valid. The congregation in its reply indicated that Pope Leo XII had agreed at a meeting of the members of the respective congregations that as long as slave marriages are not free, then clandestine marriages, although considered invalid by the Council of Trent, are to be considered valid for slaves. The bishop must see that the missionary priest deputed for the slaves puts in writing the marriages that occur in this way for a record (See *Lettere e Decreti della S. Congregazione e Biglietti di Mons. Segretario, 1828*, vol. 309, fol. 758r–758v. Congregation of the Propaganda Archives. UND Archives, microfilm. See Kenneally, *Documents in the Propaganda*, 3:335, no. 2109.)

Evidently, Benedict Joseph Flaget, bishop of Bardstown in Kentucky, posed a similar or related question regarding the marriage of slaves because a few pages further is the copy of a note addressed to the Congregation of the Holy Office requesting an urgent response to the question posed by the bishop so many years ago concerning the marriage of slaves. What if one is separated by sale from one's first wife and it happens that the new slaveowner obliges the slave to marry again while the first wife is still alive? The note ends with a plea for a response to this problem. (See ibid., vol. 310, fols. 186v and 187r, UND Archives, microfilm; Kenneally, *Documents in the Propaganda* 3:340, no. 2141).

55. See Poole and Slawson, *Church and Slave in Perry County*, 148–50, 158–60.

56. Ibid., 160–61. In her work *Louis William DuBourg, Bishop of Louisiana and the Floridas, Bishop of Montauban, and Archbishop of Besançon*, 2 vols (Chicago: Loyola University Press, 1986), Annabelle M. Melville gives a superb portrait of this Franco-American bishop, who at times had more the spirit of the French ancien régime than of the American frontier. It is somewhat remarkable that Melville makes scarcely any substantial mention of blacks or slaves in her history. Little is mentioned about DuBourg's involvement in the traffic of slaves or the fact that both in St. Louis and its environs and in New Orleans and southern Louisiana there was a large black Catholic community over which DuBourg was supposed to be a shepherd. Melville does indicate that DuBourg gave his slaves to the Jesuits along with his property in Florissant, Missouri (2:637), and that he sold his slaves Anthony and Rachel to his niece's husband to raise money for his journey to France with the stipulation that he could buy them back if he returned (767). Certainly this prelate's lack of concern about the question of slavery and the pastoral needs of black Catholics is of historical importance.

57. William Henry Elder's article in *Les annales de la Société de la Propagation de la Foi* is reprinted in *Documents of American Catholic History*, 3 vols., ed. John Tracy Ellis (Wilmington, Del.: Michael Glazier, 1987), 1:325–28. Subsequent quotations are from Elder's article.

58. *Civil War Diary (1862–1865) of Bishop William Henry Elder, Bishop of Natchez* (Natchez, Miss.). Published by R. O. Gerow, bishop of Natchez-Jackson, from photostats in the diocesan archives, 1960. The original was in the Jesuit Archives in Woodstock, Maryland. There is no indication as to who edited the text. There is no introduction or commentary. Bishop Elder refused to take the oath of allegiance to the United States government in Washington and also refused to pray publicly at the liturgy for the president of the United States. These actions got him in some trouble with the Union army officials who occupied Mississippi during the period of this diary. See Benjamin Blied, *Catholics and the Civil War* (Milwaukee, s.n., 1945), 55–57.

59. *Civil War Diary*, 59.

60. Ibid., 59–60.

61. The best study of England's ministry, theology, and impact on the United States church is Peter Clarke, *A Free Church in a Free Society: The Ecclesiology of John England, Bishop of Charleston, 1820–42: A Nineteenth Century Missionary Bishop in the Southern United States* (Hartsville, S.C.: Center for John England Studies, 1982). The areas of church conventions, the press, and the constitution are discussed at length in the book.

62. Ibid., 408–11.

63. John Forsyth (1780–1841) served as minister to Spain and governor of Georgia. He also served as secretary of state in the cabinets of President Andrew Jackson from 1834 to 1837 and President Martin Van Buren from 1837 to 1841.

64. "Letters to the Hon. John Forsyth, on the Subject of Domestic Slavery; to which are prefixed copies, in Latin and English, of the Pope's Apostolic Letter concerning the African Slave Trade, with some introductory remarks, etc.," reprinted in England, *Works* 3:106–91.

65. Peter Clarke dates the letter as 1842; see Clarke, *Free Church*, 405.

66. "Letters to Forsyth," 190–91.

67. Clarke, *Free Church*, 476–78.

68. Joseph D. Brokhage, *Francis Patrick Kenrick's Opinion on Slavery*, Catholic University of America Studies in Sacred Theology, 2d ser., no. 85 (Washington, D.C.: Catholic University of America Press, 1955), 43. Kenrick was born in Dublin, Ireland, in 1797. After studies in Rome, he came to the United States as a young priest. He became coadjutor bishop of Philadelphia in 1831 and later archbishop of Baltimore in 1851. Here he died in 1863. His brother, Peter Richard Kenrick, became archbishop of St. Louis.

69. The translation is the author's. See Francis Patrick Kenrick, *Theologia Moralis* (Mechlin: H. Dessain, 1861). 1:166, Tractatus V, "De Jure Gentium," Caput VI, "De Servitute," no. 38. See also Brokhage, *Francis Patrick Kenrick's Opinion*, 122–23.

70. Kenrick, *Theologia Moralis* 1:107, "De Servitute."

71. Ibid., 167–68. See Brokhage, *Francis Patrick Kenrick's Opinion*, 204–16.

72. Brokhage, *Francis Patrick Kenrick's Opinion*, 239.

73. Caravaglios, "Roman Critique," 67–81.

74. See *Metropolitan Catholic Almanac and Laity's Directory for United States, Canada, and the British Provinces, 1861* (Baltimore: John Murphy, 1861), 119–20.

75. *Scritture Riferite nei Congressi, America Centrale.* vol. 20, fol. 1207r–1213v, UND Archives, microfilm. See Kenneally, *Documents in the Propaganda* 3:75, no. 473. The letter was a printed text in the format of a booklet of some fourteen pages. Caravaglios, "Roman Critique," includes an English translation of a large part of the pastoral letter. She does not indicate, however, that the text cited is only a part of the entire pastoral letter.

76. *Lettere Pastorale*, 6–7, fol. 1210, UND Archives, microfilm. See Kenneally, *Documents in the Propaganda* 3:75, no. 473.

77. Ibid.

78. *Lettere Pastorale*, 8.

79. Verot later became bishop of Savannah in 1861, while remaining vicar apostolic in Florida. In 1870 he was appointed the first bishop of St. Augustine and relinquished the see of Savannah. Despite his defense of slavery, Verot became one of the first bishops to take measures for the evangelization of the freed slaves and to write publicly against racial prejudice. For an excellent study of this highly complicated man, see Michael Gannon, *Rebel Bishop, The Life and Era of Augustin Verot* (Milwaukee: Bruce Publishing, 1964.)

80. Augustin Verot, "A Tract for the Times," *Scritture Riferite nei Congressi: America Centrale*, 20, fols. 1262r–1268v, UND, microfilm. See Kenneally, *Documents in the Propaganda*, 3:77, no. 489. The publication has fourteen pages and its paragraphs were numbered by the congregation. It was published in Baltimore by John Murphy and Co.; later a translation was made into French and was published in Louisiana.

81. Verot, *Tract for the Times*, 8–9. The burning of the convent took place in 1834 in Charlestown, Massachusetts (near Boston) when a mob incited by anti-Catholic sentiment burned a convent of Ursuline nuns after forcing them and their female students to leave the buildings. See James Hennesey, *American Catholics. A History of the Roman Catholic Community in the United States* (New York: Oxford University Press, 1981), 121–22.

82. It was naive on the bishop's part to think that the importation of slaves would not have to be reintroduced if slavery continued. In fact, the clandestine slave trade in the South had continued up to the Civil War. See Charles H. Wesley, "Manifests of Slave Shipments along the Waterways, 1808–1864," *Journal of Negro History* 27 (1942): 155–74. This factor alone is one of the reasons why Gregory XVI's condemnation of the slave trade

meant a condemnation of slavery. The one depended upon the other in terms of economics and population growth.

83. Verot, *Tract for the Times*, 11.

84. Ibid.

85. Ibid.

86. Ibid., 14.

87. See Gannon, *Rebel Bishop*, 52–54.

88. Cauvin to Propaganda, April 20, 1858, Congregation of the Propaganda Archives, microfilm, *Scritture Riferite nei Congressi: America Centrale*, 18, fol. 221rv, UND Archives; Kenneally, *Documents in the Propaganda* 2:211, no. 1318. Information about Father Cauvin is found in the *Metropolitan Catholic Almanac* for 1858, 161. There is no mention of Cauvin in the 1861 edition.

89. Vincenzo Gatti, O.P (1811–82) became secretary to the Congregation of the Index in 1870, and in 1872, master of the Sacred Palace (that is official papal theologian). At the time that he investigated the writing of Bishop Martin, he was librarian at the Casanatense Library in Rome. See Caravaglios, "Roman Critique," 6, 81, n. 7.

90. *Scritture Riferite nei Congressi: America Centrale*, 20, fols. 1199r–1205v, UND Archives, microfilm. Kenneally, *Documents in the Propaganda* 3:75, no. 472. See Caravaglios, "Roman Critique," for a translation of his brief.

91. See the translation in Caravaglios, "Roman Critique," 79–80.

92. *Scritture Riferite nei Congressi: America Centrale*, Congregation of the Index to Propaganda, December 30, 1864, fols. 1198rv, 1220v, 1221r, Congregation of Propaganda Archives, microfilm; UND Archives. Kenneally, *Documents in the Propaganda* 3:75, no. 471. See the translation of the letter to the prefect of the Propaganda, in Caravaglios, "Roman Critique," 69–70.

93. Maria Caravaglios, "A Roman Critique," 70.

94. *Scritture Riferite nei Congressi: America Centrale*, 20, fols. 1261rv–70rv, Congregation of the Propaganda Archives, microfilm; UND Archives. Kenneally, *Documents in the Propaganda*, 3:77, no. 490. The note is handwritten in Italian on the back of the condensed version of the sermon.

95. Madeleine Hooke Rice, *American Catholic Opinion in the Slavery Controversy* (New York: Columbia University Press, 1944), 102–3.

96. See Hennesey, *American Catholics*, 149–51. See also Iver Bernstein, *The New York City Draft Riots: Their Significance for American Society and Politics in the Age of the Civil War* (New York: Oxford University Press, 1990).

97. For more information on Lyman Beecher (1775–1863), see Alice Felt Tyler, *Freedom's Ferment: Phases of American Social History from the Colonial Period to the Outbreak of the Civil War* (New York: Harper and Row, 1962), 365–84. At the same time, some of those opposed to slavery preached a sexual morality to which Catholics objected (208–11).

98. See John R. McKivigan, *The War against Proslavery Religion: Abolitionism and the Northern Churches, 1830–1865* (Ithaca, N.Y.: Cornell University Press, 1984). For an example of the wide spectrum of abolitionist thought, including the unique character of black abolitionists, see C. Duncan Rice, "Radical Abolitionists in the United States, 1830–1861," chap. 9 of *The Rise and Fall of Black Slavery* (New York: Harper and Row, 1975), 305–52.

99. See M. Rice, *American Catholic Opinion*, 103–7.

100. The seminal work on racism during the Colonial Period and the early part of the nineteenth century, is Winthrop Jordan, *White over Black: American Attitudes toward the Negro, 1550–1812* (Chapel Hill: University of North Carolina Press, 1968).

101. For a study of Brownson, see Thomas R. Ryan, *Orestes Brownson: A Definitive Biography* (Huntington, Ind.: Our Sunday Visitor, 1976).

102. See Brownson's article, "The Woman Question," in *The Works of Orestes A. Brownson*, ed. Henry F. Brownson (Detroit: Thorndike Nourse, Publisher, 1885), 18:381–417. He wrote: "The very fact that woman is physically the weaker vessel, physically weaker than man, renders her less morally independent, less frank, open, and straightforward, and in a contest with man, compels her to resort to art, artifice, intrigue, in which alone she can equal or surpass him. Her accession to the political body could, therefore, only introduce an additional element of political and moral corruption.... We do not believe women, unless we acknowledge individual exceptions, are fit to have their own head. The most degraded of the savage tribes are those in which the women rule, and descent is reckoned from the mother instead of the father" (402–3). Regarding the natural right to suffrage, he wrote in the same article: ... "we deny that the negroes and colored men can claim admission [to the ballot] on the ground either of natural right or of American republicanism" (382).

103. Brownson, "Native Americans," in *Works*, 18:283.

104. Ibid., 289.

105. Brownson, "Slavery and the War," in *Works* 17:163–64.

106. Hughes was born in Ireland in 1797 and came to the United States in 1817. He became coadjutor bishop of New York in 1837 and bishop in 1842. He became metropolitan in 1851. See John R. G. Hassard, *Life of the Most Reverend John Hughes, D.D., First Archbishop of New York, with Extracts from His Private Correspondence* (New York: D. Appleton, 1866), and Richard Shaw, *Dagger John: The Unquiet Life and Times of Archbishop John Hughes of New York* (New York: Paulist Press, 1977).

107. Quoted in a footnote by Hassard, *Life of Hughes*, 436–37. See also M. Rice, *American Catholic Opinion*, 118–22.

108. Hassard, *Life of Hughes*, 435–37.

109. Brownson, "Archbishop Hughes on Slavery," in *Works*, 17:202–5.

110. Brownson, "Sumner on Fugitive Slaves," in *Works*, 17:44.

111. Brownson, "Abolition and Negro Equality," in *Works*, 17:537–60.

112. Ibid., 547.

113. Ibid., 557.

114. Ibid., 559.

115. Ibid.

116. Cited by M. Hooke Rice, *American Catholic Opinion*, 82. See pp. 80–85 for discussion of Irish-American reaction to O'Connell's strictures against slavery.

117. For a discussion of O'Connell and most particularly his stand against slavery, see Lawrence J. McCaffrey, *Daniel O'Connell and the Repeal Year* (Lexington: University of Kentucky Press, 1966), 72–75.

118. For the best survey of Dupanloup's life and influence, see *Dictionnaire d'histoire et de géographie écclésiastiques*, s.v. "Dupanloup (Félix-Antoine-Philibert)."

119. "European Catholic Opinion on Slavery," a reprint of Pastoral Letter of the Rt. Rev. Félix Antoine Philibert Dupanloup, Bishop of Orleans, to his Clergy on the subject of the Civil War in the United States, April 6, 1862, *Records of the American Catholic Historical Association* 25 (1914): 21.

120. Ibid., 25.

121. See M. Rice, *American Catholic Opinion*, 108.

122. See J. Fairfax McLaughlin, "William Gaston: The First Student of Georgetown College," *Records of the American Catholic Historical Society* 6 (1895): 225–51. McLaughlin states that Gaston's name was first on the student roll when the college opened in 1791 (228).

123. See M. Rice, *American Catholic Opinion*, 134–37.

124. E. Dupuy, pastor at Iberville, to Blanc, January 3, 1856: "...I have concluded that M. Maistre was an untruthful man — what is more he is an abolitionist in his ideas and his language" (Records of Archdiocese of New Orleans, VI-1-j, in UND Archives).

125. Barnabò to Odin, January 5, 1866; Maistre to Odin, February 13, 1866, Records of the Archdiocese of New Orleans, VI-2-k, UND Archives. See also Roger Baudier, *The Catholic Church in Louisiana* (New Orleans: A. W. Hyatt Stationery Manufacturing, 1939), 413. One can get some idea of the importance of St. Rose of Lima Church for black Catholics in the announcements for Mass found in the pro-Union black newspaper *L'Union: Journal Tri-Hebdomadaire: Politique, littéraire et progressiste*. As an example, see the issue for Tuesday, April 14, 1863. "Messe à Sainte Rose de Lima," microfilm in Library of Congress, Washington, D.C.

126. Hennesey, *American Catholics*, 147–48.

127. "Father Purcell's Stand in Behalf of Emancipation of the Slaves, April 8, 1863," in *Documents of American Catholic History*, ed. John Tracy Ellis (Wilmington, Del.: Michael Glazier, 1987), 1: 378–83. Josue Moody Young (1808–66), bishop of Erie from 1854 to 1866, preached in his cathedral against the racial prejudice of the Irish and on behalf of blacks. He had the church doors locked when he threatened with mortal sin those who voted for the Democratic candidate, George McClellan, who opposed Lincoln in

1864. See Thomas Spalding, *Martin John Spalding: American Churchman* (Washington, D.C.: Catholic University of America Press, 1973), 162–63.

Chapter 3: Christ's Image in Black:
The Black Catholic Community before the Civil War

1. Michael J. Curley, *Church and State in the Spanish Floridas (1783–1822)* (Washington, D.C.: Catholic University of America Press, 1940), 67. The author cites as his authority a letter from the governor, Manuel Zéspedes, to the marquis of Sonora, José Gálvez, minister of the Indies at Madrid.

2. Ibid., 67–68.

3. Ibid., 45–46. See "The Spanish Colonial Parochial Registers of St. Augustine," Baptisms Colored, 1784–1793," book 1, 34–35, no. 73, Diocese of St. Augustine Archives, Jacksonville, Florida.

4. See Panagopoulos, *New Smyrna.*

5. "Spanish Colonial Parochial Records, Marriages Colored, 1784–1882, 52, no. 51, Diocese of St. Augustine Archives.

6. Ibid., 41, no. 85.

7. Panagopoulos, *New Smyrna*, 179.

8. Curley, *Church and State*, 111–18.

9. "Baptisms Colored, 1784–1793," 46, no. 95.

10. Curley, *Church and State*, 112–13.

11. Ibid., 116–17.

12. "Baptisms Colored, 1784–1793," 39, no. 81.

13. Ibid., 35, no. 74.

14. Ibid.

15. See Curley, *Church and State.*, 46–47; 60–61.

16. "Baptisms Colored, 1784–1793," 22, no. 50.

17. Ibid., 31–33, nos. 68, 69, 70. In nos. 68 and 69 the parents were Edenborough and Filis, who were mentioned before. In no. 68, Filis is called the slave of Beatrice Stone.

18. "Baptisms Colored, 1793–1807, book 3, 26, no. 55. The date is October 12, 1808.

19. Ibid., 95, no. 190.

20. "Baptisms Colored, 1807–1848," 26, no. 55. This is the third book of baptisms for blacks.

21. "Marriages Colored, 1784–1882," 36, no. 35.

22. "Spanish Colonial Parochial Records, Deaths Colored, 1785–1821," 75, no. 182, Diocese of St. Augustine Archives.

23. Ibid., 86, no. 205.

24. Ibid., 34, no. 81.

25. Ibid., 35, no. 82.

26. See Charles Edwards O'Neill, *Church and State in French Colonial Louisiana: Policy and Politics to 1732* (New Haven, Conn.: Yale University Press, 1966), 269. This work includes almost nothing about blacks or slavery.

27. Baudier, *Catholic Church in Louisiana*, 105. Baudier's work is old but still remains one of the best general sources on the history of blacks in the Catholic church of Louisiana.

28. See references to the slaves in ibid.

29. See ibid., 276.

30. For one example, see ibid., 206.

31. Odin to the seminary rector, August 2, 1823, published in the *Annales de la Propagation de la Foi* 2:74.

32. Baudier, *Catholic Church in Louisiana*, 250.

33. "Creole" came from the Spanish word *criollo*, meaning a Spaniard born in the New World. In its French form it came to mean also a Spaniard or Frenchman born in the New World of some African ancestry. See Magnus Morner, *Race Mixture in the History of Latin America* (Boston: Little, Brown, 1967).

34. Blanc (1792–1860) was born in France. He became bishop of New Orleans in 1835, and archbishop in 1850.

35. A. Dumartrait to Bishop Blanc, July 10, 1843, St. Martinsville, La., Records of Archdiocese of New Orleans, V-4-o, UND Archives. Besides the letter there are two unidentified newspaper clippings that give in French the minutes of the church wardens' meeting and an open letter to the pastor with whom they were in conflict. Dumartrait was the secretary to the *marguilliers*.

36. Andrieu to Blanc, Assumption Seminary, July 31, 1853, Records of Archdiocese of New Orleans, VI-1-f, UND Archives.

37. Gary B. Mills, *The Forgotten People: Cane River's Creoles of Color* (Baton Rouge: Louisiana State University Press, 1977), 2–3.

38. See ibid., 10–22.

39. Ibid., 23–28.

40. Ibid, 34–48.

41. From the last will and testament of Augustin Metoyer, cited in ibid., 153.

42. Ibid.

43. See Randall Miller, "The Failed Mission: The Catholic Church and Black Catholics in the Old South," in *Catholics in the Old South*, ed. Randall M. Miller and Jon L. Wakelyn (Macon, Ga.: Mercer University Press, 1983), 149–70.

44. Curley, *Church and State*, 143–45.

45. The archives of the archdiocese of Mobile include three baptismal registers for blacks ("Baptisma Nigrorum" [French and Spanish], 1781–1805; "Baptisma Nigrorum" [Spanish], 1806–28; "Registry of Baptisms for Colored People," 1855–63), a burial register ("Burials of Colored People," 1828–77), and a marriage register ("Marriage Register for Black People," 1830–60).

46. See Curley, *Church and State*, p. 321. Curley gives the pastor's name as Gener, but in the baptismal register the name is spelled Gerien. For Fernando, see "Baptisma Nigrorum, 1806–1828," fol. 29v–30r.

47. "Baptisma Nigrorum, 1806–1828," fol. 30r, no. 131.

48. See Mother Mary Carroll, *A Catholic History of Alabama and the Floridas* (1908; reprint, Freeport, N.Y.: Books for Libraries Press, 1970), 339–40. This work is very unscholarly in its approach.

49. "Marriage Register," no. 22 (no pagination). Michael Portier was born in 1795 at Montbrison near Lyons, France and came to the United States in 1817. He was ordained in 1818 for New Orleans. He served as the first bishop of Mobile from 1829 to 1859. See Oscar H. Lipscomb, *The Administration of Michael Portier, Vicar Apostolic of Alabama and the Floridas, 1825–1829, and First Bishop of Mobile, 1829–1859* (Ann Arbor, Mich.: University Microfilms, 1987).

50. The author expresses his gratitude to Msgr. J. Edwin Stuardi, pastor at St. Rose of Lima Church at Mon Luis Island, for information granted in an interview.

51. "Marriage Register," no. 19.

52. Ibid., no. 15.

53. Ibid., no. 21. In regard to the question of the slaves owned by Bishop Portier, these two entries give a partial answer. He possessed at least three slaves. See Lipscomb, *Administration of Michael Portier*, 282–83.

54. "Marriage Register," no. 9.

55. "Burials of Colored People," 4, no. 19.

56. Ibid., 15, no. 63.

57. Ibid., 16–17. no. 68.

58. Ibid., 17, no. 70.

59. Ibid., 22, no. 89.

60. Ibid., 3, no. 13.

61. R. P. Jourdan to Monsieur le Secrétaire du Conseil Cal. de Lyon, le 5 juin 1860, Archdiocese of Mobile Archives.

62. See Lipscomb, *Administration of Michael Portier*, 286–87.

63. "Parish Register of the Church of St. John the Baptist," Diocese of Savannah Archives.

64. Ibid. The register is in very poor condition; there are no page numbers.

65. Ibid.

66. Ibid.

67. John Rothensteiner, *History of the Archdiocese of St. Louis*, 2 vols. (St. Louis: Blackwell Wielandy, 1928), 1:146. See also William Barnaby Faherty, *Dream by the River: Two Centuries of St. Louis Catholicism, 1766–1967* (St. Louis: Piraeus Publishers, 1973), 4.

68. Faherty, *Dream by the River*, 4.

69. See Carl Ekberg, *Colonial Ste. Genevieve. An Adventure on the Mississippi Frontier* (Gerald, Mo.: Patrice Press, 1985), 11–25.

70. Ibid., 198–99.

71. See Ibid., 197–239. For population, see 200–204.

72. Ibid., 200.

73. Ibid., 223.

74. William Barnaby Faherty and Madeleine Barni Oliver, *The Religious Roots of Black Catholics of St. Louis* (Florissant, Mo.: St. Stanislaus Historic Museum, 1977), 4.

75. Ibid.

76. Ibid.

77. See Lawrence O. Christensen, "Cyprian Clamorgan, *The Colored Aristocracy of St. Louis* (1858)," *Bulletin of the Missouri Historical Society* 31 (1974–75): 3–31.

78. Sidney Kaplan, *The Black Presence in the Era of the American Revolution, 1770–1800* (Washington, D.C.: Smithsonian Institution, National Portrait Gallery, 1973), 144–46.

79. "Old Cathedral Records," copy of translation of sacramental books in the Archdiocese of Indianapolis Archives, 1:11, no. 53. The original is in the archives of the former cathedral at Vincennes, Indiana, now the Diocese of Evansville.

80. Ibid., 13, no. 58, and 19, no. 71.

81. Ibid. 2:41, no. 89.

82. Ibid. 5:75, no. 173.

83. Ibid., 98, no. 237.

84. *Maryland Gazette*, July 11, 1793, Library of Congress, microfilm.

85. Baptismal Registers of St. Peter's Church, p. 253, Archdiocese of Baltimore Archives, microfilm.

86. Ibid., 254.

87. Register for 1802, 51, Archdiocese of Baltimore Archives.

88. Baptismal Registers of St. Peter's, 255.

89. Ibid., 299.

90. Ibid., 256.

91. Ibid., 264.

92. Ibid., Registry for 1802, 34.

93. Ibid., 50.

94. RG42 box 2, p. 1, Sulpician Archives, Baltimore.

95. Ibid., 10–22, for the more complete list.

96. Ibid., 36–37.

97. Ibid., 65.

98. Easter Confession Register, 22AK1, Archdiocese of Baltimore Archives.

99. See Charles Lemarié, "Le patriarche de l'ouest," 3 vols (unpublished manuscript, 1983), 2:105–16. Lemarié quotes the first biography of Flaget by his secretary, Henri Greliche. "The slaves are made contrary to other men ... I have neglected nothing to raise them to the dignity of men; I have spoken to their spirit, to their hearts; I have tried everything and I have always failed:

there are exceptions, but they are rare; for them freedom is misery and its consequences... Moreover I believe them happier than half the workers of Europe... Freedom has no meaning for them... " (Henri Greliche, *Essai sur la vie et les travaux de Monseigneur Flaget* [Paris, 1852] 83–84). Lemarié also quotes others who remark Flaget's paternal concern for his slaves. What seems certain is that he did very little in terms of evangelization of the slaves; he was probably more concerned about the Native Americans.

100. Benedict Webb, *The Centenary of Catholicity in Kentucky* (Louisville, Ky.: Charles A. Rogers, 1884).

101. Ibid., 177–78.

102. For historical information regarding Pittsburgh black Catholics, see the St. Benedict the Moor Parish file in the Diocese of Pittsburgh Archives.

103. Letitia Woods Brown, *Free Negroes in the District of Columbia, 1790–1846* (New York: Oxford University Press, 1972), 11, table 1.

104. *Special Report of the United States Commissioner of Education on the Condition and Improvement of Public Schools in the District of Columbia*, Department of Education, "Part 1, History of Schools for the Colored Population in the District of Columbia" (Washington, D.C.: Government Printing Office, 1871), 217–18.

105. Ibid., 218.

106. Ibid., 204–5. For a fuller description of the free black society in Washington, D.C., and the schools maintained by free blacks, see L. Brown, *Free Negroes*.

107. "The Pierre Toussaint Papers," box 1, folder 2, Manuscript and Rare Books Section, New York Public Library.

108. [Hannah Farnham Sawyer Lee], *Memoir of Pierre Toussaint, Born a Slave in St. Domingo* (Boston: Crosby, Nichols, 1854). For more recent lives of Pierre Toussaint, see Arthur and Elizabeth Sheehan, *Pierre Toussaint: A Citizen of Old New York* (New York: P. J. Kenedy, 1955), and Ellen Tarry, *The Other Toussaint. A Post-Revolutionary Black* (Boston: St. Paul Editions, 1981). For an excellent analysis of the man and his spirituality, see Norbert M. Dorsey, "Pierre Toussaint of New York, Slave and Freedman: A Study of Lay Spirituality in Times of Social and Religious Change" (S.T.D. diss., Pontificia Universitas Gregoriana, Rome, 1986).

109. Pierre Toussaint Papers, box 1, folder 4, 1816–17, letters from Gabriel Nicolas.

110. Lee, *Memoir*, 86.

111. Ibid., 82.

112. Ibid., 77–78, 81–82.

113. Ibid., 101.

114. Ibid., 100.

115. Pierre Toussaint Papers, box 4, folder 11.

116. See Clarke, *Free Church*, 437–40. Clarke was one of the first to notice the significance of Paddington for Bishop England.

117. Paddington to Toussaint, July 25, 1836, Pétionville, Haiti, Pierre Toussaint Papers, box 3. folder 1.

118. See Henry Binsse, "A Catholic Uncle Tom: Pierre Toussaint," *Historical Records and Studies* 12 (1918): 90–101. See also the obituary notice from the *New York Evening Post*, cited in Lee, *Memoir*, 119–20.

119. Harriet Thompson to Pope Pius IX, October 29, 1853, New York, *Scritture Riferite nei Congressi: America Centrale*, vol. 16, fols. 770rv, 775r, 771rv, 773r, 774r, Congregation of the Propaganda Archives, UND Archives, microfilm. See Kenneally, *Documents in the Propaganda*, 2:113, no. 715. Only the punctuation and one or two words have been changed for the sake of clarity. According to the note in the Propaganda archives, the letter was submitted to the pope (folio 777v). See reference to Harriet Thompson's letter in Jay Dolan, *The Immigrant Church: New York's Irish and German Catholics, 1815–1865* (Baltimore: Johns Hopkins University Press, 1975), 24–25, 183 n. 60. Dolan discusses the animosity between immigrant Catholics and African Americans.

120. Thaddeus Anwander, C.SS.R., was the priest who helped save the Oblate Sisters of Providence in Baltimore. Father Annet Lafont, S.P.M., was pastor of St. Vincent de Paul Church, which was the French church for New York City. Bishop John Loughlin was consecrated bishop of Brooklyn on October 30, 1853. He had been vicar-general of the New York Archdiocese. Edward McColgan was pastor of the Church of the Immaculate Conception in Baltimore. There is no information regarding his connection with blacks.

121. See Bernstein, *New York City Draft Riots.*

Chapter 4: Builders of Faith:
Black Religious Women before and after the Civil War

1. For the sketchy details regarding this foundation, see Maes, *Life of Rev. Charles Nerinckx*, 510–11. See also Anna Catherine Minogue, *Loretto. Annals of the Century* (New York: America Press, 1912), 95–97.

2. The Original Diary of the Oblate Sisters of Providence, 1827–42, Oblate Sisters of Providence Archives, Baltimore. The diary is handwritten in French by Father Joubert himself. It is 163 pages in length, ledger size. The last entry is in 1842.

3. Grace Sherwood, *The Oblates' Hundred and One Years* (New York: Macmillan, 1931), 6. See also Christopher Kauffman, *Tradition and Transformation in Catholic Culture: The Priests of Saint Sulpice in the United States from 1791 to the Present* (New York: Macmillan Publishing, 1988), 113–15.

4. Original Diary, 1–2.

5. Maria Lannon, *Mother Mary Elizabeth Lange: Life of Love and Service* (Washington, D.C.: Josephite Pastoral Center, 1976).

6. See Original Diary, 23.

7. See Sister Diane Edward Shea and Sister Marita Constance Supan, "Apostolate of the Archives — God's Mystery through History," *Josephite Harvest* 85 (1983): 10–13.

8. Original Diary, 5.

9. Ibid., 9.

10. For biographical information, see *Dictionnaire de spiritualité*, s.v. "Louis-Marie Grignion de Montfort, St."

11. For the Marian devotion, see *Dictionnaire de spiritualité*, s.v. "Marie Vierge. IV. De 1650 au début du 20ᵉ siècle. (3) l'esclavage marial."

12. See L. Brunet, *Dictionnaire d'histoire et de géographie écclésiastiques*, s.v. "Françoise Romaine." For the religious community founded by St. Frances of Rome, see *Dizionario degli Istituti di Perfezione*, s.v. "Oblate del Monastero di Tor de' Specchi."

13. See Original Diary, November 3, 1833, p. 27.

14. See chap. 1 for more information regarding St. Benedict the Moor.

15. See Original Diary, May 11, 1834, p. 32. Later the archbishop changed the date for the celebration to the second Sunday of October. See the diary for May 15, 1836, pp. 42–43.

16. Ibid., March 22, 1832, pp. 13–14.

17. See Sherwood, *Oblates*, 26–27, 190.

18. Ibid., 122. See also Sister M. Reginald Gerdes, "To Educate and Evangelize: Black Catholic Schools of the Oblate Sisters of Providence (1821–1880)," *U.S. Catholic Historian* 7 (1988): 183–99.

19. Original Diary, August 26, 1832, p. 16.

20. Ibid., August 27, 1832, p. 17.

21. Ibid., September 26, 1832, p. 18.

22. Ibid., October 27, 1832, p. 19.

23. Ibid., September 20, 1835, p. 39.

24. Kauffman, *Tradition and Transformation*, 116.

25. Gerdes, "To Educate and Evangelize," 185. See also Lannon, *Mother Mary Elizabeth Lange*, 16.

26. See Sherwood, *Oblates*, 112–25.

27. St. Alphonsus Liguori (1696–1787) founded the Redemptorists in 1732.

28. Motherhouse Annals, vol. 2, the continuation of the original diary, 1842–60, December 25, 1849. The pages are no longer numbered.

29. Ibid., April 7, 1850.

30. See Gerdes, "To Educate and Evangelize," 183–99. For a comparison between the Oblate Sisters of Providence and the other early American foundations of religious women, see the very interesting study by Barbara Misner, *"Highly Respectable and Accomplished Ladies": Catholic Women Religious in America, 1790–1850* (New York: Garland Publishing, 1988). Finally, see Margaret Susan Thompson, "Philemon's Dilemma: Nuns and the Black Community in Nineteenth-Century America: Some Findings," in *The Amer-*

ican Catholic Religious Life. Selected Historical Essays, ed. Joseph M. White (New York: Garland Publishing, 1988), 81-96.

31. See Lannon, *Mother Mary Elizabeth Lange*, 16-18. Unfortunately, this source gives no references for the information regarding Sister Therese's proposal. See also Sister M. Rosalita, *No Greater Service: The History of the Congregation of the Sisters, Servants of the Immaculate Heart of Mary, Monroe, Michigan, 1845-1945.* (Detroit: Congregation of the Sisters of the Immaculate Heart, 1948), 37-46.

32. Rosalita, *No Greater Service*, 45-46.

33. Motherhouse Annals, September 9, 1845.

34. See Rosalita, *No Greater Service*, 173-207.

35. James Wood became coadjutor bishop to St. John Neumann in 1857. He served as bishop of Philadelphia from 1860 to 1883. Wood became an archbishop in 1875.

36. Rosalita, *No Greater Service*, 124-55; 208-35. See also Shea and Supan, "Apostolate of the Archives," 10-13.

37. Sister Audrey Marie Detiege, *Henriette Delille: Free Woman of Color* (New Orleans: Sisters of the Holy Family, 1976), 15.

38. Ibid., 17-27.

39. Ibid., 36-37.

40. Ibid., 43.

41. Ibid., 42-43.

42. Ibid., 47.

43. Sister Mary Francis Borgia Hart, *Violets in the King's Garden: A History of the Sisters of the Holy Family of New Orleans* (New Orleans: private printing, 1976). 13-14.

44. Detiege, *Henriette Delille*, 44-46.

45. Detiege gives the date of her death as November 17 (p. 48), but Hart gives it as November 16 (p. 16).

46. Hart, *Violets in the King's Garden*, 20-21. The archbishop, Napoléon Joseph Perché, ruled the diocese from 1870 to 1883.

47. Ibid.

48. See the 1876 Provisional Constitutions of the Sisters of the Holy Family approved by Archbishop Perché, Sisters of the Holy Family Archives in New Orleans.

49. Hart, *Violets in the King's Garden*, 71-73.

50. The original rules and constitutions were drawn up in French in 1887. An earlier provisional set of constitutions was drawn up in 1876. The modifications of 1894 were also in French. These are all found in the Holy Family Sisters Archives, along with two versions (in English translation) of the provisional constitutions of 1876. See ibid., 30-31.

51. Ibid., 128.

52. See notes entitled "An Incident in Mother Magdalen's Administration," Sisters of the Holy Family Archives.

53. See *Hoffmann's Catholic Directory* (1899). The community is listed on pp. 85 and 88. It is mentioned for the last time in the *Catholic Directory* of 1906.

54. In the Sisters of the Holy Family Archives is a handwritten account describing the sisters and their convent in 1887. In the same archives is a typewritten note by the historian Roger Baudier, giving information he received about them from oral interviews. There seems to be no written records. The present author was told in an oral interview with the Sisters of the Holy Family that the last sister died in the Lafon Nursing Home, which the Holy Family sisters operated. The Sisters of Our Lady of Lourdes are mentioned for the last time in the *Catholic Directory* in 1927, when they numbered four.

55. See Julia Floyd Smith, *Slavery and Rice Culture in Low Country Georgia* (Knoxville: University of Tennessee Press, 1985), 197. Smith had an oral interview with the step-granddaughter of Mathilda Beasley. Much information regarding the early life of Mathilda Beasley is probably due to Veronica Arnold, the step granddaughter. Except for the letters of Mother Mathilda Beasley, there is very little documentation regarding her work. See also Sister M. Assumpta Ahles, *In the Shadow of His Wings* (St. Paul: North Central Publishing, 1977), 138–39. See also "Mother Mathilda Beasley (1834–1903): The First Negro Nun in Georgia," in *Profiles of Negro Womanhood*, ed. Sylvia G. L. Dannett (Yonkers, N.Y.: Educational Heritage, 1964), 1:144–45.

56. Oswald Moosmueller was a monk of St. Vincent Abbey in Latrobe, Pennsylvania. He arrived in the Savannah diocese in 1877 and planned to open a school for blacks on Skidaway Island, just off the Georgia coast. He also began Sacred Heart Church and school in Savannah, which would be for African Americans. Later it would be a white church. See Jerome Oetgen, "Origins of the Benedictines in Georgia," copy of an article in the Diocese of Savannah Archives; the original is in the St. Vincent Archabbey and College Archives and was published in *Georgia Historical Quarterly*, 53 (1969): 165–83.

57. Fr. Oswald Moosmeuller to Mother Mathilda Beasley, August 21, 1891, copy in the Sister Charlene Walsh Collection, Diocese of Savannah Archives (original is in the Benedictine Priory Archives, Savannah).

58. *Hoffmann's Catholic Directory* (1891), 67.

59. *Hoffmann's Catholic Directory, Almanac and Clergy List — Quarterly for 1892*, 448.

60. Diary of Bishop Thomas Becker, 117, Diocese of Savannah Archives.

61. Ibid. Becker reports that he had written to the Franciscan general in Rome but had received little help.

62. Mother Mathilda to Cardinal Gibbons, August 24, 1893, copy in Diocese of Savannah Archives. The letter gives the place as Savannah, Georgia. In 1893 the *Catholic Directory* places the sisters at Washington, Georgia. Mother Mathilda was perhaps at the African American orphanage in Savannah when she wrote the letter.

63. More information regarding the work of Mother Katherine Drexel and the Blessed Sacrament Sisters will be found in chapter 5.

64. HB/Beasley/Sr. Mathilda. Josephite Archives, Baltimore. A notation from the Annals of the Sisters of the Blessed Sacrament, 1893, pp. 99–100, located in the Sisters of the Blessed Sacrament Archives, St. Elizabeth's Convent, Bensalem, Pa.

65. The Sisters of Our Lady of Charity of the Good Shepherd was founded in France in 1641 and reorganized there in 1835. See *New Catholic Encyclopedia*, s.v. "Good Shepherd, Sisters of Our Lady of Charity of the."

66. Mother Mathilda Beasley to Mother Katherine Drexel, Savannah, July 3 and September 15, 1893, Sisters of the Blessed Sacrament Archives, St. Elizabeth's Convent, Bensalem, Pa.

67. Mathilda Beasley to Katherine Drexel, Savannah, December 18, 1894, Sisters of the Blessed Sacrament Archives.

68. Mother Mathilda to Blessed Katherine, Savannah, February 26, 1895, Sisters of the Blessed Sacrament Archives.

69. Mother Mathilda to Blessed Katherine, March 5, 1895, Sisters of the Blessed Sacrament Archives.

70. Mother Mathilda to Mother Katherine, March 16, and March 22, 1895, Sisters of the Blessed Sacrament Archives. In the Diocese of Savannah Archives there is an agreement drawn up between the Sisters of the Blessed Sacrament and Bishop Keiley, the successor of Bishop Becker, who died in 1899, which refers to a gift of four thousand dollars made by the sisters to Bishop Becker "for the purpose...of the erection of a building...to be used by Mother M. Matilda Beasley and her successors, for the benefit of the Colored People of the Diocese of Savannah..." This was done in 1895. See Keiley Papers, box 3, folder 8.

71. See chapter 5 for more details regarding John Slattery and the Josephites and their mission in the United States.

72. Mother Mathilda to Slattery, November 6, 1896, 15-C-25, Josephite Archives.

73. Mother Mathilda to Slattery, July 10, 1897, 15-C-26, Josephite Archives.

74. Mother Mathilda to Slattery, May 24, 1898, 15-C-27, Josephite Archives.

75. In the Diocese of Savannah Archives, see the file for the Missionary Franciscan Sisters. An anonymous note describes the work of the sisters in Savannah. There is no mention of Mother Mathilda Beasley. See also Ahles, *In the Shadow of His Wings*, 139–54. Mother Mathilda Beasley's work is mentioned in passing.

76. Ahles, *In the Shadow of His Wings*, 152–53, 492 no. 117.

77. See the obituary notice in the *Savannah Press*, December 21, 1903, and a shorter account of the funeral in the *Savannah Morning News*, December 22, 1903, copy in the Diocese of Savannah Archives. Mathilda Beasley is

buried in the cathedral cemetery. The surviving letters of Mother Mathilda Beasley, those to Blessed Katherine Drexel and to Slattery, provide an interesting study. The seven letters to Mother Katherine and the two handwritten letters to Slattery (one letter to him was typewritten, including her name) do not seem to have been written by the same person. The handwriting in the letters to Mother Katherine was a fine script with no misspellings and very good grammar. The letters to Slattery were not in good handwriting, with poor spelling and grammar. The letters to Mother Katherine, although they were begging letters, bordered on the obsequious; the letters to Slattery were plain and forthright. Certainly the latter letters were written when Mother Mathilda was ill and about the age of seventy. It seems reasonable to infer that a member of the community wrote to Mother Katherine under the direction of Mother Mathilda and those to Slattery were from her own hand.

Chapter 5:
A Golden Opportunity for a Harvest of Souls:
The Second Plenary Council of Baltimore, 1866

1. Binsse to Propaganda, September 18, 1863, *Scritture Riferite nei Congressi: America Centrale*, vol. 20, fols. 409rv–410rv, Congregation of the Propaganda Archives, UND Archives, microfilm. See Kenneally, *Documents in the Propaganda*, 3:29, no. 174.

2. Peter Guilday, *A History of the Councils of Baltimore (1791–1884)* (New York: Macmillan, 1932), 169–70.

3. David Spalding, "Martin John Spalding's 'Dissertation on the American Civil War,'" *Catholic Historical Review* 52 (1966–67): 76–77. See also by the same author (Thomas Spalding, C.F.X., as the author returned to his original name), *Martin John Spalding: American Churchman* (Washington, D.C.: Catholic University of America Press, 1973.)

4. Alessandro Barnabò was born on March 2, 1801, was made a cardinal in 1856, and died on February 24, 1874. See notice *Dictionnaire d'histoire et de géographie ecclésiastiques*, s.v. "Barnabò (Alessandro)."

5. See Edward Misch, "The American Bishops and the Negro from the Civil War to the Third Plenary Council of Baltimore, 1865–1884" (Ph.D. diss., Pontifical Gregorian University, Rome, 1968), 182. This work is the most thorough study to date on the Second and Third Plenary councils of Baltimore and the question of African Americans.

6. Ibid., 189. Misch quoted from a letter of Spalding to McCloskey, Baltimore, October 9, 1865, in the Archdiocese of New York Archives.

7. Misch, "The American Bishops," 199–200.

8. Ibid., 191–92.

9. Ibid., 243–48.

10. *Concilii Plenarii Baltimorensis II, in Ecclesia Metropolitana Baltimorensi. A Die VII ad Diem XXI. Octobris, A.D. MDCCCLXVI. Habiti, et a*

Sede Apostolica Recogniti, Acta et Decreta (Baltimore: John Murphy, 1868), lxxxviii–lxxxix.

11. Misch, "The American Bishops," 248–49.

12. Ibid., Appendix, 607–8, sec. 519 of the original schema.

13. Minutes of the extraordinary session, 39A-D5, p. 3. Archdiocese of Baltimore Archives.

14. See Gannon, *Rebel Bishop*, 124, for the citation from his pastoral letter.

15. Minutes of the extraordinary session, 39A–D5, p. 5.

16. Ibid.

17. Ibid. See also Misch, "American Bishops," 255–56.

18. Minutes of the extraordinary session, 39A–D5, p. 6.

19. Ibid.

20. Ibid., 7.

21. Ibid., 10.

22. *Baltimorensis II*, Titulus X, Caput IV, "De Nigrorum Salute Procuranda," pp. 243–46, paragraphs 484– 85.

23. Ibid., 245.

24. Ibid.

25. Ibid., 247, paragraph 491.

26. The pastoral letter of 1866 appears in *The National Pastorals of the American Hierarchy (1792–1919)*, ed. Peter Guilday (Washington, D.C.: National Catholic Welfare Council, 1923), 198–225, quotation from pp. 220–21.

27. See Misch, "The American Bishops," 280–83.

28. Ibid., 360–70.

29. See Gannon, *Rebel Bishop*, 131–44. In point of fact, the conversion of blacks to Catholicism was not that successful. As Gannon points out, this was partly because of the lack of financial resources available to Verot. Gannon also quotes priests from that time who attributed the failure of Catholicism to the alleged innate sensuality of the African American.

30. Persico became bishop of Savannah in 1870, when Verot relinquished the see to become bishop of St. Augustine. William Hickley Gross succeeded Persico as bishop of Savannah in 1873. He was born in Baltimore in 1837 and became a Redemptorist in 1858. Gross became archbishop of Portland, Oregon, in 1885 and died in Baltimore in 1898.

31. See Oetgen, "Origins of the Benedictines in Georgia."

32. Boniface Wimmer was the founder of Benedictine monasticism in the United States. Born in Bavaria in 1809, he became a monk at the abbey of Metten in Bavaria and then began the first American Benedictine monastery in Latrobe, Pennsylvania, in 1846. This monastery, named in honor of St. Vincent de Paul, became an abbey in 1855 with Wimmer as the first abbot. Concern for blacks fitted in with the broad vision he had for the role the Benedictine Order should play in the apostolate toward all people. See Jerome Oetgen, *An American Abbot: Boniface Wimmer, O.S.B., 1809–1887* (Latrobe, Pa.: Archabbey Press, 1976).

33. In his article "Origins of the Benedictines in Georgia," Jerome Oetgen mentions the decision to close the monastery and school. See also Paschal Baumstein, *My Lord of Belmont: A Biography of Leo Haid* (Belmont Abbey, N.C.: Herald House, 1985). Baumstein does not treat directly of the closing of the monastery on Skidaway Island. In the *Catholic Directory* there is no mention of the school on Skidaway Island after 1895. St. Benedict the Moor Parish appeared for the first time in the directory in 1885.

34. Rhaban Canonge was born in 1849 and was baptized Arthur, son of a French father and a black mother, who had been a slave. He made profession at St. Vincent Abbey in 1879. See Peter Windschiegl, *Fifty Golden Years, 1903–1953* (Muenster, Saskatchewan, St. Peter's Abbey, 1953).

35. Information regarding Brother Albert was received thanks to the kind offices of Brother Philip Hurley, O.S.B., assistant archivist of St. Vincent Archabbey. Arthur Mason was born in 1854 in Charles County, Maryland. He entered St. Vincent's Abbey in 1878 and apparently went to Skidaway shortly after this time. A letter in the St. Vincent Archives from Father Melchior Reichert, O.S.B., the superior at Skidaway Island, dated July 11, 1881, indicates that he was "received into the third Order of St. Benedict and performed his religious and domestic duties well." It is difficult to know what Father Melchior meant by the "third Order of St. Benedict." Presumably he was a regular oblate. It seems from another letter from his pastor at Corpus Christi Church in Baltimore, dated August 31, 1881, that his name at Skidaway was Brother Aloysius (St. Vincent Archives). Arthur Mason became a novice at St. Vincent again in 1881, made first profession in 1882, and left afterward.

36. Oetgen, "The Origins of the Benedictines in Georgia."

37. Raymond C. Mensing, Jr., associate professor of history, Valdosta State College, "The Rise and Fall of the Pseudo Poor Clare Nuns of Skidaway Island," typescript.

38. Ibid.

39. Becker had been made bishop of Wilmington in 1868 and was transferred to Savannah in 1886. He died in 1899. Becker had little faith in the ability of African Americans to profit from education. He wrote in his diary what he had written to the Commission for the Indians and Negroes in his application for subsidies: "Merely to open schools or Orphan Homes will not do. We could have hundreds yearly...Negroes must be guided and taught to work. Boys should be put upon a farm, or learn trades..." Becker thought that girls should be under the care of sisters "and get lessons in neatness, cleanliness, decency and industry." He was utterly opposed to higher education for blacks. "The giving of a so-called education as in colored universities (God save the mark!) and Colleges, etc is a bane to the Negro anywhere but is here a positive curse to the country" (Becker Diary, p. 187 under the date of August 7, 1894, Diocese of Savannah Archives).

40. Ibid., 138–39, "In re Skidaway," Savannah, Georgia, dated August 1890.

41. Michael O'Connor, S.J., had been made bishop of Pittsburgh in 1843. In 1860 he resigned and became a Jesuit. He traveled to England in 1871 to consult with physicians and died in Maryland in 1872. See *New Catholic Encyclopedia*, s.v. "O'Connor, Michael." See also the *Dictionary of National Biography, Supplement, January 1901–December 1911*, s.v. "Vaughan, Herbert Alfred (1832–1903)."

42. For more information, see D. I. Murphy, "Lincoln, Foe of Bigotry," *America* 38 (1927–28): 432–33, and also John P. Muffler, "This Far by Faith: A History of St. Augustine's, the Mother Church for Black Catholics in the Nation's Capital" (Ph.D. diss., Columbia University, 1989), 21–24.

43. Canon Peter L. Benoit, Diary of a Trip to America, January 6, 1875, to June 8, 1875, 3 vols, CB6-CB7-CB8, typescript. Josephite Archives, original in Mill Hill Fathers Archives in England. See entry Washington, Monday, January 25, 1875, CB6-33 (hereafter CB and volume number).

44. Ibid., CB7-201.

45. James Roosevelt Bayley (d. 1877) became archbishop of Baltimore in 1872. He was a nephew of St. Elizabeth Ann Seton and belonged to the family of Theodore Roosevelt and Franklin Delano Roosevelt. He was made bishop of Newark in 1853.

46. Benoit, CB6-88.

47. CB6-92–98.

48. Patrick Lynch became bishop of Charleston in 1858 and played an important role in the Confederate States.

49. Benoit, CB6-112–19.

50. Ibid., CB6-114. Benoit seems to have been totally unaware of the true situation of the black population following the Civil War. He never refers to the black Codes, which were enacted to force blacks to labor under circumstances similar to slavery. The sweeping condemnation of black leaders that he makes did not take into consideration the fact that many black political leaders were upright and hardworking men. Many historians today consider the state constitutions of South Carolina drawn up in 1867 and 1868 as exceptional in their progressive stance.

For recent studies on the Reconstruction and African Americans, see Leon Litwack, *Been in the Storm So Long: The Aftermath of Slavery* (New York: Alfred A. Knopf, 1979); Robert H. Abzug and Stephen Maizlish, eds., *New Perspectives on Race and Slavery in America: Essays in Honor of Kenneth M. Stampp* (Lexington: University Press of Kentucky, 1986); and Eric Foner, *Reconstruction: America's Unfinished Revolution, 1863–1877* (New York: Harper and Row, 1988). For particular states, see Edmund L. Drago, *Black Politicians and Reconstruction in Georgia. A Splendid Failure* (Baton Rouge: Louisiana State University Press, 1982) and George Brown Tindall, *South Carolina Negroes. 1877–1900* (Columbia: University of South Carolina Press, 1952).

51. Benoit, CB7-148.

52. Ibid., CB7-152.

53. Ibid., CB6-80.

54. Ibid., CB7-164.

55. Ibid., CB7-179.

56. Ibid., CB7-188.

57. Ibid., CB7-214.

58. Nathaniel Southgate Shaler, "The Negro Problem," *Atlantic Monthly* 54 (1884): 700. Shaler (1841–1906) was by training a geologist and was a professor at Harvard University. He had a great influence on scientific thought in the United States at the end of the nineteenth century. See *Dictionary of American Biography*, s.v. "Nathaniel Southgate Shaler." Shaler was only one of many American intellectuals who developed racist theories based on supposedly scientific grounds. See Thomas F. Gossett, *Race. The History of an Idea in America* (Dallas: Southern Methodist University Press, 1963).

59. Benoit, CB7-229. Edward Fitzgerald was bishop from 1866 to 1907.

60. Misch, "The American Bishops," 471.

61. Benoit, CB7-239.

62. John Lancaster Spalding had been a student at the American College in Louvain from 1859 to 1864. The rector of the college, Jean de Nève, asked Spalding to dedicate the first years of his priestly ministry to the service of "those poor people . . . too long neglected and often oppressed — to the Negroes." See David Francis Sweeney, *The Life of John Lancaster Spalding* (New York: Herder and Herder, 1965), 69, 72.

63. Ibid., 94–95.

64. Benoit, CB8-325.

65. Ibid., CB8-326.

66. Joseph Lackner, "St. Ann's Colored Church and School, Cincinnati, the Indian and Negro Collection for the United States, and Reverend Francis Xavier Weninger, S.J.," *U.S. Catholic Historian* 7 (1988): 145–56.

67. The Venerable François Marie Paul Libermann (1802–52) founded the Society of the Immaculate Heart of Mary to evangelize the black peoples of Africa in 1839. His society was merged with the older, nearly moribund congregation of the Holy Ghost Fathers, which had been founded by Claude François Poullart des Places (d. 1709) in 1703.

68. Henry J. Koren, *The Serpent and the Dove: A History of the Congregation of the Holy Ghost in the United States, 1745–1984* (Pittsburgh: Spiritus Press, 1985), 118.

69. Ibid., 120–24.

70. Misch, "The American Bishops," 498–502. Misch notes that Bishop John Spalding of Peoria brought up the question of American blacks and of ministry to them during his *ad limina* visit in the early part of 1883. He wanted this topic to be discussed at a future council meeting (see 505–6).

71. Ibid., 509. For an English translation of the meeting's minutes, see "Minutes of Roman Meeting Preparatory to III Plenary Council of Baltimore," *Jurist* 11 (1951): 121–32, 302–12, 417–24, 538–47. See p. 424 for "Spiritual Care of the Negro."

72. Misch, "The American Bishops," 530–42.

73. Secs. 237–40 and 243 in "Caput II. De Cura Pastorali Pro Hominibus Nigris et Indis," as found in *Acta et Decreta Concilii Plenarii Baltimorensis Tertii, A.D. MCCCLXXXIV*, Titulus VIII, "De Zelo Animarum" (Baltimore: John Murphy, 1886), 133–36.

74. William Gross, "The Missions for the Colored People," in *The Memorial Volume: A History of the Third Plenary Council of Baltimore, November 9–December 7, 1884* (Baltimore: Baltimore Publishing, 1885), 71–74.

75. Ibid., 71.

76. Ibid., 72.

77. Ibid.

78. Ibid., 73.

79. *Memorial Volume*, 114–19.

80. Rev. C. W. Fitzhugh in the *Baltimore American*, December 1, 1884, as cited by Andrew Skeabeck, C.SS.R., "Most Rev. William Gross: Missionary Bishop of the South," *Records of the American Catholic Historical Society of Philadelphia* 66 (1955): 147–48. This article is the last of seven dealing with the work of Bishop Gross. Skeabeck accuses Fitzhugh of ranting. He might have done better to observe that for most African Americans there was little externally to conclude otherwise, and as shall be seen, many Catholics, including curial officials, did not see it otherwise. The citations from Bishop Gross's sermon in the article by Skeabeck do not agree completely with the text of the sermon in the *Memorial Volume*.

81. Sister Consuela Marie Duffy, *Katherine Drexel: A Biography* (Cornwells Heights, Pa.: Mother Katherine Drexel Guild, 1966).

82. Ibid., 74–75.

83. Martin Marty was born in 1834, served as the first abbot of St. Meinrad Abbey in 1870, became vicar apostolic of the Dakota Territory in 1879, and died as bishop of St. Cloud in 1896. Joseph Stephan served as the second director of the Bureau of the Catholic Indian Missions from 1884 to 1900.

84. Duffy, *Katherine Drexel*, 100–101.

85. James O'Connor had been rector of the diocesan seminary at Overbrook, just outside Philadelphia, when he met Katherine Drexel. In 1876 he became vicar apostolic of the Omaha territory and in 1885 the first bishop of Omaha, where he died in 1890.

86. Duffy, *Katherine Drexel*, 169.

Chapter 6: Shepherds with Black Skins:
The First African American Catholic Priests

1. For information regarding the establishment of the Congregation of the Propaganda, see *New Catholic Encyclopedia*, s.v. "Propagation of the Faith, Congregation for the," and for a more complete treatment, see

H. Bernard-Maitre et al., eds., *Les missions modernes*, vol. 2 of *Histoire universelle des missions catholiques* (Paris: Librairie Grund, 1957), 116–18.

2. For information regarding the *patronado*, see *New Catholic Encyclopedia*, s.v. "Patronato Real" and "Padroado of Portugal."

3. Its name today is the Congregation for the Evangelization of Peoples.

4. See Bernard-Maitre, *Histoire universelle*, 2:124–27, 132–38. Francisco Ingoli (1578–1649) was a priest from Ravenna who became the first secretary of Propaganda in 1622 and remained in that position until his death. He left a permanent imprint on the congregation. From the beginning he championed the cause of an indigenous clergy.

5. See chapter 1 above. There are records of African priests in Senegal in 1840. There were others before them, but little information is available. See S. Delacroix et al., eds., *Les missions contemporaines (1800–1957)*, vol. 3 of *Histoire universelle des missions catholiques* (Paris: Librairie Grund, 1957), 312–42.

6. Foley, *Bishop Healy*, was the first full biography of Bishop Healy. It was also the first to give a full picture of his racial background. Unfortunately, although he indicates in the introduction the extensive sources he used in his research, Foley did not include footnotes in his book.

7. J. Taylor Skerrett, "'Is There Anything Wrong with Being a Nigger?' Racial Identity and Three Nineteenth Century Priests," *Freeing the Spirit* 5 (1977): 30–37. Skerrett's thesis is that the Healy brothers never really identified with the African American community precisely because they were removed from it at a very early age.

8. Foley, *Bishop Foley*, 14–15.

9. Ibid., 59.

10. Ibid., 121–22.

11. See the chapter on Sherwood Healy entitled "In His Brother's Footsteps. Alexander Sherwood Healy, D.D., J.C.D., 1836–1875," in Foley, *God's Men of Color*, 13–22.

12. Fitzpatrick to Archbishop John Hughes, Boston, July 10, 1859, Letter to Archbishop Hughes, A-34, Archdiocese of New York Archives.

13. Ibid.

14. William Leo Lucey, *The Catholic Church in Maine* (Francestown, N.H.: Marshall Jones, 1957), 218. For a treatment of Healy's episcopacy, see 209–42.

15. Ibid., 224–25.

16. Ibid., 225–26.

17. Foley, *Bishop Healy*, 128; Lucey, *Catholic Church in Maine*, 216–17.

18. Lucey, *Catholic Church in Maine*, 226–33.

19. Ibid., 236. Also Foley, *Bishop Healy*, 217.

20. Albert Foley, "Bishop Healy and the Colored Catholic Congress," *Interracial Review* 28 (1954): 79–80.

21. Foley, *Bishop Healy*, 217–18.

22. Foley, *God's Men of Color*, 23–31.

23. In his article on the Healy brothers, J. Taylor Skerrett suggested that the Catholic church afforded them the home and family that they never had. He also suggests that they could not identify as blacks because "none of them had any knowledge of what being black meant" (p. 37). This comment leaves one wondering how they thought about themselves and about their role in a world of injustice and oppression.

24. The Revenue Marine Service was under the Treasury Department. It later became the Coast Guard Service. As the captain of a ship in Arctic waters off Alaska, Michael Healy became known as a hard-drinking, hard-driving sea captain, one of the best in the service. Compassionate to the Alaskan Indians and the Eskimo, tough and fair with his men, he was also known as "hell-roaring Mike Healy." Later his junior officers turned against him. See a full account of his life by John F. Murray, "Portrait of Captain Michael A. Healy," *The Bulletin. U.S. Coast Guard Academy Alumni Association* 41 (January–February 1979): 14–18 and Paul J. Johnson, "Portrait of Captain Michael A. Healy," parts 2–3, Ibid. (March–April 1979): 22–27, (May–June 1979): 26–30. The figure of Michael Healy has been given a fictional form by James Michener in his *Alaska* (New York: Ballantine Books, 1988), 429–47. For the family of Michael Healy, see Albert Foley, "Adventures in Black Catholic History: Research and Writing," *U.S. Catholic Historian* 5 (1986): 103–18.

25. The only book-length biography of Tolton is the work by Sister Caroline Hemesath, *From Slave to Priest: A Biography of the Rev. Augustine Tolton (1854–97), First Afro-American Priest of the United States* (Chicago: Franciscan Herald Press, 1973). The first name of Tolton is given as Augustine or Augustus. The baptismal register, according to Hemesath, gives neither because the name of Peter Paul and Martha's son born on April 1854 was not recorded, although he was baptized on May 29, 1854 (p. 8) Unfortunately, Sister Caroline gives no references and a very skimpy bibliography. In the records of the Urban College in Rome, Tolton's first name is given as Augustus. In the newspapers of the time, he is referred to as Augustus. In letters written as a priest, he signed his name as A. Tolton. For these reasons, it seems that it is more accurate to use the name Augustus.

26. The earliest account of Augustus Tolton's early life was in the periodical published in the United States by the Mill Hill Fathers, "Rev. Augustus Tolton," *St. Joseph's Advocate* 4 (1886): 185–87; 5 (1887): 202–4, 245–46, 322–23, 326, 360. The unsigned article was most probably by the editor, Joseph Green. More than likely the information came from Tolton himself. For information regarding the state of affairs in Missouri, see *Freedom: A Documentary History of Emancipation, 1861–1867*, ser.1, vol. 1, *The Destruction of Slavery*, ed. Ira Berlin et al (Cambridge: Cambridge University Press, 1985), 395–412.

27. See *Freedom: A Documentary History*, 402–12. In a conversation with Francis Elliott of Indianapolis, Indiana, a descendant of the slaveowners of the Tolton family, he related that according to the family tradition,

Martha Tolton and her three children had been freed and were helped in finding their way to Quincy, Illinois. Mr. Elliott graciously supplied copies of documentation relating to the Elliott family in Missouri.

28. "Rev. Augustus Tolton," 5 (1897): 202–4.

29. Father Bernardino was minister general of the Order of Friars Minor from 1869 to 1889. Born in 1822 in the province of Venezia in what is now Italy, he entered the Franciscans in 1839 and was ordained in 1844; he served as minister general for the whole Franciscan Order at the desire of Pope Pius IX. He died as a titular archbishop in 1895. The cause for his beatification was introduced in 1951. See *Bibliotheca Sanctorum, Prima Appendice,* s.v. "Dal Vago, Giuseppe (Bernardino da Portogruaro)."

30. Rev. Gustavo Conrad to the Diocese of Alton, June 3, 1886, in Scritt. Riferite nei Congressi Collegio Urbano, 1879–1892, vol. 22, p. 747, Congregation of the Evangelization of Peoples (Congregation of the Propaganda) Archives, Rome. The registry of the students at the college is found in the same series.

31. Speech by Augustus Tolton before the first black Catholic congress in 1889. See *Three Catholic Afro-American Congresses* (Cincinnati: American Catholic Tribune, 1893; reprint, New York: Arno Press, 1978), 18.

32. Bishop Baltes was consecrated bishop in 1870 and died in 1886.

33. "Father Augustus Tolton," 5 (1887): 245–46 (the title of the author changed each issue).

34. Janssen to Simeoni, July 22, 1886, Scritt. Riferite, no. 284, Congregation of the Evangelization of Peoples.

35. Richard L. Burtsell (1840–1912) was a New York priest, ordained in 1862 after studies at the Urban College. He helped establish the first black parish of St. Benedict the Moor in 1883. A canonist, he was active in the McGlynn case when the latter was suspended by the archbishop of New York. Burtsell played an important role in the civic and ecclesiastical affairs of the time.

36. Tolton to Cardinal Simeoni. n.d. Scritt. Riferite, no. 364, Congregation of the Evangelization of Peoples. In this letter, written in red ink, Tolton writes in Italian describing the events of his return trip and the reception that he received. He described how, at the port of Livorno, the Italians mistook him for an African and tried to force him to board an Italian warship on its way to the port city of Mesewa in Ethiopia, where Italy was engaged in a colonial war. He was freed only by producing his United States passport. In Marseilles the ship was quarantined for twenty-four hours. In the United States several black communities in New York and Chicago wanted him to serve with them.

37. Tolton to Propaganda, July 25, 1887, Josephite Archives; summary of documents relating to Tolton in the Propaganda Archives (this summary is a copy found in Quincy College Archives). The original of the letter in the Archives of the Propaganda was not seen.

38. Tolton to Gibbons, July 24, 1888, Archbishop Gibbons Papers, 84 T 5, Archdiocese of Baltimore Archives.

39. Ibid. The black seminarian who went to Rome after Tolton was James Reed, who had studied at St. Vincent's College in Latrobe, Pennsylvania. It is not clear whether Reed was at North American College or the Urban College.

40. John Ireland (1838–1918) was born in Ireland, became coadjutor to the bishop of St. Paul in 1875, and finally bishop of St. Paul in 1884 and archbishop in 1888. For a long time Ireland was perhaps the most outspoken friend of American blacks in the American hierarchy. See Marvin R. O'Connell, *John Ireland and the American Catholic Church* (St. Paul: Minnesota Historical Society Press, 1988).

41. Byrne to Slattery, September 13, 1888, 4-E-11, Josephite Archives.

42. Tolton to Simeoni, July 12, 1889, Scritt. Riferite, no. 174, Congregation of the Evangelization of Peoples. See also Hemesath, *From Slave to Priest*, 123–29.

43. Tolton to Slattery, January 29, 1890, 9-S-16, Josephite Archives.

44. Tolton to Simeoni, October 7, 1889. Scritt. Riferite, 2a Semest., vol. 51, nos. 176–77, Congregation of the Evangelization of Peoples.

45. Propaganda to Bishop James Ryan, August 5, 1889, Lettere e Decreti della S.C. e Biglietti di M. Segretario, 1889, vol. 385, fol. 567r, no. 3717, Congregation of the Evangelization of Peoples.

46. James Ryan to Cardinal Simeoni, August 20, 1889, Scritt. Riferite, no. 172, Congregation of the Evangelization of Peoples.

47. Ibid.

48. Propaganda to Bishop Ryan, November 7, 1889, vol. 385. fol. 765v, no. 4580; and Propaganda to A. Tolton, November 8, 1889, vol. 385, fol. 767v, no. 4580. Congregation of the Evangelization of Peoples.

49. Archbishop Patrick Feehan (1829–1902) had become bishop of Nashville in 1865 and then the first archbishop of Chicago in 1880.

50. See Hemesath, *From Slave to Priest*, 136–44.

51. Tolton to Mother Katherine, May 12, 1891, Sisters of the Blessed Sacrament Archives.

52. Tolton to Mother Katherine, June 5, 1891, Sisters of the Blessed Sacrament Archives.

53. Tolton to Slattery, January 29, 1890, 9-S-16, Josephite Archives.

54. Mary C. Elmer to J. R. Slattery, July 7, 1890, 5-R-29, Josephite Archives.

55. See Hemesath, *From Slave to Priest*, 150–54.

56. Tolton to Mother Katherine, June 5, 1891, Sisters of the Blessed Sacrament Archives.

57. Tolton to Slattery, January 29, 1890, 9-S-16, Josephite Archives; Tolton to Simeoni, July 12, 1889, Scritt. Riferite, no. 174, Congregation of the Evangelization of Peoples.

58. Tolton to Slattery, January 4, 1891, 9-S-17, Josephite Archives.

59. Ireland to Slattery, August 25, 1894, 16-T-19. Josephite Archives.

60. Slattery to Elliott, May 29, 1897, LPB-2-517, Josephite Archives. For an analysis of Slattery's views on African Americans and the church, see William L. Portier, "John R. Slattery's Vision for the Evangelization of American Blacks," *U.S. Catholic Historian* 5 (1986): 19–44.

61. See Stephen J. Ochs, *Desegregating the Altar*, 98–99.

Chapter 7:
"A Humble Experiment... an Entering Wedge":
The Emergence of the Black Catholic Laity

1. *Three Catholic Afro-American Congresses*, 59–60.

2. See Hennesey, *American Catholics*, 190–92. For the only study of the black Catholic congresses, see David Spalding, "The Negro Catholic Congresses, 1889–1894," *Catholic Historical Review* 55 (1969): 337–57. The author remains indebted to Brother Thomas [David] Spalding for his research on Daniel Rudd.

3. Rudd gave an account of his mother's life in her obituary notice in *American Catholic Tribune* (hereafter *ACT*) for April 29, 1893.

4. Baptismal Register, p. 102 for the date of September 17, 1854, St. Joseph Cathedral Records, Bardstown, Kentucky.

5. See *Cleveland Gazette* (a black newspaper) for July 10, 1886. The article, which is a reprint from the *Globe Republic* of Springfield, announced that Rudd began the newspaper in Springfield and then moved it to Columbus, Ohio.

6. Reprinted in the *Washington Bee*, September 11, 1886, on page 1. The *Washington Bee* was an influential black newspaper published in Washington, D.C., during the last quarter of the nineteenth century (microfilm in Library of Congress.) The only extant copies of the *ACT* are in the Archdiocese of Philadelphia Archives and Historical Collections, Overbrook, Pennsylvania. Here are found 283 copies, February 1887 to September 1894. All issues have been microfilmed and are available from the American Theological Library Association Board of Microtext.

7. In 1894 Camillus Maes, the bishop of Covington, wrote Rudd asking that his name be removed. "By what authority do you print the headline 'Approved by... the Rt. Rev. Bishop of Covington?' You know I never did so personally and you have every reason to know that I do not approve it" (Maes to editor of *ACT*, July 17, 1894, Diocese of Covington Archives).

8. See "Apology Accepted," *ACT*, June 10, 1887. "*American Catholic Tribune* has a Correspondent in Rome, a Colored man at that in the person of Colonel Read, formerly of Pittsburgh, and a former associate, who is now in the College of the Propaganda."

9. Ibid., September 19, 1891.

10. Ibid., March 4, 1887.

11. Ibid., January 10, 1891, "The Negro."

12. Ibid., January 3, 1891.

13. Ibid., April 18, 1891.

14. For the issues giving the text of *Rerum Novarum*, see *ACT*, June 10, June 27, July 13, July 25, August 1, and August 8, 1891. For the editorial on the encyclical, see the issue of August 1.

15. Ibid., August 1, 1891.

16. Ibid., July 9, 1892, "Lynch Law."

17. Ibid., see editorials for February 18, 1887; May 2 and October 17, 1891.

18. Ibid., see May 8, May 16, May 23, and June 13, 1891.

19. Ibid., March 11, 1887.

20. Ibid., November 7, 1891.

21. Ibid., April 4, 1891, editorial. It is not clear what standing Rudd had among black newspapers of the time. Mention was frequently made of him in the African American press as lecturer and promoter of the black Catholic congresses. According to his own account, he was elected to certain positions in the Negro Press Association. On the other hand, Rudd is almost never mentioned in any history of the nineteenth-century black press. Little mention, it seems, was made of him in the rather large and extensive black religious press of the period.

22. Ibid., May 8, 1891.

23. Ibid., June 3, 1887.

24. Ibid., Fort Wayne, see April 1, 1887. For Lewiston, Maine, see "Msgr. J. M. Lucey Scrapbook," Diocese of Little Rock Archives, in which is affixed an unidentified Lewiston, Maine, newspaper clipping for May 9, 1896. For Natchez, see A. J. Peters to John R. Slattery, 9-D-15, August 19, 1891, Josephite Archives. For Rudd's lectures in German see the *Journal*, August 20, 1892. This publication was a black Catholic weekly newspaper of Philadelphia, published from February to September 1892. All extant issues are to be found in the Archdiocese of Philadelphia Archives and Historical Collections.

25. Thomas McMillan, "Knowledge of Public Questions," *Catholic World* 47 (1888): 711–13.

26. Charles Martial Allemand-Lavigerie was born in Bayonne, France, in 1825, was ordained in 1849, became bishop of Nancy in 1863, then archbishop of Algiers in 1867 and of Carthage in 1884, having been created a cardinal in 1882. He was the founder of the White Fathers and White Sisters, now known as the Society of Missionaries of Africa and Missionary Sisters of Our Lady of Africa, in 1868 and 1869 respectively. Founded originally for missionary work in North Africa, both societies began to work in black Africa in 1878. Lavigerie represented the more liberal wing of the French church. He supported Pope Leo XIII and was used by the latter to shift Catholic allegiance in France away from a narrow Royalist focus. He also was supported by the pope in his own ardent fight against the slave trade. Lavigerie

died in Algiers on November 26, 1892. See *New Catholic Encyclopedia*, s.v. "Lavigerie, Charles Martial Allemand."

27. *ACT*, July 6, 1889. This article by Street had been copied from the *Philadelphia Sentinel*. Robert Leo Ruffin (1857?–1934) was a prominent member of the black Catholic community of Boston. He was, it seems, related to George L. Ruffin, the first black judge in New England. John Boyle O'Reilly (1844–90) was the Irish-born editor of the *Pilot* and a well-known speaker on public issues. He was an outspoken advocate of the rights of African Americans, taking a position that was not always popular in the Irish community. See "John Boyle O'Reilly's Speech in Behalf of the Negro, December 7, 1855, and His Editorial on the Excommunication of Dr McGlynn, July 16, 1887," in *Documents of American Catholic History* 2: 432–37.

28. See Robert Ruffin, "Charles Martial Allemand-Lavigerie," *A.M.E. Church Review* 4 (1892): 320–35.

29. *ACT*, July 13, 1889.

30. Ibid.

31. See for example, ibid., August 17, 1889.

32. Rudd to Elder, London, August 12, 1898, Archdiocese of Cincinnati Archives.

33. The address was 37 Mullett Street from 1894 to 1895, and 469 Monroe Avenue in 1897.

34. Elder to Rudd, September 19, 1888, in Elder Letter Book 6, p. 99, Archdiocese of Cincinnati Archives.

35. Rudd to Slattery, May 8, 1888, 9-K-8, Josephite Archives.

36. Rudd to Gibbons, September 5, 1888, 85 A 4, Archdiocese of Baltimore Archives.

37. *ACT*, May 4, 1888.

38. Ibid., June 22, 1888.

39. Ibid., October 6, 1888. In this announcement the year 1888 was given instead of 1889. This misprint was repeated in subsequent editions. An explanation was given on the editorial page of the *Tribune* for October 27, 1888.

40. *Catholic Mirror* for January 5, 1889, Catholic University of America Library, microfilm.

41. See *Three Catholic Afro-American Congresses*, 21–23.

42. Ibid., 23–27.

43. Ibid., 34.

44. Ibid., 18–19.

45. Ibid., 66–72.

46. Elder to Rudd, September 19, 1888, Elder Letter Book 5, p. 300.

47. *Three Catholic Afro-American Congresses*, 10.

48. See letters in Henry F. Brownson Papers in box III-3-c and American Catholic Congress in Henry F. Brownson Papers in box III-3-g, UND Archives. A photograph of Rudd appears in the *Souvenir Volume of the Centennial Celebration and Catholic Congress, 1789–1889* (Detroit: William H.

Hughes, 1889), 21, but there is no mention of him in the text. Both Rudd and his nephew John Rudd were present at the congress in Baltimore. It is not known how many other black Catholics participated.

49. Rudd to Brownson, October 11, 1889, Papers of Henry F. Brownson, box III-3-c, UND Archives.

50. Byrne to Slattery, St. Paul, August 30, 1889, 4-E-12, Josephite Archives.

51. J. R. Slattery, "The Congress of Negro Catholics," *Donahoe's Magazine* 24 (1890): 269–71.

52. *Cleveland Gazette*, July 19, 1890. See also *Three Catholic Afro-American Congresses*, 126. About forty delegates were at the banquet held on the last evening at the Zoological Gardens.

53. *Three Catholic Afro-American Congresses*, 94–104.

54. Ibid., 104–10.

55. The best biography of Booker T. Washington is the two-volume work by Louis R. Harlan, *Booker T. Washington. The Making of a Black Leader, 1856–1901*, and *Booker T. Washington: The Wizard of Tuskegee, 1901–1915* (New York; Oxford University Press, 1972–83).

56. "Minutes of the Meeting of the Executive Committee of the Colored Catholic Congress," 7-N-9a, Josephite Archives. This item is a two-page printed document signed by William Lofton.

57. See obituary notice in the *New York Age*, Thursday, September 23, 1915, "Veteran Brooklyn Politician Is Dead."

58. See the *Journal*, July 9, 1892, for the obituary notice of Augustin: "The Last of a Noble Family: P. Jerome Augustin Suddenly Expires. Impressive Funeral Services." Augustin took part in the California Gold Rush of 1848, returning to Philadelphia around 1860, where he helped establish St. Peter Claver Parish.

59. See publication *Golden Jubilee of St. Peter Claver's, 1886–1936*, 102.113.3, in Archdiocese of Philadelphia Archives and Historical Collections. For details regarding the third congress, see Thomas O'Keefe, "Third Congress of Colored Catholics," *Catholic World* 55 (1892): 109–13.

60. *ACT*, February 13, 1892, "Our Catholic Young Men." (Punctuation added.)

61. *Three Catholic Afro-American Congresses*, 146–48.

62. See Maud Cuney Hare, *Norris Wright Cuney: A Tribune of the Black People* (New York: Crisis Publishing, 1913; reprint, Austin, Tex.: Steck-Vaughn, 1968), 208–9. See also the *Galveston City Directory* for 1893–94. Easton was a member of Holy Rosary Church in Galveston, the oldest black Catholic parish in Texas. Bishop Nicholas A. Gallagher was particularly solicitous for the black Catholic community of his diocese and had begun a school and a parish in 1886. By 1893 the school had been expanded to become an industrial school, with donations received from Blessed Katherine Drexel. See *Alexander's Magazine and the National Domestic: Catholic Souvenir Number* 4 (1907): 97–99.

63. For biographical information, see the *Western Appeal,* a black newspaper in Minnesota and the Midwest, June 22, 1889, "The Saintly City." See also Addison R. Fenwick, ed., *Sturdy Sons of Saint Paul* (St. Paul: Junior Pioneer Association, 1899). Regarding McGhee's relationship with Booker T. Washington, see August Meier, *Negro Thought in America, 1880–1915* (Ann Arbor: University of Michigan Press, 1964), 241–42. For his part in the Niagara movement, see Elliott M. Rudwick, "The Niagara Movement," *Journal of Negro History* 42 (1957): 197.

The baptismal register of St. Peter Claver Church establishes the fact that Fredrick McGhee was baptized on February 15, 1891. McGhee revealed the depth of his convictions regarding Catholicism in "What the Catholic Church Means for the Negro," *Howard's American Magazine* 5 (1900): 360–66. Fredrick McGhee figures in the Booker T. Washington Papers, Manuscript Division, Library of Congress, and in the W. E. B. Du Bois Papers, University of Massachusetts Archives.

64. *Three Catholic Afro-American Congresses,* 153–56. In a letter to the congress, Archbishop Ireland expressed his own strong feelings against segregation in the diocesan schools of his archdiocese (158–59). For Ireland's beliefs about the public school system, see O'Connell, *John Ireland,* 322–47.

65. *Three Catholic Afro-American Congresses,* 137–39.

66. Ibid., 133, 146.

67. There is no written text of the sermon. A synopsis of the sermon entitled "The Color Line" appears in *Donahoe's Magazine* 24 (1890): 59–62.

68. *Three Catholic Afro-American Congresses,* 156–60.

69. Slattery to Onahan, Easter Sunday, 1892, LPB-1-111, Josephite Archives.

70. For example, Onahan suggested to Slattery that he arrange with Butler regarding the talk, inasmuch as Slattery was also to give a talk on the Negro and the Catholic church. "His paper should fit in with yours and naturally supplement it. You will know how best to arrange this, and I think it will be better so than a formal letter from me. It possesses this advantage too that you will thus have command of the entire subject as is fitting" (April 4, 1893, 8-P-18, Josephite Archives).

Slattery replied on April 19 that he had written suggesting that Butler deal with the educational and "industrial aspect of the Negro." He then added: "It might not be amiss, if you would extend the invitation personally to him for our black friends are tricky at times" (Slattery to Onahan, April 19, 1893, Papers of William J. Onahan, 1893, January 1–June 1, box IX-1-d, UND Archives). It would be interesting to know whether Butler and his "tricky" black friends thought that Slattery and others were "insensitive."

71. See *Progress of the Catholic Church in America and the World's Columbian Catholic Congresses,* 2 vols. in one (Chicago: J. S. Hyland, 1897), 121–25.

72. Ibid., 122.

73. See Harlan, *Washington: The Making of a Black Leader,* 218.

74. *The World's Columbian Catholic Congresses*, 153–59. For a critique of Slattery's evangelizing efforts, see William L. Portier, "John R. Slattery's Vision for the Evangelization of American Blacks," *U.S. Catholic Historian* 5 (1986): 19–44, and Sister Jamie Phelps, "John R. Slattery's Missionary Strategies," *U.S. Catholic Historian* 7 (1988): 201–14.

75. The text of the paper was printed in the Washington Catholic newspaper *Church News*, October 21, 1893. A typescript copy is also found in the UND Archives: "Paper on the Advisability of Affording Wider Fields for Negro Employment," in Papers of William J. Onahan, box IX-1-o, UND Archives.

76. See Thomas Holt, *Black over White: Negro Political Leadership in South Carolina during Reconstruction* (Urbana: University of Illinois Press, 1974), 189 n. 56 and table 5, Summary of Biographical Data for Negro Legislators, 1868–76.

77. Benoit, CB6-128–29.

78. St. Peter's Trustees to Bishop Northrop, April 21, 1888, 2-R-1i and 2-R-1j, Josephite Archives.

79. Northrop to James Spencer and others, May 3, 1888, 2-R-1k, Josephite Archives.

80. The talk of Spencer was published with the omission of several paragraphs in the *St. Joseph's Advocate* 12 (1894): 630–34.

81. See the *Boston Pilot*, September 23, 1893, "The Colored Catholic Memorial: The Eloquent Expression of Their Fourth Congress." In the UND Archives, the typescript copy is a draft that appears in the Papers of William J. Onahan in box IX-1-o. The typescript copy bears no relation to the other papers because this address or memorial was not part of the Columbian Congress. The title of the typescript copy is "Address of the 4th Congress of Colored Catholics to the Rev. Clergy of [*sic*] Laity of the Catholic Church of America."

82. Charles Randolph Uncles, S.S.J (1859–1933) was the first black Josephite and was ordained a priest in 1891 by Cardinal Gibbons in Baltimore. See Foley, *God's Men of Color*, 42–51. There was constant tension between Uncles and John R. Slattery. Slattery wished for Uncles to have a higher profile among black Catholics, but Uncles did not desire it. When Butler had made some request regarding Uncles, Slattery wrote him: "Again, I believe, that Father Uncles is in mind and education far superior to Booker Washington. But unhappily he is shy and possessed with the idea that stage work, i.e., lectures etc. is meant to trot him out before the public gaze. If Father Uncles would take the same public stand as Booker Washington his sun would dim the latter's candle. But we cannot get Uncles to see his position in that light." (Slattery to Butler, December 2, 1896, LPB-2-438/439, Josephite Archives).

83. Robert N. Wood died in 1915 at the age of fifty-one. A brief obituary notice appeared in the *New York Times*, October 1, 1915, p. 11. A lengthy obituary notice appeared in the *New York Age* on Thursday, October 7, 1915. This black newspaper, one of the most important in the nation,

was Republican in sympathy and was accustomed to excoriate Wood in its columns.

84. Wood's letter and the circular letter to all the United States bishops is found in the Vatican Archives: Robert N. Wood to Archbishop Satolli, August 14, 1893, Del. ap. U.S.A., XIII (Società) no. 8, Congresso dei Cattolici di Colore (1893–94).

85. Ibid. A copy of the questionnaire was given in the *Church News*, October 13, 1894. "Catholic Congress: The Fifth Congress of Colored Catholics Meets in Baltimore."

86. *Church News*, October 13, 1894.

87. It should be noted that there is no extant copy of the final text of Satolli's letter. The proceedings of the fourth and the fifth congresses were never published. All that exists are newspaper accounts.

88. The sermon appears in the Josephite Archives as a reprint from the *Catholic Mirror*. For Slattery's paternalistic tendencies, which need to be placed alongside the clear statements of defense on behalf of blacks in their fight for equality, see again Portier, "John R. Slattery's Vision."

89. Msgr. Joseph A. Stephan was the second director (from 1884 to 1900) of the Bureau of Catholic Indian Missions.

90. See Sister M. Adele Francis, "Lay Activity and the Catholic Congresses of 1889 and 1893," *Records of the American Catholic Historical Society of Philadelphia* 74 (1963): 3–22. As is so often the case among those writing of this period, the author ignored the existence of the black lay Catholic congresses.

91. McGhee and Lofton to Slattery, January 20, 1900, 14-M-25, Josephite Archives.

Chapter 8: Black and Catholic:
A Testimony of Faith

1. Diomede Falconio, O.F.M (1842–1917) served as apostolic delegate from 1902 to 1911. Born in Italy, he came to the United States after becoming a Franciscan. He was a naturalized citizen, although he lived very little in the United States before becoming apostolic delegate. Later in 1916 as cardinal, he was made prefect of the Sacred Congregation of Religious and was the first American citizen to head a Roman congregation. See *Dictionnaire d'histoire et de géographie écclésiastiques*, s.v. "Falconio (Diomede)."

2. Girolamo Gotti, O.D.C (1834–1916) was created a cardinal by Pope Leo XIII in 1895 and prefect of the Congregation of the Propaganda in 1902.

3. Cardinal Gotti to Msgr. Falconio, January 18, 1904, Del. ap. U.S.A., II, no. 60b, Condizione dei negri, 1904, Vatican Archives. The original is in Italian. The English translation was made in the office of the apostolic delegation prior to its transmittal to Cardinal Gibbons.

4. This letter was sent to Cardinal Gibbons on March 23, 1904. He in turn sent an excerpt from it to all the United States bishops. The letter asked that Gibbons take up the matter at the next meeting of the archbishops, which was to take place in the summer of 1904. That year is missing from the delegation files in the Vatican Archives, entitled no. 34/1 Incontri annuali degli arcivescovi (1893–96/ 1898–1900/ 1903/ 1905–08). The Baltimore archives contains a copy of the text that was sent to all United States bishops with a cover letter from Cardinal Gibbons, dated April 22, 1904. The letter stated that it was decided that the best means to comply with the wishes of Propaganda was to disseminate the text of Gotti's letter (Archdiocese of Baltimore Archives, 101 G 6).

A few weeks later Gibbons wrote Cardinal Gotti in Latin concerning his letter of January 1904. In the letter Gibbons stated that he had brought the matter up at the April meeting of the archbishops. After lengthy discussion it was decided to circulate the letter of Gotti among all the bishops "so that if something perchance must be corrected, let it be corrected." In a concluding paragraph, Gibbons gave some idea of the situation of black Catholics in the archdiocese of Baltimore, which at that time included the District of Columbia. He concluded by pointing out that the pastors everywhere "did not act with less charity with [their black parishoners] than with the other Faithful pertaining to their missions" (Gibbons to Gotti, May 14, 1904, 101 J 3, Archdiocese of Baltimore Archives). One can only add that Gibbons's reply must have seemed inadequate in the face of the complaints that Rome had received.

5. See chapter 7.

6. Del. ap. U.S.A., I, 160b/1 (1911–14/1919). Condizione dei negri. This publication, *De Miserabile Conditione Catholicorum Nigrorum in America*, is clearly out of place. It is found among the papers of Archbishop Bonzano in the year 1913. It might indicate that Bonzano had made use of it at this time.

7. Joseph Anciaux returned to Belgium in 1908 and died there in 1931. According to Stephen Ochs, *Desegregating the Altar*, Anciaux was the nephew of Cardinal William van Rossum, future prefect of the Congregation of the Propaganda (p. 126). He was also related to other influential ecclesiastics in the Roman Curia (pp. 139–40).

8. Joseph Anciaux, *De Miserabili Conditione Catholicorum Nigrorum in America* (Namur: Typis Jac. Godenne, n.d.), 11.

9. Benjamin J. Keiley (1847–1925) was bishop of Savannah from 1900 to 1922.

10. Anciaux identified him as John Marion Laval, "a man endowed with intelligence, virtue, charity..." (*De Miserabili conditione*, 19).

11. Theophile Meerschaert (1847–1924) was a Belgian, as was Anciaux. He became vicar apostolic of the Oklahoma Territory in 1891, and the first bishop of Oklahoma City in 1905.

12. At this time the struggle between the church and the Third Republic

resulted in many religious and clergy being forced to leave France because of the anticlerical laws. See Roger Aubert et al., eds., *The Church in the Industrial Age*, vol. 9 of *History of the Church* (New York: Crossroad, 1981), 507–11.

13. The work of this board created a thick file in the apostolic delegation files in the Vatican Archives. See Del. ap. U.S.A., II, no. 109 (1907–43). This file is accessible up to 1923. The decision to establish the Catholic Board of Negro Missions was made at the annual meeting of the archbishops in 1905. See Del. ap. U.S.A., II, no. 34/1, Incontri annuali degli arcivescovi (1905–8).

14. Gaetano De Lai (1853–1928) was created a cardinal in 1907 and became secretary of the Consistorial Congregation in 1908, where he remained as head until his death. He was a leader of the conservative party during the pontificate of Pope St. Pius X (1903–14).

15. Willem van Rossum, C.SS.R (1874–1932), was born at Zwolle in the Netherlands. Becoming a cardinal in 1911, he was made prefect of the Congregation of the Propaganda in 1915.

16. Giovanni Bonzano (1867–1927) was apostolic delegate to the United States from 1911 to 1922.

17. Census Bureau to Falconio, November 23, December 1, December 5, 1911, Del. ap., U.S.A., II, 160b/1 (1911–14/1919), Condizione dei negri. See also the items in the next file, De Lai to Bonzano, November 4, 1921, request for *Negro Education, a Study of the Private and Higher Schools for Colored People in the United States* (Washington, D.C.: Government Printing Office, 1917), Del. ap., U.S.A., II, 160b/2 (1919/1921). The book was sent about four weeks later. Earlier that year, Bonzano sent detailed information regarding the condition of blacks in the United States inside and outside the church in a detailed report of five pages (Bonzano to De Lai, February 4, 1921).

18. De Lai to Bonzano, June 12, 1912, Del. ap. U.S.A., II, 160b/1 (1911–14/1919), Condizione dei negri.

19. Bonzano to Burke, October 16, 1912, Del. ap. U.S.A., II, 160b/1 (1911–14/1919), Condizione dei negri. Burke replied in a letter to Bonzano on October 18. He promised a response as soon as possible.

20. Burke to Bonzano, March 8, 1913, Del. ap. U.S.A., II, 160b/1 (1911–14/1919), Condizione dei negri. The report was twenty-five pages in length, with a supplement.

21. See Carl Holliday, "The Young Southerner and the Negro," *South Atlantic Quarterly* 8 (1909): 117–31. The author was professor of English at Southwestern Presbyterian Seminary at Maryville, Tennessee, now known as Rhodes College in Memphis, Tennessee. The views expressed by white collegians in the first decade of this century give some insight into the racial climate of the time: "These, then, are the views of forty-eight young men from seven States of the South. They unanimously opposed any idea of social equality; thirty-nine were opposed to higher education of the African; twenty-five favored only reading, writing, and a trade; thirty believed that he should possess no political rights; nine were without faith in his religion;

eleven believed him to have been a better man in slavery days; thirty-one declared that he must always be a common servant to the white man; twenty-five thought that he possessed no ability in self-government; seventeen were in favor of retaining him in the South; seven favored giving a separate territory; three favored "black cities"; nine believed that his dissipation and uncleanliness would solve the problem by exterminating him; twelve were content to leave the whole question to Providence; seventeen declared that fornication and the resulting amalgamation of the races were endangering the white blood of the South; ten were opposed to lynching; and fourteen considered a race-war highly probable." The author concluded with this observation: "Are not the indications plain that the black man is to be restrained, hampered, brow-beaten, discouraged within the next quarter of a century as never before in all the bitter years of his existence on this continent?" (130–31).

22. Albert was ordained in 1907. He died in 1968.

23. Albert to Bonzano, September 1, 1913, Del. ap. U.S.A., II, 160b/1 (1911–14/1919), Condizione dei negri. This communication was four pages in length.

24. See Ochs, *Desegregating the Altar*, 176–78.

25. De Lai to Bonzano, February 13, 1914, Del. ap. U.S.A., II (160b/1 (1911–14/1919), Condizione dei negri.

26. The typewritten report was dated Rome, February 5, 1914, and entitled, "L'évangelisation des états du sud aux Etats-Unis d'Amérique," Del. ap. U.S.A., II, 160b/1 (1911–14/1919), Condizione dei negri.

27. See Ochs, *Desegregating the Altar*, 106–11. For his plans regarding St. Joseph's College, see Slattery's article "A Catholic College for Negro Catechists," *Catholic World* 70 (1899): 1–12. See also Portier, "John R. Slattery's Vision," and Phelps, "John R. Slattery's Missionary Strategies."

28. By 1913 John R. Slattery was no longer active in the ministry. He resigned as superior of the Josephites in 1904 and publicly renounced the priesthood in 1906. He died in 1926.

29. Bonzano to De Lai, May 4, 1914, Del. ap. U.S.A., II, 160b/1 (1911–14/1919), Condizione dei negri.

30. De Lai to Bonzano. July 21, 1914, Del. ap. U.S.A., II, 160b/1 (1911–14/1919), Condizione dei negri.

31. Francis August Anthony Janssens was born in Tilburg, the Netherlands, in 1843. He studied at the American College at the University of Louvain and was ordained a priest in 1867. He came to the United States and served in the diocese of Richmond, being named bishop of Natchez, Mississippi, in 1881. In 1888 he became archbishop of New Orleans. He died at sea in 1897, on his way to Europe.

32. Francis Janssens, "The Negro Problem and the Catholic Church," *Catholic World* 44 (1887): 721–26.

33. See Dolores Egger Labbé, *Jim Crow Comes to Church*, 2d ed. (Lafayette: University of Southwestern Louisiana Press, 1971; reprint, New York: Arno Press, 1978).

34. Ibid., 42–55.

35. Ibid., 68–76.

36. Some information on the foundation of the original church at what was then called Thompson's Crossroads is found in Richard Madden, *Catholics in South Carolina. A Record* (Lanham, Md.: University Press of America, 1985), 154–56, 173, 314, 321. See also J. J. O'Connell, *Catholicity in the Carolinas and Georgia* (New York: Sadlier, 1879), 180–81. Information about the church is found in printed material at the entrance. Some of the oral history is published in an article by George Lundy, "Atop Catholic Hill," *Extension* 73 (1978): 5–11.

37. Father Charles Giesen, M.H.M., stationed at St. Peter's Church for black Catholics from 1879 to 1884, discovered two other settlements of black Catholics who had retained the faith through the zeal of black laity and without clergy since the Civil War. According to *Sadlier's Catholic Directory* for 1883 (New York: Sadlier, 1883), these two settlements served from St. Peter's in Charleston were Bennett's Point and Hutchinson Island.

38. Sebastian Gebhard Messmer (1847–1930) was born in Switzerland. He became bishop of Green Bay, Wisconsin, in 1892 and archbishop of Milwaukee in 1903.

39. In the 1880s the Jesuits ministered to over 150 black Catholics in several of their parishes. See *Souvenir of St. Benedict the Moor Mission, 1909–34*, an anniversary brochure of the parish, Josephite Archives.

40. Vallé to Slattery, August 7, 1899, 16-E-32, 16-E-32a, 16-E-32b, 16-E-32c, Josephite Archives. The 1900 census indicates that Vallé was a boarder in the home of Martha Tolton and at the time was unmarried. Augustus Tolton's widowed sister also lived in the house. Vallé, who was born in 1854, was forty-five at the time of the census. His occupation was listed as editor.

41. See Albert Krieling, "The Rise of the Black Press in Chicago," *Journalism History* 4 (1977–78): 132–36, 156.

42. An account of the beginnings of St. Benedict the Moor appeared in a brochure in 1912, entitled *History of St. Benedict the Moor, Catholic Colored Mission, 311 Ninth Street, Milwaukee, Wisc.*. A copy is found in the Josephite Archives. It is thirty-two pages, with illustrations and a preface by Archbishop Messmer. The name of the author is not given, but Messmer indicates that the author is "a member of St. Benedict's Colored Mission." It is likely that the unnamed author was Lincoln Vallé himself. Vallé refers to himself in the third person as Captain L. C. Vallé. The title "captain" was given him during his stay in Milwaukee. It seems certain that Vallé had been a recruit in one of the black regiments that fought in the Spanish-American War in 1898. See John Fillmore to Archbishop Mundelein, December 9, 1915, Deceased Priests File, Morris, John, Archdiocese of Chicago Archives. Fillmore referred to Vallé as a veteran of the Spanish-American War.

43. Vallé to McCarthy, June 27, 1910, 31-D-9, Josephite Archives.

44. St. Benedict the Moor Parish, Milwaukee, Wisconsin, "House

Chronicle," p. 26. The references to the misunderstanding with the Vallés are found on pp. 15–52.

45. Ibid., 30, 39–47.

46. Ibid., 39.

47. Ibid., 47.

48. Several articles under the byline Captain Lincoln C. Vallé appeared in the *Broad Ax*, a black newspaper from Chicago in the issues for March 23, March 30, and April 6, 1918.

49. Eckert to Hoban, March 24, 1914, Madaj 2, 1914, S9, Eckert to Hoban, Archdiocese of Chicago Archives. In response, Hoban referred Eckert to Father John S. Morris, April 2, 1914.

50. L. C. Vallé, "The Catholic Church and the Negro," *America* 30 (1923–24): 327–28.

51. Ibid., 327.

52. Ibid.

53. Ibid., 328.

54. Unfortunately, we have no information that indicates when and where Lincoln Vallé died. Although he returned to Chicago, there is no evidence that he died there.

55. Thirteenth Census of the United States: 1910, Bolivar County, Mississippi, National Archives and Record Service, Washington, D.C.

56. Daniel A. Rudd and Theophilus Bond, *From Slavery to Wealth: The Life of Scott Bond. The Rewards of Honesty, Industry, Economy, and Perseverance* (Madison, Ark.: Journal Printing, 1917). Scott Bond was a former slave from Mississippi who was able to acquire land after the Civil War and become a successful farmer and businessman.

57. The present writer was granted an interview by John Gammon, Jr., the son of John Gammon. John Gammon, Jr., was seventeen when he knew Rudd. Gammon described Rudd as a tall, handsome man, highly intelligent, fluent in several languages, and adept in handling machinery. He was very businesslike, quick in his actions, and always well dressed. John Gammon, Jr., recalled that Rudd had worked for the Bond family, whom he described as very wealthy. Rudd had worked on an invention developed by the family in the manufacturing of gravel. Because of racism, the family was unable to market their invention (Interview, September 9, 1986. John Gammon, Jr., himself a successful farmer and landowner, died in 1988 at about the age of eighty-five.) In the *Memphis Commercial Appeal* for Sunday, May 23, 1920, Rudd had a letter with the caption, "Are Northern Negroes Doing Better?" Although unsigned, it was a typical Rudd comment on the successful enterprise of both Scott Bond and John Gammon. He spoke of himself as "the well-known publicist and accountant."

58. Rudd to Morris, undated, Bishop Morris Letters, Diocese of Little Rock Archives. See also a request for backing to attend NAACP conference. including printed material regarding the NAACP, Rudd to Morris, May 17 and May 23, 1919; Morris to Rudd, June 12, 1919. Morris sent some money

to Rudd, who seemed to have had some project in mind and wanted to discuss it with Morris (see letter of May 17, 1919). In subsequent letters there is no indication of what the task would be. Rudd seemed to have had much better relations with Morris than did Joseph Anciaux, S.S.J., and Father John Dorsey, S.S.J., both of whom were banished from the diocese.

59. Rudd did not date the letter to Morris, but he wrote on stationery with the "John Gammon" letterhead, which suggests a letter written in 1920. It is not clear what meeting of laymen was held in Washington in September of that year. It is also not clear whether Rudd attended.

60. Rudd to Morris, May 24, 1920; Morris to Rudd, May 28, 1920, Morris Letters.

61. Rudd to Morris. July 12, '96 [sic], Morris Letters. The number of the year is obviously a mistake for 1926.

62. This information supplied by Thomas Spalding, C.F.X., who was gracious enough to pass on to the author the research he had gathered about Daniel Rudd and other members of the congress movement. Spalding was able to interview some of the members of the Rudd family in Bardstown, Kentucky.

63. Death Register, p. 36, St. Joseph Cathedral Records. Daniel Rudd is listed as having died on December 4. The *Louisville Leader*, a black newspaper, noted that Daniel Rudd died on Sunday morning, December 3, at the home of his niece, Mrs. W. L. Bowman.

64. Nickels, *Black Catholic Protest*, 19–20. This is the best study to date on the life and works of Thomas Wyatt Turner. Nickels worked personally with Turner and had access to his unpublished papers.

65. Alonzo J. Olds was pastor of St. Augustine's Church in Washington, D.C., from 1919 to 1948. St. Augustine's has been one of the most prestigious black parishes in the nation from its beginning after the Civil War until the present. It was the parish of the important black Catholic leaders in the District of Columbia at the end of the nineteenth century and the first part of the twentieth. Msgr. Olds was a popular, outspoken pastor devoted to the parish and devoted to the black people and their needs. See Muffler, "This Far by Faith."

66. Nickels, *Black Catholic Protest*, 31.

67. John Hope Franklin and Alfred A. Moss, Jr., *From Slavery to Freedom: A History of Negro Americans*, 6th ed. (New York: Alfred A. Knopf, 1988), 313.

68. Peter Bergman, *The Chronological History of the Negro in America* (New York: Harper and Row, 1969), 387–95.

69. See Gerald P. Fogarty, *The Vatican and the American Hierarchy from 1870 to 1965* (Wilmington, Del.: Michael Glazier, 1982), 214–16.

70. Gasparri to Delegate, Msgr. Cossio, September 12, 1919, Del. ap. U.S.A., II, 160b/1 (1911–14/1919), Condizione dei negri.

71. The Chicago race riot began on July 27 at a beach when a young black accidentally swam into the waters of a whites-only beach. The lad was

stoned by the white crowd and drowned. The ensuing riot lasted almost two weeks; thirty-eight persons were killed and over five hundred injured. See Franklin and Moss, *From Slavery to Freedom*, 314–15.

72. Cossio to Mundelein, September 15, 1919, Del. ap. U.S.A., II 160b/1 (1911–14/1919), Condizione dei negri. The letter is also found in Madaj 5 1919, M 275, Archdiocese of Chicago Archives. There is no indication of a reply.

73. A single sheet of paper, dated September 19, 1919, which was evidently a memorandum, Del. ap. U.S.A., II, 160b/1 (1911–14/1919), Condizione dei negri.

74. Bonzano to Gasparri, October 2, 1919, Del. ap. U.S.A., II, 160b/1 (1911–14/1919), Condizione dei negri.

75. "To the Congress of the United States: A Memorial," Detroit, September 22, 1919, Del. ap. U.S.A., II, 160b/1 (1911–14/1919), Condizione dei negri.

76. "Pastoral Letter of the Archbishops and Bishops of the United States, 1919." This item is found in the section entitled "Progress of the Church" (Guilday, *The National Pastorals*, 287). The files of the apostolic delegation reveal that an earlier statement regarding black Americans did not appear in the final draft. This statement said in part, "Our duty [is] to purify and ennoble the spirit of the nation;... to hate race hatred, to root out race prejudice from our own minds and hearts, and to oppose, with all our strength, mob violence, rioting and lynching" (Del. Ap. U.S.A., II, 209a/1, Adunanze annuali della gerarchia, National Catholic Welfare Council [NCWC] e sua abolizione da parte della S.C. Concistoriale, Vatican Archives). The citation is from the printed text entitled "Report of the General Committee on Catholic Affairs and Interests. Presented to the Catholic Hierarchy of America Assembled at the Catholic University of America, Washington, D.C., September 24th, 1919. His Eminence, Cardinal Gibbons, Presiding," p. 46. It seems obvious why this statement was deleted.

It is interesting to note that in the same file a letter pointing out that no mention was made of coal miners and steel workers. The letter was characterized as "feeble and lifeless" by Joseph Lonergan, St. Charles Church, Sutersville, Pennsylvania, to Bonzano, February 27, 1920, Del. Ap. U.S.A., II, 209a/1, Adunanze annuali della gerarchia, National Catholic Welfare Council [NCWC] e sua abolizione da parte della S.C. Concistoriale, Vatican Archives.

77. "Pastoral Letter. 1919," 325, in the section entitled "National Conditions."

78. Committee for the Advancement of Colored Catholics, Turner to Bonzano, November 3, 1919, Del. Ap. U.S.A., II, 160b/2 (1919/1921), Condizione dei negri.

79. Ibid. The brief of the committee was part of the letter of Turner to Bonzano.

80. See Nickels, *Black Catholic Protest*, 33–35.

81. Brief to the American Hierarchy, p. 6, Del. Ap. U.S.A., II, 160b/2 (1919/1921), Condizione dei negri.

82. C. F. Borden, registrar to unnamed applicant, November 22, 1917, Del. Ap. U.S.A., II, 160b/2 (1919/1921), Condizione dei negri.

83. For a history of the decision made by the Josephites to curtail the entrance of black candidates into their seminary, see "Louis B. Pastorelli: Circling the Wagons, 1918–1924," chap. 5 in Ochs, *Desegregating the Altar*, 214–45. For Turner's personal efforts to clarify the issue of black young men studying for the priesthood, see Nickels, *Black Catholic Protest*, 36–39.

84. See Nickels, *Black Catholic Protest*, 42–43.

85. Michael J. Curley (1879–1947) was born in Ireland. He became bishop of St. Augustine in 1914 and archbishop of Baltimore in 1921. Washington was made a separate archdiocese in 1939 and Curley remained as ordinary for both sees. He was conservative politically and socially and was not very popular with black Catholics in Washington.

86. Nickels, *Black Catholic Protest*, 43.

87. Ibid., 45–49.

88. Ibid., 59–61. An earlier incident took place in New York in 1927 (52–54).

89. Ibid., 136.

90. "An Interracial Role," an unpublished autobiography by William Markoe, pp. 1–10, William M. Markoe, S.J., Papers, Series 103, box 4, Jesuit Archives, Marquette University Archives.

91. Biographical information on John Markoe is found in William Markoe, S.J., Papers, Series 103, box 3.

92. Ibid., Interracial Papers. Later Austin Bork, S.J., died from accidental drowning while attempting to save the life of a black parishioner. William Markoe indicated that his provincial granted him permission to transform the pledge into a vow. See Markoe's "Interracial Role," 10.

93. Markoe, "Interracial Role," 29.

94. John J. Glennon was born in Ireland in 1862. He was made archbishop of St. Louis in 1903, being transferred from Kansas City, Missouri. In 1946 he was made a cardinal and died in Ireland on his way home that same year. Glennon was generally insensitive to the black population of St. Louis. See Faherty, *Dream by the River*, 155, and William Markoe's autobiography, where Markoe recounts Glennon's behavior at the funeral of a black man who had worked for him as a servant ("Interracial Role," 344–45).

95. Markoe, "Interracial Role," 106.

96. Ibid., 107–8.

97. Ibid., 108.

98. Ibid., 131.

99. Ibid., 230–31.

100. Ibid., 231.

101. See Nickels, *Black Catholic Protest*, 91–94.

102. Ibid., 226–29.

103. Ibid., 229–36.

104. See John LaFarge's account of the Gibbons Institute in his autobiography, *The Manner Is Ordinary* (New York: Harcourt, Brace, 1954),
208–16.

105. Both LaFarge and Markoe were descendants of Benjamin Franklin
(Markoe, "Interracial Role," 141).

106. See Nickels, *Black Catholic Protest*, 96–135.

107. Ibid., 286–312.

108. Ibid., 298–99.

109. The papers of William Markoe are in the Jesuit Archives at Marquette University. They are a rich source of documentation for the history
of black Catholics in the first part of the twentieth century and for Markoe
himself. Markoe is a man who needs a biography.

110. See three works by John LaFarge: *Interracial Justice: A Study of the
Catholic Doctrine of Race Relations* (New York: America Press, 1937); *The
Race Question and the Negro* (New York: Longmans, Green, 1944); and *The
Catholic Viewpoint on Race Relations* (Garden City, N.Y.: Hanover House,
1956). Today there is needed another assessment of LaFarge's teaching on
race in the perspective of the last forty years.

111. De Lai to Bonzano, November 5, 1920, Del. ap. U.S.A., II, 160b/2
(1919/1921), Condizione dei negri.

112. L'Emo Card. Van Rossum all'Emo Segretario della S.C. Concistoriale, a typewritten copy without date, Del. ap. U.S.A., II, 160b/2 (1919/1921),
Condizione dei negri.

113. Benjamin Keiley (1847–1925) was born in Petersburg, Virginia. He
was ordained a priest in 1873 and became bishop of Savannah in 1900. He
resigned as ordinary in 1922. Ignatius Lissner was born in Wolxheim in the
region of Alsace in France in 1867 and entered the Society of African Missions in 1891. About 1906 he came to the United States after some ten years
of missionary activity in Africa. See *Dizionario degli Istituti de Perfezione*,
s.v. "Lissner, Ignace."

114. The Society of the African Missions had been founded in 1856 by
Melchior de Marion-Brésillac in the French city of Lyons. For that reason they
were often called at this time the Fathers of Lyons. They were founded to work
among Africans and those of African descent. Their first mission field was
Sierra Leone, on the west coast of Africa. The founder and many of the first
missionaries died from tropical diseases. See *New Catholic Encyclopedia*, s.v.
"African Missions, Society of the," and *Dizionario degli Istituti di Perfezione*,
s.v. "Società delle Missione Africane."

115. Van Rossum to Keiley, January 30, 1920, Keiley Papers, Diocese of
Savannah Archives.

116. Peter Paul Cahensly was a member of the Center party in Prussia, a
member of the Reichstag, and a representative of the St. Raphael's Society,
which gave aid to the German Catholics in the United States. As a result of his
visit to the United States in 1883, he became familiar with the complaints

of the German Catholics that they were being ill treated, especially by the Irish bishops. This charge resulted in an outcry in Europe that the Germans and other immigrants were being ignored and neglected. See *New Catholic Encyclopedia*, s.v. "Cahensly, Peter Paul."

117. Keiley to Gibbons, February 26, 1920, Keiley Papers.

118. Gibbons to Keiley, February 29, 1920, Keiley Papers.

119. See Ochs, *Desegregating the Altar*, 259–60.

120. Keiley to van Rossum, March 3, 1920, Keiley Papers.

121. De Lai to Keiley, November 8, 1920, Keiley Papers. This letter is very terse and barely conceals a certain irritation.

122. Keiley to De Lai, n.d., Keiley Papers. The letter is practically illegible because of the state of Keiley's handwriting. By this time Keiley was almost blind (Sister Felicitas Powers, Diocesan Archivist, to author, April 25, 1988).

123. Gibbons to De Lai, December 13, 1920, Keiley Papers (copy).

124. Bonaventura Cerretti was born in 1872 in Italy and died as a cardinal in Rome in 1933. He served in the papal diplomatic corps and was a secretary in the apostolic delegation in Washington, D.C., from 1904 to 1914.

125. Keiley to Cerretti, December 7, 1920, Keiley Papers.

126. Van Rossum to Bonzano, April 4, 1921, Del. ap. U.S.A., II, 160b/2 (1919/1921), Condizione dei negri.

127. Bonzano to van Rossum, May 18, 1931 (clearly an error for 1921), Del. ap. U.S.A., II, 160b/2 (1919/1921), Condizione dei negri.

128. Aside from the three Healy brothers, six black priests had been ordained by 1920: Augustus Tolton, Charles Uncles, S.S.J., John Dorsey, S.S.J., Joseph Burgess, C.S.Sp., John Plantevigne, S.S.J., and Stephen Theobald. For information about them, see Foley, *God's Men of Color*, and Ochs, *Desegregating the Altar*. In 1920 only four of these men were living. The question of whether they had given satisfaction depended, of course, on who was making the evaluation.

129. In fact, Bonzano at this point thought that the Society of the Divine Word planned to found a congregation of black brothers who would be trained to teach in black schools on the primary and secondary school levels, which, if all worked well, would result in vocations to its priesthood.

130. Bonzano to De Lai, February 4, 1921, Del. ap. U.S.A., II, 160b/2 (1919/1921), Condizione dei negri.

131. The Society of the Divine Word is a society of missionaries founded by a German priest, Arnold Janssen, born in the diocese of Münster in northern Germany in 1837 and ordained for the diocese in 1861. In 1875 he established the first mission house in Steyl, Holland, which was to become the cradle of the Society of the Divine Word. This society came to the United States in 1900 and began work among blacks in the South in 1905. See Fritz Bornemann et al., *A History of the Divine Word Missionaries* (Rome: Collegium Verbi Divini, 1981), 209–14. For the background of the foundation of the first seminary for black candidates at Bay St. Louis, Mississippi, see

Ochs, *Desegregating the Altar*, 246–54, and Koren, *The Serpent and the Dove*, 256–59.

132. Janser to Bonzano, November 25, 1921, nos. 201–2. Del. ap. U.S.A., II, 160b/2 (1919/1921), Condizione dei negri. This is the first of two letters from Janser dated November 25.

133. Janser to Bonzano, November 25, 1921, nos. 206–7, Del. ap. U.S.A., II, 160b/2 (1919/1921).

134. In 1934 first ordinations took place at St. Augustine's Seminary, Bay St. Louis. Ordained were Maurice Rousseve, S.V.D, Vincent Smith, O.C.S.O., Anthony Bourges, S.V.D., and Francis Wade, S.V.D. See Foley, *God's Men of Color*, 124–62.

135. Rebesher to Justin MacCarthy, September 16, 1909, 28-R-5 abc, Josephite Archives.

136. Rebesher to McCarthy, December 21, 1910, Josephite Archives.

137. See Knights of Peter Claver, "Brief History of the Order," *Souvenir Booklet: Seventy-Fifth Jubilee Convention* (New Orleans: Knights of Peter Claver, 1984), 8.

Chapter 9: Coming of Age:
Black Catholics in the Mid-Twentieth Century

1. See "Catholicism Unbound: The Church of the Twenties," chap. 18 in Hennesey, *American Catholics*, 234–53.

2. Michael Fink, O.S.B. (1834–1904), vicar apostolic, became titular bishop in 1871 and bishop of Leavenworth in 1877; the see moved to Kansas City, where he was the first bishop in 1891. See Mission Work among the Negroes and the Indians (1889), p. 3. Bureau of Colored and Indian Missions Papers, Series 7/9, box 1, Folder 1. Marquette University Archives.

3. See Koren, *The Serpent and the Dove*, 191–94.

4. See chapter 8 above for the quarrel that arose later between Bishop Keiley of Savannah and Ignatius Lissner.

5. Keiley to Lissner, August 25, 1916, Bishop Keiley Papers.

6. Keiley to Lissner, October 26, 1916, Bishop Keiley Papers.

7. Interview with Mother Eugenia of the Franciscan Handmaids of Mary at the convent in New York City, April 5, 1987. Mother Eugenia had entered the community five years after it was founded and knew well Elizabeth Williams.

8. Interview with Mother Eugenia. All of the sisters who knew Mother Theodore spoke of her in almost the same terms: "Courage, never discouraged, very strong." Another sister, Sister Joseph Brennan, described her as "very patient, very strict, very firm, very much in control."

9. Book of Customs and Directives, p. 1. Franciscan Handmaids of Mary Archives. The archives of the community contain little documentation relative to their beginnings. Aside from the chronicle of the house,

information was received through interviews with the elderly sisters of the community.

10. See the brochure *Who Are These Handmaids?* distributed by the community.

11. See *Marcus Garvey, Life and Lessons: A Centennial Companion to the Marcus Garvey and Universal Negro Improvement Association Papers,* ed. Robert A. Hill and Barbara Blair (Berkeley: University of California Press, 1987), lxviii, 358–59. Marcus Garvey died in London in 1940 and was buried in a Catholic cemetery. He had married his first wife, Amy Ashwood, at a Catholic ceremony in 1919 in Jamaica. It is not at all certain how and when Garvey became a Catholic. He did not live as a Catholic, although his political philosophy had a religious component. According to Rev. William A. Connolly, S.J., of Spanish Town, Jamaica, who was vicar-general of the Kingston Archdiocese in 1964, when Garvey's body was reinterred at the Marcus Garvey Memorial in Kingston, it was understood that Garvey was received into the Catholic church during his last illness. Before his burial in Kingston, Garvey's body lay in state at the Catholic cathedral, where Mass was celebrated before assembled dignitaries. Garvey was honored as Jamaica's first national hero (Connolly to author, October 27, 1989).

12. Alain Locke, *The New Negro* (New York: Albert and Charles Boni, 1925; reprint, New York: Atheneum, 1970), 7.

Alain Locke was born in Philadelphia in 1885 and died in 1954. He was the first black to become an Oxford Rhodes Scholar. For many years professor at Howard University, Locke was a philosopher, educator, and social critic.

13. Ellen Tarry, who granted the author several interviews, wrote an autobiography, *The Third Door: The Autobiography of an American Negro Woman* (New York: David McKay, 1955). She is also the author of many books for children and young adults: *Katherine Drexel — Friend of the Neglected* (New York: Farrar, Straus and Cudahy, 1960); *Martin de Porres — Saint of the New World* (New York: Farrar, Straus and Cudahy, 1963); *Young Jim — The Early Years of James Weldon Johnson* (New York: Dodd, Mead, 1967); *The Other Toussaint: A Modern Biography of a Post-Revolutionary Black* (Boston: St. Paul Editions, 1981).

14. Catherine de Hueck, *Friendship House* (New York: Sheed and Ward, 1946), 48.

15. Almost all of the biographical information about Claude McKay is taken from Wayne F. Cooper, *Claude McKay: Rebel Sojourner in the Harlem Renaissance: A Biography* (Baton Rouge: Louisiana State University Press, 1987).

16. For this sonnet and many others, see Wayne Cooper, ed., *The Passion of Claude McKay: Selected Prose and Poetry, 1912–1948* (New York: Schocken Books, 1973).

17. Claude McKay, *Harlem Shadows* (New York: Harcourt, Brace, 1922).

18. See Cooper, *Claude McKay,* 175–76.

19. Claude McKay to Max Eastman, October 16, 1944, published in Cooper, *Passion of Claude McKay*, 304–5.

20. Cooper, "Looking Forward: The Search for Community, 1937–1940," chap. 11 in *Claude McKay*, 322–46.

21. Tarry, *Third Door*, 187.

22. Bernard James Sheil (1886–1969) was made auxiliary bishop to Cardinal Mundelein in 1928. Sheil was an important figure in the Roosevelt era and after. He was a liberal in politics and spoke out often against racism; he was very willing to welcome Claude McKay. See Fogarty, *Vatican and the American Hierarchy*, 263–64.

23. Dorothy Day (1897–1980) converted to Catholicism in 1928. With the collaboration of a French peasant Catholic leader, Peter Maurin, she began a settlement house known as the House of Hospitality in 1933. At the same time, the newspaper *Catholic Worker* began appearing. The Houses of Hospitality, staffed by laypeople devoted to poverty and pacifism, spread all over the United States. As they reached out to all of the poor, the *Catholic Worker* also played a part in championing the cause of blacks.

24. "Right Turn to Catholicism," B–McKay, *G 267424, Claude McKay Papers, Schomburg Center for Research in Black Culture Archives, New York Public Library. This is a typewritten manuscript of twenty-six pages, signed by Claude McKay.

25. McKay wrote earlier a much shorter and more concise article on his conversion, entitled "On Becoming a Roman Catholic" and that was published in a small Catholic publication, *Epistle* 11 (1945): 43–45.

26. Cooper, *Claude McKay*, 368–69.

27. McKay to Charlie Smith, October 15 (no year), McKay Papers, microfilm.

28. "The Pagan Isms," in *Selected Poems of Claude McKay* (New York: Bookman Associates, 1953), 49. It was originally published in *Catholic Worker*, July 1945.

29. Elizabeth Laura Adams, *Dark Symphony* (New York: Sheed and Ward, 1942).

30. Sister Mary Anthony Scally, *Negro Catholic Writers, 1900–1943: A Bio-Bibliography* (Detroit: Walter Romig, 1945), 19–23.

31. Helen Caldwell Day, *Color, Ebony* (New York: Sheed and Ward, 1951), and *Not without Tears* (New York: Sheed and Ward, 1954). In a third book, *All the Way to Heaven* (New York: Sheed and Ward, 1956), she set forth in fictional form the story of the Catholic Union of the Sick in America, an organization for those with chronic illness.

32. William Lawrence Adrian (1883–1972) became bishop of Nashville in 1936. At that time Memphis was in that diocese.

33. Patrick A. O'Boyle (1896–1987) was named archbishop of Washington in 1947. He was created a cardinal in 1967 and retired in 1973.

34. Interview with Roy Foster, who worked as assistant in the mission from 1946 to its closing in 1967. Foster worked very closely with Llewellyn

Scott, taking him to visit the Baroness de Hueck at her retreat in Canada and Dorothy Day in New York State. See also the obituary notice for Llewellyn Scott in the *Washington Evening Star*, December 20, 1978, and the *Washington Post* for the same date; and Vernon Pizer, "Miracle in the Slums," *Catholic World* 181 (1955): 268–73.

35. Archbishop Patrick John Ryan (1831–1911) became coadjutor bishop in St. Louis in 1872 and then archbishop of Philadelphia in 1884.

36. Information about Mother Lewis is not plentiful. See fiftieth anniversary brochure for St. Monica Church, Atlantic City, New Jersey, 1938–1988, and the parish brochure for the thirtieth anniversary in 1958.

37. The activities of Lena Edwards were covered in many articles in periodicals and newspapers. See "Lady Doctor to Migrant Workers," *Ebony* 17 (February 1962): 59–60, and *Jubilee* 11 (July 1963): 24–31. Her life was published by Sister M. Anthony Scally, *Mother, Medicine, and Mercy: The Story of a Black Woman Doctor* (Washington, D.C.: Associated Publishers, 1979). The details of her life were taken from this volume and the unpublished final chapter, which Scally graciously supplied to the present writer.

38. Turner to the Annual Meeting of the American Hierarchy, October 20, 1931, United States Catholic Conference Archives, Washington, D.C.

39. "Letter Proposed for the Hierarchy," October 24, 1932, United States Catholic Conference Archives. (The actual text of the letter is not available.)

40. The Federated Colored Catholics to the American Hierarchy, August 8, 1939, United States Catholic Conference Archives.

41. Francis Joseph Spellman (1889–1967) became auxiliary bishop of Boston in 1932 and then archbishop of New York on May 22, 1939. In 1946 he was created a cardinal.

42. "The Catholic Interracial Program in New York City: Report for the Most Reverend Archbishop, by J. LaFarge, S.J.," July 3, 1939, typescript, Archdiocese of New York Archives. For a short history of the Catholic Interracial Council of New York and the formation of the National Catholic Council for Interracial Justice that grew out of it, see Martin A. Zielinski, "Working for Interracial Justice: The Catholic Interracial Council of New York, 1934–1964," *U.S. Catholic Historian* 7 (1988): 233–60.

43. For details regarding Hunton's activity, see his autobiography, *All of Which I Saw, Part of Which I Was: The Autobiography of George K. Hunton, Crusader for Racial Justice, as Told to Gary MacEoin* (Garden City, N.Y.: Doubleday, 1967).

44. Manhattanville College is now located in Purchase, New York, and is no longer under the direction of the Religious of the Sacred Heart.

45. Mother Dammann, President, Manhattanville College of the Sacred Heart, New York, N.Y., "Principles versus Prejudices: A Talk Given to the Alumnae on Class Day, May 31st, 1938," in *Higher Education for Catholic Women: An Historical Anthology*, ed. Mary J. Oates (New York: Garland

Publishing, 1987), 377–96. For the background, see Hunton, *All of Which I Saw*, 91–103.

46. Dammann, "Principles versus Prejudice," 387.

47. Ibid., 395.

48. Walter White, president of the NAACP, to Mother Katherine, July 25, 1934, NAACP Letters, 1934–35, Sisters of the Blessed Sacrament Archives, Bensalem, Pa. White thanked Mother Katherine for the donation to the NAACP and expressed regret that she did not want her donations made public.

49. Mother Katherine to Archbishop Blenk and replies, 1909–17, Sisters of the Blessed Sacrament Archives. James Hubert Blenk (1856–1917) was made bishop of San Juan, Puerto Rico, in 1899 and archbishop of New Orleans in 1906, where he remained until his death.

50. See *New Catholic Encyclopedia*, s.v. "Xavier University of Louisiana."

51. "The American Catholic Bishops and Racism, November 14, 1958," *Documents of American Catholic History* 2:646–52. It is important to note that the letter was issued by the Administrative Board of the National Catholic Welfare Conference in the name of the American bishops. It was not a pastoral letter. The American bishops issued their pastoral letter on racism in 1979 after the period of this history. It was entitled "Brothers and Sisters to Us: United States Bishops' Pastoral Letter on Racism in Our Day," November 14, 1979.

52. Ibid., 649.

53. Ibid., 651.

54. Joseph Ritter (1892–1967) became bishop of Indianapolis in 1934 and archbishop of the same see in 1944. Two years later in 1946, he became archbishop of St. Louis and was created a cardinal in 1961.

55. Vincent S. Waters (1904–74) was ordained bishop of Raleigh in 1945.

56. Thomas Joseph Toolen (1886–1976) was named bishop of Mobile in 1927 and bishop of Mobile-Birmingham in 1954. Bishop Toolen, who had little sympathy for the aspirations of the black community, resigned in 1969.

57. Harold Perry was born in 1916 and was ordained a priest in 1944. The episcopal ordination took place in New Orleans on January 6, 1966. For details regarding his life, see Sister Caroline Hemesath, *Our Black Shepherds: Biographies of the Ten Black Bishops of the United States* (Washington, D.C.: Josephite Pastoral Center, 1987), 27–43.

58. Herman Porter (1914–1986) was ordained a priest in the Society of the Sacred Heart in 1947. Later he joined the diocese of Rockport in Illinois.

59. For some of the details regarding the summoning of the caucus and its agenda during the Catholic Clergy Conference, see National Catholic Conference for Interracial Justice Collection, Series 16, Catholic Clergy Conference on Interracial Apostolate (CCCIA) (Black Caucus), Marquette University Archives. So far there is no published account of the initial meet-

ing of the National Black Catholic Clergy Caucus. Some of the description is from the personal papers of the present writer, who was present at the meetings of April 16–17, 1968. For the published text of the black priests' statement, see "A Statement of the Black Catholic Clergy Caucus, April 18, 1968," in *Black Theology: A Documentary History, 1966–1979*, ed. Gayraud Wilmore and James Cone (Maryknoll, N.Y.: Orbis Books, 1979), 322–24.

60. Ibid., 322.
61. Ibid., 323.
62. Ibid., 323–24.

BIBLIOGRAPHY

MANUSCRIPT COLLECTIONS

Archdiocese of Baltimore Archives.
    Archbishop James Gibbons Papers.
    Baptismal Register of St. Peter's Procathedral. Microfilm.
    Bohemia Plantation Record, 1790–1815.
    Second Plenary Council of Baltimore. Extraordinary Session Minutes.
        Handwritten manuscript.
Archdiocese of Chicago Archives.
    Deceased Priests File.
    Madaj Collection.
Archdiocese of Cincinnati Archives.
    Archbishop William Elder Papers.
Archdiocese of Indianapolis.
    Old Cathedral Records (copy and translation).
Archdiocese of Mobile Archives.
    Baptismal Registers for Blacks, 1781–1863.
    Marriage Register for Blacks, 1830–1860.
    Burial Register for Blacks, 1828–1877.
    Correspondence of the Bishops of Mobile.
Archdiocese of New York Archives.
    Letters to Archbishop John Hughes.
    Letters to Cardinal John Farley.
Archdiocese of Philadelphia Archives and Historical Collections.
    Golden Jubilee of St. Peter Claver's, 1886–1936.
Congregation for the Evangelization of Peoples Archives Rome.
    Lettere e Decreti della S.C. e Biglietti di M. Segretario, 1889.
    Scritture Riferite nei Congressi Collegio Urbano, 1879–1892.
Diocese of Covington Archives.
    Bishop Camillus Maes Letters.
Diocese of Little Rock Archives.
    Bishop John B. Morris Papers.
    Msgr. J. M. Lucey Papers.
Diocese of St. Augustine Archives. Jacksonville, Florida.

323

The Spanish Colonial Parochial Registers of St. Augustine (1594–1821).

Diocese of Savannah Archives.

Bishop Benjamin Keiley Papers.

Diary of Bishop Thomas Becker.

Franciscan Sisters of the Immaculate Conception Papers.

Parish Registers.

Sister Charlene Walsh Collection.

Franciscan Handmaids of Mary Archives. New York.

Book of Customs and Directives.

Josephite Archives. Baltimore.

Diary of a Trip to America by Canon Peter L. Benoit, 1875. Typescript copy of original in Mill Hill Archives, London.

History of St. Benedict the Moor. Catholic Colored Mission, 311 Ninth Street, Milwaukee, Wisconsin.

John R. Slattery Papers.

Minutes of the Meeting of the Executive Committee of the Colored Catholic Congress. 2 pages, printed document.

St. Peter's Trustees to Bishop Northrop, 1888.

Souvenir of St. Benedict the Moor Mission, 1909–1934. Milwaukee.

Summary of documents relating to A. Tolton.

Library of Congress. Manuscript Division.

Booker T. Washington Papers.

W. E. B. Du Bois Papers. Microfilm.

Marquette University Archives. Milwaukee.

Bureau of Colored and Indian Missions Papers.

Jesuit Archives. William M. Markoe, S.J., Papers.

National Catholic Conference for Interracial Justice Collection.

The Moorland-Spingarn Research Center. Howard University, Washington, D.C.

Arthur B. Spingarn Collection.

The Murray Papers.

National Archives and Record Service. Washington, D.C.

Census Records.

New York Public Library. Manuscript and Rare Books Section.

The Pierre Toussaint Papers.

New York Public Library. Schomburg Center for Research in Black Culture Archives.

Claude McKay Papers.

Oblate Sisters of Providence Archives. Baltimore.

The Original Diary of the Oblate Sisters of Providence, 1827–1876. 4 vol.

St. Benedict the Moor Parish. Milwaukee, Wisconsin.

House Chronicle.

St. Joseph Cathedral Records. Bardstown, Kentucky.

Parochial Registers.

Sisters of the Blessed Sacrament Archives. Bensalem, Pennsylvania.

Mother Katherine Drexel Papers.
NAACP Letters, 1934–1935.
Sisters of the Holy Family Archives. New Orleans.
The Original Rules and Constitutions of the Holy Family Sisters.
Miscellaneous Historical Papers.
Sulpician Archives. Baltimore.
Journal of the Society of the Holy Family, 1843–1845.
United States Catholic Conference Archives. Washington, D.C.
Minutes of Archbishops' Meetings.
Minutes of the Board of NCWC.
Thomas Wyatt Turner Correspondence.
University of Notre Dame Archives.
Archdiocese of New Orleans Records.
Congregation of the Propaganda Fide Archives. Microfilm.
Henry Brownson Papers.
William J. Onahan Papers.
Vatican Archives.
Apostolic Delegation. U.S.A. Papers.
Yale University. Beinecke Rare Book and Manuscript Library.
Claude McKay Papers (James Weldon Johnson Collection).

NEWSPAPER AND PERIODICAL COLLECTIONS

Archdiocese of Philadelphia Archives and Historical Collections. Overbrook,
Pennsylvania.
American Catholic Tribune.
Journal.
Boston Public Library.
Boston Pilot.
The Catholic University of America Library. Washington, D.C.
Catholic Mirror. Microfilm.
Church News. Microfilm.
The Indiana State Library and Archives. Indianapolis.
Indianapolis World. Microfilm.
Library of Congress. Washington, D.C.
Broad Ax. Microfilm.
Cleveland Gazette. Microfilm.
Maryland Gazette. Annapolis, Md. Microfilm.
New York Age. Microfilm.
Washington Bee. Microfilm.
Western Appeal. Microfilm.
The Moorland-Spingarn Collection. Howard University, Washington, D.C.
Alexander's Magazine and the National Domestic.
Howard's American Magazine.

Toledo Public Library. Toledo, Ohio.
  Toledo Blade. Microfilm.
University of Louisville Archives.
  Louisville Leader. Microfilm.

PUBLISHED SOURCES

Abzug, Robert H., and Stephen Maizlish, eds. *New Perspectives on Race and Slavery in America: Essays in Honor of Kenneth M. Stampp.* Lexington: University Press of Kentucky, 1986.

Acta et Decreta Concilii Plenarii Baltimorensis Tertii, A.D. MDCCCLXXXIV. Baltimore: John Murphy, 1886.

Adams, Elizabeth Laura. *Dark Symphony.* New York: Sheed and Ward, 1942.

Adams, William Y. *Nubia: Corridor to Africa.* Princeton, N.J.: Princeton University Press, 1984.

Ahles, Assumpta. *In the Shadow of His Wings.* St. Paul: North Central Publishing, 1977.

Baudier, Roger. *The Catholic Church in Louisiana.* New Orleans: A. W. Hyatt Stationery Manufacturing, 1939.

Baumstein, Paschal. *My Lord of Belmont: A Biography of Leo Haid.* Belmont Abbey, N.C.: Herald House, 1985.

Bergman, Peter. *The Chronological History of the Negro in America.* New York: Harper and Row, 1969.

Bernstein, Iver. *The New York City Draft Riots: Their Significance for American Society and Politics in the Age of the Civil War.* New York: Oxford University Press, 1990.

Bernucci, Sadoc. "Martino di Porres, santo." In *Bibliotheca Sanctorum* 8:1240–45. Rome: Istituto Giovanni XXIII della Pontificia Università Lateranense, 1966.

Binsse, Henry. "A Catholic Uncle Tom, Pierre Toussaint." *Historical Records and Studies.* 12 (1918): 90–101.

Blied, Benjamin. *Catholics and the Civil War.* Milwaukee, s.n., 1945.

Bowser, Frederick P. *The African Slave in Colonial Peru. 1524–1650.* Stanford, Calif.: Stanford University Press, 1974.

Boxer, C. R. "The Problem of the Native Clergy in the Portuguese and Spanish Empires from the Sixteenth to Eighteenth Centuries." In *The Mission of the Church and the Propagation of the Faith*, Studies in Church History, vol. 6, ed. C. J. Cuming. Cambridge: Cambridge University Press, 1970.

Brokhage, Joseph D. *Francis Patrick Kenrick's Opinion on Slavery.* The Catholic University of America Studies in Sacred Theology. 2nd series, no. 85. Washington, D.C.: The Catholic University of America Press, 1955.

Brown, Letitia Woods. *Free Negroes in the District of Columbia. 1790–1846.* New York: Oxford University Press, 1972.

Brown, Peter. *Augustine of Hippo: A Biography.* Berkeley: University of California Press, 1967.

Brownson, Orestes. *The Works of Orestes A. Brownson.* Collected and arranged by Henry F. Brownson. 20 vols. Detroit: Thorndike Nourse, 1882–87.

Callan, Louise. *Philippine Duchesne: Frontier Missionary of the Sacred Heart, 1769–1852.* Westminster, Md.: Newman Press, 1957.

Caravaglios, Maria. "A Roman Critique of the Pro-Slavery Views of Bishop Martin of Natchitoches, Louisiana." *Records of the American Catholic Historical Society of Philadelphia.* 83 (1972): 67–81.

Carey, Patrick. *People, Priests, and Prelates: Ecclesiastical Democracy and the Tensions of Trusteeism.* Notre Dame Studies in American Catholicism. Notre Dame, Ind.: University of Notre Dame Press, 1987.

Carroll, John. *The John Carroll Papers.* Vol. 1, 1755–1791; vol. 2, 1792–1806; vol. 3, 1807–1815. Edited by Thomas Hanley. Notre Dame, Ind.: University of Notre Dame Press, 1976.

Carroll, Mary. *A Catholic History of Alabama and the Floridas.* Freeport, N.Y.: Books for Libraries Press, 1970.

Christensen, Lawrence. "Cyprian Clamorgan, the Colored Aristocracy of St. Louis (1858)." *Bulletin of the Missouri Historical Society* 31 (1974–75): 3–31.

Clarke, Peter. *A Free Church in a Free Society: The Ecclesiology of John England, Bishop of Charleston, 1820–1842: A Nineteenth Century Missionary Bishop in the Southern United States.* Hartsville, S.C.: Center for John England Studies, 1982.

Concilii Plenarii Baltimorensis II, in Ecclesia Metropolitana Baltimorensi. A Die VII ad Diem XXI. Octobris, A.D. MDCCCLXVI. Habiti, et a sede Apostolica Recogniti, Acta et Decreta. Baltimore: John Murphy, 1868.

Conrad, Robert Edgar. *Children of God's Fire: A Documentary History of Black Slavery in Brazil.* Princeton: Princeton University Press, 1983.

Cooper, Wayne. *Claude McKay: Rebel Sojourner in the Harlem Renaissance: A Biography.* Baton Rouge: Louisiana State University Press, 1987.

———. *The Passion of Claude McKay: Selected Prose and Poetry, 1912–1948.* New York: Schocken Books, 1973.

Correspondance de Dom Afonso, Roi du Congo, 1506–1543. Académie Royale des Sciences d'Outre Mer. Classe des Sciences morales et politiques, n.s., 41, 3, ed. and trans. Louis Jadin and Mireille Dicorato. Brussels: Snoeck-Ducaju et Fils, S.A., 1974.

Curley, Michael. *Church and State in the Spanish Floridas (1783–1822).* Catholic University of America Studies in American Church History, 30. Washington, D.C.: Catholic University of America Press, 1940.

Curtin, Philip. *The Atlantic Slave Trade: A Census.* Madison: University of Wisconsin Press, 1969.

Dammann, Grace. "Principles versus Prejudices: A Talk Given to the Alumnae on Class Day, May 31st, 1938." In *Higher Education for Catholic Women: An Historical Anthology*, ed. Mary J. Oates. New York: Garland Publishing, 1987.

Dannett, Sylvia. *Profiles of Negro Womanhood*. Vol. 1, 1619–1900. Negro Heritage Library. Yonkers, N.Y.: Educational Heritage, 1964.

Davidson, Basil. *The African Slave Trade*. Boston: Little, Brown, 1980.

Davis, David Brion. *The Problem of Slavery in Western Culture*. Ithaca, N.Y.: Cornell University Press, 1966.

Day, Helen Caldwell. *All the Way to Heaven: A Story about the Catholic Union of the Sick*. New York: Sheed and Ward, 1956.

——. *Color, Ebony*. New York: Sheed and Ward, 1951.

——. *Not without Tears*. New York: Sheed and Ward, 1954.

de Hueck, Catherine. *Friendship House*. New York: Sheed and Ward, 1946.

de Meester, Paul. "'Philippe et l'eunuque éthiopien' ou 'Le baptême d'un pèlerin de Nubie'?" *Nouvelle Revue Théologique* 103 (1981): 360–74.

The Desert Christian: The Sayings of the Desert Fathers: The Alphabetical Collection. Edited and translated by Benedicta Ward. New York: Macmillan Publishing, 1980.

Detiege, Audrey. *Henriette Delille: Free Woman of Color*. New Orleans: Sisters of the Holy Family, 1976.

Documents of American Catholic History. 3 vol. Edited by John Tracy Ellis. Wilmington, Del.: Michael Glazier, 1987.

Dolan, Jay. *The Immigrant Church: New York's Irish and German Catholics, 1815–1865*. 1975. Reprint. Notre Dame, Ind.: University of Notre Dame Press, 1983.

——. *The American Catholic Parish: A History from 1850 to the Present*. Vol. 1, *The Northeast, Southeast, and South Central States*; vol. 2, *The Pacific, Intermountain West, and Midwest States*. New York: Paulist Press, 1987.

Doresse, J. "Edesius et Frumentius" and "Elesbaan." In *Dictionaire d'histoire et de géographie ecclésiastiques* 14:1416–20 and 15:135–43. Paris: Letouzey et Ané, 1960 and 1963.

Dorsey, Norbert. "Pierre Toussaint of New York, Slave and Freedman: A Study of Lay Spirituality in Times of Social and Religious Change." S.T.D. diss., Pontificia Universitas Gregoriana, Facultas Theologiae. Rome, 1986.

Drago, Edmund L. *Black Politicians and Reconstruction in Georgia: A Splendid Failure*. Baton Rouge, Louisiana State University Press, 1982.

Duffy, Consuela. *Katherine Drexel. A Biography*. Cornwells Heights, Pa.: Mother Katherine Drexel Guild, 1966.

Dupanloup, Félix. "'European Catholic Opinion on Slavery,' a Reprint of the Pastoral Letter of the Rt. Rev. Félix Antoine Philibert Dupanloup, Bishop of Orleans, to His Clergy on the Subject of the Civil War in the United States, April 6, 1862." *Records of the American Catholic Historical Association* 25 (1914): 18–29.

Ekberg, Carl. *Colonial Ste. Genevieve: An Adventure on the Mississippi Frontier.* Gerald, Mo.: The Patrice Press, 1985.

Elder, William Henry. *Civil War Diary (1862–1865) of Bishop William Henry Elder, Bishop of Natchez.* Natchez, Miss.: published by R. O. Gerow, 1960.

England, John. *The Works of the Right Rev. John England, First Bishop of Charleston, Collected and Arranged under the Advice and Direction of His Immediate Successor, the Right Rev. Ignatius Aloysius Reynolds, and printed for him in Five Volumes.* Baltimore: John Murphy, 1849.

Eusebius Pamphilus. *The Life of the Blessed Emperor Constantine in Four Books.* Vol. 1 of *The Greek Ecclesiastical Historians of the First Six Centuries of the Christian Era, in Six Volumes.* London: Samuel Bagster and Sons, 1845.

Faherty, William. *Dream by the River: Two Centuries of St. Louis Catholicism, 1766–1967.* St. Louis: Piraeus Publishers, 1973.

Faherty, William and Madeleine Oliver. *The Religious Roots of Black Catholics of St. Louis.* Florissant, Mo.: St. Stanislaus Historic Museum, 1977.

Felder, Cain. *Troubling Biblical Waters: Race, Class and Family.* The Bishop Henry McNeal Turner Studies in North American Black Religion, vol. 3. Maryknoll, N.Y.: Orbis Books, 1989.

Fenwick, Addison, ed. *Sturdy Sons of Saint Paul.* St. Paul: Junior Pioneer Association, 1899.

Fogarty, Gerald. *The Vatican and the American Hierarchy from 1870 to 1965.* Wilmington, Del.: Michael Glazier, 1982.

Foley, Albert. "Adventures in Black Catholic History: Research and Writing." *U.S. Catholic Historian* 5 (1986): 103–18.

———. "Bishop Healy and the Colored Catholic Congress." *Interracial Review* 28 (1954): 79–80.

———. *Bishop Healy, Beloved Outcaste: The Story of a Great Man Whose Life Has Become a Living Legend.* New York: Farrar, Straus, 1954.

———. *God's Men of Color: The Colored Catholic Priests of the United States, 1854–1934.* New York: Farrar, Straus, 1955.

Foner, Eric. *Reconstruction: America's Unfinished Revolution, 1863–1877.* New York: Harper and Row, 1988.

Forbes, Jack. "Black Pioneers: The Spanish-Speaking Afroamericans of the Southwest." *Phylon* 27 (1966): 233–46.

Francis, M. Adele. "Lay Activity and the Catholic Congresses of 1889 and 1893." *Records of the American Catholic Historical Society of Philadelphia* 74 (1963): 3–22.

Franklin, John Hope, and Alfred Moss, Jr., *From Slavery to Freedom: A History of Negro Americans.* 6th edition. New York: Alfred A. Knopf, 1988.

Freedom: A Documentary History of Emancipation, 1861–1867. Series 1, vol. 1. *The Destruction of Slavery.* Edited by Ira Berlin, Barbara Fields,

Thavolia Glymph, Joseph Reidy, and Leslie Rowland. Cambridge: Cambridge University Press, 1985.

Frend, William. "Blandina and Perpetua: Two Early Christian Heroines." In *Town and Country in the Early Christian Centuries*, 15: 167–75. London: Variorum Reprints, 1980.

———. "Coptic, Greek, and Nubian at Q'asr Ibrim." In *Religion Popular and Unpopular in the Early Christian Centuries*, sec. 22, 224–29. London: Variorum Reprints, 1976.

———. "Nubia as an Outpost of Byzantine Cultural Influence." In *Religion Popular and Unpopular in the Early Christian Centuries*, sec. 12, 319–26. London: Variorum Reprints, 1976.

———. "Recently Discovered Materials for Writing the History of Christian Nubia." In *The Materials, Sources, and Methods of Ecclesiastical History*, Studies in Church History, vol. 11, ed. Derek Baker, 19–30. New York: Barnes and Noble, 1975.

Friede, Juan, and Benjamin Keen, eds. *Bartolomé de Las Casas in History: Toward an Understanding of the Man and His Work*. DeKalb: Northern Illinois University Press, 1971.

Gannon, Michael. *The Cross in the Sand: The Early Catholic Church in Florida, 1513–1870*. Gainesville: University of Florida Press, 1967.

———. *Rebel Bishop: The Life and Era of Augustin Verot*. Milwaukee: Bruce Publishing, 1964.

General History of Africa. Vol. 2, *Ancient Civilizations of Africa*, ed. G. Mokhtar. Vol. 3, *Africa from the Seventh to the Eleventh Century*, ed. M. Elfasi. Berkeley: University of California Press, 1981.

Gerdes, M. Reginald. "To Educate and Evangelize: Black Catholic Schools of the Oblate Sisters of Providence (1821–1880)." *U.S. Catholic Historian* 7 (1988): 183–99.

Gillard, John. *The Catholic Church and the American Negro*. Baltimore: St. Joseph's Society Press, 1930.

———. *Colored Catholics in the United States*. Baltimore: Josephite Press, 1941.

Gossett, Thomas. *Race: The History of an Idea in America*. Dallas: Southern Methodist University Press, 1963.

Guilday, Peter. *A History of the Councils of Baltimore (1791–1884)*. New York: Macmillan, 1932.

Hallenbeck, Cleve. *The Journey of Fray Marcos de Niza*. Dallas: Southern Methodist University Press, 1987.

Hanke, Lewis. *All Mankind Is One: A Study of the Disputation between Bartolomé de Las Casas and Juan Ginés de Sepúlveda in 1550 on the Intellectual and Religious Capacity of the American Indians*. DeKalb: Northern Illinois University Press, 1974.

Hare, Maud Cuney. *Norris Wright Cuney: A Tribune of the Black People*. New York: Crisis Publishing Co., 1913. Reprint. Austin, Tex.: Steck-Vaughn, 1968.

Harlan, Louis. *Booker T. Washington*. Vol. 1, *The Making of a Black Leader, 1856–1901*; vol. 2, *The Wizard of Tuskegee, 1901–1915*. New York: Oxford University Press, 1972–83.

Hart, Mary Francis Borgia. "Violets in the King's Garden: A History of the Sisters of the Holy Family of New Orleans." New Orleans: private printing, 1976.

Hassard, John R. G. *Life of the Most Reverend John Hughes, D.D., First Archbishop of New York, with Extracts from His Private Correspondence.* New York: D. Appleton, 1866.

Hemesath, Caroline. *From Slave to Priest: A Biography of the Rev. Augustine Tolton (1854–97), First Afro-American Priest of the United States.* Chicago: Franciscan Herald Press, 1973.

———. *Our Black Shepherds: Biographies of the Ten Black Bishops of the United States.* Washington, D.C.: Josephite Pastoral Center, 1987.

Hennesey, James. *American Catholics: A History of the Roman Catholic Community in the United States.* New York: Oxford University Press, 1981.

Higginbotham, Leon. *In the Matter of Color: Race and the American Legal Process: The Colonial Period.* New York: Oxford University Press, 1978.

Histoire universelle des missions catholiques. 4 vols. Edited by Msgr. S. Delacroix. Vol. 2: *Les Missions Modernes (XVIIe et XVIIIe siècles)*, ed. by H. Bernard-Maître, B. de Vaulx, Duc de la Force, A. Perbal, M. Quequiner, G. Cussac, J. Bouchard, C. Lugon, E. Jarry, and S. Delacroix. Paris: Librairie Grund, 1957.

A History of the Third Plenary Council of Baltimore, November 9–December 7, 1884: The Memorial Volume. Baltimore: The Baltimore Publishing Co., 1885.

Hodge, Frederick W., ed. "The Narrative of Alvar Núñez Cabeça de Vaca" and "The Narrative of the Expedition of Coronado, by Pedro de Castañeda." In *Spanish Explorers in the Southern United States, 1528–1543.* New York: Charles Scribner's Sons, 1907.

Hoffmann's Catholic Directory, Almanac and Clergy List — Quarterly. Milwaukee: Hoffmann Brothers, 1886–99.

Holliday, Carl. "The Young Southerner and the Negro." *South Atlantic Quarterly* 8 (1909): 117–31.

Holt, Thomas. *Black over White: Negro Political Leadership in South Carolina during Reconstruction.* Urbana: University of Illinois Press, 1974.

Hunton, George. *All of Which I Saw, Part of Which I Was: The Autobiography of George K. Hunton, Crusader for Racial Justice, as Told to Gary MacEoin.* Garden City, N.Y.: Doubleday, 1967.

The Image of the Black in Western Art. Vol. 1, *From the Pharaohs to the Fall of the Roman Empire.* Edited by Jean Vercoutter, Jean Leclant, Frank Snowden, Jr., and Jehan Desanges. Lausanne: Office du Livre, Menil Foundation, 1976. Vol. 2, *From the Early Christian Era to the "Age of Discovery".* Part 1, *From the Demonic Threat to the Incarnation of Sainthood.* Edited by Jean Devisse and translated by William Granger

Ryan. Part 2, *Africans in the Christian Ordinance of the World (Fourteenth to the Sixteenth Century)*. Edited by Jean Devisse and Michel Mollat and translated by William Granger Ryan. New York: William Morrow, 1979.

Janssens, Francis. "The Negro Problem and the Catholic Church." *Catholic World* 44 (1887): 721–26.

Jordan, Winthrop. *White over Black: American Attitudes toward the Negro, 1550–1812*. Chapel Hill: University of North Carolina Press, 1968.

Kaplan, Sidney. *The Black Presence in the Era of the American Revolution, 1770–1800*. Washington, D.C.: Smithsonian Institution, National Portrait Gallery, 1973.

Kaplan, Stephen. *The Monastic Holy Man and the Christianization of Early Solomonic Ethiopia*. Studien zur Kulturkunde, 73. Wiesbaden: Franz Steiner Verlag, 1984.

Kauffman, Christopher. *Tradition and Transformation in Catholic Culture: The Priests of Saint Sulpice in the United States from 1791 to the Present*. New York: Macmillan, 1988.

Kelsey, Harry. "A New Look at the Founding of Old Los Angeles." *California Historical Quarterly* 55 (1976): 326–39.

Kenrick, Francis Patrick. *Theologia Moralis*, 2 vols. Mechlin: H. Dessain, 1860–61.

Knights of Peter Claver. *Souvenir Booklet: Seventy-fifth Jubilee Convention*. New Orleans: Knights of Peter Claver, 1981.

Koren, Henry. *The Serpent and the Dove: A History of the Congregation of the Holy Ghost in the United States, 1745–1984*. Pittsburgh: Spiritus Press, 1985.

Labbé, Dolores Egger. *Jim Crow Comes to Church*. Lafayette, La.: University of Southwestern Louisiana, 1971. 2nd ed. Reprint. New York: Arno Press, 1978.

Lackner, Joseph. "St. Ann's Colored Church and School, Cincinnati, the Indian and Negro Collection for the United States, and Reverend Francis Xavier Weninger, S.J." *U.S. Catholic Historian* 7 (1888): 145–56.

LaFarge, John. *The Catholic Viewpoint on Race Relations*. Garden City, N.Y.: Hanover House, 1956.

———. *Interracial Justice: A Study of the Catholic Doctrine of Race Relations*. New York: America Press, 1937.

———. *The Manner is Ordinary*. New York: Harcourt, Brace, 1954.

———. *The Race Question and the Negro*. New York: Longmans, Green, 1944.

Lamanna, Richard, and Jay Coakley. "The Catholic Church and the Negro." In *Contemporary Catholicism in the United States*, University of Notre Dame, International Studies of the Committee on International Relations, ed. Philip Gleason, 147–93. Notre Dame, Ind.: University of Notre Dame Press, 1969.

Land, Aubrey. *Colonial Maryland: A History*. Millwood, N.Y.: KTO Press, 1981.

Lannon, Maria. *Mother Mary Elizabeth Lange: Life of Love and Service*. Washington, D.C.: Josephite Pastoral Center, 1976.

Le Liber Pontificalis: Texte, introduction, et commentaire. 3 vols. Edited by L. Duchesne. Paris: E. de Broccard, 1955–57.

Lemarié, Charles. "Le patriarche de l'ouest." 3 vols. Unpublished manuscript, 1983.

Lipscomb, Oscar. *The Administration of Michael Portier, Vicar Apostolic of Alabama and the Floridas, 1825–1829, and First Bishop of Mobile, 1829–1859*. Ann Arbor, Mich.: University Microfilms, 1987.

Liptak, Dolores. *Immigrants and Their Church: Makers of the Catholic Community*. The Bicentennial History of the Catholic Church in America, Authorized by the National Conference of Catholic Bishops. New York: Macmillan Publishing, 1989.

Litwack, Leon. *Been in the Storm So Long: The Aftermath of Slavery*. New York: Alfred A. Knopf, 1979.

Lucey, William Leo. *The Catholic Church in Maine*. Francestown, N.H.: Marshall Jones, 1957.

McCaffrey, Lawrence. *Daniel O'Connell and the Repeal Year*. Lexington: University of Kentucky Press, 1966.

McGill, Anna. *The Sisters of Charity of Nazareth, Kentucky*. New York: Encyclopedia Press, 1917.

McKay, Claude. "On Becoming a Roman Catholic." *Epistle*, 11 (1945): 43–45.

McKivigan, John. *The War Against Proslavery Religion: Abolitionism and the Northern Churches, 1830–1865*. Ithaca, N.Y.: Cornell University Press, 1984.

McLaughlin, J. Fairfax. "William Gaston: The First Student of Georgetown College." *Records of the American Catholic Historical Society* 6 (1895): 225–51.

Madden, Richard. *Catholics in South Carolina: A Record*. Lanham, Md.: University Press of America, 1985.

Maes, Camillus. *The Life of Rev. Charles Nerinckx*. Cincinnati: Robert Clarke, 1880.

Mattoso, Katia M. de Queiros. *To Be a Slave in Brazil, 1550–1888*. Translated by Arthur Goldhammer. New Brunswick, N.J.: Rutgers University Press, 1986.

Maxwell, John. *Slavery and the Catholic Church*. Chichester: Barry Rose Publishers, 1975.

Melville, Annabelle. *Louis William DuBourg. Bishop of Louisiana and the Floridas, Bishop of Montauban, and Archbishop of Besançon*. 2 vols. Chicago: Loyola University Press, 1986.

The Memorial Volume: A History of the Third Plenary Council of Baltimore, November 9–December 7, 1884. Baltimore: Baltimore Publishing, 1885.

Mensing, Raymond. "The Rise and Fall of the Pseudo Poor Clare Nuns of Skidaway Island." Unpublished paper. Diocese of Savannah Archives.

Miers, Suzanne, and Igor Kopytoff, eds. *Slavery in Africa: Historical and Anthropological Perspectives.* Madison: University of Wisconsin Press, 1977.

Miller, Randall, and Jon Wakelyn, eds. *Catholics in the Old South: Essays on Church and Culture.* Macon, Ga.: Mercer University Press, 1983.

Mills, Gary. *The Forgotten People: Cane River's Creoles of Color.* Baton Rouge: Louisiana State University Press, 1977.

Minogue, Anna Catherine. *Loretto: Annals of the Century.* New York: America Press, 1912.

Misch, Edward. "The American Bishops and the Negro from the Civil War to the Third Plenary Council of Baltimore, 1865–1884." Ph.D. diss., Pontifical Gregorian University, Rome, 1968.

Misner, Barbara. *"Highly Respectable and Accomplished Ladies": Catholic Women Religious in America, 1790–1850.* New York: Garland Publishing, 1988.

Monneret de Villard, Ugo. *Storia della Nubia Christiana.* Orientalia Christiana Analecta, 118. Rome: Pont. Institutum Orientalium Studiorum, 1938.

Morabito, Giuseppe. "Benedetto il Moro, santo." *Bibliotheca Sanctorum* 2:1103–4. Rome: Istituto Giovanni XXIII della Pontificia Università Lateranense, 1962.

Morner, Magnus. *Race Mixture in the History of Latin America.* Boston: Little, Brown, 1967.

Muffler, John. "This Far by Faith: A History of St. Augustine's, the Mother Church for Black Catholics in the Nation's Capital." Ph.D. diss. Columbia University, 1989.

The National Pastorals of the American Hierarchy (1792–1919). Edited by Peter Guilday. Washington, D.C.: National Catholic Welfare Council, 1923.

Nickels, Marilyn. *Black Catholic Protest and the Federated Colored Catholics, 1917–1933: Three Perspectives on Racial Justice.* The Heritage of American Catholicism. New York: Garland Publishing, 1988.

O'Connell, J. J. *Catholicity in the Carolinas and Georgia.* New York: Sadlier, 1879.

O'Connell, Marvin. *John Ireland and the American Catholic Church.* St. Paul: Minnesota Historical Society Press, 1988.

Oetgen, Jerome. *An American Abbot: Boniface Wimmer, O.S.B., 1809–1887.* Latrobe, Pa.: Archabbey Press, 1976.

———. "Origins of the Benedictines in Georgia." *The Georgia Historical Quarterly* 53 (1969): 165–83.

O'Keefe, Thomas. "Third Congress of Colored Catholics." *Catholic World* 55 (1892): 109–13.

O'Neill, Charles. *Church and State in French Colonial Louisiana: Policy and Politics to 1732.* New Haven, Conn.: Yale University Press, 1966.

Palladius. *Palladius: The Lausiac History.* Edited and translated by Robert T. Meyer. Ancient Christian Writers, vol. 34. Westminster, Md.: Newman Press, 1965.

Palmer, Colin. *Slaves of the White God: Blacks in Mexico, 1570–1650.* Cambridge: Harvard University Press, 1976.

Panagopoulos, E. P. *New Smyrna: An Eighteenth Century Greek Odyssey.* Gainesville: University of Florida Press, 1966.

Patterson, Orlando. *Slavery and Social Death: A Comparative Study.* Cambridge, Ma.: Harvard University Press, 1982.

Phelps, Jamie. "John R. Slattery's Missionary Strategies." *U.S. Catholic Historian* 7 (1988): 201–14.

Poole, Stafford, and Douglas Slawson. *Church and Slave in Perry County, Missouri, 1818–1865.* Lewiston, N.Y.: Edwin Mellen Press, 1986.

Portier, William. "John R. Slattery's Vision for the Evangelization of American Blacks." *U.S. Catholic Historian* 5 (1986): 19–44.

Price, Richard, ed. *Maroon Societies: Rebel Slave Communities in the Americas.* 2nd ed. Baltimore: Johns Hopkins University Press, 1979.

Progress of the Catholic Church in America and the World's Columbian Catholic Congresses. 2 vols in 1. Chicago: J. S. Hyland, 1897.

Raboteau, Albert. *Slave Religion: The "Invisible Institution" in the Antebellum South.* New York: Oxford University Press, 1978.

Randles, W. G. L. *L'ancien royaume du Congo des origines à la fin du XIXe siècle.* Paris: Mouton, 1968.

Rice, C. Duncan. *The Rise and Fall of Black Slavery.* New York: Harper and Row, 1975.

Rice, Madeleine. *American Catholic Opinion in the Slavery Controversy.* New York: Columbia University Press, 1944.

Rosalita, Sr. M. *No Greater Service: The History of the Congregation of the Sisters, Servants of the Immaculate Heart of Mary, Monroe, Michigan, 1845–1945.* Detroit: Congregation of the Sisters of the Immaculate Heart, 1948.

Rosenblum, Morris. *Luxorius: A Latin Poet among the Vandals.* New York: Columbia University Press, 1961.

Rothensteiner, John. *History of the Archdiocese of St. Louis.* 2 vols. St. Louis: Blackwell Wielandy, 1928.

Rudd, Daniel, and Theophilus Bond, *From Slavery to Wealth: The Life of Scott Bond: The Rewards of Honesty, Industry, Economy, and Perseverance.* Madison, Ark.: Journal Printing, 1917.

Ruffin, Robert. "Charles Martial Allemand-Lavigerie." *A.M.E. Church Review* 4 (1892): 320–35.

Russell-Word, A. J. R. *Fidalgos and Philanthropists: The Santa Casa da Misericordia of Bahia, 1550–1755.* Berkeley: University of California Press, 1968.

Ryan, Thomas. *Orestes Brownson: A Definitive Biography*. (Huntington, Ind.: Our Sunday Visitor, 1976.

Sadlier's Catholic Directory, Almanac, and Ordo. New York: D. and J. Sadlier, 1866–86.

Sauget, J.-M. "Mosé di Scete o l'Etiope." In *Bibliotheca Sanctorum* 9:652–54. Rome: Istituto Giovanni XXIII della Pontificia Università Lateranense, 1967.

Scally, Mary Anthony. *Mother, Medicine, and Mercy: The Story of A Black Woman Doctor*. Washington, D.C.: Associated Publishers, 1979.

———. *Negro Catholic Writers, 1900–1943: A Bio-bibliography*. Detroit: Walter Romig, 1945.

Shaler, Nathaniel. "The Negro Problem." *Atlantic Monthly* 54 (1884): 696–709.

Shaw, Richard. *Dagger John: The Unquiet Life and Times of Archbishop James Hughes of New York*. New York: Paulist Press, 1977.

Shea, Diana, and Marita Supan. "Apostolate of the Archives — God's Mystery through History." *Josephite Harvest* 85 (1983) 10–13.

Sheehan, Arthur, and Elizabeth Sheehan. *Pierre Toussaint: A Citizen of Old New York*. New York: P. J. Kenedy, 1955.

Sherwood, Grace. *The Oblates' Hundred and One Years*. New York: Macmillan, 1931.

Skeabeck, Andrew. "Most Rev. William Gross: Missionary Bishop of the South." *Records of the American Catholic Historical Society of Philadelphia* 66 (1955): 131–55.

Skerrett, J. Taylor. "'Is There Anything Wrong with Being A Nigger?' Racial Identity and Three Nineteenth Century Priests." *Freeing the Spirit* 5 (1977): 27–37.

Slattery, John. "A Catholic College for Negro Catechists." *Catholic World*, 70 (1899): 1–12.

———. "The Congress of Negro Catholics." *Donahoe's Magazine* 24 (1890): 269–71.

Smith, Julia. *Slavery and Rice Culture in Low Country Georgia*. Knoxville: University of Tennessee Press, 1985.

Snowden, Frank. *Before Color Prejudice: The Ancient View of Blacks*. Cambridge: Harvard University Press, 1983.

———. *Blacks in Antiquity: Ethiopians in the Greco-Roman Experience*. Cambridge: Harvard University Press, 1970.

Souvenir Volume of the Centennial Celebration and Catholic Congress, 1789–1889. Detroit: William H. Hughes, 1889.

Spalding, David [Thomas]. "Martin John Spalding's 'Dissertation on the American Civil War.'" *Catholic Historical Review* 52 (1966–67): 66–85.

Spalding, Thomas. *Martin John Spalding: American Churchman*. Washington, D.C.: Catholic University of America Press, 1973.

———. "The Negro Catholic Congresses, 1889–1894." *Catholic Historical Review* 55 (1969): 337–57.

Special Report of the United States Commissioner of Education on the Condition and Improvement of Public Schools in the District of Columbia. Department of Education. Washington, D.C.: Government Printing Office, 1871.

Steins, Richard. "The Mission of the Josephites to the Negro in America, 1871–1893." Master's thesis, Columbia University, 1966.

Sweeney, David. *The Life of John Lancaster Spalding.* New York: Herder and Herder, 1965.

Tannenbaum, F. *Slave and Citizen: The Negro in the Americas.* New York: Alfred A. Knopf, 1946.

Tarry, Ellen. *The Other Toussaint: A Post-Revolutionary Black.* Boston: St. Paul Editions, 1981.

———. *The Third Door: The Autobiography of an American Negro Woman.* New York: David McKay, 1955.

TePaske, John Jay. *The Governorship of Spanish Florida, 1700–1763.* Durham, N.C.: Duke University Press, 1964.

Thompson, Margaret. "Philemon's Dilemma: Nuns and the Black Community in Nineteenth-Century America: Some Findings." In *The American Catholic Religious Life: Selected Historical Essays,* ed. Joseph M. White, 81–96. New York: Garland Publishing, 1988.

Three Catholic Afro-American Congresses. Cincinnati: American Catholic Tribune, 1893. Reprint. New York: Arno Press, 1978.

Tindall, George. *South Carolina Negroes, 1877–1900.* Columbia: University of South Carolina Press, 1952.

Ugarte, Ruben Vargas. *El santo de los pobres.* Lima: Ediciones Paulinas, 1986.

United States Documents in the Propaganda Fide Archives: A Calendar. 11 vols. Edited by Finbar Kenneally, O.F.M., et al. Washington, D.C.: Academy of American Franciscan History, 1966–87.

Uqbit, Tesfazghi. *Current Christological Positions of Ethiopian Orthodox Theologians.* Orientalia Christiana Analecta, 196. Rome: Pont. Institutum Studiorum Orientalium, 1973.

Vallé, Lincoln. "The Catholic Church and the Negro." *America* 30 (1923–24): 327–28.

Vantini, John. *The Excavations at Faras: A Contribution to the History of Christian Nubia.* Museum Combonianum N. 24. Collana di Studi Africani dei Missionari Comboniani. Bologna: Editrice Nigrizia, 1970.

Verlinden, Charles. *L'esclavage dans l'Europe médiévale.* Vol. 1, *Péninsule ibérique, France.* Brugge: De Tempel, 1955.

———. "L'esclavage dans la péninsule ibérique au XIVe siècle." *Anuario de estudios medievales* 7 (1970–71): 577–91.

Webb, Benedict. *The Centenary of Catholicity in Kentucky.* Louisville, Ky.: Charles A. Rogers, 1884.

Weber, David, ed. *Foreigners in Their Native Land: Historical Roots of the Mexican Americans.* 6th ed. Albuquerque: University of New Mexico Press, 1981.

Wesley, Charles. "Manifests of Slave Shipments along the Waterways, 1808–
    1864." *Journal of Negro History* 27 (1942): 155–74.
Wilmore, Gayraud, and James Cone, eds. *Black Theology: A Documentary
    History, 1966–1979*. Maryknoll, N.Y.: Orbis Books, 1979.
Windschiegl, Peter. *Fifty Golden Years, 1903–1953*. Muenster, Saskatchewan:
    St. Peter's Abbey, 1953.
Zielinski, Martin. "Working for Interracial Justice: The Catholic Interracial
    Council of New York, 1934–1964." *U.S. Catholic Historian* 7 (1988):
    233–60.

INDEX

Of Related Interest

Carl J. and Dorothy Schneider
In Their Own Right
The History of American Clergywomen
The first cross-denominational history of American clergywomen;
an important contribution to church history and women's history.
0-8245-1653-2; $39.95

Timothy Walch
Parish School
*A History of American Catholic Parochial Education
from Colonial Times to the Present*
The dramatic story of a social institution that has adapted itself to
constant change without abandoning its goals of preserving the faith of
its children and preparing them for productive roles in American society.
0-8245-1532-3; $39.95

Christopher J. Kauffman
Ministry and Meaning
A Religious History of Catholic Health Care in the United States
"... the way in which Catholics, chiefly religious sisters, saw and
practiced their vocation as a real pastoral ministry of religious service."
— James Hennesey, S.J., Rector, Saint Peter's College
0-8245-1459-9; $29.95

Please support your local bookstore, or call 1-800-395-0690.
For a free catalog, please write us at
The Crossroad Publishing Company
370 Lexington Avenue, New York, NY 10017

We hope you enjoyed The History of Black Catholics in the United States.
Thank you for reading it.

crossroad
herder